# Austria
## in the
# Twentieth
# Century

**Studies in Austrian and Central European History and Culture**

Günter Bischof, Series Editor

*Austria in the Twentieth Century*

Edited by Rolf Steininger, Günter Bischof,
and Michael Gehler

Rolf Steininger
Günter Bischof
Michael Gehler
editors

# Austria
## in the
# Twentieth
# Century

Transaction Publishers
New Brunswick (U.S.A.) and London (U.K.)

First paperback printing 2009

Copyright © 2002 by Transaction Publishers, New Brunswick, New Jersey.

This book is printed on acid-free paper that meets the American National Standard for Permanence of Paper for Printed Library Materials.

Library of Congress Catalog Number: 2002020451
ISBN: 978-0-7658-0175-3 (cloth); 978-1-4128-0854-5 (paper)
Printed in the United States of America

Library of Congress Cataloging-in-Publication

Austria in twentieth century / Rolf Steininger, Günter Bischof, Michael
    Gehler, editors.
        p. cm.—(Studies in Austrian and central European history and
    culture ; 1) Includes bibliographical references and index.
    ISBN 0-7658-0175-2 ( cloth : alk. paper)
        1. Austria—Politics and government—20th century. 2. Austria—Intellectual life. 3. National socialism—Austria. 4. Austria—Ethnic relations. I.
Steininger, Rolf, 1942-  II. Bischof, Günter, 1953-  III. Gehler, Michael. IV.
Series.

DB91 .A87 2002
943.605—dc21

                                                                    2002020451

*For Gordon "Nick" Mueller*

# Table of Contents

## III. THE SECOND REPUBLIC 161

# Introduction

"In small Austria the great world holds its trial runs," noted the optimistic dramatist Friedrich Hebbel. Austria is "the laboratory for the end of the world" wrote the acerbic wit Karl Kraus during World War I. In the days of the old Habsburg Monarchy, Austrian writers showed grand ambition inventing such hyperbole to describe Austria's unique importance in the world. In the waning days of the twentieth century, the performance artist Hermann Nitsch expressed the country's mood of "small is beautiful" when he desired only to be the "emperor of the wine district," the *Weinviertel* in Lower Austria north of the Danube. Such decline in ambition expressed as artistic imagination indicate Austria's trajectory in the twentieth century from great European power to small state.

Few countries in the world have experienced such dramatic and precipitate reversals of fortune as Austria did in the twentieth century. At the beginning of the century, Vienna was still the capital of a multinational/multiethnic empire in East Central Europe as well as the world capital of particular sorts of artistic imagination and grandiose intellectual pursuits. Sigmund Freud, Ludwig Wittgenstein, Gustav Mahler, Gustav Klimt, and Egon Schiele all contributed to the birth of modernism with their unusual talents. Bertha von Suttner won the Nobel Prize for her pacifism. At the same time, the feverish imagination of the failing young artist Adolf Hitler developed his noxious repertoire of racial anti-Semitism and imperial German grandeur, eventually leading him towards genocide and continental conquest. In Austria as elsewhere, the martial spirit trumped the desire for peace.

The reckless imperial Austro-Hungarian/German alliance contributed much to precipitate World War I, the "Great War" that killed more than ten million people. This orgy of bloodshed on the continent also rang in the beginning of the end of European predominance in the world. With the collapse of the Habsburg, Ottoman, German and Russian Czarist empires, the "long nineteenth century" (David Blackbourn) came to an end, and the brutal "short twentieth century" (Eric Hobsbawn) began.

The collapse of the Austro-Hungarian Monarchy in the waning days of World War I saw the emergence of six successor states that changed the map of East Central Europe and destabilized the region with their deep-seated envies and short-sighted rivalries.

Austria was one of them. A democratic polity emerged after November 1918, but one that was troubled from the beginning. The new Austrian government wanted to join Germany ("Anschluß"), but the great powers making peace in Paris did not permit it. Austria's troubled identity between imperial grandeur and small statehood, between the rock of Germany and the hard place of a destabilized East Central Europe, never gelled in the years between the two World Wars. Austrians lacked a will to live in a state that did not fit their ambitions. Cut off from its traditional East Central European markets and financial control over East Central Europe, the new, much smaller Austria was also economically anemic. On top of these destabilizing mental and economic factors, the irresolvable rivalries between the principal political parties (political "camps" or "*Lager*") led to creeping civil war.

The political camps' unwillingness to mend fences and co-operate in spite of worsening international situation led to the demise of democracy, like in the rest of much of Central and Eastern Europe. With the advent of the "corporatist *Ständestaat*"—the Austro-Fascist regime in 1933—Austria opened itself up to the pulls from both Fascist Italy and National Socialist Germany. When Hitler and Mussolini entered the "Axis Berlin-Rome" in 1936, and the Western powers appeased these fascist powers, Austria's demise became only a matter of time. In March 1938 the long-anticipated Anschluß came suddenly and chaotically. Hitler's army invaded and occupied Austria and incorporated it into the "Third Reich." Austrians were divided over the end of their state. Many regretted it and wept quietly. Many were forced to flee the country: a mass exodus of Jews ensued, for many Communists and Socialists had already fled the Austro-Fascist state after 1933. But many were out in the streets cheering the Nazi conquest of their own country. What the Pan-Germanists had always desired occurred: Austria became a province of Germany and no longer could be found on the map for the next seven years.

During the devastating years of World War II, Austrians in the "Ostmark"/"Danube and Alpine *Gaue*" of Nazi Germany shared in the pride, power, and eventual defeat of Hitler's conquest of much of Europe. Deeps rifts between fervid Nazis, band-wagon party joiners, and anti-Nazis often divided families. "Austrians" served in the German armed forces and resisted Hitler at the same time. They experienced economic development and growing prosperity in the early part of the war and the devastation of their homeland in the later part of the conflict. They made signal contributions to Nazi genocidal practices and experienced Allied bombardment of their cities. By and large the majority of the Austrian public supported Hitler until the final days and weeks of his regime. The end of the war came with more destruction by the invading liberating Allied armies. Those who had supported the Nazis experienced defeat while the few resisters were thrilled with the coming of liberation.

In April/May 1945, Austria became "free" again. It turned out to be only a freedom of sorts. Liberated from the Nazis and re-established as a country, Austria still was under the occupation of the principal victorious Allied powers (Soviet Union, United States, Great Britain, France). Only in 1955 was Austria "liberated from the liberators" and able to regain its full sovereignty. With the emergence of the Cold War after 1945, the erstwhile allies guarded against each other's perceived territorial and ideological ambitions in Austria too. The East-West conflict impacted Austria with full force. While the Western powers were prepared to leave, the Russians made Austria pay for the devastation its nationals had wreaked in Hitler's armies in the Soviet Union during the war. While the Soviets exploited their zone economically, the United States poured enormous amounts of aid into Austria through the Marshall Plan.

The fear of a partition haunted Austrians until the State Treaty was signed in May 1955. The price Austria paid to get the occupation powers to leave was neutrality and more "reparations" to the Soviets. The price was acceptable to get rid of four-power tutelage. Neutrality also put Austria on the path of a neutralism and pacifism in the world's conflicts and produced an "island-of-the-blessed" mentality still prevailing to this day. Austria stayed out of the Western military bloc system and did not join NATO.

Austria's "Westernization" came slowly and was politically arrested for a long time. Neutral Austria joined the Western

European trajectory of the "golden age" (Hobsbawm) towards prosperity and consumerism and the "leisure-class society." Yet neutrality arrested full political and economic integration. It prevented Austria from joining the European Economic Community.

Austria became a model political economy. Its "consensus democracy," practiced by the two major parties (conservatives and Socialists) forming "grand coalition" governments, brought political stability. Its strong corporate system of the "social partnership" brought social peace and one of the most highly developed welfare states in the world. Socialist governments used the huge sector of state-owned industries as a Keynesian tool to secure high employment. Such state-directed capitalism had elements of the economies east of the Iron Curtain as much as Western European-style political economy. In spite of such "Austro-Keynesian" economic fine-tuning, Austria experienced economic recession and political stagnation like the rest of the West.

In the 1980s and 1990s, dramatic sea changes began to take shape in the Austrian political landscape. With the "Greens" and the short-lived "Liberal Forum," new parties appeared on the horizon. An ambitious leader turned the old liberal/German nationalist fringe Freedom Party into a populist powerhouse that began to break-up the "grand coalition" monopoly led by the Socialists. In the fall of 2000, the FPÖ entered a national middle-right government coalition and thus sped up these sea changes in Austrian domestic politics. The days of typical Austrian consensus politics are numbered. Austria has become a normal Western European contentious democracy. This seems to complete the "Western Europeanization" of Austrian politics.

In foreign policy, similarly dramatic events allowed Austria to finally join the Western European community. With the fall of the Iron Curtain in 1989, Austria's peripheral role of the West suddenly changed into a central position in Europe again. In 1995 Austria joined the European Union and is now caught in the middle of the EU's process of integrating Austria's neighbors to the East into the West. Austria retains a hollow neutrality of sorts—maybe better termed nonaligned or alliance-free geopolitical status. To date Austria refuses to join NATO. Neutrality, however, is surviving vigorously in Austrians' identity and worldview.

The political entity that at the beginning of the twentieth century had contributed much to control the destiny of the continent has been much diminished by the turns of its fortunes in its sensitive geopolitical situation. By the end of the century, its people have become quite content to live in their small but highly prosperous state. They have gladly abdicated their role as being the gadfly of continental disasters.

Austria joins the European Union in 1995: A symbol of the new Austria—the European Union flag waving in Vienna—contrasted against symbols of the old Austria of imperial glory.

Source: Harald Hofmeister, *Die Presse*

This is a textbook intended to further the reader's deeper understanding of the basic trajectory of Austria's political and economic fortunes in the twentieth century. We are well aware of the fact that the short space available in a college textbook does not allow us to delve into the intricacies of the social, gender, cultural, and mental history of the country. This text does not seek to impress the student with "structural," "culturalist," or "postmodern" methodological approaches to Austria's history. Rather, it tries to provide students with a more traditional, basic framework for understanding the fundamental political, economic, and international trends and shifts that characterize Austria's history in the twentieth century. Students can immerse themselves in methodological approaches once this basic history is understood. The bibliography provides numerous references for further such engagement. The annual serial publications *Contemporary Austrian Studies* (Universities of New Orleans and Innsbruck) and the *Austrian History Yearbook* (University of Minnesota) are the best places to start investigating this new history. The Vienna journal *Österreichische Zeitschrift für Geschichtswissenschaft* primarily publishes articles that utilize the new methodologies.

The Salzburg historian Ernst Hanisch has pigeonholed the historiography of twentieth century Austria into four basic schools: first, the "German national" school prevailing before World War II; second, the consensual school of "coalition history" after the war; third, the new social and structural histories penned by a younger generation of scholars in the 1970s and 1980s; and fourth, the "postmodernist" fragmentation and atomization pervasive in much historical writing in the West and prevailing in Austria as well. The generation of Austrian historians writing the chapters in this book is in the third and fourth schools in the sense that most of them have left the paradigms of consensus history behind.

The editors think that a fresh textbook approach to Austrian history is long overdue for the English-speaking world. No serious overview of an up-to-date Austrian history has appeared in almost twenty years. Barbara Jelavich's *Modern Austria* (1987) has the benefit that it covers both the nineteenth and twentieth centuries very ably. But its post-World War II narrative is still largely beholden to the "consensus" school. Lonnie Johnson's *Introducing Austria* (1989) is still very useful, but it is too short for college audiences that demand historiographically advanced perspectives. Gordon Brook-Shepherd's *The Austrians* (1996) covers 1,000 years of Austrian history in a breezy style. But it not only betrays hidebound prejudice in some of its twentieth century portions, but also an arrogant British condescension *vis-à-vis* Austrian parliamentarism by a man that seems to be a monarchist at heart. Anton Pelinka's *Austria: Out of the Shadow of the Past* (1998) is unrivaled in its smart analysis of Austria's changing post-World War II political culture. While

Brook-Shepherd's history is too diffuse and uninformed about recent historiography, Pelinka's historical perspectives are too brief to delve deeply into all of Austria's twentieth century history. Peter Thaler's *The Ambivalence of Identity* (2001) is methodologically highly sophisticated, but only concentrates on Austrian identity. Three recent anthologies (two British, one American) pursue largely postwar Austrian history with cultural, social, economic, and political approaches, and their essays complement this volume well: Anthony Bushell, ed., *Austria 1945-1955* (1996); Kurt Richard Luther/Peter Pulzer, eds., *Austria 1945-1995* (1998); and David F. Good and Ruth Wodak, eds., *From World War to Waldheim* (1999). Lonnie R. Johnson's *Central Europe* (1996) ought to be read as a companion volume to this book since it provides a grand overview of the history of Austria's neighbors to the East.

In the end, the editors would like to thank those people who have made this book possible. We much appreciate the challenging questions from our students on both sides of the Atlantic. They have consistently forced us over the years to think harder and more coherently on the issues covered in this book. We are very grateful to the contributors to this volume for providing us with their chapters in a timely and professional manner.

Most of these chapters were initially penned in German for a textbook on twentieth century Austria: Rolf Steininger and Michael Gehler, eds., *Österreich im 20. Jahrhundert* (1997). This massive two-volume 1235-page publication contained 22 essays. Not all those chapters are included here. Two long essays on "anti-Semitism and the Holocaust" and one on "South Tyrol" are scheduled to appear in separate English publications. For brevity's sake, the extensive scholarly apparatus (references, chapter bibliographies, key documents selection, and discussion agendas) has been dropped for this volume. There is, however, an updated list for further readings— especially English language titles—in the back of this volume. All works cited in the text are in this bibliography. Bischof, Gehler and Kaiser, and Pelinka contributed their chapters in English, and Bischof and Gehler and Kaiser's chapters are substantially rewritten while Pelinka's is a new essay written for this volume. The rest of the chapters have been translated by Mel Greenwald and Margaret Davidson from German into English.

This publication came together under the auspices of the University of New Orleans/ University of Innsbruck friendship treaty arrangements. This *model trans-Atlantic university partnership* has not only been highly beneficial to the faculty and students of these two universities but to U.S.–Austrian scholarly relations in general. Both the Chancellor of the University of New Orleans, Gregory St. O'Brien, and the *Rektor* of the University of Innsbruck, Hans Moser, have been enthusiastic supporters of this uniquely dense academic partnership. The UNO Summer School in Innsbruck has been the flagship program for almost thirty years. It will first test this textbook with American students. Since its students and faculty will benefit from it, the UNO Summer School in Innsbruck has agreed to help fund the initial printing of this book. This textbook will also be used by the UNO "Academic Year Abroad" program in Innsbruck. Since its inception five years ago, "Twentieth Century Austria" has been a core course in the AYA curriculum.

We would like to thank the Summer School's coordinator, Peter Alongia, as well as Alea Cot, the Director of International Programs at UNO, for their generosity in helping us launch this textbook. AYA director Margaret Davidson is also eagerly anticipating this textbook for her students. At UNO, Robert Dupont, the Dean of Metropolitan College administering the international studies programs, has been instrumental in providing the funding for copy-editing the manuscript. Dean Dupont has yet to encounter an Innsbruck project he does not like. At the University of Innsbruck, Franz Mathis, the coordinator of relations with UNO, has been helpful in finding the funding for the type-setting of the volume. Mathias Schennach from the University of Innsbruck *Auslandsamt* has provided this funding. Ministerialrat Alois Söhn from the Austrian Federal Ministry of Education, Science, and Culture has been instrumental in helping to secure the funds for translating most of this volume.

The nitty-gritty chores on this volume have been done, as has so often been the case in our careers, by talented women. Jennifer Shimek from Loyola University of New Orleans deserves our enormous gratitude for her highly professional work in copy-editing and type-setting the entire volume and indexing it on top of it. Eva Plankensteiner at the Institute of Contemporary History in Innsbruck and Gertraud Griessner from CenterAustria at UNO have both made the editors' work much easier in the transmission and handling of the individual essays and photos. Any mistakes that slipped us by in the editing process are the fault of the editors.

Transaction, our publisher, has become one of the premier publishing houses on Austrian Studies in the United States. Irving Louis Horowitz, its founder, publisher, and chairman, and Mary Curtis, the President, have been highly enthusiastic about *Contemporary Austrian Studies* (*CAS*) and this project. Anne Schneider has shepherded this volume through to publication as professionally as she handled many previous *CAS* volumes. Ellen F. Kane designed the cover with her usual savvy.

For permission to reproduce the illustrations for this volume we are most grateful to the following institutions: the Innsbruck City Archives and the Tirol *Landesbilddokumentation;* the Museum of Military History and the Austrian Institute of Contemporary History, as well as the *Verein für die Geschichte der Arbeiterbewegung* and the Bruno Kreisky Foundation in Vienna; *Verein Wiener Kreis*, Vienna; Harald Hofmeister of *Die Presse*, Vienna; the Institute of Contemporary History in Innsbruck, and the National Archives in College Park, Maryland. Without the generous help of all these institutions and individuals the printing of this volume would not have been feasible.

Without the vision of Gordon "Nick" Mueller, founder of the UNO Summer School in Innsbruck and co-founder and founding director of CenterAustria at UNO, the UNO–Innsbruck partnership would never have materialized and prospered. We dedicate this volume to a great pioneer in Austrian–American university cooperation.

Rolf Steininger (Innsbruck)
Günter Bischof (New Orleans)
Michael Gehler (Bonn)
April 2002

# I. WORLD WAR I AND THE FIRST REPUBLIC

Austria's desire for Anschluß during the interwar years—"*Ein Volk, ein Reich, ein Führer*": Innsbruck giddily expecting *Führer* Adolf Hitler's arrival on 5 April 1938 before the 10 April plebiscite confirming the Anschluß.

Source: Innsbruck City Archives

# On the Threshold of the Twentieth Century: State and Society in Austria before World War I

*Hermann J.W. Kuprian*

### Introduction

In order to be able to sketch that transitional phase of Austrian history prior to the First World War in which, on one hand, a series of social and political upheavals began to gather strength, and, on the other hand, the ossification of the state system kept it oriented on the past, it will first be necessary to briefly define the terms "state" and "society," and then to look into the question of what is meant by the term "Austria" on the threshold to the twentieth century.

First of all, the "state" was considered to be synonymous with the coherent forces and forms of "society," with the power and prestige of the ruling house and the imperial court, with organized administration and bureaucracy, with uniform lawmaking, with the discipline and loyalty of the army, with shared political representation in both foreign and domestic affairs, with a territorially delimited entity, and so forth. "Society," on the other hand, was the sum of all inhabitants and citizens—men as well as women—and, above all, of all social classes including their diverse traditions, values and norms, interests and prospects in life, but was by no means associated with any territorial limitation and included thoroughly centrifugal tendencies and forces. The necessary elaborateness of this attempt at a definition gives some idea of the complexity inherent in this highly conflicted and dichotomous conceptual pair—complex, indeed, because a conception of society understood in this way has no really antithetical character and

Archduke (later Emperor) Charles with his wife Zita and their son Otto visiting a regiment of Tyrolese riflemen c. 1916.

Source: *Landesbilddokumentation*

therefore also does not exclude the representatives of the state's instruments of power, but rather incorporates them as an admittedly small, but disproportionately influential, segment of society.

Secondly, in the common parlance in general use at around 1900, Austria meant the western, Cisleithan (that is, situated on this side of the Leitha river) portion of the Habsburg Monarchy, including Lower Austria (with Vienna), Upper Austria, Salzburg, Tyrol, Vorarlberg, Styria, Carinthia, Carniola, Görz and Gradiska, Istria, Dalmatia, Bohemia, Moravia, Silesia, Galicia, and Bukovina, and was referred to in the bureaucratic terminology of the day as "the kingdoms and lands represented in the *Reichsrat*" (Parliament). Its counterpart was the Hungarian or transleithan half of the empire—essentially Hungary, Siebenbürgen, Croatia, and Slavonia, which comprised the "lands of the holy Hungarian crown of St. Stephan." On the basis of this state construct which resulted from the so-called *Ausgleich* (compromise) of 15 March 1867 following the military defeats at Solferino (1859) and Königgrätz (1866), a dualistic system in the form of a double monarchy had been established, the two halves of which were connected solely through their shared dynasty, the financial and military affairs they had in common, as well as their unitary foreign policy. Otherwise, they remained two equal, independent states whose common affairs and policies had to be harmonized and agreed upon at regular intervals.

This official state bifurcation gave rise, among some thinkers contemporary with the double monarchy, to a theory that still has proponents to this day whereby, as a result of this system, the decline and fall of the multiethnic Habsburg Monarchy was already a foregone conclusion. Thus, as early as March 1867—and therefore even before the negotiations with Hungary had been officially consummated—a "German Austrian" in a brochure entitled "The Break-up of Austria" noted what the author termed the first mention "in the agenda of the public discussion of the disintegration of Austria as a European necessity."

In any case, the Danube Monarchy at this point was enveloped by the aura of a realm in decay, the psychological effects of which have influenced the historical discussion to this day. This can be clearly seen in a whole series of works on the history of the final decades of the Habsburg Monarchy by Austrian historians as well as their European and American colleagues, which often bear indicative titles such as *The Decline of the Danube Monarchy* (Helmuth Andics), *The Decline of Austria-Hungary* (Anton Mayr-Harting), *Requiem for a Monarchy* (Francois Fejtö), *The Decline and Fall of the Habsburg Empire* (Alan Sked), *The Dissolution of the Habsburg Empire* (Richard G. Plaschka et al.), *The Dissolution of the Habsburg Monarchy* (Oscar Jászi), or *Turning Point in the History of the Danube Basin* (Alfred Opitz). Indeed, the differences in the historical assessments proffered by these works lie in their more or less multifaceted discussion of the causes of and the attribution of blame for this decline—stressing either its internal structural weaknesses or the lack of equilibrium inherent in the coexistence of rival ethnic groups, the political-social backwardness of Austria-Hungary *vis-à-vis* the modernity of Western Europe, economically and regionally disparate, and thus highly problematic; social developments; the virulent system of dualism; and, finally, parading out a whole series of erroneous political decisions attributable to personal and human inadequacies on the part of both Kaiser Franz Joseph as well as his ministers and delegates (Mayr-Harting, Sked). Even the hypothesis of the conscious and purposeful destruction of the Double Monarchy from within and without can be found on this list (Fejtö).

Nevertheless, no matter how much fierce and justified criticism—above all from the disadvantaged Slavic peoples—was leveled at the total restructuring of the Monarchy that was carried out in 1867 and did indeed raise a number of new problems in the already tense relationships among the various nationalities, the reform still offered at least a genuine chance to go forward with the federalist restructuring of what had been until then an absolutist and centrally ruled unitary state. Moreover, this opened up new opportunities with respect to a comprehensive democratization of public life and to solving pressing social problems, especially since the priority of foreign policy, which up to that point had gone hand in hand with the prestige of the imperial house and Austria as a great power, had to gradually recede into the background to be replaced at center stage by domestic restructuring. The long-unsolved social problems that were the result of ongoing industrialization and the liberal market economy made it a pressing necessity by the last two decades of the nineteenth century at the very latest to fundamentally reorient the policies the state pursued in order to further its interests. The conditions under which this could be carried out were quite dissimilar in the two halves of the Monarchy. Consequently, when reference is made hereafter to Austria, this refers to the Cisleithan half of the Habsburg Monarchy with particular reference to the regional development of the present-day territory of the Republic of Austria.

## Social Policy Changes

Examining more closely the social policy changes that took place in Austria during the second half of the nineteenth century, two key questions immediately arise: 1.) To what extent was the state power apparatus, which had been structured in accordance with an absolutist state until then, able and prepared to react to these challenges that by no means proceeded in linear fashion? 2.) To which challenges are we actually referring? Answering the second question sheds light on the first. Moritz Csáky has pointed out a few of the essential elements that characterized the breakdown—

triggered in 1848 and accelerating up to the turn of the century—of old corporatist social structures in Austria.

First of all, there were demographic developments—that is, population growth that by necessity led to an expansion of administrative and educational institutions as well as economic production and distribution. Consequently, this brought about an extension of old legal and administrative structures beyond their original conception oriented on an elitist, corporatist social stratum. In actual practice, this laid the groundwork for the inclusion of the entire population in the process of delegating political authority (that is, the expanded right to vote) as well as the demand for the creation of corresponding constitutional and parliamentary institutions.

Second, new economic systems of production and distribution as well as commercial innovations contributed to the transformation of the social landscape. Alongside the aristocracy, the nobility, and the peasant classes, a new social stratum arose as the result of increasing industrialization—the working class.

Third, a widening of the intellectual horizon—chiefly evident in the (enlightened) bourgeoisie and bureaucracy—led to a new conception of self that was no longer oriented on the privileges of birth but on educational attainment. The proponents of this new understanding were interested in assuming greater political responsibility.

Fourth, the increased mobility resulting from the construction of new transportation arteries and the expansion of the rail network played a considerable role in overcoming old social constraints.

Aside from these general factors, the Habsburg Monarchy was particularly characterized by ethnic-linguistic diversity, the territorial boundaries of which were not always clearly drawn. However, this ethnic pluralism only first started to loom as a threat to state unity in the 1870s when nationalist thought began to coalesce into a self-contained ideology.

So then, how did the state react to these novel social policy challenges? A first, decisive step was taken shortly after the *Ausgleich* on 21 December 1867 with the confirmation by Kaiser Franz Joseph of the state's Constitutional (or Fundamental) Laws establishing citizens' general rights. They applied to the Austrian half of the empire and constituted, together with the basic tenets of the February Constitution of 1861, the so-called December Constitution—a body of legislation that contained practically all of the liberal basic rights of that day and age. Among other provisions, it established that all citizens were to enjoy equal treatment before the law, that all citizens were to have an equal right to hold public office, that the right to hold property and the right of a householder to forbid someone entrance or to order someone to leave must be sacrosanct, and that the freedom of movement of persons and property within the territory of the state may not be restricted. Furthermore, all Austrian citizens were to enjoy not only the right to assemble and to form associations, but also—at least theoretically— the right to freely express their opinions verbally, in writing and print, and in graphic images within certain legal bounds; the freedom of conscience and of religion; as well as the right to freely choose one's occupation. However, the most important point, which, in light of the traditionally privileged position of the Germans within the Austrian half of the Monarchy, would lead to fierce debates both in public as well as in Parliament, was the commitment to the preservation and cultivation of the culture and language of each of the state's ethnic groups, which was tantamount to an inviolable right.

Despite these laws that were quite "revolutionary" for their time, Austria, in its political decision-making structures, nevertheless remained until 1918 a dynastic, bureaucratically ruled, authoritarian state, since the crown and the imperial court continued to be the centers of power. The constitution, ordained as an "act of grace on the part of the Kaiser" in the form of a constitutional Monarchy, could thus also be rescinded at any time and, in the face of the turn-of-the-century parliamentary crisis, even constituted the basis of some considerations of a "*coup d'état* from above." Initially, though, Franz Joseph made this position the starting point of his efforts to encounter and deal with the inexorable progress of social and political change.

## Democratization of Public Life

In light of the assertion that the imperial court remained the center of political power, the question that suggests itself is which array of powers the dynasty actually relinquished and how this contributed to the democratization of public life. It was, in any case, democracy on the installment plan that went hand in hand with the successive expansion of constitutional preconditions and, despite much progress up to 1918, was based upon the unequal distribution of power, since the lion's share was still in the hands of the Kaiser and the administration that—like all ministers and high-level officials—he appointed and dismissed as he pleased. Indeed, the Kaiser could conduct governmental affairs only through "his" ministers who, in turn, were responsible to the "people's representatives," the *Reichsrat*. Nevertheless, only one man had the power to convene and dissolve this Parliament—the Kaiser himself. The *Reichsrat* had to discuss and pass all legislation before it had to be submitted once again to the monarch for "sanctioning." The oversight of the state's administration and financial affairs was also the responsibility of the "people's representatives"; whereas, the sovereign had to answer to no one for his decisions.

Moreover, the Kaiser not only retained the ultimate right to reach decisions or raise objections in all domestic matters, but also, as head of state, he represented it in foreign affairs, concluded treaties, waged war and made peace, was commander-in-chief of the army and navy, and nominated those who held high church positions. Justice was administered in his name, which is not to say, of course, that the arbitrary use of power characterized the entire court system. Austria was a state founded on the rule of law with a Supreme Court, Court of Appeals, and Administrative Tribunal. For the people, the dynasty was also a symbol that stood for the idea of the state and stood as the guarantor of the unity of Austria-Hungary that was so widely being called into question. The Kaiser became more honored and revered the longer he reigned, so it was not only after the Monarchy's demise that the Habsburg legend was born.

The Parliament's limited authority—corresponding to that of the respective provincial legislatures—leads to the issues of whether this truly was a body representative of the people, and what tangible steps were taken to broaden the franchise. From our present-day perspective, this was not actually democratic representation. However, it most certainly was in line with the political realities of the time, especially since it was not achieved as the result of a struggle from "below" but rather was decreed from "above." The "masses" were not yet politicized, and the system was not yet set up for mass-level political parties. At the top of the agenda was the assertion of the interests of the ruling elites—the liberal upper-middle class and the predominantly aristocratic large landowners. In order to guarantee this, the votes cast in an election were not only "weighted" according to social position, property ownership, and education (so-called *curiae*), but were also divided up into electoral bodies and constituencies of various sizes, which led to unequal representation of the various provinces, cities, and nationalities. Up to 1873, only the provincial legislatures had been permitted to send members from their ranks as representatives to the *Reichsrat*, until the "popular vote" was introduced in that year.

The Austrian *Reichsrat* consisted of two chambers: the upper house and the house of representatives. The members of the upper house, either as a result of hereditary right or appointment by the Kaiser, represented the concrete interests of the estates making up the social order; whereas, the members of the house of representatives had to stand for direct election, even if the number of eligible voters was severely limited by the condition of having to pay a relatively high tax rate (*Zensus*).

The voting rights reform of 1873, however, established conditions favorable to the formation of political parties, which occurred immediately in its wake. Initially, this took place primarily within the *Reichsrat* itself in the form of parliamentary factions, which were ad hoc political alliances usually focused on the objectives and interests of particular nationalities than parties with specific ideological and programmatic principles. Frequently shifting coalitions were the significant consequences of the absence of programmatic and internal cohesion within these factions as well as the intensifying conflicts among religious and ethnic groups. As a result, the ability of the *Reichsrat* to work effectively was repeatedly called into question.

Various proposals by liberal and democratic representatives in the 1870s that were aimed at expanding the right to vote finally bore fruit in March 1882 when a Clerical-Federalist parliamentary majority that was working together with the Conservative government of Count Eduard Taaffe succeeded in passing a reduction of the *Zensus* payment that was a condition of eligibility to vote from ten to five Gulden. This constituted a further step toward democratization of public life since the modest proportion of the population that had enjoyed the right to vote—just under 6 percent of the 20 million inhabitants of the Cisleithan half of the Empire—increased considerably, by 26 percent among peasant farmers and about 34 percent among the (urban) petit bourgeoisie. However, the vast majority of the workers, servants, and farmhands were still excluded. Nevertheless, the consequences of the expansion of the electorate confronted the old parliamentary parties with totally new social and political challenges.

The next step in the broadening of the franchise came in 1896 when Prime Minister Count Kasimir Badeni presented the Austrian *Reichsrat* with a voting rights reform bill that, at least according to its claims, introduced the general right to vote. To the four existing *curiae*—the large landowners, the cities and major market towns, the professional associations and chambers of commerce, and the rural communities—there was simply appended a fifth, so-called general class of voters, that included all male citizens twenty-four years of age and older with proof of a fixed place of residence for at least six months, regardless how much tax they had paid. Although this raised the number of eligible voters from approximately 1.7 million to over 5.3 million, the overwhelming majority of the population was still excluded. Moreover, new regulations by no means complied with the fundamental principle of equality since the first four curiae included a total of 353 representatives whereas only seventy-two votes were allocated to the fifth. In actual practice, this meant that each member from the first two *curiae* represented, respectively, sixty-four and twenty-six voters as compared to nearly 70,000 in the fifth.

At around the turn of the century, ongoing initiatives to further expand the right to vote were the work of the up-and-coming and, by this time, formally organized, predominantly German mass political parties—above all the Social Democrats and the Christian Socials. While they wanted to make a major issue of the social welfare aspects of the general right to vote, various ethnic minorities—especially Slavic groups—demanded their fair share according to their level of political participation. Countless rallies and demonstrations that frequently mobilized hundreds of thousand of participants raised the "pressure on the street" and brought it to bear on the monarch and his government. Even if Kaiser Franz Joseph, through the wait-and-see attitude he adopted, sought to give the impression that the crown would not cave in to this "violence," he was no longer able to rule out the possibility that the only appropriate response to these social and ethnic tensions could be the political emancipation of all citizens. Moreover, the Hungarians were already openly thinking about uncoupling their half of the Empire from the dualistic state configuration, and the most radical proponents of this idea, Franz Kossuth and his Independence Party, had been victorious at the polls in January 1905. Revolution then broke out in Russia, which forced the Czar to make extensive political concessions to the *Duma* (Parliament). These events had tangible impact on Austria.

In light of these developments, Kaiser Franz Joseph approved a corresponding bill in January 1907 to introduce the general and equal right to vote directly by secret ballot in Austria. The elitist *curia* system and the exclusionary electoral *Zensus* had, indeed, been eliminated, and the number of voters drastically increased, but these new provisions applied to not even half the population. Women not only remained excluded, but also lost the limited right that they had under the ownership provisions of the old law—namely, the (at least theoretical) right to run for office in the first curia for large landowners. On the other hand, men were also subject to numerous restrictions, such as 1.) the requirement of "full legal entitlement," which meant that, for example, all domestic servants subject to the authority of a head of household were automatically excluded; and 2.) the residency clause that primarily affected itinerant workers. Furthermore, clever gerrymandering undermined the principle of the equality of all votes by allocating a different number of votes or legislative districts to the individual crown lands, cities, rural communities, and ethnic groups, so that approximately 38,000 Germans had one parliamentary seat as compared to 100,000 Ruthenians. This meant that the Germans, who made up a mere 35 percent of the population of the Monarchy's Cisleithan half, had 43 percent of all seats while paying 63 percent of all taxes. Aside from this complicated weighing process, the introduction of the right to vote came with considerable delay in most provinces when it occurred at all. A "true democratization" of the franchise in Austria—including women's suffrage—had to wait for the First Republic, and would thus not happen until 1918/1919.

The political hopes that had been invested in the new voting rights law of 1907 were only partially fulfilled. To be sure, the major, mass-level parties chalked up impressive gains in the next *Reichsrat* elections in May of that year, but the spectrum of ethnic parties did not contract. Quite the contrary—it increased, and by the first decade of the twentieth century, Austria's parliamentary system had already sunk into a deep crisis, since the democratization of the political system had not kept pace with ethnic nationalism, and the conflicts between the various ethnic groups, that had been intensifying since 1867, now threatened to paralyze the *Reichsrat*.

## Transformation of the Terrain of Party Politics

Before examining this problem in more detail, one must examine the question of how the transformation of the party landscape ran its course in the context of the changed social and constitutional circumstances in place prior to World War I is crucial. Taking into account the continuities displayed by party politics in postwar Austria, this discussion focuses primarily on those parties that were influenced predominantly by German Austrians.

First of all, it can be asserted that there also had been various expressions of political demands and stances on public issues even before 1867; nevertheless, it was not until the previously-mentioned December Constitution that political life set out on a course that would display a degree of continuity, although the initially restrictive voting rights provisions at first prevented—or inhibited—a major portion of the population from getting involved politically. In fact, the widespread sense of resignation engendered by the insight that political action could hardly accomplish or change anything may well have contributed to this. The palpable omnipresence and omnipotence of the absolutist, bureaucratic power structure had an oppressive effect. Only a small, privileged class with a predominantly liberal orientation had the possibility of vigorously pursuing its political and economic interests both inside and outside formal legislative structures without existential fears and risks. But this group also had to ultimately come to grips with the expansion of the right to vote and—like the Catholic Church—confront worsening social and ethnic problems with new ideas and concepts.

Thus, the rapidly progressing socioeconomic changes in the social fabric demanded a "politicization of the masses" in turn-of-the-century Austria, too. Initially, this was largely carried out by associations that had been legally institutionalized on the basis of the association law established in the constitution. The new Austrian parties established themselves externally in the 1880s and 1890s primarily by confronting the ruling elites: the imperial court, the bureaucracy, and the Church. The encounter of *Weltanschauungen*, however, pitted them against liberalism, which was proving incapable of coming up with solutions to the social problems to which it had given rise, and had thus been plunged into a severe crisis. A community of shared interests manifested itself in this early phase in close working relationships among the parties' personnel and focused especially on the charismatic personality of the young Georg von Schönerer. His early supporters included men like Karl von Vogelsang, Karl Lueger, Victor Adler, and Engelbert Pernerstorfer, before differences in their approaches to political problem-solving led them to go their separate ways. Adam Wandruszka was the first to point out these common origins of the Austrian parties and, in doing so, introduced the term "political camp" into Austrian historiography. Thus, the three classic "camps"—each conceived as a political grouping encompassing several parties—formed along these lines of conflict, but were, in a larger sense, the expression of competing *Weltanschauungen*: socialist, conservative-Christian social, and liberal-German nationalist.

On this ideological basis, the parties sought to influence and organize all aspects of their members' lives, and to take over the patronage function that had previously been the state's job. This was not merely a matter of conducting propaganda campaigns to create a strong sense of identification; rather, "from birth to death" and "from cradle to grave," as the mottos went, the masses were to find a (new) home in their party of choice. Whether in childrearing or schooling, in matters of career, family, or recreation, each party's aim was to achieve the total involvement of its followers. This would eventually lead to an extreme polarization of the populace, to the development of stereotypical images of one's adversaries, and to mistrust, intolerance, and aggression directed at the respective "political opponents." The parties started their own newspapers so that the "foe" could be given concrete names: the Anti-clericals, Liberals, Schönerians, Social Democrats, and the enemy *par excellence*: the deicidal Jews. This tradition managed to survive the hostilities of World War I and continued to exert a pernicious influence on the political climate of Austria during the interwar period, reaching its sad climax in the double Civil Wars of February and July 1934.

It was especially the workers, a new social class that arose over the course of industrial development, who led the way in the effort to free themselves from the bureaucratic paternalism of the ruling elites after 1867. With their efforts initially oriented upon improving the material basis of everyday life, the labor movement began to form in—for the most part seemingly apolitical—auxiliary organizations, thereby bringing as many aspects of human existence as possible within their purview. Although these organizations initially lacked a clear ideological orientation, Victor Adler ultimately succeeded in late 1888 and early 1889 to unite them into a cohesive party. According to this group's view, the struggle of the proletariat to achieve a classless society would not come about in a revolutionary but an evolutionary way, that is, working within the state's prescribed decision-making structures. This was the highly-touted path of "Austrian Marxism," called Austromarxism.

In the years leading up to the turn of the century, the united Austrian Social Democrats succeeded, in any case, in making a name for themselves in connection with the line of conflict centered on property and labor issues, thus bringing about a large-scale mobilization of the industrial workforce and establishing themselves as the quintessential class party. Their first representatives could take their seats in the *Reichsrat* in March 1897 and thus launch the Social Democrats' ascent to a mass-level party on the parliamentary level. Although a powerful German workers' party took its place alongside those of the Czechs, Yugoslavs, Italians, and Poles—all of which cooperated as a federation governed by the principles of the Socialist International—this collaboration nevertheless broke down even prior to the outbreak of World War I. One of the most important reasons for this was the increasing difference among their positions on ethnic issues. The Austrian Social Democrats were thus reduced to a primarily German-Austrian party whose goal all the way up to 1918 remained the preservation of the Danube Monarchy, though without ultimately being able to do anything to prevent its "disintegration" as a state. But the bloc of protest voters that had formed in the wake of the economic and social changes brought on by the war made them, immediately after the Monarchy's collapse in November 1918, the most powerful political force in German Austria. Thus, the Social Democrats played a decisive and fundamental part in determining the political course of the new republic, until they maneuvered themselves into a fateful opposition role after 1920.

The Christian Social Party likewise established itself in the 1880s and 1890s in opposition to the economic and social consequences of liberalism. It was committed to Catholic-conservative traditions and values, was initially extremely heterogeneous both with respect to its voters and its personnel, and was concentrated predominantly in Vienna. Its ascent to a modern party, however, is less attributable to a clearly formulated platform or the strict discipline of its rank and file than to the charismatic personality and demagogical skills of the man who was its chairman and, from 1897, the mayor of Vienna, Karl Lueger.

Lueger's political successes in the imperial capital enabled the Christian Social movement to then extend its power of attraction beyond the metropolis to the predominantly German (Alpine) provinces. There the movement found congenial allies who had long since begun laying the political groundwork for a Christian-oriented reform party. These allies were rebellious clergymen in the lower ranks of the Catholic Church hierarchy who, in their daily encounters with the cares and problems of the mostly religiously affiliated rural population and the so-called middle stratum of society in the provincial towns, had been railing against obsolete power structures and come out in favor of drastic social reforms in accordance with the views Pope Leo XIII espoused in his 1891 encyclical *Rerum novarum*.

In the provinces at around the turn of the century, the Christian Socials built up a network of co-ops and thrift institutions as well as powerful Farm Bureau-type lobbying organizations that would provide them up to 1907 with an enormous political power base and the capability to implement their agenda. The party staged large-scale public events with an emphatically programmatic Catholic orientation featuring demonstrative appearances by prominent politicians in order to underscore its claim to acceptance as an ambitious, up-and-coming "people's party."

Through its association with the Catholic-Conservatives and its inclusion in the government following the 1907 elections, the Christian Social movement lost the original dynamism of its social policy platform and developed into a conservative party, swapping its principles that had seemed so progressive for those aimed at maintaining the status quo. This shift was also a response to the growing ideological proximity to the conservative heir to the throne, Archduke Franz Ferdinand, and to the economic consolidation of the artisans, small shopkeepers, and farmers. As a predominantly German-oriented party, it took a relatively one-sided nationalist position in the multi-national construction of the Habsburg Monarchy. Following Karl Lueger's death, this led to an internecine struggle to determine the future direction of the party, the outcome of which was a fundamental crisis and, in 1911, substantial losses at the polls in the last *Reichsrat* election prior to World War I.

Even before 1914, the Social Democrats, particularly in Vienna, became the strongest political competitors of the Christian Socials, whose focus shifted to the agrarian-federalist interests of the rural population that constituted their prime constituency after the war as well. The Social Democrats, like all the other parties, had gone into the war with high hopes for the consolidation of the nationalities and states of the Habsburg Monarchy, and it was not until November 1918 that they became the last to concede to the facts of life and to agree to a republican form of government as well as the Anschluß of the "new" Austria to the German Reich.

The formation of the liberal-German nationalist spectrum in Austria is still considered a case that is extremely difficult to characterize. Like the other two camps, German nationalism also initially positioned itself in the tradition of the confrontation with liberal demands for the political emancipation of broad segments of the population as well as with its social consequences. The realization of many of these demands in the Constitution of 1867, which conceded the fundamental equality of the various nationalities, bore within it, however, the seed of the ethnic-linguistic conflict that would accompany the Monarchy to the very end. The German-

Austrians, who, like the Hungarians, enjoyed a privileged position in the political and bureaucratic decision-making structures, thus increasingly feared the loss of their dominant influence as the non-German nationalities became more adamant in demanding their rights. This faction made its presence felt in a prevailing political mood which manifested itself in concrete form by 1882 at the latest with the constitution of the German Nationalist Association. Georg Ritter von Schönerer, Victor Adler, Engelbert Pernerstorfer, and Heinrich Friedjung not only were present at the birth of this group, but also provided it with an ideological platform embodied in the Linz Program. Although its fundamental points had recourse to much older nationalist demands, it nevertheless also contained elements that went much further, especially with respect to social welfare policies. This mixture of demands for the benefit of one national group as well as those serving the good of the general public, a blend that was capable of appealing to broad segments of the population and, above all, the educated middle class, failed, however, as a result of internal conflicts regarding the degree of emphasis to be placed on one or another programmatic objective over the course of their political implementation. But it was the conflict surrounding the form and intensity of the nationalist orientation and the increasingly aggressive, racist anti-Semitism of Schönerer and his supporters that ultimately splintered the "Nationalists" into more or less radical and moderate factions.

It can by no means suffice, though, to attribute the subsequent development of the German Nationalist spectrum solely to the radical anti-Semite Georg von Schönerer. He indeed developed into a kind of symbolic figure whose considerable skills as a political agitator enabled him to attain a high degree of recognition, but he lacked the organizational talents of a Karl Lueger. Nevertheless, Schönerer determined the issues that, on one hand, essentially characterized German nationalism in the Habsburg Monarchy at around 1900 and, on the other hand, gradually splintered it and led to the bankruptcy of its anti-liberal ideas.

Personal rivalries between the leaders of the individual factions, the lack of a unitary organizational structure, divergent assessments of liberal traditions, and various conflicts of interest between the Germans in the Austrian crownlands and the German Bohemians—

the urban centers of both regions were considered the bastions of German nationalism—led to frequently shifting party formations in the Nationalist-Freedom camp in the Cisleithan half of the empire until the outbreak of the war. The most significant among these parties up to 1918 were the "German Progressives," the "German Agrarians," the "German People's Party," and the "German Radicals," who, after a series of failed attempts, finally got together in February 1910 to form the "German National Association" as a collective movement that, following the 1911 elections, had over 100 representatives in Parliament. In contrast, Schönerer's "Pan-Germans," who did not join this ad hoc alliance, won only four seats.

During the period of upheaval in the autumn of 1918, the German Nationalists, along with the Social Democrats, were the most vehement proponents of the Anschluß of *"Deutsch-Österreich"* to Germany, but the nationalist camp quickly declined in political significance due to, on one hand, the national question having lost its explosiveness in the Republic of Austria and, on the other hand, the victorious powers having expressly prohibited such an Anschluß in the Paris peace treaties of St. Germain and Versailles.

## State, Society, and the National Question

What role, then, did ethnic issues play in the social and political changes taking place during the final years of the Danube Monarchy?

While there is a broad consensus in the field of historiography that the nationality problem advanced inexorably to an existential threat to the Habsburg Monarchy, there have been considerable disagreements over its causes as well as the factors that possibly prevented finding a way out of this crisis. This might be attributable in part to divergent definitions and assessments of nationalism, although it might also have to do with the diverse manifestations and consequences of nationalist thought and action in connection with the process whereby it came to be defined in increasingly condensed ideological terms.

In any case, developments in Austria-Hungary were very accurately described by Jean-Michel Leclercq, according to whom nationalism can be considered as "the upshot of an unsuccessful peaceful transition from absolutism to constitutionalism." The foundation of this hypothesis is the insight that, as a result of the tremendous persistence of absolutist structures in Austria, what was originally liberal patriotism hardened into a *Weltanschauung* that placed the liberation of the ethnic group above that of human beings. Changing socioeconomic circumstances and their unequal regional distribution along the Monarchy's ethnic-linguistic borders accelerated this process of national consciousness formation that had taken hold among large segments of the population up to the turn of the century. Thus, an "integral" nationalism emerged that was characteristic of the Habsburg Monarchy, which gradually encompassed all expressions of cultural, religious, economic, social, and, ultimately, political life, and the aim of this nationalism was either to maintain the "national way of life" or to achieve equality with other ethnic groups.

Neither the pan-ethnically oriented state power structure nor the newly emerged (popular) parties could long resist this phenomenon, since it became increasingly difficult to withhold in real-life politics the equal rights that were constitutionally guaranteed to the various ethnic groups. The parties sought to encourage and to instrumentalize both the "politicization" as well as the "nationalization of the masses," which occurred not only directly on an official level, but indirectly through an extremely elaborate network of clubs and organizations, such as choral societies and gymnastics groups (*Deutscher Turnverein, Sängerbund, Sokol* Movement, and so forth), co-ops, unions, farmers' groups, and industrial, commercial, and artisanal associations. Special rituals, ceremonies, songs, and the like were instituted as a means to underscore the historical greatness and traditions of the particular ethnic group and were designed to contribute to the formation of its own culture of celebration that was cultivated especially in nationalist school associations, paramilitary marching societies, and college fraternities. This form of social nationalization simultaneously created a climate of intolerance and an unwillingness to come to an understanding with others, the ultimate results of which were the parliamentary and extra-parliamentary conflicts—some of an extremely violent nature—that erupted before the war, the consequences of which continued to be felt into the 1920s and 1930s. It also manifested itself in other ways, including an increasingly aggressive anti-Semitism, as well as the rejection and mistrust with which many members of local populations far behind the lines in World War I encountered civilians from other ethnic groups fleeing from the front.

Equally important was the fact that an essential psychological element was gradually destroyed among large segments of the population as a result of this integral nationalization, namely, the identification with the idea of the entire state as still embodied by the ruling house. Indeed, Kaiser Franz Joseph himself made a decisive contribution to this in his sanctioning of the dualistic *Ausgleich* agreement of 1867, which evoked bitter disappointment on the part of all those nationalities that rightfully felt disadvantaged *vis-à-vis* the Germans and the Hungarians. What had been conceived by the monarch as the first step in a process of fundamental stabilization of the entire realm quickly proved to have consequences that achieved just the opposite. It was above all the Slavic nations—the Poles, Croats, Slovenes, and particularly the Czechs in Bohemia and Moravia—who took issue with this discrimination and one-sided preferential treatment. By means of a stubborn policy of obstructionism that employed tactics like paralyzing the imperial Parliament and provincial legislatures through the demonstrative absence of their representatives, and with pointed threats and, occasionally, mass demonstrations, the Slavic nations were indeed successful in wringing isolated economic and social policy concessions, but not the national autonomy for which they hoped. The governments installed and replaced with great frequency by Franz Joseph—the members of which were recruited from among the aristocracy and high-level bureaucracy representing all nationalities—believed that, by invoking the provisions of Paragraph 14 of the constitution, they would be able to carry on the necessary affairs of state even without a Parliament. As a consequence, not only were the political parties hardly in a position to reach their ideological and social goals through the parliamentary process, but the hopes connected with them repeatedly "flowed back into the current of narrowly-defined national interests." After all, the majority of the representatives in the *Reichsrat* at this time were non-Germans.

What, then, were the chief manifestations of this tension in the emancipation process which pitted these national groups against German dominance? Without a doubt, it reached its pre-1914 climax

in the so-called Badeni Crisis triggered in April 1897 by a language
ordinance issued by the then-prime minister. Polish Count Kasimir
Badeni, the governor of Galicia whose government took over in
September 1895 as the successor to an interim cabinet headed by
Lower Austrian governor Count Erich Kielmansegg, at first
succeeded in using his pleasant personality and diplomatic skills to
win over most of the ethnic groups and parties in the *Reichsrat*. What
he had in mind was a coalition of all liberal factions representing the
Cisleithan half of the Empire, and this indeed enabled him to achieve
a notable success in 1896 in expanding the right to vote.
Nevertheless, the predominant composition of the newly constituted
*Reichsrat* of 1897, which, as already mentioned, included a
contingent of supranationally oriented Social Democrats for the first
time, gave an initial indication of the future direction of politics
pursued to further the interests of individual nationalities. The
Badeni government, though, was faced with difficult *Ausgleich*
negotiations with Hungary, for which it needed the votes of Czech
and German representatives. The prime minister believed he could
win the support of the Czechs through an expansion of the language
regulations for Bohemia and Moravia that had been in effect since
1880 and had, even at that early date, done away with the exclusive
use of German as the language of the judiciary and the public
administration. Badeni's April 1897 directives mandated that all
public officials would henceforth have to be bilingual, which, in
actual practice, meant above all that German bureaucrats in Bohemia
and Moravia would be forced to learn Czech within a few years (by
1901), whereas the overwhelming majority of Czech bureaucrats
were already fluent in German.

When the government's bill also received the support of a majority
of the representatives of Czech, Polish, Slovenian, and Catholic
conservative groups (Catholic People's Party, *Zentrum*), a storm of
indignation began brewing throughout the oppositional German
public and especially the German Nationalist camp. Of course,
Badeni had not anticipated such a violent reaction. In Parliament, the
Germans began resorting to obstructionist measures as well as to
filibusters, noisy spectacles, and shouting matches that frequently
ended in physical confrontations. To exact revenge for the Catholic
conservatives' "betrayal" of the German nation, the German radicals

surrounding Schönerer began propagating the "Get Rid of Rome" movement that called for conversion from "un-German" Catholicism to Protestantism. Ultimately, this was a matter—at least symbolically—of assuring continued German supremacy, as well as guaranteeing career chances, which is why German student organizations were actively involved. Street demonstrations and bloody clashes between various ethnic groups and demonstrators and the troops trying to maintain order brought nationalist emotions to the boiling point. The German areas of Bohemia, Prague, Vienna, and Graz were scenes of tremendous unrest; the government was flooded with resolutions and letters of protest; Badeni himself fought a duel with the German radical representative Karl Hermann Wolf in which the prime minister was injured. Observers abroad took an active interest in what was transpiring in Austria and began to interpret the often shameful and ridiculous scenes being staged in the *Reichsrat* as indicative of the decline of the Monarchy.

Despite all efforts to calm things down, society's alienation from the state as well as hostilities among the various ethnic groups threatened to intensify. When, at the end of November 1897 during a heated dispute over the rules of parliamentary order, Badeni called in the police to clear the chamber in which the representatives met, the Kaiser even began to fear the outbreak of a revolution and adjourned the *Reichsrat*. He simultaneously dismissed the prime minister from office and named Baron Paul Gautsch von Franckenthurn, who had been serving as minister of education, to head the new administration, which governed on the basis of the emergency decree provisions of Paragraph 14. The crisis of Austrian parliamentarism had gotten out of hand, so that the successor governments had to calm nationalist passions that had been whipped into a frenzy. What remained, however, was the stale aftertaste attached to the belief in the viability of democracy and parliamentary government even before these had established their place in society's thinking. The hypothesis that the negative experiences from the Badeni turmoil exerted a decisive influence upon the generation that assumed political leadership of the post-1918 successor states and thus made a considerable contribution to the development of authoritarian tendencies in Central Europe has some merit, too.

Only two and a half years later in October 1899, the short-lived cabinet under Prime Minister Count Manfred Clary-Aldringen had to once again suspend the language regulations, whereupon the Czechs resorted to obstructionism. Aldringen resigned because he had promised not to govern on the basis of Paragraph 14, but a new era would be inaugurated in January 1900 with the appointment of liberal bureaucrat Ernest von Körber. Indeed, he did succeed, through "rapprochement conferences" that he conducted personally and through generous economic and cultural programs, in calming these nationality conflicts to a certain extent. But just as he did so, the imperial house itself was shaken by dynastic turbulence. To the great displeasure of the aging Franz Joseph, the designated heir to the throne, Franz Ferdinand, entered into a "marriage beneath his station" with Sophie Chotek, and had to renounce in advance any claim to succession to the throne on the part of any children stemming from this union. This was seen as a stain on the reputation of the ruling house.

Meanwhile, Körber had presented the doubly displeased Kaiser with plans for a *coup d'état* that included a number of highly explosive elements. The plan foresaw a new voting rights act, new rules of parliamentary procedure for the *Reichsrat*, and new language regulations, all decreed without ratification of Parliament on the basis of absolute imperial power. Indeed, Körber's proposals did not depart from the *curia*-based system that had been in effect until then, but were designed to introduce the general franchise for the majority of the population. The ulterior motive for this move was to get the voters to the polls directly as individual persons, thus isolating them from the national groupings in the regional electoral bodies. In such a newly structured *Reichsrat*, obstructing business by means of filibusters and delaying tactics would be a thing of the past, since time limits would force representatives to put bills to a vote. Körber hoped that this would make it possible to get over the nationality question, but his program failed for the simple reason that it would have applied to only one part—namely, the Austrian half—of the Monarchy. Körber's Hungarian counterpart, Prime Minister Koloman von Szell, finally rejected the *coup d'état* before the Crown Council with the explanation that setting aside the constitution of one of the two halves of the empire would, at the same time, necessarily mean the abrogation of the Austrian-Hungarian *Ausgleich* of 1867.

Nevertheless, Körber's cabinet remained in office until 1904 despite the already difficult negotiations betweens the Germans and the Czechs and the tense relationship to the Hungarian half of the empire being repeatedly put to the test by nationalistically motivated strikes and street fighting in different parts of the Monarchy, such as in Trieste and in Innsbruck due to the establishment of an Italian-language law school. But the Liberal Körber was unable to permanently withstand the pressure and growing mistrust of the Conservative-Christian Social elements grouped around the heir to the throne, and he finally had to go. The parties of the masses, meanwhile, were pressing to assume power, and the question of the introduction of equal voting rights for all reared its head again. Kaiser Franz Joseph, expecting to be able to once again pacify the nationality conflict, named Max Wladimir Baron von Beck, another representative of the bourgeois-bureaucratic civil servant class, to succeed Gautsch and Körber as the head of government. Beck succeeded in introducing universal and equal suffrage for all men in 1907 in the face of resistance from the aristocracy and the conservatives, who had long ago recognized this as their political demise and fought against it to the very end.

The hopes that the Kaiser and his prime ministers placed in the revised constellation of the Austrian Parliament were, however, not fulfilled during the following years, although Beck also named representatives of the new parties to fill cabinet posts and successfully concluded the *Ausgleich* negotiations with Hungary. The "Wahrmund Affair," as well as the jealousy and oppositional attitude of Franz Ferdinand, made it so difficult for him to govern that he resigned in the autumn of 1908, just as the Habsburg Monarchy was becoming embroiled in a foreign policy crisis over the annexation of Bosnia and Herzegovina. While subsequent administrations up to 1914 tended to govern in absolutist style by means of political maneuvering, indefinite assurances, and frequent invocation of the emergency provisions of Paragraph 14 (for which the deeply divided Austrian Parliament was not entirely free of blame), foreign policy increasingly became the focus of social and governmental interest. To be more precise, it was purposely shifted to that focal point! In 1906, the cool-headed Baron Aloys Lexa von Ährenthal became foreign minister, replacing Count Agenor Goluchowski who had pursued cautious and reserved policies since 1895. Ährenthal's maxim, in contrast to his predecessor, was that it was precisely because of Austria-Hungary's internal weaknesses that it needed to pursue an active foreign policy. Of course, the only theater available for such activities was the Balkans, which had long been among the Monarchy's areas of imperialistic interest. The only problem was that there was no field in which the two halves of the Empire were more dependent upon one another than they were in this question. Furthermore, these ethnic conflicts, as a result of irredentist currents among the Monarchy's minorities including the Serbs, Italians, Rumanians, and Ruthenians, would have immediate domestic and foreign policy feedback effects. For a number of reasons including their own political advantage, the Germans in Austria supported loyalty to the German Reich with which the state had already been allied for decades through the bilateral and trilateral treaties concluded in, respectively, 1879 and 1882.

This alliance provided Ährenthal with just the self-confidence he needed when he sought in 1908 to give evidence of Austria-Hungary's international position as a major European power and, following a diplomatically controversial agreement with Russia, annexed Bosnia and Herzegovina, territories the Empire had already occupied since 1878. This would prove to be the penultimate and the last "successful" act of power by the Danube Monarchy, since, in retrospect, it was actually only a temporary victory. From this point on, the Habsburg Empire's foreign policy placed it permanently on the brink of war with Serbia, an ambitious land that emerged invigorated from the Balkan Wars of 1912/13 and instilled with pan-Slavic ideas, as well as with its protector, Russia, without actually being prepared for such a war. Nor was Ährenthal's successor, the less energetic Count Leopold Berchtold (1912-1915), willing or able to change this, and he did everything possible to maintain the latent state of crisis in Central Europe through policies meant to uphold the status quo.

It was not until 28 June 1914 when the deadly shots of Sarajevo suddenly hit the couple that was to ascend to the Habsburg throne that all seemed to have a common enemy: the Serbs! The final mobilization of all military, ethnic, political, economic, and social forces of the Habsburg Empire gave renewed hope to all those who believed in the power of dynastic cohesion. When, exactly one month later, Austria-Hungary declared war on Serbia, thereby triggering a wave of international reactions that culminated in World War I, the nineteenth century had truly come to an end, while a tragedy for the state and an even greater one for mankind was just beginning.

# Austria in the First World War, 1914-1918

*Manfried Rauchensteiner*

The murder of Archduke Franz Ferdinand on 28 June 1914 precipitated a European crisis in which Austria-Hungary intended to get even with Serbia, not only because of its assumed participation in the planning of the assassination, but also because of its years of policies made against the Habsburg monarchy. Shortly after the onset of the July crisis, Germany promised unconditional support of Austrian politics, and it was clear from 7 July 1914 in Vienna that there should be—and would be—war.

What was intended, however, was a war with Serbia, not a European war with unforeseeable consequences. Reality fell by the wayside, however, for how could one assume that one's own alliance would hold up and function and not that of the opponent? The course embarked upon was resolutely followed out. In mid-July, a diplomatic course and action addressed to Serbia was drawn up; Emperor Franz Joseph had made an appeal "to my peoples," and posters for mobilization had been prepared. However, the Foreign Ministry in Vienna did not yet consider the time favorable enough. Not until 23 July was the *démarche* delivered in Belgrade. The demands contained in it had been formulated deliberately in such a manner that Serbia could not comply unconditionally. The response, which arrived forty-eight hours later, was deemed unsatisfactory. Diplomatic relations were terminated. Yet there was still no war.

On 27 July, however, an incident was fabricated, and Austria maintained that Serbia had begun fighting. With that the war began, and the automatic pilot of the alliances took care of the rest. Russia supported Serbia and mobilized. Germany took the side of Austria-

Preparing for a gas attack during World War I.

Source: Museum of Military History, Vienna

Hungary and declared war on Russia and France. England took the blow to Belgian neutrality by Germany as an excuse to enter the war; Austria-Hungary declared war on Russia. Suddenly, nations found themselves at war with one another, including Austria-Hungary with France and England, who had scarcely ever had a conflict with one another. However the war did not break out—it was unleashed.

The mood of July 1914 and the reason why Europe entered into war with such unbelievable enthusiasm have been explained by many. One such attempted explanation goes so far as to say that this was an expression of a death-wish. This view certainly does not do justice to the realities. If one looks at what was expressed across Europe, in particular what was said and written by the intellectuals and the artists, something else is evident. It was the question of the meaning of life which had arisen, and virtually everyone who expressed him- or herself on this was convinced that the stand of his or her government was justified and, further, that life had finally assumed a meaning through the war. A man such as Sigmund Freud, whose death instinct theory was used to support one chain of argumentation, wrote, following the Austrian declaration of war on

Serbia: "I feel perhaps for the first time in thirty years like an Austrian. I would like to try one more time with this Empire of little hope."

Everywhere in the Danube Monarchy, one marched out to war with more or less enthusiasm, but at least with confidence. Certainly no one was in a position to assess what really had begun here; it was no war in the sense of the nineteenth century, but a total war, the great dispute between alliances, with virtually no spatial or temporal limit. Total war could only end with total peace following the total defeat of an alliance, and no one knew that either.

The Austrian-Hungarian troops began their march to the Balkans. They did this primarily in the vague hope that war would remain confined to this theater, or else that it would be possible to defeat Serbia before the war had developed into another larger theater less advantageous to the Habsburg Monarchy. Yet, even as the march on the Balkans was under way, it became evident that one had followed an illusion; Russia immediately entered the war as well. Now the Austro-Hungarians had set themselves against the Russians.

The imperial Habsburg army suffered the first serious setbacks. Instead of conducting a swift ground war against Serbia, the Austro-Hungarian troops quickly got into trouble. In the Balkans, they failed at two offensives and were turned back at their points of attack. At the same time, it became clear that a further hope of the Central Powers had not been fulfilled: the German chiefs of staff had assumed that it would be possible to defeat France within six to eight weeks; immediately thereafter, additional superior German forces were supposed to appear in the Russian theater. This was not the case. The defeat of France failed. Alongside France stood England, and these two would be able to block the advance of the German Western army at the Marne.

After the German advance had been brought to a standstill and the Germans subsequently had been turned back, the war became one of position and stamina. The armies of Austria-Hungary, meanwhile, were in increasingly difficult situations. A third great offensive failed in Serbia. To be sure, it had been conducted from Belgrade all the way into old Serbian territory. The Balkans stood at the brink of destruction. Yet the imperial Habsburg army did not have sufficient power to defeat the last Serbian forces. Ultimately, the overextended and dwindling Austrian-Hungarian divisions had to begin their retreat again back to the borders of the Empire.

The situation appeared bleak at the Russian front in December 1914, and there was only the success of the battle at Limanowa-Lapanów to thank for avoiding a catastrophe. Nonetheless, the majority of Galicia remained in Russian hands. The tide did not turn until the beginning of May 1915, when there was the first major joining of German and Austro-Hungarian troops at the battle of Tarnów-Gorlice. Then something occurred which no one had considered possible; in a series of battles, one directly after the other over the course of several weeks, the Russians were defeated. They were driven back so far that the largest parts of Austria-Hungarian territory were liberated again, and the majority of Russian Poland could be occupied.

At the Balkan front, the Serbs had been so weakened by the campaigns of 1914 that there were hardly any more engagements. Then a further opponent entered the picture: Italy. It had been allied with the Central Powers, but by commencement of the war, it had declared its neutrality. Italy wanted to maintain neutrality ultimately only if Austria-Hungary was prepared to make extensive territorial concessions in Trient, South-Tyrol, and in the Triest and Dalmatian area. It was then the Entente which made the desired concessions to Italy in the secret London Treaty (26 April 1915), with the condition, however, that there would be something like an Austro-Hungarian *Konkursmasse* (bankrupt's estate). Then Italy was supposed to be compensated for its participation in the war. It entered the war on 23 May 1915, and from that point forward, the fronts at Isonzo in the Dolomites and at the Kärnten border were the sectors, which more intensely than any others drew the attention of the central Habsburg states.

It was considered over and again whether or not it would be possible to conclude a separate peace with one or the other of the warring factions. Germany felt Italy should be granted the concessions it desired, for there might come a point in time when territories relinquished could be retrieved. Berlin and Vienna also speculated whether or not Russia might be prepared for peace following the summer battles of 1915 and whether or not Serbia would retire from the war. From the discussions conducted in Austria

as well as in Germany, new plans for the restructuring of middle
Europe ultimately developed. To some, the war could only make
sense if the victims that it claimed, which had reached immeasurable
proportions, were balanced out by a middle Europe dominated by the
German Empire and Austria-Hungary.

These debates, which were conducted above all regarding the
future of Poland and Serbia, certainly underscored the fundamental
problems of the Danube Monarchy. For as statesmen began to
calculate the territorial gain of the Monarchy, the question had to be
posed as to whether these gains were even compatible with the
dualistic structure of the Monarchy. Should a trilateral solution be
sought, or should Poland be cut off completely from the Monarchy?
How could the alliance with Germany be developed? How could
they get a position of world power? Which measures should be taken
in order to give Germans living in the Danube Monarchy a dominant
position? With this debate, the demand was soon made for the
complete reorganization of the Monarchy, for the setbacks in the war
were attributed to a lack of national identity and to the fear of the
Slavic troops. All of these fears and concerns began to ferment.

In the fall of 1915, the war reached its climax for Austria-
Hungary. From that point forward, the symptoms of crisis and partial
setbacks increased. One sought to overcome this with ever greater
efforts and ultimately by putting aside the vital interests of the
Empire. Initially the front was paralyzed in the East, while the
campaign against the Serbs, which had been renewed in late fall of
1915 under German command and together with Bulgarian troops,
brought about this mission of Serbia and subsequently the defeat of
Montenegro by Austro-Hungarian troops. However, the joint success
of Germany and Austria created a climate in which each side began
to assert itself more strongly against the other. Austria-Hungary
accused Germany of arrogance, complete ignorance concerning
Austrian matters, and, ultimately, the desire for supreme authority.
Germany pointed increasingly to weaknesses of the Monarchy and,
in the end, brought the course of the war to the simplest common
denominator, that only where German troops were brought in as
support were the imperial Habsburg armies in a position to offer any
resistance.

The conflict ultimately led to a lack of communication among the
chiefs of regarding military strategy. For example, the German

General Chief of Staff Falkenhayn planned an offensive in the Verdun area, while his Austro-Hungarian colleague Conrad von Hötzendorf prepared an attack on Italy. Both plans failed, and if there had been such a thing as an advantage of "inner line" for the Central powers, then it was lost by spring of 1916.

The Entente powers—Great Britain, France, Russia, and Italy— had agreed that their armies should begin the offensives as simultaneously as possible, in order to deprive Germany and Austria of the possibility of moving large units. When Russia undertook its part of the plan in June of 1916, Germany was engaged at Verdun and additionally on the Somme, and Austria-Hungary through its South Tyrol offensive. As a result, the Imperial Habsburg front nearly collapsed in the east. A catastrophe was avoided only by dispatching all available German troops, an activity that was the result of German commanders assuming command. This incident and the internal problems of the Habsburg Monarchy, which were becoming ever more apparent, contributed to Germany's increasing involvement in the politics and military government of Austria-Hungary. These developments led to the creation of the senior war command, which transferred to the German Kaiser the decision making powers for the military leadership of the Central Powers.

In that, however, a step had been taken which could not remain without lasting consequences for the *Kaiser- und Königliche Monarchie*'s (*k. und k.*, Imperial and Royal Monarchy's) internal politics. For the non-German nationalities of the Monarchy believed they recognized the meaning to this war: that the multinational state was to be maintained and that the living conditions for the individual nationalities ought to be improved. In no way, however, did the non-German nationalities want to conduct a war as "vassals" of the German Empire and offer themselves up to the imperialistic war aims of the war powers.

The problems increased and ultimately made their way into the domestic agenda, which the Austrian government and especially its prime minister, Count Stürgkh, could no longer counter. The overthrow of the prime minister had been rehearsed since the summer of 1915. Several times it appeared as though this overthrow was imminent; however, it did not happen. Friedrich Adler, the son of the leader of the Austrian Social Democrats, Viktor Adler, plotted in 1916 not for a normal removal of the prime minister, but for his elimination by force. On 21 October, Adler shot Stürgkh. Yet the turning point was not brought about by Stürgkh's death, but by the death—exactly one month later—of the eighty-six-year-old Emperor Franz Joseph.

The new Emperor, Karl I, inherited a difficult situation, for his empire was coming apart at its seams. Karl tried to deal with his inheritance by gradually breaking away from Germany. The supreme command of the Austro-Hungarian army was dissolved and moved from Teschen to Baden by Vienna. The emperor assumed supreme command personally and selected General Arz von Straussenburg as his new chief of staff. He was also not of the mind simply to accept a joint conduct of war and made clear thereby that the days of the alliance were numbered.

The young emperor selected new prime ministers in swift succession. He had the Austrian imperial council convened; made extensive declarations of amnesty even for those who had committed high treason; and, in direct conversations with representatives of the Entente and by developing contacts in neutral countries abroad, he sought ultimately to make clear the readiness of the Danube Monarchy for peace. For a while, he was also able to hope that the opponents of the Central powers did not want the destruction of Austria-Hungary. For, without question, one needed to maintain hopes in this regard, since the United States, which since April 1917 had been at war with the German Empire, had not initially broadened its warfare to include the Habsburg Monarchy. A further hope was based on the fact that following the February Revolution in Russia and following the October Revolution in 1917 there was a cease-fire and ultimately a peace concluded with Russia. This peace was viewed as a means for the people of Austria-Hungary to survive with the assistance of Russian grain supplies.

Hunger prevailed in Austria from 1916 onward, and there were bottlenecks in virtually every area of life. The work forces were just as near of the end to their capabilities as were the soldiers. In the factories, there were work weeks with up to 110 hours in order to provide supplies for the front. The so-called Hindenburg program was supposed to mobilize the last reserves of the work forces and raw materials. Ultimately, the Empire was over-extended. None of these conditions changed, not even with the military success which had been considered impossible in late fall 1917. After eleven defensive battles against Italy in the area of Isonzo, Austria-Hungary and Germany sought once again to deliver to the Italians a limited blow in a joint offensive. Yet the local successes sought after in this offensive spread themselves out to the point that the entire Italian front collapsed. The armies of the Central Powers were able to take over a considerable portion of upper Italy and moved the front as far as the Piave. Then, of course, they no longer had sufficient forces to conquer Italy.

Germany was engaged in heavy fighting in the west. The last hopes for a victory of the Central Powers were crumbling. In mid-December 1917, the United States declared war on Austria-Hungary as well, and in January 1918, U.S. President Woodrow Wilson delivered his famous Fourteen Points speech. Out of these points, one could infer the intent to dissolve the Monarchy.

The mood in the country was despairing. Workers and soldiers, mindful of the example of the Russian Revolution, wanted ultimately to make clear at the beginning of 1918 that they were no longer willing to bear the burdens of the war. In January and February 1918, there were strikes and military revolts. Once again, it was possible to subdue or to put down the revolts. On the other hand, neither the Emperor nor the governments of the two halves of the Empire found the strength or the possibility to end the war. Over and again, people clung to the hope that the war would take a turn in the last moment. The Treaty of Brest-Litovsk concluded with Russia had been such a hope. One could argue up to the summer of 1918 that the situation on the fronts was incomparably better than the situation within the country. Finally, last, decisive offensives would be conducted, from Germany once again into France and from Austria-Hungary across the Piave.

However, the offensive in June 1918 failed practically at its beginning. The collapse of the Danube Monarchy stemmed from this failure. To be sure, the government exercised its central powers still, and the Emperor attempted to the end to offer himself as an integration factor. All these efforts, however, could no longer keep the Empire together. New Serbian troops and troops from the Entente were approaching from the Balkans, and the Italian army began to push the Austro-Hungarian forces into the mountains.

There was no sudden collapse of the Empire, but a slow death. Finally, one group after another withdrew its allegiance to the Monarchy and declared its independence. Emperor Karl, to be sure, attempted with his Peoples' Manifest of 16 October 1918 to make clear that he was willing to function even as emperor of a federation of independent states. This declaration, however, fell on deaf ears. It was all too late.

The final collapse went hand in hand with the declaration of independence of the different national states. This caused the dissolution of the Austrian army, not her destruction in a last battle. A cease-fire was ultimately called for, negotiated, and concluded with the Allies in the Villa Guisti near Padua. Due to a failure of the army commands in these last hours of the war, the Austro-Hungarian troops were ordered to cease fighting earlier than the actual cease-fire was to have taken place. As a result, hundreds of thousands of *k. und k.* soldiers were taken prisoner by Italy.

The last national state that on 12 November 1918 began to rise from the ground of the fallen Monarchy was German Austria. It did not begin its existence in peace, however, but rather merely in a state of non-war, and its existence was viewed not as permanent, but merely as a transitional solution, as part of the new German Republic.

# 12 February 1934: Social Democracy and Civil War

*Wolfgang Maderthaner*

## The Road Leading to Crisis

During the years of the Great Depression after 1929, when pre-existing structural weaknesses and developmental tendencies marked by recurring crises were endowed with the potential for disaster to an extent inconceivable until then, the First Republic was destabilized and finally destroyed. The profound economic and psychological transformations of these years of crisis had an impact on all strata and classes of society, and led to fundamental changes in political and cultural life.

Following the collapse of the Habsburg Monarchy, the now-diminutive Austrian state's industrial and commercial sectors were cut off from 85 percent of the formerly tariff-protected markets in which they had done business. The end of the historically integrated economic territory of the Danube Monarchy with its high degree of regional division of labor meant the separation of natural resource deposits from the plants that processed them and the severance of ties connecting the various stages of the production process. As soon as the export premium of the inflation during the immediate postwar years had been eliminated by the stabilization of the value of the currency, an enormous process of shrinkage of the urban and industrial sectors of the economy set in, a process that was dramatically exacerbated by the consequences of the international economic crisis after 1929 with its succession of import bans, protective tariffs, quota agreements, payment restrictions, and so forth.

The crisis hit the economy just as it was going through a process of restructuring, and led to a retrogressive structural shift. Industrial

Civil war in February 1934: Artillary bombardment of the workers' quarters in Karl-Marx-Hof in Vienna.

Source: *Verein für Geschichte der Arbeiterbewegung*, Vienna

production fell by nearly 40 percent from 1929 to its 1933 low. In the iron industry, one of the leading economic sectors, customer orders had slowed to such a degree that by November 1932 production had sunk to 8 percent of normal. Whereas unemployment had averaged 9 percent during the relatively strong business cycle upswing of 1927-29, it then hit 38 percent when things were at their worst. In human terms, this meant 700,000 jobless, of whom only 40 percent were receiving regular unemployment benefits or emergency relief payments at the end of 1934. Thus, a third of the entire workforce was continually excluded from the production process. Even more dramatic was the situation among industrial workers, who traditionally comprised the core of the Social Democratic labor movement. Fully 44.5 percent of them were out of work in early 1934, and a considerable proportion of those who still had a job were forced to work part-time (28 percent in 1933). Mass unemployment and the decline in real wages meant a dramatic drop in consumer demand. From 1929 to 1934, monthly wages and salaries in Vienna declined by 44 percent from 158 million to 89 million ÖS; the workforce decreased from 636,000 to 439,000.

The populations of what had previously been prosperous industrial regions were impoverished, long-term structural unemployment became a mass phenomenon, and the weight of organized labor within Austrian society diminished. Worn down by years of unemployment with no prospect of recovery, resignation became widespread, and this paralyzed the resistance people could mount in the face of authoritarian experiments by the political right. An increasingly blatant contradiction developed between the labor movement's steadfast effort to maintain the social welfare accomplishments of the revolutionary years of 1918-20 and its constantly declining political and social power. Breaking the power of the labor movement, the *Gleichschaltung* of the unions, and broadly scaling back welfare entitlements thus became an increasingly clear and ever-more-promising strategy in the government's effort to deal with the crisis. Wage pressure and the elimination of the welfare system's safety net in the absence of the "disruptive influence" of a still-powerful parliamentary opposition were designed to restore economic competitiveness. Taking advantage of the reactionary ground swell of the time, the government shattered the parliamentary and democratic forms of its system of rule just as Hitler was taking power in Germany.

Rost von Tonningen, the League of Nations commissioner responsible for oversight of the state's finances and a future Dutch Nazi, confided to his diary that, in conference with Chancellor Engelbert Dollfuss and Central Bank President Viktor Kienböck, it was decided that the dismissal of Parliament was necessary since it was sabotaging the work of reconstruction.

In the face of the pressure exerted by the economic crisis, substantial processes of divergence had been at work within the bourgeois and peasant strata of society. Since the world war, tremendous amounts of capital had been devalued and destroyed, and holders of fixed-income securities were devastated by inflation. With the stabilization of the value of the currency, the profits of black-market dealers and profiteers began to dry up. Industry was mired in a sort of endless crisis—the destruction of companies' savings and the exposure of their working capital during the phase of hyperinflation did lasting damage to their financial position, and, following stabilization, credit interest remained at an exorbitant level. Among industrialized countries, Austria was the only one whose industrial output was shrinking. By 1933, exports had sunk to 57 percent of their 1920 level. The inability of industry to become self-financing and its ongoing weakness made a critical contribution to social breakdown.

The industrial crisis was followed by a crisis in the Austrian banking sector that had grossly expanded during the time of inflation. Even before World War I, the relationship between bankers and industrialists was characterized by a highly pronounced one-sided dependency, and subsequent events had made it even more extreme. Industry was heavily in debt to the banks, which often involuntarily became majority owners of their industrial debtors. This banking crisis, which had become virulent in the wake of the currency stabilization, could indeed be covered up at first by concentrating the bad loans among the holdings of an ever-shrinking number of large banks, but the collapse of the *Creditanstalt (CA)* in 1931 triggered the outbreak of a worldwide credit crisis. The *CA* was the largest Central European bank; following its takeover of the *Bodenkredit*, it controlled 70 percent of all industrial and large wholesale enterprises. Restoring it to financial viability necessitated the involvement of the state and the National Bank; the government assumed liability for all domestic and foreign bank deposits, whereby the losses amounted to more than 10 percent of the 1931 GNP. The consequences of the *CA* crisis for the currency sector and the credit market, in the production sphere, and for the state's finances were dire. They led to the adoption of economic policy measures that, in turn, exacerbated the crisis and accelerated the economy's path along the deflationary spiral.

The reorganization of the Austrian banking sector under the leadership of the National Bank was completed in 1934. In the end, all large banks in Vienna (with the exception of the *Länderbank*) were under the direct control of the National Bank and thus of the state. Big business' dependence upon banks that were now controlled by the state (and to a much lesser extent by foreign capital) delivered a telling blow to its position of power. The captains of industry naturally wished to continue exerting influence upon government measures—for instance, the substance of emergency regulations having to do with worker protection or social security—but an economic policy course heavily favoring agrarian interests and initiatives aimed at department stores and bread-making factories that were reminiscent of guild restrictions strongly suggested that the bankers and industrial capitalists had begun to lose their leading role in the bourgeois camp.

Meanwhile, the crisis had impoverished large segments of the bourgeoisie and peasantry. The plunge in consumer demand drove the number of court-supervised liquidations of and bankruptcy filings by retail and commercial enterprises in 1932 up to more than double what it had been in 1929. In the wake of a crisis in agricultural prices and sales, farm indebtedness, which had been practically extinguished in the hyperinflation of 1924, jumped dramatically, and amounted to more than half the annual market production by 1933. In that year in the province of Salzburg, for example, almost 80 percent of all farms were threatened in one form or another with mandatory debt collection measures. A re-agrarianization process had been underway since 1929, but the government subsidy policies were primarily aimed at the grain-producing farmers of the eastern Austrian plains. The situation in the west was much different; there, small and middle-size farms on a rather low technological level with limited product specialization dominated agriculture. Processes of impoverishment resulting from the crises in the markets for farm animals and breeding stock, milk products and timber had a much more drastic impact here. Financially devastated members of the middle class and peasant farmers in the Alpine provinces who were dependent on tourism from Germany and on German demand for Austrian agricultural products joined together with businessmen in industries that desperately needed protective tariffs in advocating Anschluß with Germany. Following the failure of the German-Austrian customs union plan of 1931, these groups increasingly provided the grassroots support for National Socialism in Austria. This movement's basic appeal was to the embittered, rebellious mood of the impoverished masses of the petit bourgeoisie, the peasantry, and large segments of the traditionally German nationalist, anti-clerical and anti-Habsburg intelligentsia.

But this meant that the bourgeois right wing was divided into two hostile factions. As soon as the Pan-Germanists left the government and split off from the Christian Socials, the nationalist dividing lines within the Austrian bourgeoisie re-emerged and a conflict that had determined the development of that segment of society for the last century assumed renewed relevance—the conflict between German nationalists and legitimists (supporters of the Habsburgs and advocates of a restoration). At the moment of the "nationalist revolution" in Germany, state power in Austria was in the hands of the legitimist faction that opposed Anschluß. In order to have been able to effectively combat National Socialism using parliamentary democratic means, they would have had to form a coalition with the Social Democrats against whom they had been pitted in a decades-old, bitterly fought *Kulturkampf*. As early as April 1932, provincial legislature and city council elections had resulted in alarming gains for the Nazis at the expense of the established parties. In Parliament, the Christian Socials formed a coalition with the *Heimwehr*, producing the slimmest possible majority of just one vote and forcing parliamentary governance that was susceptible to crises and dependent upon strokes of fate in every imaginable variety. The Dollfuss government resorted to the means of dictatorship.

## Radicalization of the Political Climate and the Rise of the *Heimwehren*

The actual victors on 15 July 1927 (the Ministry of Justice fire in Vienna) had been the *Heimwehr* units, whose active intervention had made an important contribution to quickly controlling and putting down the twenty-four hour general strike and the unlimited transportation strike called by the Social Democratic Party (SDAP) leadership. Formed in the immediate postwar period as a border patrol in the provinces of Carinthia and Styria, they soon developed under the influence of militant organizations of the Bavarian right wing into anti-Marxist paramilitary groups of middle-class burghers and peasant farmers. As a protest movement of those classes and groups who were acutely threatened by social decline into underprivileged status, they initially succeeded in recruiting a significant number of active members and supporters only in those regions where they were able to call upon uninterrupted conservative and anti-modernist traditions—as was the case with the Tyrolean *Heimatwehr* under the leadership of its chief of staff, Major

Waldemar Pabst, a German fugitive who had been involved in the murder of Rosa Luxemburg and Karl Liebknecht and later was a central figure in the Kapp *Putsch*.

During the second Seipel administration, the *Heimwehr* began to exhibit the first signs of developing into a mass movement. Seipel had lost the elections of 27 April 1927 with the burgher bloc he headed, and within the framework of parliamentary democracy, he seemed unable to guarantee for any length of time that faction's continued pre-eminence if it would ever come to a serious political confrontation with the ever-more-powerful Social Democrats. He saw his best chances in a constitutional revision and an alliance with the *Heimwehr*, whose military and, above all, political-symbolic potential for mobilization he sought to instrumentalize to this end. The Austrian Banking Association, large landowners, the German capitalists who controlled the Alpine Montan coal and steel operations and other industrialists, and, beginning in 1928, Hungary and fascist Italy under Mussolini generously subsidized the *Heimwehr* with substantial sums of money and a diversified arsenal of weapons. Under these circumstances, the *Heimwehr* had no trouble attracting new members, although the units increasingly consisted of the "*déclassé* of all classes." Like its rank and file, the *Heimwehr*'s grassroots supporters were also thoroughly heterogeneous, encompassing members of the traditional and new middle classes facing the acute endangerment of their social status, heavily indebted farmers, the unemployed, and—particularly in areas where the Alpine Montan's influence was greatest—laborers who feared for their material existence. Its leadership was comprised of representatives of the intelligentsia, demobilized and out-of-work World War I officers, and an increasingly significant number of landowning aristocrats. What they had in common was their militant rejection of the democratic republic, and their joint struggle to break the political power of organized labor and to check the rise to social pre-eminence of upper middle class parvenus, many of whom had financed their social climb with profits from speculation and black market dealings during the time of inflation. With this political clientele, two attorneys, Dr. Richard Steidle and Dr. Walter Pfrimer, managed to unify the previously independent and rival *Heimwehr* groups in October 1927.

With constant threats of a *putsch* or a *coup d'état*, invocations of the "emergency right of the people," and calls to dispense with the "fetish of legality," they campaigned for fundamental changes to the Constitution of 1920, though it would not be until Chief of Police Johannes Schober—one of those chiefly responsible for the bloody incidents of July 1927, and a man who seemed to personally guarantee the success of the *Heimwehr* plan—once again took over as chancellor that this became the central issue of domestic politics in Austria. The draft constitution that Schober submitted on 18 October 1929 essentially foresaw a broad expansion of the authority (including the right to rule by emergency decree) of a president who would now be elected by popular vote, as well as the elimination of Vienna's status as a separate province, which would have undermined the power of the Social Democrats in their most important stronghold. Other provisions called for the reintroduction of aristocratic privileges; censorship, especially in the theater and cinema; doing away with jury trials; the establishment of a corporatist council; the expansion of police authority; and a series of other changes all having an authoritarian bias. Schober, nevertheless, would not prove to be a mere pawn of the *Heimwehr*. In protracted negotiations with the Social Democrats, whose position of power in society had still hardly been diminished by the global economic crisis that was still in its early stages, the two sides succeeded in working out a compromise that did not establish the authoritarian state the *Heimwehr* was striving for, but rather a mixed presidential-parliamentary system of government.

Defeat in the constitutional conflict brought out into the open the opposing positions that co-existed within the ranks of the *Heimwehr* as a result of its heterogeneous social structure. Ongoing efforts to achieve unity culminated in a convention held on 18 May 1930 in Korneuburg, at which all *Heimwehr* units were to come out in support of an anti-parliamentary course and condemn "Western parliamentarism" as well as the "multi-party state." Oversight corporations set up for each profession were to be the basis of the "self-regulation of the economy," at the head of which was to be a "strong state administration." The estates making up society were to be "aligned with the needs of the community," which would overcome the "subversion of our people by Marxist class struggle and the liberal-capitalist economic system." Behind these principles formulated in the "Korneuburg Oath" were positions that had been developed by Viennese sociologist and economist Othmar Spann and his followers and were an expression of the close ideological and personnel ties between Spann's circle and the *Heimwehr* leadership.

Spann, with recourse to the deterministic realism of the older scholasticism and concrete reference to the romantic anti-liberalism of Adam Müller, developed his teleological holistic metaphysics as a reaction to the conditions and consequences of modern industrial society. Under the influence of the events of the immediate postwar period, he designed in his work *The True State* a conception of the organization of the structure of society along occupational lines, the objective of which was to preserve existing property rights and conditions from the social welfare claims of an increasingly aggressive labor movement. Cartels and unions would be merged together into self-administered occupational associations in which membership would be mandatory, and the growth of Social Democratic power in the republic was to be neutralized by means of a decentralized arrangement of corporate bodies and the transfer of state sovereignty rights to these very same mandatory membership associations. Altered political circumstances in the late 1920s prompted Spann and his circle to make a decisive change to this conception, modifying it in accordance with the social structure of the *Heimwehr* movement: the reintroduction of an authoritarian state governmental body to which the business and professional corporations would be subordinate as a means of overcoming the economic contradictions inherent in corporatist society. The top leadership role was conceived for the *Heimwehr*, which was to constitute a "state's estate." Spann's model was a sweeping abstraction of the social reality of a modern industrial society, and his highly complicated work naturally did not provide concrete instructions for implementing his ideas. Rather, his vague definition of terms, the complexity of the argumentation, and the nebulousness of his language precipitated in a rather vulgar form the conscious understanding of the *Heimwehr* leaders, and this crystallized into a superficial concept of the enemy that targeted "the leftists."

## The Establishment of the Authoritarian
## "Corporatist State"

In light of de-industrialization and re-agrarianization processes
and the progressive weakening of modern segments of society like
industry, financial capital, and the labor force, the bourgeois and
peasant masses were divided and incapable of exercising political
power. The power vacuum that developed was occupied by "new"
classes: the federal bureaucracy, now unfettered by parliamentary
controls    and    thus    with    enormously    expanded    power;    the
predominantly aristocratic large landowners via leadership positions
in the paramilitary *Heimwehren*; and, finally, the Church hierarchy.
The general destabilization of the country during the years of crisis
had made democracy incapable of functioning and, in principle, had
paved the way for pre-capitalist classes to erect a "corporatist"
dictatorship. These groups' capability of filling this emerging power
vacuum was rather facilitated by the fact that Austria's whole
political system was absolutely pervaded by pre-modern structures.
This was a system based on privileged notabilities, intervention and
intrigue, one in which parties, associations, and co-operatives
assured the social integration of their clientele, and corruption was
not merely socially tolerated but rather something taken completely
for granted. The social crisis had once again imparted relevance and
attractiveness to those conservative utopias that had been ever-
present, but had nevertheless been edged out of the limelight during
the phase of (relatively) functional parliamentary democracy.

If corporatist ideology was elevated to what amounted to an
official state theory, then one key reason for this was that the
Catholic Church had taken this line of thinking from aristocratic
romanticism—as the two went side by side into the fray against the
bourgeois revolution—and made it its own. In intentional contrast to
formal, parliamentary democracy, the authoritarian regime countered
with the idea of a constitution based on occupational corporations,
that is, the constitutional idea that all anti-democratic bourgeois
currents had in common. Now, Austrofascism's backing was coming
from those elements of society that Otto Bauer referred to as "heirs
to the legacy of the Austria of yore," and was thus competing with
National Socialism and its annexation plans. Therefore, its
conception of a constitution could not possibly be that of nationalist

fascism, since its own aim was a Catholic, corporatist constitution implemented in accordance with the Catholic Church's teachings on social welfare. But even if the papal encyclical, which included extremely sharp and pointed criticism of capitalism in the tradition of older "Christian socialism," approved of the fascist corporatist system, and called for the "peaceful cooperation of the classes," for the "suppression of socialist organizations and undertakings," and for the "regulating influence of a separate state bureaucracy," it nevertheless firmly rejected the totalitarian claim to power of the fascist state. Rather, it introduced the principle of subsidiarity, called for the free self-administration of the occupational associations, and thus moved toward the principle of "industrial democracy," of "economic democracy." It refused to go into elaborating on questions of a "technical nature" just as it gave no concrete instructions for setting up a corporatist order. It treated the economic configuration of society; it completely ignored the form of the state and the process of establishing and building up the authority of the state. As a compilation of corporatist ideologies of diverse provenance and social content, it was, consequently, open to a wide variety of interpretational approaches.

Until Dollfuss took office, he had stood solidly in the democratic tradition of the Christian Social rural peasantry. But as soon as he renounced parliamentary-democratic forms, he came under the powerful influence of the *Heimwehren* as well as of political Catholicism, which, with its tightly interwoven network of organizations and associations, was also in a position to provide the regime with a certain mass-level, grassroots support of its own. Under this pressure, the authoritarian momentum intensified, and, through the Italian influence to which Dollfuss had submitted in return for support against the Third Reich, it increased even further. After all, Italian fascism was among the leading patrons of the *Heimwehren*. In a letter dated 1 July 1933, Mussolini had insistently pressed Dollfuss "to carry out [a program] of effective and substantial internal reforms of a decisively fascist nature," to "deliver a blow [to the Social Democrats] in their citadel Vienna," and to expand the scope of the purges to encompass "all centers of activity" that "are pursuing destructive tendencies in opposition to the authoritarian principle."

On 18 August 1933, Dollfuss met Mussolini in Riccione. *Il Duce* emphatically urged him to deliver "a major political address" in early September to announce the independence and renewal of Austria, the "dictatorial character" of the regime, the appointment of a government commissioner for the municipality of Vienna, and the project to reform the constitution and to put it on a "fascist basis from a political, economic, and social perspective." In fact, Dollfuss did deliver a major programmatic address at Vienna's trotter racetrack on 11 September in conjunction with the festivities marking the 250th anniversary of Vienna's liberation from the Turkish siege. In this speech, he touched on all those points that would go on to constitute the core pattern of legitimation of Austrofascism: the creation of a "new Austrian" identity as opposed to that of the Third Reich and its craving for annexation; the evocation of a romanticizing "Reich concept" and the construct of a specifically Austrian, Catholic-Western, "German mission"; the suppression of both the independently organized Social Democratic labor movement as well as the "heathen" Prussian nationalist fascism; and the creation of a "public-spirited, Christian, German state of Austria on a corporatist basis under strong, authoritarian leadership." The corporatist state was defined as a holy mission derived from the past and pointing the way to the future, and understood as a backward-looking alternative to the consequences of modern industrial society and to modernism as a whole; based upon a specifically Catholic longing for class harmony and conflict resolution, coupled with feudal reminiscences and anti-modern emotions; intertwined with traditional conceptions of an above and a below mandated by God; and infused with vaguely anti-capitalist sentiments. It embodied the longing for the organic society based on natural law, with its unquestioned social hierarchization. In his speeches, Dollfuss repeatedly used the image of the farmer and the farm hand who lived and labored together, and who, after a hard day's work, kneeled down side by side, each with rosary in hand, and prayed together. Parliamentary democracy, autonomous labor unions, and competing political parties had no place in this worldview that regarded the social contract and the Enlightenment as marked with the stigma of blasphemy.

In a "cold" *coup d'état* on 4 March 1933 (dissolution of Parliament by Chancellor Dollfuss), the regime assumed what amounted to absolute governmental power. From March 1933 on, in a permanent state of unconstitutionality, approximately 300 ordinances were enacted on the basis of the wartime Enabling Act of 1917. The Supreme Court was dismissed. These emergency decrees led to the dismantling of general civil rights and social welfare legislation, but by their very nature they also destroyed in advance the self-administrative bodies that were in place in a number of professions and which would have been capable of further development—the disqualification of the railway workers' representative body, dismissal of the freely elected representatives of the post office personnel and health insurance fund staff as well as federal employees, placing the Chamber of Labor under government control, undermining the autonomy of the Social Security system, placing district industrial commissions (made up of equal numbers of labor and management representatives) under central government control, and so forth. In the rapid, sequential form of these emergency decrees, in their cumulative effect, in the combination of integrating and regressive measures, Dollfuss, a man suffused with the sense of being on a religious mission, gave the appearance of an uncompromising and resolute crisis manager.

Freedom of the press and the right to assemble were severely restricted, and the *Arbeiterzeitung* (*Workers' Daily*) became subject to prepublication censorship. Jurisdiction over political offenses was transferred to the police, trial by jury was almost totally eliminated, and the independent judiciary was gradually transformed into an agency to assist in implementing the government's authoritarian claims to power. Although each of these steps was justified with the necessity of taking more aggressive action against the National Socialists, they were applied first and foremost to the Social Democratic labor movement. The *Republikanischer Schutzbund*, the Social Democrats' paramilitary auxiliary, was dissolved on 30 March 1933, although it was immediately reorganized in another form. Legally valid collective contracts agreed upon by unions and private firms were set aside, and wage cuts were ordered. Unemployment compensation was reduced considerably and cut altogether for certain categories of recipients. A ban on strikes in a number of industrial sectors went into effect, with walkouts punishable by imprisonment. On 11 November 1933, a law went into effect providing for summary judgments for murder, arson, and malicious damage to property; an emergency decree dated 12 February 1934 added "revolt" to this list. "Holding camps" for the internment of political opponents were set up, and a campaign to financially destroy "Red Vienna" was launched. Dollfuss wrote Mussolini on 22 July 1933 that what they had in mind was to "take quite a big chunk out of" the financial resources that the "Marxists" had at their disposal due to their vast influence in Vienna. On the very day Dollfuss departed for Riccione, the Council of Ministers voted to impose a 36 million Schilling tax on the city of Vienna retroactive to 1 January 1933. Summing up the situation, Dollfuss wrote that the government was unshakably committed to its goal of "overcoming the Marxist mentality, Marxist forms and organizations, and replacing them with patriotism arrayed above class loyalties and with a society structured along occupational-corporatist lines under the leadership of a strong authoritarian government."

## The Social Democratic Party on the Defensive

The Social Democrats stood powerless and bewildered before this authoritarian rule by emergency decree, and they increasingly pursued a wait-and-see political course that ultimately became tinged with fatalism. Since withdrawing from the coalition in 1920, the party leadership had decided on a strict and fundamental policy of opposition. Seipel's offer in 1931 to join a "concentration" government in which all major parties would be represented was refused for obvious reasons, though the Social Democrats displayed a will to cooperate that transcended narrow political boundaries by supporting, not the first, but all seven subsequent *CA* bail-out laws— and thus foregoing a short-term rise in their popularity—with the justification that having done otherwise would have meant the collapse of the country's entire industrial sector. But they concentrated their real energies on an internationally admired effort to expand and improve municipal facilities and social welfare programs in Vienna, made possible by the city's status as a separate province up to the early 1930s that guaranteed it wide-ranging financial sovereignty. The Viennese experiment in municipal socialism was also designed to serve as a model for the rest of the country, since the city was the only political jurisdiction in which

Austromarxist theory could be put into practice. The policies pursued in Vienna thus took on decisive importance in the effort to achieve socialist hegemony in the country as a whole. By building municipal socialism, the Austrian Social Democrats could maintain their commitment to an active and radical reform program while at the same time acknowledging the limits of its reformist course that was oriented on the unconditional preservation of the parliamentary democratic republic. The Social Democrats were the first socialist party to administer a city with over a million inhabitants, and "Red Vienna" was the first practical example of a long-term socialist strategy to transform an entire metropolitan infrastructure. Contemporary observers considered the municipal reform strategies in public housing policies and the welfare system along with Otto Glöckel's school reform as the centerpiece of "Red Vienna."

In the socialist *Internationale* and throughout the world, the Vienna administration was regarded as a model for Social Democratic municipal policymaking. If the Austrian Social Democrats' organizational strength had made them renowned as the "model party of the *Internationale*," then this reputation was considerably enhanced when the party took over the administration of a major metropolis. Nowhere else had a party succeeded to such an extent in capturing the support and identification of the working class, and this was especially true of the Vienna organization, which could proudly call itself the "largest party organization in the world." In 1932, 25 percent of the population was organized within the SDAP—among men, 38.8 percent; among women, 14.2 percent. The 648,496 party members throughout Austria in 1929 included 400,484 Viennese. The proportion of members under age 20 was three times as high as in the SPD—its German counterpart with a disproportionately high percentage of elderly members—and 57 percent of the Viennese members of the SDAP were under 40. At the polls in Vienna, the party continually chalked up a nearly two-thirds majority; the 1927 results were above average with 59. 87 percent of the votes cast in Vienna (as compared to 42.32 percent in Austria as a whole). According to the party's own calculations, approximately 80 percent of all workers voted Social Democratic in the parliamentary and city council elections held from 1923 to 1930.

The municipal social welfare policies, acclaimed as the "Viennese System," are closely associated with the work of anatomist Julius

Tandler. Conceived as a much-needed supplement to social policy legislation and labor laws passed during the coalition period, child welfare protections were soon proposed. Furthermore, Tandler rejected traditional concepts of charity and proceeded under the assumption of society's duty to provide and the individual's right to receive social welfare services. Beginning in 1922, a tightly woven network of welfare institutions and measures was set up. Most of these aimed at raising the birth rate and improving the socialization conditions in lower-class families. Welfare agency intervention and medical counseling for women and mothers were designed to implement higher standards in the areas of infant and child care, hygiene, and parental childrearing practices, thus bringing about a higher level of familial reproduction. Despite its tremendous popularity and the undeniable progress it made, the "Viennese System" as a whole exhibited that close connection between welfare and repression, disciplining and surveillance that characterize "modern" welfare systems in general.

Nevertheless, city hall socialism's successes were most evident, particularly in the area of public housing. On 21 September 1923, shortly before parliamentary elections, the Vienna City Council passed a five-year residential building program that would construct 5,000 new apartments a year beginning in 1924. The plan's targets were already met by 1927, and on 27 May of that year, it was decided to construct an additional 6,000 apartments and 5,257 townhouses a year. Before long, 10.8 percent of all city residents lived in such developments. The city administration believed it had found the solution to the shortage of acceptable working-class housing in gigantic projects, the so-called people's residential palaces. Furthermore, a maximum building density of 40 percent of the particular parcel—as compared to 85 percent permitted for the old tenements built by real estate speculators—guaranteed spacious, landscaped, sunlit interior courtyards. Welfare agency offices and community facilities were located in almost all municipal housing projects; the apartments themselves, despite their small size, were very nicely appointed.

New methods were initiated to improve the city's finances, and Hugo Breitner, city councilman in charge of financial affairs, introduced direct taxes. The residential construction tax receipts were set aside in a special-purpose fund, and the rates, like those of the various user taxes, were highly progressive. It was not until the residential construction tax had practically lost its original character in the wake of the decisive changes that took place in 1932 that outlays for residential construction were adjusted to match tax receipts. With its new system of taxation—the financial basis of municipal policymaking as a whole during the interwar period—the city set a restructuring of its economy in motion, the objective of which was to expand the communal sector and raise local industrial investment at the expense of the consumption of luxury goods and the foreign investment market.

The Social Democratic political concept was connected with a pedagogically formulated transformation of the individual, with the creation and anticipation of a "New Man" within existing circumstances and in the framework of a strategy of "anticipatory socialism." A complex, highly integrated network of auxiliary and cultural organizations was set up—what amounted to a universal "system for drop-outs" from the culture of everyday life, a "state within a state" designed to place the life of the individual within a historic and existential context and to endow the individual with a sense of security, self-confidence, and assurance about prospects for the future.

This strategy of erecting a comprehensive countercultural network was implemented in a very appropriate manner, particularly in "Red Vienna," but as the political situation deteriorated and the transformation of the economic order was projected into a far distant though still absolutely determined socialist future, the subjective factor of "socialist reform of life" was ascribed with exaggerated significance. Furthermore, it should not be overlooked that important aspects of this seemingly autochthonous working-class culture with its unique characteristics of an often very rigid nature were nothing more than expressions of a modern industrial culture that was developing internationally or of popularized versions of what previously had been reformist approaches of bourgeois movements. Moreover, coming to grips with and modifying the living conditions and lifestyle of the working class called for leadership from above and bureaucratic intervention. In spite of all the quite serious and ambitious plans to democratize its internal organizational structures (such as those expressed in the party's 1926 statutes), Social Democracy in Austria nevertheless also displayed traits characteristic of all modern socialist mass parties: oligarchic tendencies, hierarchical organizational structure, and the formulation of political demands and objectives proceeding from top to bottom. Indeed, there were massive, though not irreconcilable, differences between the modes of cultural behavior, views, and needs of the political elites and those of the grassroots supporters; thus, Vienna municipal politics during the interwar period were worked out not only in correspondence with but also in discordant contrast to the propagated model of the New Man. This was made an even graver problem for the Social Democrats because the linkage of culture and politics constituted a central element of their strategy. This dichotomy between the leadership and the rank and file was never eliminated, not even in the cultural experiment of "Red Vienna." Historically rooted and vibrant worker subcultures as well as forms of popular culture were opposed rather than integrated.

Through the constant indoctrination of the masses organized in the party's network of auxiliary groups, it was possible to propagate the model of the beautiful, strong, educated, collective New Man— celebrated in aesthetically polished mass parades and artistically exaggerated mass festivals. The disciplined masses symbolized simultaneously strength and restraint, threat and domestication; they were a symbol of the revolutionary idealism as well as the puritanical sobriety of the Industrial Age. One of the more important reasons for the failure of Social Democracy in interwar Austria is that it ultimately succumbed to the mass suggestion that it had created. It attempted to compensate for its steadily diminishing social and political power with the strength and beauty of staged ritual, and ultimately replaced concrete action with pseudo-revolutionary pathos.

With the Linz Program of 1926, the party had, moreover, established a strategy of "defensive violence." In case—and this was formulated conditionally—the bourgeois parties sought to use armed violence to subvert a socialist victory attained through democratic means, the Social Democrats would be forced to safeguard the republic through civil war and, for the time being, by resorting to the "means of dictatorship" of the proletariat. It was added, though, that this dictatorship could by no means be permitted to oppose democracy; rather, it could only serve the cause of its re-establishment. This was a highly controversial passage, a compromise formulation meant primarily to insure the continuing integration of the party's left wing. The conception of defensive violence played a key role in the reorganization of the *Republikanischer Schutzbund* following the disaster of 15 July 1927 as a disciplined and rather apolitical military auxiliary, just as the propagandistic reception accorded to that conception by the bourgeois parties made a considerable contribution to polarizing the political situation.

The more the party leadership retreated in the face of the authoritarian regime's rule by emergency decree, the greater the sense of unrest that pervaded the Social Democratic ranks in Vienna and the major industrial regions. At an extremely turbulent special convention in October 1933, which, by this point, could only be held in an atmosphere of "semi-legality," the left wing angrily attacked the defeatist policies being pursued by the executive committee and, above all, Otto Bauer himself. The leadership succeeded in hammering out a compromise; it foresaw calling a general strike that would, of necessity, mean civil war, in four cases: 1.) if the government illegally and unconstitutionally imposed a fascist constitution, 2.) if the government illegally and unconstitutionally dismissed the constitutional administration of the city and province of Vienna and transferred authority to a government commissioner, 3.) if the government dissolved the party or the unions, or 4.) if the government sought to implement their *Gleichschaltung*.

They wanted to risk civil war only if it were unavoidable, and made the attempt to prevent the looming catastrophe by offering ever-greater concessions ultimately bordering on total capitulation. Delegates established contact with Christian Social politicians known to be committed to democracy, in order to thus persuade Dollfuss to abandon this uncompromising fight against Social Democracy, and to enable him to proceed with forces united against National Socialism. The message sent to the chancellor was that the Social Democrats would be prepared to constitutionally grant the government extraordinary powers as long as these were utilized under the supervision of a special parliamentary committee and the

Supreme Court. In return, the party's freedom to pursue political
activities as well as freedom of assembly and of the press were to be
guaranteed. As late as the morning of 12 February representatives of
the party's right wing—led by the Lower Austrians—conferred with
Christian Socialist politicians. Dollfuss, who on 26 January 1934 had
once again been reminded by Italian Undersecretary of State Fulvio
Suvich that decisive action could no longer be deferred, did not
respond. Thus, even Otto Bauer's final offer of a compromise
formulated in the February issue of the theoretical journal *Der Kampf*
(*The Struggle*) did not elicit the slightest reaction:

> The working class can by no means share the petit bourgeois
> illusion that the "occupational-corporatist" organization could
> constitute the basis of a "new social order" that would eliminate
> class disparities. But neither must the working class therefore
> unconditionally reject the formation of cooperatives organized
> along occupational lines. . . . It is precisely through the process
> of reaching an understanding with the petite bourgeoisie and the
> farming community about a democratic system of occupational
> cooperative self-administration that the working class can win
> allies among the petite bourgeoisie and the farming community
> against an anti-democratic "corporative" forced-membership
> administrative organization based on the Italian model, which
> would mean the destruction of political democracy and the
> establishment of a fascist dictatorship.

## The Path Leading to 12 February 1934

On 24 January 1934, Major Emil Fey, (ret.), the minister of the
interior, vice-chancellor and "*Führer*" of the Viennese *Heimwehren*,
issued the order to begin systematic searches in Social Democratic
Party local branches, in public offices in which Social Democrats
were in charge, and in private residences. The discovery of large
caches of arms in Schwechat provided Fey with the pretext to expand
this to a large-scale search for weapons throughout all of Vienna and,
among other steps, to have the party headquarters in the heart of the
city occupied by a large police detachment on 8 February. In the
wake of these searches for weapons, there were numerous arrests of
*Schutzbund* functionaries, which meant *de facto* its entire technical

staff including military chief Major Alexander Eifler, (ret.), and Captain Rudolf Löw, (ret.). By 10 February, all district and unit leaders of the Vienna *Schutzbund*, a total of 200 persons, were under arrest. In a communiqué dated 11 February, Fey spoke of a "proven plot by Marxist-Bolshevik criminals" and announced on the same day—to a euphoric crowd at a *Heimatschutz* military exercise in Strebersdorf/Langenzersdorf—that they would really go to work the next day and finish the job.

By the end of January 1934, the *Heimwehren* were taking action to implement their decidedly fascist program. Their battalions occupied Innsbruck, demanding the dismissal of the constitutionally elected provincial government and the appointment of *Heimwehr* commanders to leadership positions, the forced dissolution of the Social Democrats and the voluntary dissolution of the Christian Socialist Party, as well as the removal from office of all Social Democratic local administrations. State officials took no action, even though the Tyrolean *Heimatwehr* had deployed 800 men. Over the following days, armed *Heimwehr* formations moved into other provincial capitals and lodged the same demands. They seemed to be following in the footsteps of the Italians and preparing for a "March on Vienna." On 10 February, the Upper Austrian *Heimwehr* arrayed its forces in Linz and Steyr and submitted an ultimatum to the governor. One day before, the Upper Austrian *Schutzbund* leaders headed by Richard Bernaschek had become aware of a secret order from the province's director of security that called for the arrest of all key Social Democrats and their internment in "detention camps." On Sunday, 11 February, when it appeared that the arrest of the party leadership in the province was imminent, Bernaschek ordered that the *Schutzbund* be armed, and advised party leaders in Vienna that any further provocation would be met with armed force. In the early morning hours of 12 February, as police units raided Hotel Schiff in Linz to search for weapons, heavy fighting suddenly erupted and quickly spread to industrial areas in Upper Austria, Styria, and Tyrol. In Vienna, the remainder of the executive committee of the Social Democratic Party's board met in an apartment in Gumpendorf; after a turbulent session marked by bitter disputes, it was decided—by a one-vote majority—to call a general strike and to mobilize the *Schutzbund*. The once-so-formidable party, which, according to the latest election results, represented 80 percent of the working class, 60 percent of the population of Vienna, and the overwhelming majority of the urban and industrial population of Austria as a whole, had 600,000 members organized within its ranks, and had at its disposal a tightly-woven network of print shops and printed media, was no longer even in a position to spread the word properly that a strike had been called. Two officials of the Socialist Workers' Youth Group, Franz Olah and Bruno Kreisky, ran off copies of the greatly abridged call to strike on a duplicating machine at the Construction Workers and Carpenters Union.

At 11:46 a.m., electric company workers gave the sign for a general strike, and Vienna's trolley cars came to a halt. Throughout the city, the electric lights went out, including those in St. Stephan's Cathedral where the chancellor and the government had gathered to celebrate a festival mass.

At an emergency session of the Council of Ministers held on 12 February 1934 from 6 to 9:15 p.m., Dollfuss and Fey were given a situation report that was anything but reassuring. The government initiated "extensive countermeasures"—army units were dispatched to areas where fighting was going on; in Vienna, the downtown area was cordoned off and City Hall was occupied. "Numerous leading Social Democrats," including the chairman of the Federal Council, General Theodor Körner, (ret.), were already under arrest.

The Council of Ministers met in the Army Ministry and resolved to disband, effective immediately, the Social Democratic Party (that had received, it should be noted, 41 percent of all votes cast at the last election), all of its affiliated associations, and all independent unions, to confiscate all their assets and to close the *Arbeiterbank*; the *Konsum* co-op markets were to undergo *Gleichschaltung*. During the following days and weeks, a wave of arrests rolled across the country, impacting thousands of lower-level officials and staff members, most of whom had not taken part in the fighting and in many instances had only an indirect occupational or personal connection to the Social Democrats. In Vienna alone up through mid-March 1934, a total of 7,823 persons served some length of time in jail "as a result of the February unrest," whereby retaliatory verdicts that even went beyond the arbitrary sentencing that was already institutionalized had devastating mass psychological consequences that persisted for decades.

The Council of Ministers also decreed the dissolution of Vienna's provincial legislature and city council, the dismissal of the mayor and the city's senate, and the appointment of a federal commissioner.

The government measures were coordinated and executed according to an operational plan that had taken a great deal of time to develop, rework and fine-tune, and the fighting was the result and manifestation of the systematic deployment of executive power. And though the government troops and their allied militia units had seized the initiative from the very start, they were nevertheless greatly surprised by the scope and decisiveness of the reaction by the *Republikanischer Schutzbund*, since, according to consensus, the Social Democrats' militia was demoralized, demobilized, and beaten even before the fight began.

The *Schutzbund*, which had been outlawed for almost a year, was prepared for a fight. Following the events of 15 July 1927, when a spontaneous uprising of the Viennese workers led to a fundamental breach of party discipline, this force was systematically drilled, militarized, and depoliticized under the leadership of Julius Deutsch, the Republic's first minister of the army, and Alexander Eifler. What emerged was a well-organized party militia that, in its heyday, was capable of mobilizing 80,000 men to safeguard the legal democratic order, but it was also an organization that began to develop an independent existence largely separate from the rest of the party's rank and file. In the case of a civil war-like conflict, the plan called for offensive tactics that took advantage of the element of surprise. According to Chief of Staff Eifler, the entire action could by no means last longer than twenty-four hours. He and Deutsch oriented their thinking on guerilla warfare waged according to purely military rules. The *Schutzbund* would continue to have a monopoly on weapons; "irregulars" supervised by a hierarchical command structure and led according to action plans worked out to the smallest detail would be deployed as the military situation dictated. Then came the grassroots supporters of the Social Democratic cause, who were assigned the role of "reserves," that is, carrying out scouting assignments and diversionary maneuvers, performing security services, and so forth. The plans of action called for occupying the Vienna *Gürtel* (beltway), seizing or blowing up strategically important points, and then, in a concerted action, moving in and taking the inner city. Similar plans based on the same fundamental principle existed for most cities and industrial regions. In the last directives he issued before his arrest on 3 February, though, Eifler modified these plans; the *Schutzbund* was now to observe the development of the general strike for twelve hours and to seek open military confrontation only after government troops had intervened.

This concept of "half-baked militarization"—of head-to-head conflict with a numerically superior, better equipped, and better trained opponent—was vehemently opposed by General Theodor Körner, (ret.). In his view, the effort to challenge the state's police and army with an armed force purporting to be their equal was destined to fail; rather, small, mobile, (politically and militarily) highly trained units ought to engage in bold, independent action. According to Körner, the essence of civil insurrection and street fighting is "individual armed men who materialize, fire and disappear"; the only viable form of combat is passive defense according to the motto, "Think offensively, act defensively." But, in any case, the *Schutzbund* could only be the recipient of the momentum of mass action, the determinant of its intensity and direction; the military objective in a civil war had to always be determined by democratic political considerations—namely, the re-establishment of the democratic constitution.

Nevertheless, the government was aware of the basic features of the *Schutzbund*'s action plans, and, following the act of betrayal by Eduard Korbel, commander of Vienna's western district, in the first weeks of February 1934, it presumably knew the details as well. The state's armed forces had a carefully worked-out battle plan prepared for their deployment in case of a Social Democratic uprising. Parallel to the militarization of the party militias that had been underway since July 1927, the Vienna Police Department was re-organized into twelve companies specially set up for action in a civil insurrection, forming an emergency response team trained by the army and equipped with infantry weapons. Three specially designed Czech armored cars were acquired to provide efficient leadership during the street fighting. Key components of the government's battle plan were predicated on the rapid and effective coordination of the deployment of the police and the army in order to thus seize the initiative from the very outset. According to plan, most of the fighting would be done by police units and the "volunteer corps," which was made into a kind of auxiliary police force equipped with weapons from government armories and thus was practically identical to the *Heimwehren*. The rest of the citizens' militias—the *Ostmärkische Sturmscharen*, the Christian-German Gymnastics Association, the *Reichsbund* and the *Freiheitsbund*—were assigned subsidiary or back-up roles. The decisive element in the fighting, however, was the deployment of the army, which was provided for in legislation mandating the military's "duty to offer assistance" and duly ordered by Dollfuss in his capacity as minister of the army. At the time of the fighting, the army's total strength was approximately 25,000 men, of whom about 4,000 could be deployed in Vienna. These units used heavy artillery and howitzers to fire upon public housing projects in which *Schutzbündler* had barricaded themselves, for instance, the Karl-Marx-Hof, which was targeted by a motorized artillery battery positioned on the foothills nearby. Aside from the (ultimately decisive) military aspect, this artillery bombardment assumed great symbolic value, and the dissemination of picture postcards showing the destroyed apartment buildings that were once the pride of the Social Democrats' communal reform program was one of the central elements of the government propaganda campaign during the weeks immediately after the February events.

Richard Bernaschek's revolt in Linz launched an act of desperation on the part of the *Schutzbündler* that was lost even before it began. But it was also an act of symbolic significance, a struggle for self-assertion and self-esteem undertaken contrary to explicit orders from the party leadership, and which, not least importantly, was aimed at the permanent defiance of the constitution and the insidious—and finally open—effort to drive the Social Democrats into illegal status.

By the evening of 12 February, the general strike had collapsed. It would have been almost impossible to hold out even without more than a third of the workforce being unemployed and in times of more advantageous political framework conditions. It quickly became obvious that the strategy that had made the *Schutzbund* into what amounted to the professional army of a political party was bound to go down in flames. The masses of working men and women, as much as they sympathized with the fighting troops, did not get the least bit involved in the fighting, and the railroad workers' refusal to honor the call for a general strike proved to be particularly decisive. Once the vanguard of the Austrian labor movement, their numbers had dropped from over 100,000 in the early 1930s to 58,000 men; moreover, since their last strike—the event that triggered the parliamentary crisis of March 1933—the union representing them had been smashed. Thus, the army was unhindered in transporting its artillery and armored vehicles, and an ammunition shortage that arose on the second day of fighting could be easily alleviated with supplies shipped in from Hungary. The Army General Staff's report then noted succinctly that it was inconceivable why the Social Democratic leaders had placed so much faith in the success of their "seemingly indispensable panacea."

Besides their heavy artillery, armored vehicles, and trains, the government troops could also bring the "Austrian Homeland Defense Air Corps," based at the Aspern Airport, into action, but their decisive advantage was in the area of communications and propaganda. Radio stations and broadcasting facilities were occupied by military units and remained in government hands; attempts by the *Schutzbund* to counter with short-wave transmissions were a flop. Thus, from the very beginning of the fighting, reports of the defeat of the *Schutzbund* could be broadcast permanently, and Dollfuss' offer of an amnesty—subsequently not honored—was repeated every half hour. At 2 p.m., the radio reported that martial law was in effect and that the federal government, having deployed all police and army forces at its disposal, was acting decisively "to nip the planned attacks by Bolshevik elements in the bud." The first victim of summary justice was the forty-three-year-old shoemaker Karl Münichreiter, a father of three. Severely wounded twice, he was carried into the courtroom on a stretcher and condemned to death within an hour; three hours later he was hanged. The second death sentence was handed down against thirty-five-year-old engineer Georg Weissel, commander of the Floridsdorf Fire Department. Minister of Justice Schuschnigg justified the executions with the urgent need to set an example that would act as a deterrent. A whole series of summary death sentences followed on 16 February, but they drew massive international protests and only a small number were carried out. By 21 February, when summary justice and the death sentencing were discontinued, 140 *Schutzbündler* had been convicted. Of a few dozen death sentences, only eight were carried out. In the case of Koloman Wallisch, the man who had uncovered the Hirtenberg arms smuggling affair, it would even be appropriate to speak of murder by law. After several days on the run, he was captured in the mountains of Styria. He was charged with "somehow assuming command" and taking part in the fighting. The court martial in Leoben, without hearing any testimony from defense witnesses, found Wallisch guilty "beyond a shadow of a doubt." Shortly before midnight on 19 February, the day of the trial, he was hanged.

By Saturday, 17 February 1934, the *Neue Freie Presse* was reporting that "total calm" prevailed.

# The Christian Corporatist State: Austria from 1934 to 1938

*Dieter A. Binder*

In his analysis of the partial *Schutzbund* uprising in February 1934, Otto Bauer wrote shortly after the fighting ended that

Austrian fascism lacks a . . . despotic fascist organization. What it does have is the *Vaterländische Front*, a curious hodgepodge of Jewish bourgeoisie . . . of monarchist aristocrats, clericalist middle class burghers, of *Heimwehr* units who . . . are committing extortion upon Dollfuss, of *Ostmärkischen Sturmscharen* organized to counter the *Heimwehr*, and of a bunch of poor bastards, half of whom are Nazis and the other half are Social Democrats, all of whom are wearing the red-white-red ribbon for no other reason than to avoid losing their job or to get one.

This fragile government coalition can be traced back to its roots when the economic and agricultural crisis polarized political interests. These diverging particularistic interests of the various estates making up the social fabric came increasingly to the fore and strengthened the formation of small factions within the anti-Marxist camp. A similar process can also be observed in the case of Austromarxism—blocs and splinter groups formed and the party could no longer be held together by the myth of revolution. The free union organization's dramatic loss of members, resignations by the party's own rank and file in individual provinces, and the disaster at the polls in the 1932 provincial elections made it clear that the left-wing claim to being the sole representative of the working class could no longer be justified and that the high organizational potential

Chancellor Kurt Schuschnigg arrives in Innsbruck on 9 March 1938, announcing a plebiscite for 13 March, thus sparking the German invasion of 12 March.

Source: Institute of Contemporary History, Innsbruck

of the Social Democratic Workers' Party (SDAP), upon which that claim had been based, no longer existed. As the SDAP proceeded more and more defensively, the members of the government coalition became increasingly convinced of their ability to work toward a change in the constitution. This development was brought to a head by the events of February 1934, whereby the "teamwork" of actionist leftists and fascist *Heimwehr* members destroyed the last chance to implement a policy of rapprochement in the spirit of *Realpolitik*. Crushing the SDAP's organizations and persecuting its functionaries led, first of all, to that two-front war against the Nazi Party (NSDAP) and the SDAP, which, of necessity, decisively weakened the resistance the state could mount against National Socialism.

In light of the economic, propaganda, and underground warfare that Adolf Hitler as German chancellor and head of the domestic Austrian opposition was waging against Austria, outlawing the NSDAP in the spring of 1933, a move made during the phase of the "*coup d'état* on the installment plan" that also characterized this phase, was accepted as an emergency defensive measure and regarded as justified by the SDAP both internationally and, by the time of the conference of provincial organizations in September 1933 at the very latest, domestically as well. The ban on the Communist Party (KP), which had gone into effect even before the Nazis were outlawed, ultimately presented no problem to the dominant right wing of the SDAP, which absolutely rejected any collaborative action involving the SDAP and the KP. It was only the impression left by the events of February 1934 that caused the government certain image problems abroad, but it succeeded with astounding alacrity in stabilizing the turbulence on this level as well. After all, didn't the murder of Engelbert Dollfuss by the Nazis on 25 July 1934 made it crystal clear that Austria actually was engaged in a defensive struggle against a terrorist system?

Karl Renner asserts this clearly when he writes that "what the great powers regarded in 1934 as a form of protection against the Anschluß . . . is precisely that which is promoting it the most. It is not Austria's errors alone that have caused the loss of our independence; it has been, above all, the self-deceptions of Geneva, Paris and London, which naively cheered Dollfuss on." According to Renner, Dollfuss, "by trusting in Mussolini's promise to protect Austria, through military means if necessary, from annexation by Germany, [went ahead with] his *coup d'état* against the will of the overwhelming majority of the people . . . which embittered not only the working class but the bourgeois intelligentsia as well."

The conceptual conglomerate of the May 1934 Constitution encompassed—on the basis of an underdeveloped parliamentary culture—not only the demand for a limitation on parliamentarism but also, above all, that the responsibility for economic legislation and planning be turned over to a board consisting of business leaders and corporatist representatives. The model that was finally adopted beginning in January 1934 was the one for which fascist *Heimwehr* ideologist Odo Neustädter-Stürmer had been actively campaigning; it dispensed with the last remnants of parliamentary norms and, setting up four advisory chambers and a voting body, the *Bundesrat*, which was incapable of initiating legislation, culminated in the Constitution of 1 May 1934. The chamber of provincial delegates, which was also instituted, was a federalist accessory without any real political power. It established a pseudo-integration of provincial interests in the corporatist constitution, so that the political representatives of the individual provinces were ultimately pawns manipulated by the federal government in its day-to-day dealings. The encyclical *Quadragesimo anno* was set up alongside the corporatist-authoritarian teachings of Othmar Spann in an effort to make up for any theoretical deficiency the bourgeoisie might be experiencing. As a result of the benevolent attitude maintained by the Vatican, which raised no objection to such an interpretation, many Christian Socials became convinced of the fiction that a radical corporatist restructuring conformed to the wishes of political Catholicism's supreme authority: the pope himself.

In the conflict situation centered on the defensive struggle against National Socialism, the government succumbed to the temptation to draw a clear dividing line on the left, whereby, in the fight against Hitler, it lost precisely that potential ally that would have proved to be quite easy to mobilize in light of the clear and present danger that emerged in March 1938 in conjunction with the Schuschnigg referendum. Austromarxism had been on the defensive since the early 1930s. As the backwards-looking myth of revolution lost its integrative power, neither the tactical maneuvering of the party leadership *vis-à-vis* the Dollfuss government nor the partial *Schutzbund* uprising were able to prevent certain groups of supporters from deserting its ranks. The activist minorities went over to the Communists or to that other "movement," National Socialism. Accordingly, the proportion of workers within the illegal NSDAP rose from 18 percent to 31 percent between 1934 and 1937. Decisive in this respect was undoubtedly the break-up of the leftist labor organizations in February 1934, while among railway and postal workers as well as employees in the private sector, German nationalist unions had already facilitated the process of going over to the NSDAP. One regional peculiarity was Carinthian socialism, which was focused on social welfare issues, decidedly German nationalist, anticlerical, and mistrustful of a Viennese brand of Austromarxism formulated by "Jews." Helmut Konrad notes that, in some regions of Austria, this phenomenon made the "distinction between Socialism and National Socialism so blurry that the switch

from one to the other (and back again in 1945) was not even
perceived as a significant discontinuity in individual biographies."
The "hate they had in common," as Bruno Kreisky said, for the
repressive Dollfuss-Schuschnigg regime gave rise at certain times to
that symbiotic relationship that downplayed ideological differences
(even after 1945) and accentuated mutually held positions.

The latitude within which Schuschnigg could maneuver, though,
was tightly circumscribed due to foreign and domestic policy factors.
What he ultimately took over upon his appointment as chancellor on
30 July 1934 was a "coalition of militant confraternities" and the
assets left over after the Christian Socials had declared political
bankruptcy. Starhemberg became vice-chancellor and assumed the
post of *Bundesführer* at the head of the *Vaterländische Front*, in
which Schuschnigg, in turn, figured as his second in command.
Ultimately, though, Starhemberg remained arrested in the pose of the
radiant militia leader, which also manifested itself in controversy
directly involving Schuschnigg. Whereas Starhemberg was strictly
opposed to the disarmament of his *Heimwehr,* which Schuschnigg
had systematically demanded since 1935, in light of the real loss of
significance of its military potential, Schuschnigg was finally able to
eliminate Starhemberg once and for all in 1936 at a time when
Schuschnigg's own power had reached a low point.

A housecleaning among cabinet ministers and the domestic policy
changes that went along with it were also designed to signal a
reorientation of Austria's foreign policy in 1935. Josef
Dobretsberger, who was directed to pursue a policy of reconciliation
with the left, replaced *Heimwehr* fascist Neustädter-Stürmer as
minister of social affairs. Along with Neustädter-Stürmer, Emil Fey,
the Viennese *Heimwehr* leader, also took his leave. Dobretsberger is
properly to be included among the proponents of "Christian
solidarity," and it was from this fundamental stance that he sought to
strengthen the position of the Federation of Labor (the unified labor
union modeled on the Christian Labor Movement). However,
Dobretsberger's approach was possible only as long as foreign and
domestic policy considerations made Schuschnigg prepared to
pursue a policy of reconciliation towards the left, though without
deviating from the basic state model that had been chosen. On 7
November 1935, Dobretsberger announced legislation that clearly

accommodated the interests and wishes of left wing, union-oriented labor: intensified enforcement of measures to protect workers, collective contracts, and the free election of shop stewards. With these announced policies, the government launched its "reconciliation offensive," the clearest expression of which was the 1935 Christmas amnesty for those who had still been in prison since the February hostilities. The minister of social affairs' various promises and certain concrete steps by the government in late autumn 1935 were meant to signal that the authoritarian regime was prepared for the first time to bring itself to make concessions oriented on the demands of the illegal leftists. Nevertheless, the "reconciliation offensive" got bogged down in the spring of 1936 without having made much political headway. The breakthrough for which Dobretsberger had hoped was thwarted by the regime's "German nationalist" change of course, which, along with the new government formed on 14 May 1936, paved the way for the July Agreement.

Nazi terrorist acts ceased after the July 1934 *putsch* was put down; their illegal activities, consisting mainly of disseminating propaganda and distributing aid to the families of Nazis who had fled or been arrested, continued to occupy the attention of state security agencies, but did not pose a threat to the government. Positional struggles within Austrian Nazi ranks, differences regarding questions of tactics, and personal feuding in the shadowy world of illegality diminished the Nazis' effectiveness.

Whereas individual government officials sought to establish what amounted to a purist basis for negotiations in order to pursue the reconciliation of the government and committed German nationalists by attempting to expand the grassroots support among them for the regime—under the misconception that it would be possible to win over the "idealistic German nationalists" and isolate the "aggressive Nazis"—certain business leaders, who had in the 1920s already come to the conclusion that the savior of the *Vaterland* was to be found beyond democracy, pursued policies that made them the driving force behind the Anschluß movement. In light of the catastrophic economic situation, there were calls for a settlement with Hitler in order to hitch Austria's wagon to the star of German rearmament. From the very outset, Franz von Papen, Hitler's envoy in Vienna, had gone about establishing a "bridgehead" among Catholic circles whose "romantic reveries of the Reich" and anti-Marxist sentiments enhanced their receptiveness to National Socialism. On the other hand, there were also people like Ernst Karl Winter, who spoke out in favor of a popular front extending all the way from the far left to the patriotic, anti-Nazi, and fascist members of the *Heimwehr*, and Dietrich von Hildebrand, who, in his newspaper *The Christian Corporatist State*, came out vehemently and incessantly against the Catholic bridge-builders and anti-Semites in the "*Schönere Zukunft*," and against Bishop Alois Hudal's efforts "to Catholically infiltrate" National Socialism. Nevertheless, Schuschnigg, obviously under pressure from representatives of Austrian big business who desired a liaison, refused to be steered off the path leading to the July Agreement.

The agreement dated 11 July 1936 between the Third Reich and Austria was Janus-faced. It was meant to end the German-Austrian conflict as a bilateral problem, while at the same time contributing to calming Austria's domestic tensions. The July Agreement was formulated as a non-intervention pact to which Germany agreed. Austria's independence was thus solemnly recognized, and the domestic policies pursued in each land were acknowledged to be the internal affairs of the respective country. In addition, there were secret accords—the so-called gentlemen's agreements—that were not made public but ironed out key details. Press issues, the guarantee of amnesty for Nazis (with the exception of the worst cases), the status of Germans in Austria, and the strengthening of cultural ties were resolved. The decisive point, though, was IXb, in which the Austrian chancellor pledged to appoint at least two representatives of the "German nationalist opposition" whom he trusted to posts in his government. Thereafter, "German nationalist" elements were partially integrated into the *volkspolitische* departments of the *Vaterländische Front*. This, however, can hardly be said to have been an expansion of the government's basis of support; rather, it amounted to legal organizational assistance for illegal Nazis. Commercial arrangements ended the boycott that had been in effect since 1933, but they also ultimately left the doors wide open to German penetration of Austrian economic life. The secret accords contradicted the official non-intervention pact not only in those areas in which influence was exerted upon the executive (composition of the chancellor's cabinet) and judicial (amnesty) branches of government, but also in those having to do with cultural and economic cooperation.

The barriers that were removed in July 1936 led to an expansion of bilateral trade relations, which was also questionable from a currency policy perspective, and to a German plan for a currency union, for which the integration of Austria into the German bank clearing system was designed to serve as a preliminary stage. With trade between the two countries accelerating as a result, German indebtedness in Austria rose, and this incited the resistance of National Bank President Viktor Kienböck, who sought to stabilize the currency by maintaining a close linkage to the West. Economic and ideological considerations came together in his thinking, which contributed to his opposition to further economic interconnections.

Hermann Göring, who was appointed to administer the German four-year plan on 9 September 1936, increasingly took Austrian economic resources into account in planning for the German economy. Besides strategic advantages—the border with Italy, direct access to southeastern Europe, semi-encirclement of Czechoslovakia, recruitment potential for at least eight to ten divisions—such a consolidation also paid economic dividends, particularly in the iron and steel industry. Accelerated exploitation of iron ore deposits in Styria and Carinthia made it possible in 1938-39 to reduce foreign exchange-intensive iron ore imports by almost 50 percent, and the mining of magnesite and graphite deposits even raised the prospects of generating surpluses for export. There were similar considerations regarding the exploitation of petroleum and timber reserves and the energy potential from hydroelectric power. Another issue being addressed was the labor potential of Austria's unemployed workforce, whereby skilled workers and engineers were greatly coveted by the German armaments industry. The same applied to Austria's unutilized industrial capacity, particularly in stainless steel production.

In its struggle to fight off National Socialism, the government recognized the necessity of replacing the German nationalism that transcended the boundaries of the various political camps and its Anschluß-oriented thinking with an Austrian identity derived from a historical conception of self that could also endow the "new Austria" with corresponding feelings of self-confidence. Efforts to do so got away from approaches that had already been articulated in the monarchy, and instead developed, in the tradition of Austrian state historiography, a "history of the German-Austrian Reich," according to which the land now called Austria was said to be what was tantamount to "the better German state" and the bearer of the traditions and hopes of the Catholic Habsburg myth. Finally, it is most striking that the corporatist regime, in conjunction with its demonstratively backwards-looking, anti-modern, and anti-liberal worldview, began—hesitantly and inconsistently but nevertheless gradually—to cozy up in a number of ways to the multiculturalism of Austrian modernism, and, in light of the obvious multiethnic influences within the former Habsburg lands, to juxtapose a unique "Austrian way" to the construct positing a "single German people." This was reflected to some extent by policies pursued toward ethnic groups and by the integration of religious minorities, for example Jews, in the state administration and the prominent public role they played despite the only barely toned down anti-Semitic climate. On the other hand, much of Austrian cultural policy remained arrested in the "stultifying provincialism" of "*vaterländischen* blood-and-soil mysticism." In addition, there was no way to divert attention from this development, not even with the presence of the stateless bourgeoisie who found in Austria a place to live and display their artistic talents in the style to which they were accustomed—men like Max Reinhardt and Carl Zuckmayer who constituted living testimony for the corporatist state as land of exile for anti-Nazis, or those like Franz Werfel who cast some light into the drab salons of government circles.

Although, in light of the National Socialist threat, the SDAP suspended the Anschluß paragraph from its party platform at its extraordinary convention held in the fall of 1933, this new Austrian consciousness also embittered some of the party's followers, since, as Karl Kraus put it, Karl Marx had been taking gymnastics instruction from *Turnvater* Jahn, and many began to equate the emphasis being placed upon Austrian independence with the beginning of a Habsburg restoration. Even Ignaz Seipel was suspected by Karl Renner of not being able to sever his attachment to the Austria of the past, whereas, for Renner, the future was clear: "There is no geographic, ethnic, or economic force, no power in the world, no *diktat* of a victorious coalition that can alter the fundamental facts of our existence—we are a major branch of the great German nation, nothing more, but also nothing less! We are not a nation, we never were and never will be one!" Despite all the inconsistencies within the anti-Nazi government coalition, though, this cultivation and promotion of an Austrian identity was a politically attractive means to mobilize intellectuals and younger supporters of the government in particular. The Communists, as part of their popular front strategy, also got involved in this discussion; they saw this posture as one transcending the boundaries separating the various political camps, and one that could form a basis for the intra-Austrian anti-Hitler coalition. From Otto Bauer's perspective, though, this remained one of the Communists' deadly sins even after the Anschluß that was carried out in March 1938: "But the slogan that we [Socialists] put forth in opposition to foreign rule by the fascist satraps of the Third Reich cannot be the reactionary motto calling for the re-establishment of Austria's independence, but only the revolutionary slogan of the pan-German revolution."

Schuschnigg's foreign policy was still corseted by policies pursued for the sake of the alliance with Italy. This was originally meant to provide protection against the Third Reich, but had already begun to lose significance when Italy sought to prevent an international escalation of the German-Austrian conflict by, for example, appealing to the League of Nations, and thus took the steam out of the diplomatic maneuvers England and France had undertaken from 1933 to 1935. Furthermore, by the time Italy itself had become internationally isolated and was forced to seek political and economic backing from Germany, this situation contributed to Austria's international isolation in that Schuschnigg's diplomats at the League of Nations could not come out against the Italian invasion of Abyssinia, and Austria thereby lost the goodwill it had previously enjoyed in the eyes of this body and, above all, the Western powers. In consistent pursuit of policies based on "Danube basin" thinking, Mussolini now strove once again to steer Austria *viribus unitis* into a pact expanded to include Germany. The Western card that Dollfuss would have been in a position to play was no longer the ace-in-the-hole it had once been. On 27 September 1934 in Geneva, the major powers renewed their declaration of 17 February 1934, in which they had emphasized Austria's independence. Further guarantee declarations and treaty provisions aimed at bringing about a Danube Pact were defeated by German obstructionism as well as by the fears and special interests of the Small Entente states. With the joint declaration by Great Britain, France, and Italy at the Stresa Conference on 14 April 1935, the policy of limited internationalization would once again win the day.

In light of Yugoslavia, Hungary, and Italy's closer relationship to the Third Reich, strengthened contact to Czechoslovakia was rather scant consolation for the loss of British interest in Austrian sovereignty. In the wake of Austria's conduct at the League of Nations' proceedings to condemn Italy, voices critical of Austria gradually won the upper hand in London, and this attitude was solidified when the July 1936 Agreement apparently confirmed the view that the German-Austrian conflict was rather along the lines of a family feud. Acceptance of German re-armament, the German-British naval agreement, and, finally, tolerating remilitarization of the Rheinland were the commencement of international collaboration with National Socialism, which, under the heading of appeasement policies, acknowledged the Anschluß as a *fait accompli* even before it happened and, with the Munich Agreement, left Czechoslovakia militarily defenseless. Additionally, it was in the context of this international state collaboration that the official Austrian struggle against National Socialism was subjected to precisely that isolation that made military resistance seem pointless. Those diplomats like George Messersmith, the U.S. envoy in Vienna, who praised the resistance Austria was putting up against Hitler and were basically in favor of an international isolation of Germany, were ultimately thwarted by their own countries' attitude which was focused on appeasement.

On 7 March 1936 Hitler sent his *Wehrmacht* into the demilitarized Rheinland without France staying his hand. Austria, in turn, put general national service into effect on 1 April, thereby abrogating the military provisions of the Treaty of Saint-Germain. The Austrian Army had already begun to upgrade its personnel and matériel in 1935. This made it possible by March 1938 to marshal a small armed force "with a very high level of training." The army was able to mobilize a total of 127,000 men, and progress was also made in erecting a line of fortifications along the border with the Third Reich which, in case of a German attack, would have enabled Chief of Staff Alfred Jansa to carry out a defensive plan (Case D) with the objective of holding out long enough to give the major powers time to respond. But energetic intervention on their part could no longer be counted upon; thus, the Jansa Plan lacked the political framework necessary for successful implementation.

The increased semi-legal radius of action the Austrian Nazis enjoyed in the wake of the July Agreement, the fact that Austria's economic affairs were becoming increasingly interwoven with Germany's, the growing German interest in Austria's economic and personnel resources in connection with the German four-year plan, and, finally, the coexistence of moderate and radical Nazis side by side in Austria turned up the pressure on Schuschnigg. This pressure increased even more due to the stance that Italy assumed. At the final meeting of the signatories of the Rome Protocol on 9-12 January 1938 in Budapest, Italy tried to convince Austria and Hungary to resign from the League of Nations and to join the Anti-Comintern Pact (Berlin-Rome-Tokyo). Schuschnigg sought to ease the tensions at a face-to-face meeting with Hitler. He hoped for renewed German confirmation of Austrian independence as a *quid pro quo* for the concessions requested by the German side. But Hitler, whose domestic political position was strengthened by his brutal shake-up of the top ranks of the *Wehrmacht*, was in no mood for compromise. On 12 February 1938 in Berchtesgaden, he instead dictated to Schuschnigg the terms of total submission.

Agreeing to the terms of the *diktat* would have been tantamount to capitulation, since Austria would have, by necessity, succumbed almost immediately to Hitler's influence and power. Even if Austria had strictly complied with all points, Hitler's loyal minions in the Austrian government—who were formally subordinate to the Austrian chancellor, but were *de facto* carrying on treasonous relations with Berlin—could have blackmailed the Austrian government at any time with the threat to resign. The step-by-step fulfillment of the *diktat's* provisions and its effect upon the public mobilized the Austrian Nazis to prepare for the final push, while the

German government pushed ahead with the interpretation of the *diktat*. What followed on 9 March 1938 was the attempt by Schuschnigg to compel an anti-Nazi *levée en masse* by calling for a referendum entitled "For a free and German, independent and public-spirited, for a Christian and united Austria!" to be held on 13 March. For the first time, conversations with the leftists gave rise to concrete action, despite the fact that, even in this situation, Schuschnigg remained standoffish in his dealings with leftist functionaries. But this domestic political mobilization came too late. While Austrian patriots and anti-Nazis representing the entire political spectrum were still writing slogans, putting up posters, and handing out fliers for Schuschnigg's referendum, the German government was turning up the heat on Austria. Military blackmail was now added to the political extortion. The German invasion was preceded by an intra-Austrian partial takeover of power by the Nazis, after Schuschnigg was forced to resign on 11 March and to allow Arthur Seyss-Inquart to assume power.

# 12 November 1918-12 March 1938: The Road to the Anschluß

*Rolf Steininger*

"As Führer and chancellor of the German nation and the Reich, I hereby announce before history the entry of my homeland into the German Reich!"

With these words spoken on 15 March 1938—a Tuesday—Adolf Hitler ended the "liberation rally" on *Heldenplatz* (Heroes' Square) in Vienna attended by a few hundred thousand people. Hitler delivered his report of "a historical mission accomplished" from the balcony of the New Imperial Palace; the assembled multitude responded with unending cheers and shouts of "*Sieg Heil!*" For all the world to see, Austria had been brought "home into the Reich," and it seemed as though a longstanding wish—one that had been ardently expressed since the end of World War I—had finally come to fruition. This prologue, which begins in autumn 1918, is especially important for an understanding of the events of March 1938. It shows that what occurred then did not take place in a vacuum, and that the Nazis intentionally built upon pre-existing circumstances and established continuities, although these were highly modified from their original form—such as Hitler's visit to Innsbruck on 5 April 1938, when he was presented with the documents of the Anschluß referendum held in the Province of Tyrol on 24 April 1921, and was celebrated as the one who had consummated this expression of the people's will.

"Home into the Reich!" "One people, one Reich!" "Greater Germany, our future!" These and similar slogans were already

Adolf Hitler addressing the masses in Vienna's *Heldenplatz* (Heroes' Square) after
the Anschluß on 15 March 1938.

Source: Institute of Contemporary History, Innsbruck

commonplace in Austria as early as 1918-19, when it was still known
as *Deutschösterreich* (German-Austria). From then on, the subject of
Anschluß somehow remained on the agenda and had an impact—at
times as a pressing issue, at others from the back burner—on
political life in Austria. Six relatively well-defined stages mark the
path leading up to the events of March 1938:

1. Socialist Anschluß euphoria in 1918-19 in Austria;
2. the Anschluß (or, more properly, unification) movements in
   the Austrian provinces in 1921;
3. Anschluß propaganda and practical alignment policies pursued
   in the 1920s;
4. the German-Austrian Customs Union project of 1931;
5. Hitler in power; the "quick solution" of 1933-34;
6. the evolutionary solution via the "mental saturation" of
   Austria, with the Anschluß in March 1938.

These stages, discussed in more detail below, were influenced by considerations of political and economic expediency: in stages one to three, Austria was the active suitor; at stage four, Germany took the lead; and by stages five and six, there was no longer even a trace of Austrian desire for an Anschluß—at least on the official government level.

## Stage One: The Socialist Anschluß Euphoria of 1918-19

A notable date in the history of Austria is 12 November 1918. On that day, the men who had been elected in 1911 to represent the German territories of the Habsburg Monarchy in the imperial Parliament (*Reichsrat*) and who had convened in Vienna on 21 October 1918 as the "Provisional National Assembly for German-Austria" ordained and established a new constitution; in Article 1, the new state of German-Austria—which was also meant to include the Sudeten German areas—was declared to be a democratic republic, and Article 2 went on to state that "German-Austria is a component part of the German Republic." In other words, at the very moment of its birth, the new state declared itself to be unviable, a stigma that it would be unable to rid itself of in the following years. What had come into being was the state "that nobody wanted."

Social Democratic Chancellor Karl Renner, in a speech delivered before Parliament on 12 November, passionately voiced his belief in German unity. He lamented the fate of the German *Volk* and declared: "The people that has always been proud to be called the people of poets and thinkers now lies prostrate. But in this hour, our German people throughout all the districts we inhabit should know this: we are one community sharing a common fate."

Otto Bauer, intellectual leader of the Social Democrats and secretary of state for foreign affairs, informed German legislator Hugo Haase about the resolution passed unanimously on 12 November in a telegram sent to Berlin the following day, in which he stated that German-Austria had "expressed its will to be reunited with the other Germanic nations from whom it had been separated fifty-two years ago [Königgrätz 1866; R. St.]. We request that you . . . enter into direct negotiations with us concerning the unification of German-Austria with the German Republic." At the same time, he asked that coal and foodstuffs be shipped quickly to

Austria, and expressed hope "that the old . . . ties that still exist between political party colleagues will now facilitate our efforts to establish a close and lasting connection between Germany and German-Austria."

Furthermore, it was decided to send a historian named Hartmann, son of one of the representatives who had met at Paul's Church in 1848, as an envoy to Berlin in order to awaken "understanding and enthusiasm for the Anschluß." Three days later, U.S. President Woodrow Wilson was advised that German-Austria "wished to reestablish with Germany the close constitutional ties that were severed by the sword fifty-two years before," and he was asked for his support. Four months later, on 12 March 1919, the resolution passed on 12 November by the constituent National Assembly was "ceremonially reiterated, confirmed and reinforced." In a programmatic address, Otto Bauer stated that "the unification of German-Austria with the great German Republic . . . is today once again in our platform."

What were the reasons for this policy? Karl Renner, also the first chancellor of the Second Republic, answered this question in 1945. According to his interpretation, hunger and joblessness in 1918 had led everyone to think that the Anschluß was the only possible solution. "If you understand Austria's disastrous economic situation, you will understand the movement favoring the Anschluß." At the time, the Social Democrats were convinced of the necessity of large spheres of economic activity. A land without coal, one that was unable to produce sufficient foodstuffs within its own territory and was without major export industries could not exist independently according to Otto Bauer's thinking in July 1919; the inhabitants of such a land would lead a life of servitude, penury, and misery under the yoke of foreign capitalists. The only thing that could prevent this from happening to Austria was unification with Germany.

There is no denying that there was hunger and suffering during the postwar years, although the anguish of the times made many lose sight of the fact that the Republic was not as poor as many then believed. It had within its territory 12 percent of the population of the former Habsburg Empire, but approximately 30 percent of its industrial capacity. Vienna had been the financial center of the old Double Monarchy, and there was still a lot of money in Vienna.

Thus, aside from economic considerations, there were other reasons for the Social Democrats' Anschluß euphoria. Their goal was to form a united front with the German Social Democrats. As a speech from the February 1919 election campaign put it: "We want to come together with red Germany. Unification with Germany now means unification with socialism."

Only the Austrian German Nationalist Party was as enthusiastic as the Social Democrats in its support for the Anschluß. Both parties conducted their campaigns for the National Assembly using the slogans cited above, winning twenty-five and sixty-nine seats respectively, as compared to sixty-three for the Christian Socials, who were anything but enthused by the subject of Anschluß, to say nothing of the red Germany that so raised the spirits of the Social Democrats. Indeed, the parliamentary resolution of 12 November passed unanimously, but the delegates had been pressured by the threats of revolution coming from the Red Guard and the crowd on the street. The minutes of the session record repeated shouts like, "We're being fired upon!" and Ludwig Brügel, the chief press officer of the state council (*Staatsrat*), took a bullet in the eye. Thus, in the Christian Social election platform published on 25 December 1918 in the *Reichspost,* the party's newspaper, the Anschluß was, significantly, not mentioned. Moreover, the Christian Social Party— which was, after all, the one with which the majority of the Austrian population outside of Vienna was affiliated—did not even participate in Anschluß rallies conducted throughout Austria on 11 May 1919.

The decision made in Vienna on 12 November was received with cool restraint in Berlin, since it had already been made known on 9 November in Bern that, in the case of an Anschluß, the Entente would impose harder peace terms upon Germany. Therefore, when Bauer's telegram was discussed at the legislative session held on 15 November, it was decided "not to go into the question of unification due to the overall international situation." Vienna reacted accordingly; there was "disappointment that the Anschluß question was not mentioned. The press of all political affiliations is reserved, hardly any discussion of the answer," reported German Ambassador von Wedel.

Hartmann addressed the *Reichskonferenz* in Berlin on 25 November 1918 and requested that German-Austria be accepted into the German Reich with the words: "As representative of the Austrian people, I extend to the German people the hand of brotherhood and ask that you take it." German Secretary of State for Foreign Affairs Solf immediately objected. He warned against taking such a step prior to the peace negotiations since it might jeopardize the peace that was so desperately needed, and he stated that he could not accept responsibility for the consequences. The effect of Solf's words was "like being doused with cold water." According to Colonel von Häften, one of the participants, Friedrich Ebert, Social Democrat and head of government, also "declined to accept the hand offered in brotherhood," whereby "this historically momentous event, which could have endowed the world war with some historical sense for Germany, came to a pathetic conclusion."

But this was not true as far as the German public was concerned. On 17 January 1919, the entire press was calling for the Anschluß, and all parties came out in favor of it on 5 February. This was the mood that greeted Bauer when he arrived in Germany on 21 February to carry on discussions in Berlin and Weimar with Foreign Minister Brockdorff-Rantzau. The impression he got was that German-Austria would be "welcomed with brotherly convictions" into the Reich and would find "the most sincere willingness to provide fraternal assistance." On 2 March, the discussions ended with the signing of a secret agreement stating that the unification of the two states should be carried out "as speedily as possible." According to its provisions, German-Austria was to be amalgamated with the Reich as an "independent constituent member state" with certain special rights (including Vienna as second capital enjoying equal status, in which the president of the Reich would reside from time to time). Various commissions composed of equal numbers of representatives from both states would prepare the alignment in the fields of jurisprudence, commerce, transportation, education, and social policy.

Nevertheless, it was the Germans, whose view was focused on the peace conference in Versailles, who failed to then go ahead with the decisive step. The attitude of France was well known: it had worked itself up into absolute abhorrence of the idea of an Anschluß. No French politician was prepared to permit vanquished Germany to expand its territory and to add some 6.5 million people to its population. Then, in Article 80 of the Treaty of Versailles, the victors strictly established the independence of Austria and the inviolability of its borders. Indeed, the German delegation protested, explaining that Germany "never had, and will never have, the intention to shift the border of German-Austria," and demanded the right of self-determination for Germany too. The opposition merely "took note" of this explanation, and, on 28 June 1919, the peace treaty was signed.

Two months later, on 2 September in Saint Germain, Karl Renner was given a draft of the treaty with Austria along with a five-day ultimatum. South Tyrol and the Kanal Valley were to go to Italy, parts of Styria and Carinthia to Yugoslavia, the Sudeten German lands to Czechoslovakia. A ban on an Anschluß was spelled out in Article 88 here as well: "The independence of Austria is immutable, unless the Council of the League of Nations agrees to a change. Therefore, Austria pledges, except with the express approval of the above-mentioned Council, to refrain from any and all activities that could, directly or indirectly or in any other way . . . jeopardize its independence."

The Austrian National Assembly accepted the treaty under protest on 10 September 1919. Six weeks later on 21 October 1919, since an Anschluß was obviously no longer within the realm of possibilities, in implementing the Treaty of St. Germain, not only was the name *Deutschösterreich* changed to the *Republik Österreich*, but the previously passed resolution stating that "German-Austria is a component part of the German republic" was repealed.

During these weeks of chaos and resignation, the young republic experienced one success that enhanced its self-image. Two days after the ceasefire between Austria-Hungary and the Allies, Southern Slav units had moved into southern Carinthia, and Austria's repeated protests to the Allies against the military action taken by its Yugoslav neighbors brought no relief. The new Yugoslav state (Serbs, Croats, and Slovenes) lodged ever-growing territorial claims.

On 5 December 1918, the Assembly of the Province of Carinthia decided to take up armed resistance against the intruders. The defensive action claimed approximately 270 lives on the Carinthian side and 250 Yugoslav dead. By early May, the Yugoslav units had been pushed back to a small pocket south of Eisenkappl, but then powerful Slav forces moved forward on a broad front and the

Carinthian defenses collapsed. Yugoslav troops marched into the capital city of Klagenfurt on 6 June 1919 as Carinthian units retreated. In contrast to other German-speaking regions, the Allied Council in Paris decided to hold a plebiscite in Carinthia. After repeated calls by the Allies for them to withdraw, the Yugoslav units left Klagenfurt at the end of July 1919 and pulled back behind the demarcation line.

Two zones were established for the plebiscite. In the southern Zone A, Slovenian-speakers predominated (79 percent) according to the results of the 1910 census. A second round of balloting would be conducted in the "eye of the needle" Zone B—including Klagenfurt and an overwhelming German majority—only if the vote in Zone A turned out in favor of Yugoslavia. The Yugoslavs administered Zone A; the Austrians administered Zone B.

The plebiscite was set for 10 October 1920. During the weeks leading up to that date, the agitation by both sides reached its highpoint, and thousands of flyers flooded the area in which voting would take place. Astoundingly, the plebiscite itself then came off quite peacefully, and voter turnout was a remarkably high 96 percent. Slightly more than 22,000 voters (59 percent) in Zone A chose to remain part of Austria, versus about 15,200 (just under 41 percent) for Yugoslavia. On 18 November the southern Carinthian Zone A reverted back to Austria. Due to this outcome, the planned plebiscite in the predominantly German-speaking Zone B was cancelled.

## Stage Two: The Anschluß Movement in the Austrian Provinces and the Geneva Protocol

If Otto Bauer's demonstrative resignation on 25 July 1919 was an admission that his Anschluß policy had failed, then the acceptance of the peace treaty and the legislation of 21 October seemed to drive the last nail into the coffin of the Anschluß issue. But appearances were deceiving. The "Republic of Austria," a state that came into existence under the motto "*L' Autriche, c'est ce qui reste*" (Austria, that's what's left over), was now, in the aftermath of territorial losses, truly an unviable state in the eyes of the vast majority of its population, and for all those who were unwilling to believe in this state, the Anschluß, in spite of Article 88, now really did seem to be the only way out of this worsening state of despair. At this point, the focus of the Anschluß movement largely shifted to the provinces—first and foremost to Tyrol, Salzburg, and Styria.

As the economic situation became ever more unbearable over the following months during which a hungry population was demonstrating in the streets, the National Assembly called upon the federal government on 1 October 1920 to conduct a plebiscite on the Anschluß within six months. Through the use of threats—in particular, of a "starvation blockade"—and with a sharply worded note from Paris on 17 December, France succeeded in halting this plebiscite. Then on 10 February 1921, the German Nationalist Representative Dinghofer introduced a bill in Parliament calling for a referendum in which the following question would be put to a vote: "Shall the federal government petition the Council of the League of Nations to approve the Anschluß of the Republic of Austria to the German Reich?"

Although it was thought that the former Entente powers could have no objection to this approach since the peace treaty had, after all, specifically provided for going about the Anschluß in this way, the Allies under French leadership tried almost every means to prevent this referendum. They wished to avoid at all costs any discussion in the League of Nations of an Austrian petition for Anschluß; the "no" from France would deal a blow to the prestige of that body that could perhaps call its very existence into question.

The provincial governments saw that pressure from the victorious powers was depriving the central government of its freedom to act. They resolved to conduct the referendum on a province-by-province basis, but this drew sharp protests from the Allies as well. On 14 April 1921, the French envoy in Vienna, Lefèvre-Pontalis, called upon Christian Social Chancellor Michael Mayr, a representative from Tyrol, "to quash these subversive intrigues aimed at bringing about an Anschluß"; otherwise, all aid for Austria would be suspended. The federal and provincial governments objected, and on 24 April in Tyrol, the plebiscite mandated by the province's legislature took place anyway. In it, 98.15 percent of the ballots were cast in favor of the Anschluß. Immediately thereafter, the barriers blocking the border crossings at Kufstein and Scharnitz were removed, and this was later done in Salzburg as well. What followed were similar resolutions by the legislatures in Salzburg and Styria to conduct referendums if a national plebiscite did not take place. Obviously to prevent further provincial referendums, the above-mentioned bill was passed into law, whereupon the Allies increased the pressure on Austria even more. Paris was resolved to take even the most drastic steps, threatening to terminate the loan negotiations, and even to carve up the country and pass out the pieces to Austria's neighbors. Mayr did succeed in seeing to it that the referendum in Salzburg would only be conducted on a "private basis," whereby 98.8 percent of those who voted, representing 73 percent of all registered voters, cast ballots for the Anschluß. Nevertheless, the Christian Social government of the Province of Styria stuck to its guns, whereupon Mayr resigned on 1 July 1920. It thus became obvious that different policies would have to be pursued to keep the state from sinking into an even greater crisis.

It is clear that the motives of the Anschluß movement in the provinces—above all in Tyrol and Salzburg—differed from those of the movement that emerged in postwar Vienna. These were provinces with conservative majorities who had nothing in common with either the Viennese or the German Socialists. There was no longer talk of Anschluß under the banner of socialism. Germany had not gone socialist, and the Soviet Republic in Bavaria had been a fleeting episode. On the other hand, in light of the desperate economic straits, a financial "merger" with that larger country did seem promising; thus, the word "Anschluß" was now avoided at all costs. The provinces wanted to be done once and for all with "red, Jewified" Vienna, and they did not hold this Republic of Austria in very high regard either. Nowhere is this expressed more clearly than in a letter written on 25 May 1921 to Chancellor Mayr by Richard Steidle, the influential leader of the Tyrolean *Heimatwehr* (as the conservatives' *Heimwehr* home defense force was called there) who in 1940 lost his life in the Buchenwald concentration camp. In his view, the decisive element in the attitude of the population of Tyrol was "above all the wish to get rid of the whole despised 'Vienna business,' which the people want nothing more to do with. This mood assumes dimensions that are tantamount to spitefulness, especially in religiously and nationalistically oriented circles, and I come across more and more people who openly express this opinion." Steidle ended the letter with his own unequivocal wish, illustrating why the domestic affairs of this state could not possibly have settled down during the ensuing years. "Actually," Steidle wrote, "I shouldn't even tell you all this because, as far as my own personal opinion is concerned, there's nothing I long for more than the elimination of this ridiculous state—along with the stink it gives off—and Tyrol being rid of Vienna for good."

Austria was not dissolved along with its "stink." Following a year-long interlude with Johannes Schober as chancellor, Prelate Ignaz Seipel, "the strongest non-Socialist personality, who had long been active behind the scenes," assumed the leadership of the government in May 1922 and remained in office until 1929. Seipel, a Christian Social, was certainly no proponent of the Anschluß, even though he never came out against it in public. His prime concern was to stabilize Austria without an Anschluß. When he took office, unemployment was over 20 percent, inflation was at its peak, and the system was on the verge of collapse. The end of Austria seemed to be near.

Seipel's tactic was to make the victorious powers responsible for subsequent developments, but at the same time to convince them that the preservation of Austria as a state was a vital necessity for Europe. In a stirring note dated 7 August 1922, he pleaded with British Prime Minister Lloyd George to arrange a loan for Austria. If this were not granted, then his government would have to convene the Austrian Parliament and to declare in concurrence with it that neither the current government nor any other one is in a position to carry on the administration of this country. Furthermore, they would see themselves forced to state, before the Austrian people and international public opinion, that the powers of the Entente were responsible for the collapse of one of the oldest centers of civilization in the heart of Europe, and to lay the fate of Austria in the hands of those powers.

In the end, these efforts did bring forth a loan from the League of Nations for over 650 million gold Crowns, under conditions like those imposed on Third World countries nowadays. Seipel accepted these conditions in the Geneva Protocols signed on 4 October 1922. In Protocol Number 1, the Republic of Austria pledged for the next twenty years, "in accordance with the wording of Article 88 of the Treaty of St. Germain, to not relinquish its independence; it will refrain from any actions, and abstain from any and all economic or financial ties that might possibly diminish its independence either directly or indirectly." However, Austria maintained its freedom with respect to tariff, trade, and financial agreements "and all general affairs having to do with its economic system and trade relations."

In light of the subsequent course of events, it is particularly interesting that Great Britain, France, Italy, and Czechoslovakia pledged to preserve the "political independence, the territorial integrity and the sovereignty of Austria." Without a doubt, Austria had to make enormous sacrifices for this financial aid, but this was obviously the only course it could take towards economic rehabilitation. Even the proponents of Pan-Germanism concurred in this and approved of Seipel's policies, though this was not the case with the Social Democrats, who had been in the opposition since July 1920. What a Christian Social termed the chancellor's "great deed" was for Social Democrats "high treason" for which Seipel deserved only scorn.

### Stage Three: Anschluß Propaganda and Practical Alignment Policies Pursued in the 1920s

As economic retrenchment efforts got underway with the help of the League of Nations loan, the Anschluß began to lose its current relevance among large segments of the population since it appeared unlikely to come about in the foreseeable future. But that changed beginning around 1925 when the economic situation worsened once again. Even the Pan-Germans, for whom the Anschluß was above all an ideological and nationalistic postulate, now placed economic considerations in the foreground and demanded the Anschluß as a "necessity for trade and economic policies." A resolution passed at their 1925 party convention stated that it was evident "that the stabilization of our domestic economy cannot be accomplished without unification with the German economic sphere." In addition, 1925 also marked the beginning of organized propaganda campaigns conducted by "working groups" and "peoples' associations" that were tolerated by the government in Vienna and financially supported by Berlin. Intellectuals and politicians joined together in the *Österreichisch-deutsche Arbeitsgemeinschaft* and its counterpart in Germany, the *Deutsch-österreichische Arbeitsgemeinschaft für das Reich*. These working groups took a primarily "scholarly" approach to the Anschluß issue; they published a wide variety of articles and texts, put out their own newspapers, put on "Austrian Weeks" from 1929 on, and were surprisingly influential.

In addition, there were associations for the general public, the *Österreichisch-deutscher Volksbund Berlin* and the *Österreichisch-deutscher Volksbund Wien*, which quickly attracted several hundred thousand members and disseminated Anschluß propaganda among the public at large. One of their most impressive public events was the Tenth German Choral Union Festival held in Vienna in 1928. In his address, the president declared: "Our soul thirsts for this Greater Germany, but our rational mind tells us that we can only do the work in preparation for this. We want to go about this work with the power and enthusiasm that flows from the German song." A third important organization was the Delegation for Austrian-German Economic Unification, which was founded in 1927 and within a short time included more than 140 member associations in almost all sectors of the economy. Thereafter, demands for this economic amalgamation were asserted more loudly and more frequently across the industrial and commercial spectrum, including the executive committee of the Chamber of Commerce, leaders of the coal and iron industry (the chairman of the committee for heavy industry, Apold, stated: "For us, the Anschluß is an economic necessity of the highest order. This must come about!"), the Farm Bureau, and the Lower Austrian Chamber of Agriculture. Simultaneously, German capital continued to penetrate the Austrian economy without a great deal of fuss being made about it. The best example of this was the 1926 takeover of the *Alpine Montanwerke* mining operation by the *Vereinigten Stahlwerke* steel company. Nevertheless, this penetration did not reach the level that had been anticipated.

Meanwhile, in the fields of transportation, culture, and jurisprudence, practical efforts to harmonize the two systems were underway. Thus, as early as 1925, visa requirements were abolished and postal service agreements were reached; in 1926, dull green was even replaced as the color of the Austrian *Bundesheer*'s uniforms by German army gray; in 1927, a unified law regulating guardianship and probate law was passed; and in 1930, an agreement on the use of each other's patents was signed. In the same year, standardized rules for insurance companies went into effect in both countries. One year before, common railway traffic regulations had been implemented, and legal scholars were working together to update and re-issue their penal codes. In 1928, a German-Austrian exchange program for government officials was initiated, and a conference of the deans of German and Austrian universities was held in Frankfurt that year as well. Shortly thereafter, the Universities of Vienna and Berlin recognized each other's diplomas as academically equivalent.

Even with all these activities, the bottom line was that this approach was not effective politically in bringing about an Anschluß. For one thing, existing treaties and Seipel's policies did not permit such a thing; for another, the Anschluß was not at this time a high-priority German political objective, although it was kept on the back burner for future consideration. Gustav Stresemann, foreign minister from 1923 to 1929, described the larger context of this issue from the German perspective in a secret memorandum he prepared in January 1925 for the cabinet. The object of "German hope" in his view was "the creation of a state the political borders of which encompass all the German peoples living within the contiguous area of German settlement in Central Europe and who wish to be connected to the Reich." This was nothing other than the Central Europe concept from World War I, especially since in this Central European Reich "besides our fellow Germans, members of other foreign ethnic groups would also become subject to German dominion" because this Reich would otherwise be impossible to bring into existence.

A study conducted in March 1926 for the German Army's general staff made clear the military's take on this situation; in it, the "Anschluß of *Deutschösterreich*" (!) was foreseen as Stage Three, with, indeed, a lower priority than Stage One: "liberation of the Rheinland and the Saar region" and Stage Two: "elimination of the corridor and reacquisition of Polish Upper Silesia" but, nevertheless, higher on the agenda than "elimination of the demilitarized zone."

In any case, Berlin had not forgotten about Austria during its climb back to major power status. In going about this, Germany was careful to avoid doing anything that might be detrimental to the Anschluß movement in Austria itself. Thus, the government of the Reich refused to recognize the Brenner border, and made no reference to South Tyrol that could be interpreted as their approval of the *status quo*.

## Stage Four: The Customs Union Project of 1931

Germany's Austrian policy was then revived under Stresemann's successor, Julius Curtius. There were several reasons for this.

First, further deterioration of economic conditions in Austria, particularly in the textile and iron and metal processing industries, played a key role. In late 1929, the downturn also hit the electrical, leather and shoe, and chemical sectors, while sales and prices of farm products continued to plunge. In 1930, the crisis and the depression caused by the 1929 collapse of the *Bodenkreditanstalt* spread throughout the economy. Almost all industrial sectors cut back on production, which, in turn, led to a sharp rise in unemployment. In the opinion of Johannes Schober, who took over as chancellor again in September 1929, Austria was not in a position to manage a financial and economic turnaround on its own; only the Anschluß with a larger neighboring economy could help solve its problems. Curtius meant to see to it that this would be the German Reich and not, for instance, the Danube Federation being proposed by the Czechoslovakian foreign minister.

Second, the growing influence of the *Heimwehr* in Austria also affected the revival of Germany's Austria policy. The *Heimwehr* was a militant, anti-Marxist movement, an assemblage of nationalistic and conservative forces of all stripes whose political influence was growing steadily. It rejected the democratic republic—which it characterized as "red"—and wanted to replace it with an authoritarian state. The danger that this might pose to the Anschluß movement was clear. Thus, Count Hugo Lerchenfeld, the German envoy in Vienna, reported to Berlin on 21 November 1929 that a total victory of the *Heimwehr* would be tantamount to the accession of a semi-fascist dictatorship. This, in turn, would mean that Austria would establish solid ties to the Italian-Hungarian bloc, and would thereby very seriously threaten the development of German-Austrian relations.

Third, Aristide Briand's plan for Europe was a key influence. At the League of Nations meeting held in September 1929, French Foreign Minister Aristide Briand proposed the creation of a *lien fédéral* among the peoples of Europe. This federative association was designed as a *lien de solidarité* linking together the European states. Putting this plan into effect would solidly establish the political and territorial *status quo* in Europe, and would have simultaneously meant the end of German revision policies and Germany as a great power. But this Germany's autonomy and power was precisely what Berlin did not want to allow to become endangered through its integration into the proposed "New European Order." On 8 June 1930, Chancellor Brüning made it clear to his cabinet that Germany had to have "sufficient natural *Lebensraum*." Curtius pointed out that the German answer "will be a first-class funeral for Briand's initiative, but would, on the other hand, also have to serve German foreign policy as a platform for the ongoing pursuit of its political and economic goals."

The pursued goal was the elevation of Germany to the status of a major power in the Danube Basin. The springboard for this was, logically, Austria. "Union with Austria," according to a paper prepared by the Foreign Office on 7 July 1930, "ought to be the highest priority task on the German policy agenda, since an Austria belonging to Germany could open up totally new possibilities to influence and determine developments in the southeast in accordance with Germany's interests." The first step in that direction was to be the customs union. It was expected that Czechoslovakia, Hungary, Yugoslavia, and Rumania would be forced to follow suit. Then, once economic relations with the Baltic States were improved, the Poles would be caught in a vice, and it would be possible to offer them economic aid in exchange for political concessions (that is, redrawing the German-Polish border). A "pan-European cloak" was to be draped over the entire undertaking, as Secretary of State von Bülow of the Foreign Office formulated it in January 1931.

The insistence on the part of the Germans—from Curtius above all—was too much for Schober to resist. The negotiations were then conducted under the utmost secrecy until a treaty draft was finalized, but an indiscretion put an end to the confidentiality and led to a rushed announcement of the project on 21 March 1931. It may be assumed that the leak came from Vienna since—and this is the interesting thing about it—resistance started to emerge on the Austrian side just as it finally started to look like there really would be an economic union. This resistance emerged in the machinery sector, the chemical industry, heavy manufacturing, the garment industry, agriculture and forestry, and even among the piano makers.

Across the commercial spectrum, businessmen were pointing to Austria's technological backwardness and the resulting structural disadvantages in competition with German industry.

There is still no definitive answer to the question of whether there was collaboration between these circles, Christian Social politicians, and the French government during the following weeks. France felt—and rightly so—that it had been deceived by the German government, and now pulled out all the stops, including issuing an ultimatum to the Austrian government, to bring about the project's downfall. Then, beginning in May 1931, a banking crisis in Austria and Germany was piled on top of this crisis of political confidence, and in September 1931, both the German and Austrian sides officially renounced the project.

As Renner later wrote, the events and circumstances surrounding the project placed the Anschluß issue "in a very dangerous way once again on Austria's current agenda, and aroused nationalist passions from which Hitler's movement would ultimately benefit the most." Soon, a parliamentary majority government was not even possible anymore. Finally, the League of Nations forfeited "the hard-earned goodwill it had enjoyed among most segments of the Austrian population."

In Germany, the domestic political crisis in which the republic was embroiled was considerably exacerbated by the project, and Weimar would not be able to surmount these difficulties. Moreover, there were foreign policy consequences. The whole undertaking was "truly German foreign policy's fall from grace, a challenge issued to the European state system, and a poorly calculated one at that." The concept of international cooperation and the ideas of Geneva were finally laid to rest. A development began to emerge that, in a very short time, would prove to have disastrous consequences for all powers involved. The Customs Union project was thus a station of "historical significance" along this path of estrangement, and "laid the first charge for the coming European explosion." For Germany, that meant Hitler; for Austria, Dollfuss.

### Stage Five: Hitler in Power—The Failure of the "Quick Solution" in 1933-34

The Nazis' seizure of power in 1933 added a new element to the previously mentioned political, economic, and military

considerations on the German side of the Anschluß question—
namely, raising *völkisch*-nationalistic racial thinking to a position of
paramount importance. On the very first page of *Mein Kampf*, Hitler
voiced his demand: "German-Austria must be restored to the great
German motherland, and, indeed, not on the basis of any economic
calculation whatsoever. No, no—even if this union were a matter of
economic indifference, even if it were disadvantageous, it must take
place nonetheless. People of the same blood belong together in the
same Reich."

This was precisely the line that Nazi propaganda pursued up to
March 1938, although those disseminating it successfully concealed
the fact that precisely this aspect of Nazi Anschluß policy was
assuming ever-diminishing importance. Hitler's concept of world
domination attributed almost exclusively military-strategic and
economic significance to the Anschluß of Austria. Nowhere was that
expressed as clearly as in his famous speech delivered on 5
November 1937 to the commanders of the various branches of the
*Wehrmacht*, in which he announced his "irrevocable decision . . . to
solve the German territorial question by 1943 to 1945 at the latest."
Here, Austria was put on a par with Czechoslovakia; Hitler stated
that his primary objective was "to subjugate Czechoslovakia and,
simultaneously, Austria," and he referred to "attacking
Czechoslovakia and Austria." The Anschluß was the first
precondition for the creation of "Greater Germany," which, in turn,
was one of the preconditions for the implementation of his foreign
policy program.

In 1933-34, Hitler launched the effort—obviously in the hope of
being able to take advantage of the Nazi movement's momentum—
to bring about the Anschluß in the fastest way possible. He named
Theodor Habicht, a top Nazi party (NSDAP) official in Vienna, as
his "special delegate" for Austrian affairs, and from this point on
terrorist attacks by Austrian Nazis were the order of the day. When
Engelbert Dollfuss, who had been presiding over an authoritarian
system since March 1933 when the Parliament dissolved itself,
expelled the Bavarian Minister of Justice and *Reichsjustizkommissar*
Frank from Austria in May 1933, Hitler reacted with the so-called
thousand Mark barrier: henceforth, every German who wished to
travel to or through Austria had to pay in advance the outrageously

high "fee" of 1,000 Reichsmarks. This measure dealt a staggering blow to the Austrian tourist industry, but Hitler's expectations, as formulated at a cabinet meeting on 26 May 1933, were not fulfilled: "This measure can be expected to lead to the collapse of the Dollfuss government and to new elections. These new elections will bring about the internal *Gleichschaltung* of Austria, and thus eliminate the necessity of an external Anschluß. . . . The struggle will be decided this summer."

Dollfuss reacted in June by banning the activities of the NSDAP. Nazi economic warfare and terror were carried on even more intensively, but without producing the success for which Hitler had hoped. The Pan-Germanists could be counted on to support an Anschluß under Nazi conditions, but not the Social Democrats and the Christian Socials, who had by then eliminated the Anschluß paragraphs from their platforms. Nevertheless, at this point no joint defensive front was organized, nor was an effort made to invoke consciousness of an Austrian identity because the land was already divided into irreconcilable "camps," and Dollfuss had established a regime that calculatedly accepted as a fact of life a situation that had already reached its first climax with the Ministry of Justice fire in July 1927.

In 1977, the Viennese *Arbeiter-Zeitung* published a retrospective look at those events that stated:

15 July 1927 claimed more human lives than the revolution of 1918-19, and not that many fewer than February 1934. It is the key event of the First Republic, the pivotal episode between democracy and fascism. On this bloody Friday, a lot more was left in ruins than the Ministry of Justice alone—the working class lost its trust in Austria as a state founded upon the rule of law, and Social Democrats lost their faith in the omnipotence of their organization. The dismissal of Parliament in 1933 and the dissolution of Social Democracy in 1934 were only the final upshots of this great defeat of the young democracy.

In February 1934, four days of civil war-like fighting pitted the *Heimwehr*, the military and the police against armed Austrian Social Democratic workers. There were hundreds of fatalities, and nine workers were executed. These events were never forgotten; from then on, the shadows of those dead were cast over all that came about afterwards.

In the process of revamping the state in accordance with the fascist model—in return for a vague promise from the Italian dictator Benito Mussolini to defend Austria's independence by force of arms—Dollfuss did a thorough job. The Social Democratic Party, the independent unions, and the workers' athletic and cultural associations were dissolved and their assets confiscated. Dollfuss was now waging a two-front war against the Nazis and the Social Democrats. In the "corporatist state" that was now set up, nearly two-thirds of the population were denied any say about what that new state would be like, while in the Nazi's Third Reich, the "community of the *Volk*" was being propagated. With such policies, overcoming the idea of Anschluß was condemned to failure since, as Gerhard Botz has emphasized, "[T]he image of independent Austrian men and women as the better Germans was still associated with German nationalism, and from this point of departure—as it actually transpired during the final years of the corporatist state—it could be undermined by the Nazis."

Hitler's attempt at a "quick solution" ended with the *putsch* by the Austrian Nazis on 25 July 1934. Even if there had been no orders from Hitler to go ahead with the *putsch*, the ultimate responsibility was in his hands. The *putsch* was poorly organized and, in the wake of the massacre of SA members in the Third Reich on 30 June, the severe tensions between the SA and the SS in Austria contributed significantly to its failure. Indeed, Dollfuss lost his life, but the *putsch* itself collapsed after a few hours in the face of determined resistance by the government and the army. The German government distanced itself from these proceedings, whereby Mussolini's decision to dispatch four divisions in the direction of Brenner and one to Carinthia played a considerable role in eliciting that reaction.

## Stage Six: The "Evolutionary Solution" up to the Wehrmacht Marching into Austria on 12 March 1938

The events in Austria, together with Mussolini's "Watch on the Brenner," convinced Hitler that the time was not yet ripe for an Anschluß. Faced with this situation, Franz von Papen—now Hitler's special envoy in Vienna—argued in favor of an "evolutionary" solution to this question, for the "mental saturation" of Austria: the land was to be undermined from within.

This policy played right into the hand of Dollfuss' successor, Kurt von Schuschnigg. He undertook nothing to reconcile the "camps" and to bring together the politically divided land. He purposefully pursued a "German way" with Austria as the second German state, and his economic policies saw to it that Austria was the European country with the highest relative unemployment rate. He oriented his foreign policy more and more on Italy. It is doubtful whether Papen's "evolution theory" alone could have ever led to success. In any case, among the most decisive factors were the foreign policy isolation and the growing dependence on Mussolini which Schuschnigg had engineered. With each step that Mussolini took to alienate the Western powers and to draw closer to Hitler (for example, the attack on Abyssinia, the Spanish Civil War), his interest in an independent Austria subsided and Schuschnigg's latitude for action diminished. Thus, in early 1936, Mussolini let Berlin know that, for a guarantee of the Brenner border, he would have no objections to a treaty whereby Austria "although formally remaining an independent state, practically [would become] a satellite of Germany."

Simultaneously, Mussolini advised Schuschnigg to make a deal with Hitler in order to improve relations between Germany and Austria. The result was the "confidential gentlemen's agreement" of 11 July 1939 that Papen had long been pushing. Schuschnigg pledged to:

1. "conduct the Austrian government's foreign policy with due consideration of the peaceful endeavors of the German government's foreign policy," whereby it was not made clear what was meant by either "consideration" or "peaceful";
2. appoint Austrian Nazis "to positions of political responsibility"; and
3. cease his media campaign and propagandizing against Germany;
4. proclaim an amnesty.

Schuschnigg had no illusions about what he was getting into, but his aim was "to win time and to get relief from the German pressure for the moment," especially since his antagonist Hitler confirmed that

"Germany [has] neither the intention nor the desire to interfere in Austria's internal affairs, or in any way to effect the annexation of or unification with Austria."

However, with this agreement, Hitler had managed to get the decisive foot in the Austrian door. With the appointment of Edmund von Glaise-Horstenau, a National Socialist would be taking his place on the Austrian Council of Ministers, and the approximately 17,000 amnestied Nazis now intensified the struggle of the "movement" against the "system," while the land stood there without foreign policy protection as the "Berlin-Rome axis" took shape in the fall of 1936. That was when the macabre joke began making the rounds that this axis was the skewer on which Austria was going to be broiled to a golden brown.

In the fall of 1936, Germany began its four-year plan, and thus launched the phase of direct preparation for war. In this connection, Austria became increasingly important, and not for the above-cited reason mentioned by Hitler on page one of *Mein Kampf*, but rather on strategic and economic grounds. Thus it was no mere coincidence that Hermann Göring, as special delegate responsible for administering the four-year plan for re-armament, now became the driving force pushing for a fast Anschluß.

Austria was most enticing because of its unemployment at 600,000 including tens of thousands of highly skilled workers, much newly-built industrial capacity, and important natural resources—iron ore, timber, crude oil, and magnesite in particular. But most enticing of all were its monetary and foreign currency reserves that were desperately needed in light of Germany's catastrophic currency situation. Thus, at the end of 1937, the German Reichsbank's foreign currency holdings were a relatively paltry 90 million Reichsmarks, whereas the fabulous booty they got their hands on in March 1938 came to the equivalent of about 1.4 billion Reichsmarks. Instead of using the money on measures to stimulate employment so that the many jobless and all those whose unemployment benefits had run out would become supporters of the state, the Schuschnigg government had given top priority to the stability of the currency and had amassed foreign exchange. According to Schausberger,

> [I]t was only [this booty] that imparted real world-class political
> weight to the dimensions and the significance of the redoubled
> German effort to bring on the Anschluß from late 1937 to early

1938. With the acquisition of Austria, the Third Reich could overcome its critical economic situation as well as maintaining the speed of its build-up and its arms-race lead of at least nine months.

At the end of 1937, Austria's domestic and foreign policy situation was almost hopeless. Mussolini, during his visit to Berlin in September 1937, had given Hitler a free hand with respect to Austria. Nor could any help be expected from the British after Lord Halifax—chairman of the Privy Council, confidant of Prime Minister Chamberlain and soon to be foreign minister—had let Hitler know on 19 November 1937 that, with respect to Danzig, Austria, and Czechoslovakia, England was only concerned "that these revisions be brought about by means of peaceful evolution, and that methods that might cause ongoing disruptions . . . be avoided." Meanwhile, on the domestic front, the fifth column of still-illegal National Socialists intensified its activities.

The dismissal of Generals Blomberg and Fritsch, and the shake-up at the top of the Foreign Office (Neurath replaced by Ribbentrop) in early February 1938 made it clear that Hitler was determined to take the first step on the path that he had elaborated on in the 5 November 1937 speech cited above, and in doing so was prepared to use force if necessary. Hitler now had absolute control over the *Wehrmacht*.

The significance of this development was not recognized at the time—neither in Austria nor by the opponents of this policy in Germany. Otherwise, Schuschnigg would hardly have consented to that meeting with Hitler on 12 February in Berchtesgaden that Papen and the Austrian Nazis had so cleverly arranged. If the Austrian chancellor had hoped to be able to clear up existing differences and to buy some time, then he got a rude awakening. Hitler dictated an ultimatum to Schuschnigg—a man not known for his nerves of steel in any case—whereby he had three days to conform Austria's foreign, military, economic, and press policies to those of Germany, to grant the National Socialists the freedom to engage in political activities and an amnesty, and to appoint one of their moderates, Arthur Seyss-Inquart, as minister of the interior with unlimited authority over the police. If he refused, Hitler threatened to send in the *Wehrmacht*—a bluff, since preparations for this move had not even begun.

Schuschnigg capitulated, especially since no outside assistance could be expected. Basically, this was already the beginning of the end, which then came even more quickly than expected. By this point, the smell of Anschluß was in the air, and a few days after Berchtesgaden, there began a wild flight of capital out of the country. On 20 February, Hitler gave an address that was eagerly awaited, especially in Austria, and was the first to be carried by the Austrian National Broadcasting Company—another consequence of Berchtesgaden. In his speech, Hitler did not utter even a single word about Austria's independence; rather, he pointed out how unbearable it was for a major power to know that there were members of its own ethnic group alongside it who, because of their love for the people as a whole and their sense of attachment to its fate and its worldview, were being subjected to terrible and prolonged suffering.

Numerous listeners reacted accordingly; in many parts of Austria, Hitler's speech was followed by Nazi demonstrations, celebrations, and rallies. "In Vienna, the red-white-red banner was ripped from its mast at City Hall and the swastika flag raised in its place; many in Graz felt that the 'Third Reich had broken out already,' and the federal police force, now under the command of Seyß-Inquart, did not intervene."

Schuschnigg responded on 24 February; in a major policy address before the legislature, he declared that his utmost duty was "to preserve [the] undiminished freedom and independence of the Austrian fatherland. . . . We know very well that there is a limit to how far you can go, that there comes a point where it is clearly posted 'This far and no further!' . . . Red-white-red to the death! Austria!" This could also be interpreted as meaning that Austria would be prepared to fight to maintain its independence. There were then demonstrations in support of this course, and corresponding Nazi counter-demonstrations.

On 2 March in Linz, Seyss-Inquart reviewed a parade of the outlawed SA, giving the marchers the Nazi salute as they passed. The event turned into a Nazi demonstration that ended with chants of "One people, one Reich!" "*Sieg Heil*!" and "Arise Germany, down with the Jews!" Similar demonstrations followed throughout the country, and the situation grew more critical from day to day. Schuschnigg attempted to launch a desperate offensive meant to regain the momentum, and thereby triggered the final act of this drama himself. Echoing the historic call-to-arms of heroic Tyrolean freedom fighter Andreas Hofer, "*Mander, 's ischt Zeit!*" (Men, the time has come!), he announced at a meeting of the *Vaterländische Front* on 9 March in Innsbruck his intention to hold a plebiscite on Sunday, 13 March. It was to be entitled "For a free and German, independent and public-spirited, for a Christian and united Austria!" Even at this late date, Schuschnigg considered it imperative—despite the regrets of many of his supporters—to refer to a "German" Austria.

But the whole undertaking came too late. In light of the political course pursued over the previous four years, it was an act of desperation that was also, as Italian Foreign Minister Galeazzo Ciano noted, a "bomb" destined "to explode in [Schuschnigg's] hands." There was good reason why Mussolini had warned against such a step.

It is idle speculation to consider what would have happened if the plebiscite had taken place. Hitler and his minions had a clear idea of how plebiscites held by dictatorships were designed to come out, and they had good reason to fear that Schuschnigg might well have gotten a majority, even if—or perhaps precisely because—there were no lists of eligible voters (since no general elections had taken place during the previous eight years).

Essentially, 10-12 March were days marked by chaos in Vienna; there was total confusion as to who had political clout and who was officially in charge of what. Certainly, 11 March was the decisive day. The chronology of the key events has subsequently become known for the most part, and can be briefly summarized as follows. On the morning of 10 March, Hitler reacted to Schuschnigg's speech by ordering preparations for "Operation Otto," the invasion of Austria, which was set for 12 March. At 6:30 p.m., the corresponding mobilization order was issued. Glaise-Horstenau, who happened to be in Germany at the time, was ordered to return to Vienna immediately and to deliver to Schuschnigg an ultimatum to postpone the plebiscite. The success of this ballot question seemed to be assured when, on the morning of 11 March, the Central Committee of the Revolutionary Socialists addressed the following appeal to the working class of Austria:

Workers, Comrades! Schuschnigg's plebiscite confronts you with the decision to either vote "yes" or to help Hitler's fascists take power. A victory by Hitler's fascists means not only the bloody repression and unrestrained exploitation of Austrian workers; it also poses a threat to the entire world. Austrian workers therefore cannot answer Schuschnigg's question with "no." . . . This coming Sunday is not the day on which we will settle the score with Austrian fascism, and call the authoritarian regime to account for the crimes it has committed against the workers since February 1934 by voting against Schuschnigg. This coming Sunday, we're voting against Hitler's fascists. On that day, the whole working class must vote "yes."

This was followed that very same day by three ultimatums delivered by the Austrian Nazis in Vienna—each after consultations with Berlin.

First, at 10:00 a.m., Seyss-Inquart and Glaise-Horstenau peremptorily demanded that Schuschnigg cancel the plebiscite; otherwise, they threatened to resign, which would have constituted a breach of the Berchtesgaden Agreement and given Hitler official grounds to intervene militarily. Schuschnigg accepted at 11:30 a.m. At 1:00 p.m., Hitler signed Directive Nr. 1 for the attack on March 12. It read in part:

If other means prove fruitless, I intend to send armed forces into Austria to restore constitutional conditions there and put a stop to further acts of violence against those segments of the population displaying the convictions of true Germans. I will be in command of the entire operation. . . . The army's initial objective is to occupy Upper Austria, Salzburg, Lower Austria, and Tyrol, to quickly take Vienna, and to secure the Austrian-Czech border. . . . It is in our interest that the entire operation proceed without resorting to violence as a peaceful occupation welcomed by the population. . . . If resistance is encountered, however, it is to be ruthlessly broken with armed force.

Second, a few minutes after 1:00 p.m., Seyss-Inquart delivered his second ultimatum. The cabinet was to resign by 5:30 p.m., and he would appoint a new one. Almost simultaneously, the Nazis began to take over power in the cities and provinces, as the old regime collapsed virtually without resistance. When diplomatic queries undertaken in Paris, London, and Rome made it clear that no help could be expected from there in this situation, Schuschnigg resigned at 4:00 p.m.

The third ultimatum, this time addressed to President Wilhelm Miklas, arrived shortly thereafter. He had until 7:30 p.m. to appoint Seyss-Inquart as the new chancellor or else German troops would march in. While Miklas was still refusing to accept the ultimatum, Schuschnigg capitulated once and for all. At 8:00 p.m., via radio, he bade farewell to his countrymen, and made public the ultimatum and the German threat to send in troops:

> The president has called upon me to inform the Austrian people that we are yielding to force. Because we fervently wish, even now, in this desperate hour, to avoid at any price the spilling of German blood, we have given our armed forces the order that, in case of an attack by German troops, they are to withdraw without resistance. . . . *Gott schütze Österreich*! (God protect Austria!)

The *Bundesheer* was instructed that "not a shot was to be fired" if German troops marched into Austria, and "their own troops were to pull back to the east."

Instead of considering the issue of how troops in Vorarlberg and Tyrol were supposed to withdraw "to the east," one should coonsider the more interesting and more frequently posed questions are: "Why was no order issued to put up military resistance? What would have happened if it had been?" The latter question cannot be answered by historians, and the only serious response that can be given to the former is that in the concrete situation that existed on 11-12 March immediately before and after the takeover of power by the National Socialists, there was absolutely no political basis on which to issue or to carry out such an order; furthermore, the Austrian leadership did not wish to spill "German blood." In such a discussion about the possibility of resistance, the wish is often father to the thought. The political will for such a step was absent, there no longer existed a functional government, the troops had been infiltrated by "illegal elements" (that is, National Socialists), and the Nazis had practically assumed power already throughout the whole country.

In the meantime, the National Socialists were already taking over the provincial governments—first of all in Tyrol, which reported to Vienna at 9:00 p.m. that power was in the Nazis' hands. Miklas named Seyss-Inquart the new chancellor at 11:00 p.m. Although the Austrian Nazis' victory was thus complete, this changed nothing with respect to Directive Nr. 2 signed by Hitler at 8:45 p.m. ordering the invasion to begin at daybreak on 12 March. The last bit of uncertainty as far as Hitler was concerned was cleared up late that evening when Rome gave the word that Mussolini had no objections to the move.

The jubilation and enthusiasm displayed by the Austrians as German troops marched into their country on the morning of 12 March exceeded all expectations on the German side and contributed to Hitler's decision to immediately go ahead with a complete Anschluß without waiting for the transitional phase that had been foreseen initially. It was left up to Seyss-Inquart on 13 March as the final act of his two-day term as chancellor to sign into law the "Reunification of Austria with the German Reich," whereby Article 1, stating that "Austria is a land of the German Reich," fatefully recalled the events of 1918, although this time everything had turned out much differently.

Besides the enthusiastic celebrations, expressions of support, hope for better times, and much opportunism, there were also those Austrians who did not approve of what was going on in those days; nevertheless, they remained largely inconspicuous in order to avoid the clutches of Himmler's henchmen, so that what remained were the images of jubilation and Hitler on *Heldenplatz*. In places where there was still skepticism, an unprecedented propaganda campaign was conducted—not without the active involvement of Austrians—during the weeks leading up to the plebiscite held on 10 April. The Catholic bishops expressed their delight "that the activities of the National Socialist movement would avert the threat of cataclysmic, godless Bolshevism" and wanted to give "their blessings and best wishes for these activities in the future"; Cardinal Innitzer signed off with "Heil Hitler." Karl Renner declared on 2 April:

> Although not brought about by the methods which I advocate, the Anschluß has nevertheless been completed, it is a historical fact, and this I regard as genuine satisfaction for the

humiliations of 1918 and 1919, for St. Germain and Versailles. . . . As a Social Democrat and thus as a proponent of a nation's right to self-determination, as the first chancellor of the Republic of Austria, I will vote "yes."

With testimonials like these, how many Catholics or Socialists were going to vote "no"? Indeed, that is how it turned out. To the question "Do you agree with the reunification of Austria with the German Reich that was carried out on 13 March 1938, and do you cast your vote for the list of candidates of our Führer Adolf Hitler?" there were 4,453,772 (99.73 percent) "yes" votes, 11,929 "no" votes, and 5,776 invalid ballots in Austria. (In Germany, where the plebiscite was combined with a *Reichstag* election, there were 44,362,667 (99.02 percent) votes for and 440,429 against.) In assessing these results, we may well proceed under the assumption that massive election fraud did not take place. Actually, under these circumstances, it was not even necessary.

But for many Austrians, it did not take long for disillusionment to set in. Hitler had never particularly cared for the Austrian Nazis, so it was Nazis from the "old Reich" who took over the leading positions in Austria. It was certainly significant that among the passengers aboard the first plane to land in Vienna on 12 March (at 4:30 a.m.) were Heinrich Himmler, *Reichsführer* SS and head of the German police, and SS-*Gruppenführer* Reinhard Heydrich, head of the Security Service (SD). By December, approximately 21,000 persons had been taken into "protective custody." There were systematic terror, acts of revenge, and outbreaks of horrible anti-Semitic violence—only possible because anti-Semitism was so deeply rooted in a long tradition. "With their bare hands," an eyewitness recalled,
university professors had to scrub the streets; pious, bearded Jews were dragged into the Temple and forced by howling young goons to do deep knee-bends while shouting in unison 'Heil Hitler.' They rounded up innocent people on the street like rabbits and marched them to the SA barracks to clean the toilets. Every sick, filthy, hate-filled fantasy that had been the object of countless nights' orgiastic longings was now raging in broad daylight.

The name *Österreich* and the traditions of that country were soon eradicated. Austria first became the *Ostmark*, and then the *Alpen- und Donaugaue* (Alpine and Danubian administrative districts). From the heights of its rich culture, it sank into provincialism. Those who had voted "yes" on 10 April had doubtlessly not intended this, to say nothing of a war. Indeed, most Austrians involved in this war did their "duty" to the bitter end, but to them can also be applied what Adolf Schärf, Social Democrat and later Austrian president, recounts having said to a representative of the German resistance in the spring of 1943: "The Anschluß is dead. The Austrians have had their love for the German Reich driven out of them."

# II. WORLD WAR II

Gusen concentration camp slave laborers who perished in the final days of the war before the American liberation of Upper Austria.

Source: National Archives, College Park, MD (#206475)

# The Emigration and Exile of Austrian Intellectuals

*Friedrich Stadler*

## Introduction

The book-burnings which occurred in German cities in May 1933 were an early and acute eruption of anti-enlightenment forced in the anti-democratic field of tension surrounding politics and science. The German Student's Union, dominated even in Austria by National Socialists and supported by a large number of professors, delivered to the flames not only thousands of books by authors such as Erich Kaestner and Stefan Zweig, but also many scientific works by Marxist, psychoanalytic, and pacifist authors. The works were denounced with slogans such as: "Against class-warfare and materialism . . . character-swindle and political betrayal . . . the soul-shredding over-exaggeration of the drives . . . " In the war against so-called "Jewish cultural Bolshevism," Karl Marx, Sigmund Freud, and Albert Einstein were made into figureheads of the hated rational/empirical, humanistic science of nature and society. Appearing since 1935, the *Reichsschrifttumskammer*'s list of censored "harmful and undesirable" writings (which included about 4,000 authors), officially excluded works of pure science. Nevertheless, it included authors such as Alfred Adler, Friedrich Adler, Max Adler, Victor Adler, Otto Bauer, Siegfried Bernfeld, Ernst Bloch, Helene Deutsch, Albert Einstein, Sandor Ferenczi, Ernst Fischer, Sigmund and Anna Freud, Karl Marx, Erich Fromm, Magnus Hirschfeld, Max Horkheimer, Fritz Wittels, Wilhelm Reich, Theodor Reik, and many others. More extensive censorship was implemented in Austria: the Austrofascist *Verbotslisten* of 1934-1938 which had mainly included social-democratic and Nazi literature, were replaced after the Anschluß by secret blacklists consulted in the further "purification"

The philosopher Karl Popper emigrated to New Zealand (1937-45); after the war he moved to London, not to Vienna.

Source; Institut Wiener Kreis, Vienna

of scientific libraries. The long-term consequences of intellectual emigration and of the "purification of the universities"—but also of science outside of the university—were, in these fields, as catastrophic as in the field of literature.

Considered as a whole, the Austrian universities between the two wars were a hotbed for reaction, but this was especially true in the University of Vienna. This was exemplified by a general anti-Semitic and anti-liberal trend, particularly by a conglomeration of German-nationalists and clerics which fought successfully against "Jewish" liberalism and socialism. Causes for this include high unemployment of academics, as well as the rise of the ideologies of political Catholicism and National Socialism. After 1934, anti-democratic pressures were increased by the Schuschnigg regime's attempts to ward off the German nationalist phalanx by propagating an "Austria-ideology" which, in turn, further strengthened militant anti-Semitism. The decline of scientific reason was a logical consequence of the sociopolitical conditions within the university milieu as a particular manifestation of the general social condition.

The defensive posture of the liberal/socialist camp can also be explained by its rejection of all forms of totalitarian thought and action. This can be illustrated by the way in which university appointments were made and accreditation to teach (habilitation) was granted at the time. Already marginalized democratic groupings, after professing liberal or Marxist leanings or logical-empirical or "materialistic" views, were condemned as "Freudo-Marxists" and expelled by 1938 at the latest. Research in university history yields concrete evidence of this practice in failed applications for accreditation (Max Adler, Edgar Zilsel, Viktor Kraft, Karl Menger, Sigmund Freud), as well as dismissals (Heinrich Gomperz, Friedrich Waismann) and partisan appointments (after Moritz Schlick).

Philosophical and political pluralism was replaced by the monoculture of political Catholicism and Fascist universalism (Othmar Spann and his circle), followed by a seamless transition of National Socialist ideology. The consequent expulsion of intellectuals could not and cannot be compensated for, even today. A main reason for this was the continuity of a conservative, clerical, or even "national" mentality, following the failed postwar attempt at de-Nazification. After 1945, the field of philosophy was again dominated by universalism, Christian existentialism, and *Weltanschauungsmetaphysik*. With few exceptions, it proved impossible to revive the fruitful intellectual climate of the *Zwischenkriegszeit*, or inter-war period.

During the economically catastrophic inter-war period, the "intellectual workers" of the Austrian universities were drawn, on the average, from the politically and economically "de-classed" middle class. In the ideological context of German nationalism and political Catholicism, the bulk of professors and students formed themselves into an anti-democratic and anti-Semitic front: "Liberalism" in all of its variants was its declared enemy. Hopelessly trapped in the middle of the "nationalist" encirclement in the "Alma Mater," were mainly socialist, Austromarxist, neo-positivist, and psychoanalytic professors such as Carl Gruenberg, Max Adler, Sigmund Freud, Karl and Charlotte Buehler, Moritz Schlick, Karl Menger, Hans Kelsen, but also Julius Tandler and many others, mostly Jewish academics.

The authoritarian ideologies of the economist Othmar Spann, the historian Heinrich Ritter von Srbik, or the professor of German language Josef Nadler, prepared the way for the gradual elimination of scientific reason. The politics of university appointments, which took place in the gap between dubious university autonomy and interventions of the Ministry of Education, guaranteed selections which favored the right wing. Nazi students distributed "black-lists" of Jewish and/or socialist professors to be boycotted and, with the public support of sympathetic professors, rectors, and the Minister of Education, demanded admission restrictions for non-Aryan students. All of this occurred before the authoritarian regime's dissolution of parliament in March 1933. Following the defeat of the democratic opposition, the Austrian regime, helplessly caught in the undertow between Italian and German fascism and itself infiltrated by "illegal" National Socialists, attempted to construct a "Christian German corporate state" (*Ständestaat*).

## The Intellectual "Anschluß" in the Universities before 1938

The Nazi assassination in 1925 of Hugo Bettauer, a publicist of sexually enlightened ideas, had been legitimized by the right-wing press and greeted by many academics (Hall 1978). The public justification by the state press and university faculty of the 1936 murder of Moritz Schlick—intellectual leader of the world renowned Vienna Circle—therefore comes as no surprise. The Catholic-nationalist newspaper *Schoenere Zukunft* wrote apologetically that in the Schlick case

the disastrous influence of Judaism can be seen . . . Now, the Jewish circles will certainly not tire of praising him as the greatest of thinkers. We understand that very well. For the Jew is the born ametaphysician. In philosophy, he loves logicism, mathematicism, formalism and positivism—those very ideas which Schlick had united so completely in himself. We would, however, like to remind everyone that we are Christians living in a Christian-German state and that it is we who decide which philosophy is good and suitable. The Jews should be allowed their Jewish philosophy in their own Jewish cultural Institute! But in the chairs of philosophy in the Viennese university in Christian, German Austria, there belong Christian philosophers! Recently, it has been repeatedly explained that a peaceful solution of the Jewish question in Austria is also in the interest of the Jews, for otherwise, a violent solution is unavoidable. Hopefully, the terrible murder in the Viennese university will

serve to bring about a truly satisfactory solution of the Jewish
question! (Austriacus 1936)

Catholic faculty members demanded the unity of religion and
science. The same professor of philosophy who had classified
Schlick's teachings as "negativistic," for example, also polemicized
against Freudian psychoanalysis:

Psychoanalysis is, to someone versed in intellectual matters,
nothing other than crude-cutting materialism and, apart from the
fact that it is scientifically untenable, is the most degrading
conception of mankind that history has ever seen . . . In the final
end, psychoanalysis—the judgment of which naturally can not
be left to romanciers like Stefan Zweig or Thomas Mann—is
nothing more than pornography dressed in scientific garb. We
pity its founder as a mistaken genius who, like Nietzsche, was a
victim of the materialistic Zeitgeist. But Science and Philosophy
have a responsibility to the Volk to counter this monstrous
error—which, like every error, contains in some points,
distorted grains of truth—with a serious investigation of
conscience. (Sauter 1936)

Clearly, this exponent of political Catholicism regretted the lack of
a bonfire for Freud's life work. In the land of the *Vaterländische
Front*, the attacks against the representatives of scientific
psychology, sociology, and psychoanalysis differed only in details
from the later National Socialist denunciations of Magnus
Hirschfeld, Wilhelm Reich, and Sigmund Freud. After all, the flames
in 1933 in Germany also consumed the (today, world-renowned)
study *Die Arbeitslosen von Marienthal* (1933) by Marie Jahoda, Paul
F. Lazarsfeld, and Hans Zeisel. But the political and scientific
conditions within the Austrofascist state had been the cause of the
author's exile. This was also the reason why those who had been
branded on 10 May 1933 by the Nazis in Germany could find no
friendly refuge in Austria. After 12 February 1934, the first great
wave of emigration of Austrian politicians, scientists, and artists
occurred. Sexual fears were combined with clerical pettiness to
create a defensive syndrome against enlightened rationalism and
empiricism which were denounced as weapons of destruction against

national "earth-bound" thought. The "healthy body politic" (a metaphor of Spannian universalism) was called on to immunize itself against the "ulcers of Jewish *Weltanschauung*." The fear of contact was the last barrier against outright physical aggression. The operation "final solution" had become conceivable.

What the destruction of democracy and the consequent "black and brown" cultural landscape, with its anachronistic Reich ideology, Christian worldview, metaphysical speculation, and irrationality gathered under the banner of "Unity of Faith and Knowledge" could mean to an enlightened mind was expressed by the Austrian writer and expatriate Jean Amery:

> The land expelled before its time that very spirit which it had given birth to. Freud became an inter-Jewish matter, against which Christian vigilance was advised. Behind the men of the Vienna Circle stood the Thomist young assistant professors, and behind them stood the Rosenberg followers who found it possible to reconcile their Christianity with their loyalties just as the Church found it possible to do with the Nazis. Literature received public support and approval as long as it busied itself with alpine-Christian yodeling, whose celebratory Catholic melodies were quickly, and without formal difficulty, transposed into the Nazi key. The native literati behaved like drunks: Their merriness gradually changed—in a manner unnoticed but not accidental—into a howling rage. (Amery, 1971, 49f)

The details of the resulting twilight of intellectual culture speak for themselves and are still sobering today. They include destruction of the democratic Viennese adult education and school-reform movement, as well as the entire range of social and cultural policies of "Red Vienna" including those of Julius Tandler, Otto Gloeckel, Otto Neurath, and Max Adler; the dissolution of the Vienna Circle and the Ernst Mach society; and the obstruction of Paul Lazarsfeld's social research long before the Anschluß. All of this was a result of the cultural policies of Austrofascism and of those that had prepared the way for it. Moreover, all of it occurred before Hitler's arrival an the scene. Indeed, the majority warmly welcomed the *Herrenmenschen* which had only to complete the work of destruction and eradication begun by their Austrofascist predecessors.

## Emigration, Exile, and Annihilation

The emigration and exile of Austrian intellectuals must also be
seen in the larger historical context of the inter-war years. In this
context, the shadow of rising Fascism, economic crisis had existed
since the twenties as had the destruction of democracy and the
crushing of the labor movement in 1933/34, and, finally, the violent
Anschluß of March 1938. Austrian intellectual emigration is a
special case of the general phenomenon of emigration for political,
religious, cultural, and so-called "racial" reasons, but also a specific
part of the larger migration movements of the twentieth century.

This emigration as a whole, which was always a forced exile out
of the home country, can be divided into three main phases: the years
before 1933/34, the Austrofascist period of 1934-1938, and the era of
National Socialist tyranny, 1938-1945.

In the time before the dissolution of parliamentary democracy by
the Dollfuss–regime, the "brain drain" consisted mainly of Jewish
intellectuals escaping the hopeless economic situation and general
climate of anti-Semitism. But the period of cultural emigration out of
"Red Vienna" after 12 February 1934 is characterized by the
increased departure of the political left, especially of approximately
3,000 members of the *Schutzbund* to Czechoslovakia and the Soviet
Union. Unfortunately, the figures and statistics needed to quantify
this first wave of emigration, as well as those to cover emigration as
a whole up to March 1938, are unavailable. However, many
biographical testaments and relevant sources explain how the dull
intellectual and reactionary political climate that was deeply hostile
to Jews and intellectuals was responsible for the departure of so
many liberals and socialists, long before the advent of National
Socialism. In the ideological battle against the critical and
enlightened spirit, we see a historical process which was perfected
into a mass phenomenon after March 1938. Here the distinctly
Austrian role played in the "banishment of the mind" becomes
apparent; it cannot simply be passed of as the work of evil foreign
powers.

During the National Socialist annihilation and expulsion policies,
the violent "cultural exodus" became systematic. Well over 150,000
Austrians (at least 130,000 of whom were Jewish) had to flee the
country (if they could). There were approximately 100,000 victims

of National Socialism (among them 65,000 Jews) who were unable to cross the border to safety, or, because of their part in the anti-Fascist resistance, were forced to give their lives. The whole topic of "emigration and exile" cannot be discussed without reference to the millions of victims of Hitler's Fascism, the Holocaust, and the mass migration of half a million people—among them 300,000 Jews—out of Central Europe.

The years of National Socialist racism represent the awful and historically unprecedented height of this mass migration. This migration can be seen as a part of general European emigration during the interwar years, but can also be viewed in the context of increased mobility and internationalization of cultural elites. The fact that many representatives of the scientific community expelled by fascism have been responsible for most of the international research on exile in the last fifteen years bears witness to this cosmopolitan exchange.

Unfortunately, even fifty years after the Anschluß, institutionalized research in the field of emigration and exile remains, with few exceptions, nonexistent at the university level. The large contributions of the "Documentation Center for Austrian Resistance" on general Austrian exile provide an important foundation for research. However, in terms of intellectual emigration, this project still remains in its early stages because an interdisciplinary history of science in the context of Austrian modern history is missing. This is, in the international context, unique to Austria.

Second, the representatives of various university disciplines were, with few exceptions, unable to systematically review and analyze the recent history of their own disciplines. This is, of course, connected with the taboo problem of a continuity within cultural elites.

Third, the postwar coalition in Austria had no partisan or political interest in coming to terms with the legacy of two kinds of Fascism. The failure of the official Austrian republic to encourage the return of its many exiles is a logical consequence of "Austria-making" after the failed attempts at de-Nazification and in light of the official myth of "reconstruction" from "ground zero."

Fourth, as already mentioned, the majority of emigrants were Jewish, owing to steadily increasing racism in both word and deed. This raises once more the question of "home-made" Austrian anti-

Semitism. Since the turn of the century, if not earlier, anti-Semitism had been present in all forms and variations, except for the absolute culmination of racist madness, the systematic genocide of National Socialism. The currently resurfacing forms of anti-Semitism must, therefore, be seen in the historical perspective of a societal process which has yet to be overcome.

Fifth, in the public consciousness, including that of high-ranking politicians, the notions of emigration or anti-Fascist resistance were, and continue to be, viewed with suspicion. The meager "reparations" made to those few emigrants who did return, signify certain social reservations against the expatriated. Abroad however, they continue to represent the "other" democratic Austria both in theory and practice and are occasionally used by official Austria to polish its international image.

Sixth, the restrictive policies guarding archives in Austria for fifty years have blocked any systematic historiography of the years 1938-45. This raises the question whether modern historians are even allowed to try and come to terms with the past.

For all the reasons listed above, a complete portrayal of Austrian intellectual emigration, as well as of the history of emigration in general, remains to be written. The Austrian aspect of this emigration was subsumed by the relevant international research under the category of German-speaking emigration, a fate shared by Austrian literature. (The lack of Austria's own research in this field made the subsumation seem less awkward.) On the one hand, it was held that there were too few criteria to justify a separate Austrian category within that of German-speaking countries. On the other hand, in view of the available material and sources, there were also purely practical reasons for including all German-speaking emigration from Nazi-occupied countries in one group.

For many reasons, however, a genuine research project on "Austrian Intellectual Emigration" separate from the general German-speaking category, seems both meaningful and necessary. First, Austria's past must be seen, although in connection with it, separately from that of Germany's, especially when considering the years 1933/34-1938. Second, there are significant differences and typical characteristics of Austrian emigration which, in comparison to other German-speaking emigration, reveal themselves in effects both at home and abroad.

In summary, one could say that, since the 1930s, as a result of the rise of Fascism and National Socialism, the gradual destruction of the once thriving Viennese culture coincided with increasing emigration of Austrian intellectuals. This emigration turned into a mass phenomenon during the tragic climax of the Anschluß with Nazi Germany. The already world-famous representatives of Austrian literature, art, and science, the entire intellectual avant-garde, were forced to abandon the sinking ship of the clerical-Fascist *Ständestaat* or, in 1938 at the latest, the National Socialist *Ostmark*, provided they were still able to.

## Effects of Emigration, Exile, and Annihilation on Intellectual Disciplines

A short, incomplete sketch of this cultural exodus, seen in the exile of Austrian scientists, can only begin to outline the loss and long-term consequences it had. The consequences for the Second Republic can only be alluded to.

In the fields of philosophy, mathematics, and logic, the intellectual state of affairs forced the emigration of the famous Vienna Circle, a group of renowned scientists who, with enlightened intentions, strove to make philosophy a pure science. The exodus of this linguistically critical, interdisciplinary group began in the 1930s with the dissolution of the popularizing *Verein Ernst Mach* (Ernst Mach Society) on 12 February 1934 and with the murder of Moritz Schlick on 22 June 1936. The last representatives of this "Scientific World-Conception" were forced to leave after the Anschluß. After 1930, fourteen exponents of logical empiricism left Austria for political, "racial," and intellectual reasons: Gustav Bergmann, Rudolf Carnap (from Prague), Herbert Feigl, Philipp Frank (from Prague), Kurt Goedel, Felix Kaufmann, Karl Menger, Richard von Mises (from Turkey), Marcel Natkin, Otto Neurath, Rose Rand, Josef Schaechter, Friedrich Waismann, and Edgar Zilsel. Only Bela Juhos, Heinrich Neider, and Viktor Kraft (who was banned from his profession) remained.

After 1945, only Juhos and Kraft could obtain short-term university positions. In postwar Austria, philosophy was dominated by Christian *Weltanschauungsphilosophie* and by idealistic systematic philosophy. The most famous philosopher of the twentieth century, Ludwig Wittgenstein (and one of the main contacts of the Vienna Circle) had left the country in 1929 without academic status or a chance of pursuing an academic career and had gone to Cambridge, England. There, on the basis of his *Tractatus logico-philosophicus*, he made his name and initiated the linguistic turn in philosophy. Karl Popper, the father of "Critical Rationalism," who had also socialized with the edges of the Vienna Circle, emigrated to New Zealand in 1937, mostly because of the hopeless career opportunities at home. After the Second World War, he received an appointment in England at the renowned London School of Economics. Not one of these outstanding representatives of modern philosophy were invited back home, although some, as in the case of Karl Buehler, had hopes for this request to return.

If we consider the representatives of modern mathematics and logic alone, the balance of loss of "colleagues in a dark time" (Pinl/ Dick) is no less shocking. Out of the institutes of mathematics and theoretical physics of the Viennese university, eighteen mostly Jewish scientists were banished. The physicist and mathematician Hans Thirring remained and lived through the National-Socialist period as a pacifist "inner emigrant."

A similar dark picture emerges when considering the exile of the psychoanalytic movement out of Vienna. As a declared enemy of conservative, right-wing culture, this provocative discipline had been massively attacked since the turn of the century and successively forced into a defensive posture through the 1930s. For "soul-shredding psychoanalysis" (as the Nazi jargon put it), this process could almost be predicted. A large portion of emigrating psychoanalysts found professional positions in the Anglo-American world due to the high degree of internationalization of this field (which, however, did not contribute much to its social and critical dimension). Out of the fifty official members of the Vienna Psychoanalytic Association, all but three were forced to leave the country after the annexation. In this context, the school of individual psychology under Alfred Adler must be mentioned. Over two-thirds of a total of twenty-nine people emigrated. The fact that individual psychology as a movement had a stronger connection to Viennese socialist educational programs was a main cause of its early disintegration after 1934. The entire science and practice of *Tiefenpsychologie*, which was effective well beyond the therapeutic field and which enriched education, social work and science, was thereby eliminated in two stages: 1934 and post-1938.

Scientific psychology, at that time poorly institutionalized, also lost its best minds as intellectual collaborators used racist criteria to "professionalize" their discipline (this also occurred in the field of sociology). In this field, cognitive and *Gestalt* psychology and child and adolescent psychology pioneered by Karl and Charlotte Buehler, is of special importance. Both placed their knowledge in the service of Viennese school reform and, along with the Economic Psychological Research Center, created a platform for the new empirical social research being done by Paul Lazarsfeld, Marie Jahoda, and Hans Zeisel until their exile. The socially oriented work of all these psychological schools in connection with the social policies of Julius Tandler, Otto Gloeckel, and Hugo Breitner was abruptly put to a stop after the labor movement was crushed in 1934. Since 1945, it has not been able to recover the same quality and quantity which it, at that time, lost. A concrete vision of socialist culture in the "field of Austromarxism" (Glaser) with its fruitful cooperation between science and worker's culture, had already been eradicated before the marginalized humanistic tradition was finally driven out in 1938. In this tradition, we find psychologists like Egon Brunswik, Else Frenkel-Brunswik, Gustav Ichheiser, and Ernest Dichter, the father of advertising psychology. The "destruction of reason" thereby becomes much more concrete, as the title of a book of interviews with emigrated social scientists formulates. A symptom of this cultural rupture can be seen in the fact that, fifty years after the exile of psychoanalysts and individual psychologists, there exists not a single chair at any Austrian university for these schools.

Because of the interdisciplinary methods of research of the time, it is impossible to give a canonized presentation according to subjects or disciplines. This difficulty can be seen when considering the Vienna Circle, but is also present in the fields of sociology and the social sciences. The emigration of social scientists took place in the context of a not-yet-differentiated and institutionalized subject. Aside from this, the main sociological innovations were to be found outside of the university, in social-liberal circles or in the associations of Viennese adult education. The final elimination of social-scientific research within the universities in 1938 had the consequence that a discipline under construction was forced to move elsewhere to establish itself internationally. On the other hand, after the Second World War, its country of origin had to slowly come to terms with its own legacy of "universalism and Fascism." In the non-academic fields surrounding empirical social research, the consequences of the disintegration were severe. The Social and Economic Museum in Vienna, for example, founded and directed by Otto Neurath and intended as a platform for worker education (utilizing the "Viennese method of Statistical Graphics"), was put under Austrofascist patronage after 1934, and later taken over by the Nazis. Neurath and his team fled to Holland and later to England where, for the rest of his life and under difficult circumstances, Neurath untiringly promoted and developed the "Unity of Science" movement and his picture pedagogical theory ("isotype"). Paul Lazarsfeld and his assistants successively left their posts in 1934. In these fields, a number of sociologically oriented lecturers of the Viennese Community Colleges must be mentioned, including Karl Polanyi, Leo Stern, Eduard Maerz, Walter Hollitscher, and Edgar Zilsel. In the course of "cleaning-up" in the spirit of "Christian German" ideology during the Austrofascist period, all of these men were dismissed from their positions. So in this field as well, Austrofascism was successful in preparing the way for the National Socialists. In this context, the original connection between schools, community colleges, and universities and its importance for emigration research becomes clear. With the last wave of dismissals in 1938, a *Gleichschaltung* of the universities was achieved, but also forced departure of the non-academic social science intelligentsia, a portion of which was able to pursue an academic career abroad. The fate of social scientist Kaethe Leichter, who was murdered in a concentration camp, is typical of many victims of National Socialism. In summary, with approximately fifty social scientists forced into exile, the liberal and the Austromarxist schools, including their followers, were completely eradicated either through exile or physical annihilation.

Such a diagnosis is also appropriate for the field of economics. This creative scientific culture, with its open form of exchange, disappeared entirely; whereas, the universalistic approach of the Othmar Spann circle became the only tradition after the Nazi intermezzo which was able to secure footing in the Second Republic. Also, in the cultural and political periphery of the liberal/socialist camp, scientifically-oriented reform in the areas of schooling, adult education, and social reform (monists, freethinkers, pacifists, and women's movement) had the rug pulled from under its feet. This had negative effects for both the displaced intellectuals, as well as for the failed "reconstruction" of the labor-culture movement after 1945. The productive connection between progressive science and democratic education was halted by emigration, exile, and annihilation.

Emigration in the fields of law and political science is strongly connected to that of the social sciences in terms of personnel and topics. Using a sample of approximately fifty representatives, a few preliminary characteristics can be seen. With the disappearance of the Vienna School of the *"Reine Rechtslehre"* (pure legal theory) of Hans Kelsen, father of the Austrian constitution, a reflection of the anti-Semitic and ideologically-colored battle against legal positivism fought by the exponents of natural law emerges. In addition to this, after 1945, mostly non-emigrants were chosen to re-build the faculties of law and political science. The disregard shown towards one of the most important Austrian constitutional jurists went so far that in 1965, during the celebrations of the six-hundredth anniversary of the University of Vienna, Hans Kelsen was forced to give a lecture outside of the official proceedings. This is an indication of the repression within Austrian scientific history.

The lack of research an emigration and exile is connected with the central role of the historical sciences, which have hardly come to terms with their own histories. Caught in the paradigm of German historicism, these disciplines could not and would not deal with these sensitive and self-critical issues. Those who wished to do so were, after 1938, no longer in the country. In 1938, most of the established historians were in favor of the Anschluß and, after the war, these same historians established new guilds in the old tradition of historicism and in the new dressings of the "Austria-ideology." In contrast, we find a number of emigrants in the field of history and historiography who stand in a different tradition: Robert A. Kann, Alfred F. Pribram, Friedrich Engel-Janosi, Ernst Stein, Josef Kaut, Joseph Buttinger, Hermann Langbein, Leopold Spira, Karl R.

Stadler, Felix Kreissler, Gerda Lerner, Ernst Wangermann, Arthur von Rosthorn, Heinrich Benedikt, Hugo Gold, Josef Fraenkel, Herbert Rosenkranz, Jonny Moser, Peter Pulzer, Franz Goldner, Herbert Steiner, Thomas Chaimowicz, and Walter Grab. This list provides a preliminary picture of the great potential which was lost by Austria, as only a small number of these historians returned.

This intellectual collapse was worsened by the exile of a number of Austrian journalists and publicists and by their failure to return after the war. Over a third of the journalists writing after 1945 had also been active in the Austrofascist and National Socialist periods.

More strongly present in public consciousness—and also more fitting to the cliché of Austria as a land of muses—is literary and artistic emigration. The exile of natural science and technical sciences with its many Nobel prize winners has, by contrast, been wrongly marginalized. This is connected to the fact that the importance of Austrian literature of the inter-war period, written by authors like Hermann Broch, Robert Musil, Manes Sperber, Elias Canetti, Joseph Roth, and Stefan Zweig, is generally recognized today. But many forgotten and repressed authors and literary scientists are ignored by this elitist perspective. This could occur more easily as there was a certain continuity of the "national paradigm" in Austrian German studies associated with Josef Nadler, as well as of "blood and soil" literature well into the Second Republic. This influence, however, has been reduced by the influx of emigrated foreign literary historians like Heinz Politzer, Joseph Strelka, Egon Schwarz, Franz Mautner, and Berthold Viertel.

A main exponent of German studies as a national science in the field of theater science was Heinz Kindermann. He took over the Central Institute for Theater Science in 1943 and led it in the true National-Socialist spirit. Alternatives could be found only outside of the universities, in the writings of exiled theater publicists like Berthold Viertel, Ferdinand Bruckner, Heinrich Schnitzler, Karl Paryla, Leonard Steckel, and Wolfgang Heinz and also in the work on literary theory by Paul Reimann and Ernst Fischer.

In the 1940s and 1950s, there was a strong feeling of suspicion within the high culture toward the literary, artistic, and scientific avant-garde. Twelve-tone music was blocked with the exile of Arnold Schoenberg as was every form of experimental music and theater. This problem raises the issue of the little-researched musicological emigration which, considering how often Austria is stylized as a land of music, can only be called scandalous. This is contrasted with the domestically-accepted fellow traveler syndrome of composers and conductors like Herbert von Karajan and Karl Boehm.

In the face of National Socialist leanings of Joseph Strzygowski and Hans Sedlmayr, the renowned Viennese school of art history was inevitably exiled, but was revived in the English Warburg Institute by the continued work of Ernst Kris, Otto Kurz, Ernst Gombrich, Otto Paecht, Fritz Saxl, and Hans Tietze. Also in England, Arnold Hauser, who was ignored in Austria, published his standard works on the history and sociology of art.

The Austrian architectural avant-garde received no better treatment. Around one-fifth of the architects of the internationally-recognized Viennese Community Housing Projects and one-half of the builders of the Viennese *Werkbundsiedlung* were exiled either by Austrofascism or by National Socialism. Within the span of only a few years, Vienna had lost her entire progressive architectural avant-garde. The failure of these architects to return was the cause of a kind of architectural theory no-man's land: a spiritual and practical vacuum which was left to be filled by the national, romantic tradition in the absence of modernist criticism. Only in the last few years has the domestically established architectural provincialism been enriched by the influx of international discourse.

However largely the prominent natural scientists of the First Republic—such as Nobel prize-winners Erwin Schroedinger, Max Perutz, Viktor F. Hess, Wolfgang Pauli, Georg von Hevesy, Otto Loewi, and Karl Landsteiner—may loom in the international scene, a complete portrayal of natural scientific, and technological emigration is missing. The entire Institute of Radium Research, for example, was banned from the Austrian Academy of Sciences. Many intellectuals in the field of natural science left the crisis-plagued country even before the Anschluß and headed for Weimar Germany. Structural migration had occurred even before the end of the monarchy. Around one-third of physicists were affected by the violent expatriation and the whole of theoretical physics had to yield to the insane fiction of "Aryan physics."

The continuos "brain-drain" of technicians since the beginning of the First Republic included at least 500 persons. The number of

Austrians alone among the "technical intelligentsia in exile" in England (thirty engineers) is enough to show the practical economic and political problems which were—with the lack of skilled personnel—entailed in the re-construction of the Second Republic. It also begins to explain the current innovation deficit in Austria.

The emigration of physicians out of Central Europe, including approximately 3,000 out of Austria, included medical scientists, psychiatrists, psycho-therapists, and practical physicians, who were forced to leave in three main periods (before 1933, in 1934, and until 1938) for economic, political, or "racial" reasons. Universalistic and anti-Semitic exclusion policies became stronger as the economic crisis grew worse. They favored *vaterländische,* or German nationalist physicians, over their liberal, socialist, and/or Jewish colleagues. With the Austrofascist takeover, the emigration of leftist physicians began. The march of German troops into Austria and the National Socialist takeover were accompanied by the largest expatriation of physicians. Many other lives ended in suicide, concentration camps, or inner emigration. Around a third of Viennese university teachers of medicine emigrated—more than half of them to the United States—whereby almost the entire Austrian school of medical history and social medicine was exiled in one blow. The little-known professional organization for exiles served as a platform for many physicians to voice their desire to return to democratic Austria. However, this return was minimal in comparison to the many important innovations made by emigrants in their new countries, especially in the areas of psychoanalysis and individual psychology, but also in the natural sciences, which was the case for Wolfgang Pauli and Otto Loewi, for example. With the departure of an entire profession, one source of possible practical and cognitive resistance against the Nazi biological racial madness was lost, and international scientific progress was abruptly halted. This gives cause enough to reflect upon the supposed and actual "crisis in medicine" in a historical context.

Although, since the 1960s, Austrian science has slowly received modernizing impulses and gradually been internationalized, the substantial loss which it suffered due to the emigration of an entire intellectual elite with great potential, could not be made up for. For example, Austria is currently struggling to connect itself with international research in the fields of science and technology. With figures alone, however, the qualitative aspect of emigration and exile can only be alluded to. The subjective suffering of those involved, beginning with their often perilous journey over the border, and continuing with the struggle to obtain visas and affidavits; existential problems due to loss of property; the Fascist persecution or annihilation of their friends and family; the pains of transit into a strange land with a strange language; and the daily balance between integration and failure, between a scientific career and professional demotion; all of this has often been described. It was possible for a small minority of emigrants to pursue successful careers, emigrants such as Marie Jahoda, Paul Lazarsfeld, Rudolf Carnap, Josef Frank, and Kurt Goedel. Yet this was often due to the international status their disciplines had already before their departure, But for each one of these lucky few, a silent majority suffered often tragic fates: thwarted attempts to return, unsuccessful assimilation, or even suicide (Edgar Zilsel represents many others here). All of these individual fates were characterized by diverse, often accidental, factors including: 1.) age (Charlotte Buehler, for example, was able to pursue a career in the United States; whereas, her husband, Karl Buehler, experienced an unsuccessful acculturation and remigration); 2.) diverse conditions within the countries of arrival; and 3.) the state of development of one's own discipline (geographical as well as social subject-specific conditions will have to be the subject of further research). Whereas most European countries until National Socialist occupation served only as short-term transit stations, it was sometimes possible to offer more extensive help to the expatriated. An example of this occurred in Turkey where, owing to Kemal Atatuerk's planned program of modernization, it was possible to organize German-speaking "educational assistance in exile." Due to their quota-free immigration policies, Shanghai and Palestine were the most frequented stops in the Asian and Middle Eastern regions. In terms of quantity, however, the Anglo-American realm (mainly the United States and Great Britain) was the most important receiving region for intellectual emigration.

Although new publications concerning the geographical aspects of general emigration have appeared, Austrian immigration remains to be investigated with the help of not-yet-existent research on cultural transfer. The works on trans-Atlantic influence published until now have been written mainly from the perspective of the receiving countries. A comprehensive study of reception in a general social context from the perspective of the home country would, therefore, be useful. There are many topics which would belong in such research and such have, until now, been scarcely investigated. Among these topics are the institutional and psycho-social conditions surrounding the "intellectual worker" in a foreign environment and the basic patterns of language and lifestyle in terms of cognitive identity. We know what strong effects a loss of language has had (though not as decisively as in literature) in the change of theoretical orientations and paradigms, especially when backed up by existential pressures. For example, a majority of physicians or lawyers who had been trained in their home country found it impossible to exercise their professions in a foreign country, which meant either retraining or working in the service sector. Many were forced to work in non-academic fields or other positions, simply to survive, a dreary situation which improved only slightly after the end of the Second World War.

Exile was an opportunity of a lifetime for only a small minority. Those in the shadows are not seen. Others experienced, from the very beginning, a politically motivated exile and were firmly convinced that they would return after the defeat of the Nazis, to help re-build a democratic Austria. It is important to mention here the many foreign exile organizations which aided expatriated intellectuals, along with the more politically oriented partisan organizations (monarchist, Catholic, socialist, or communist). The latter were more concerned with plans for Austria's future and had other aims and functions than the more private associations like the London Society for the Protection of Science and Learning or the New York University in Exile. What has been more deeply researched in the fields of political, literary, and artistic exile still need to be matched in the field of scientific exile. An inter-disciplinary project is called for, with a diversity of theories and methods and the opportunity for international exchange and comparison. "Oral history" will soon come to an unwilling end; the recent loss of so many contemporaries of the period (such as Karl Menger, Gustav Bergmann, Eduard Maerz, Karl Stadler, Marie

Langer, and Hans Motz) drastically illustrates the self-induced dilemma of belated research on emigration and exile.

In light of public prejudices against anti-Fascist resistance and the absurd characterization of emigration and exile as "desertion" or "their own choice," one thing must be kept clear: beneath these omens, which are in the end apologia, there is also a distorted view of the genuine "inner emigration" which did take place and which was a legitimate form of protest against the regime. To place these dissidents, who acted out of humanistic or political and ideological motives, in the same category as the losers of inter-Nazi power struggles, or with fallen representatives of Austrofascism, is detrimental to any form of political education. Nevertheless, opposition resulting from a change of convictions or from the shock of Nazi tyranny, as well as all forms of resistance—even that which was belated or unsuccessful—should be valued as contributions towards the liberation of Austria.

To indicate the contemporary importance of this subject, it is important to remember that the credibility of attempts at coming to terms with the past is inseparably connected to the global role of the Second Republic as a land of asylum and immigration, to the question of material "reparations," and to Austria's policies toward minorities, marginalized groups, foreign workers, migrants, and of course, returning emigrants. The ideal condition in these areas is far from being realized. In light of this, perhaps a correlation between a consciousness of past emigration and current attitude towards the minorities, exiles, and refugees of today should be made. In 1933, Austria missed the opportunity to offer itself as a refuge for anti-Fascist exiles of Hitler's Germany (she took in only a rather small number of Catholic immigrants).

The common cliché saying that emigrants led "cushioned lives safely abroad" is, in the end, a cynical attempt to reverse the unshakable connection between cause and effect. For there is one characteristic which all of these exiles shared: as a result of not reconciling themselves to Fascism for political, "racial," or cultural reasons, they were forced to leave their home involuntarily. A clear differentiation of the various reasons for emigration is impossible, just as is the often discriminatory distinction between voluntary emigration and forced exile. The fact that exile could sometimes provide a political or scientific opportunity does not alter the common experience of those intellectuals who were annihilated or driven out by Fascism. National Socialist mass annihilation and mass expulsion are two aspects of the same phenomenon, namely that of an historically unique and unrivaled criminal regime.

From the perspective of intellectual emigration, a second issue enters the picture: the role played by "intellectual traitors" as perpetrators and flag-wavers acting on behalf of Fascist ideology because of opportunism or of having been blinded (Stadler, 1988a). On the other side, we find the victims of this pseudo-scientific, anti-humanistic clique: the hunted and hounded cultural class. The connected questions of a remaining cultural vacuum and of the exile of reason form parts of one repressed phenomenon which, because of its current relevance, is often artificially dissected. Future historical portrayal will have to encompass the themes of fascism, science, and exile.

Modern history will also have to explain the phenomenon of the repression syndrome, which has continued to oppose all unconventional or avant-garde forms of progress and experimentation within science, literature, and art, under Hans Sedlmayr's unfortunatel slogan, "the loss of the center." This is basically the structural reaction to what is still referred to as "degenerate," in the same sense in which the Nazis used this term in their propaganda exhibition of "degenerate art" in Munich which was a declaration of war on all modern art. Fifty-five years have passed since the giant book-burning in Salzburg where, on 30 April 1938, with the help of a large part of the population, the gruesome German example of 10 May 1933 was zealously imitated. Heinrich Heine had warned: "A country that burns books will sooner or later burn people." It is well-known how inexorably Heinrich Heine's prophesy was fulfilled. These lists of "harmful and undesirable writings" of 1938 and 1942 read like a "who's who" of European culture. If today, intellectual intolerance and reactionary censors attempting to make anti-Semitism acceptable once more, populate the boulevard, a bridge between the First and Second Republic has been formed and the seemingly well-buried past has suddenly returned to haunt us. If such censors exist, then Bertold Brecht's warning retains its relevance: "The womb from which it crawled is still fertile."

# Resistance, Persecution, Forced Labor

*Erika Weinzierl*

### Definition of Terms

When this author published an initial overview of the history of Austrian resistance almost thirty years ago, the relevant literature was still quite meager. Since then, a great deal of source material and a whole series of monographs on this subject have come out. With the growth of Austrian resistance research, scholars of modern history in Austria have also been forced to confront the question of terminology. In going about this, it also became necessary to establish differentiations, and numerous reservations were raised about the relatively recent definition of resistance "because it meant, as a rule, mute acceptance, resignation and apathy, and by no means precluded integration in the regime."

As early as 1966, Karl R. Stadler, a scholar of modern history from Linz, formulated a comprehensive definition that was adopted by the Documentation Center of Austrian Resistance (DÖW) and with which I fully concur: "In light of the total obedience demanded by those in power and the sanctions that threatened those who disobeyed, all forms of opposition in the Third Reich must be considered as acts of resistance, even if this was a matter of isolated attempts to maintain ones 'decency.'" Stadler also regarded all these acts of resistance in the context of an Austrian national liberation struggle.

Felix Kreissler added further weight to this argument with his hypothesis that the Austrian nation came into being in precisely this struggle (or rather at its end in 1945). During the first half of the 1980s, an Austrian historian of the next generation developed a tripartite model of resistance that resembles the work of Richard Löwenthal. It established the following classifications: 1.) political

Beginning of persecution of Jewish citizens in "*Ostmark*" after Anschluß: Forced to clean the sidewalks with their bare hands.

Source: Institute of Contemporary History, Innsbruck

resistance (resistance in the narrow sense), 2.) social protest, and 3.) deviant behavior. Eight additional subcategories range from *putsch* and assassination attempts to criticism of the regime, listening to foreign radio stations, slaughtering farm animals without permission, absenteeism, and desertion. Radomir Luza summed up this problematic issue with the assertion that resistance, "just like socialism and democracy, [cannot be] conceived of for historical purposes in abstract terms alone"; on the other hand, an empirical representation without a precise explanation of terms was said to be nothing more than a "jumbled mass of facts." He therefore differentiated between opposition and resistance. In his view, the latter is "any politically conscious, primarily conspirative, organized activity . . . that was perceived as hostile and declared illegal by National Socialist and Fascist governments." Luza thereby very closely approaches the previously cited definition by Karl Stadler. According to Luza, the prime movers behind Austrian resistance— the particular difficulties of which he describes in detail—were the elites.

With respect to Austria, there is an additional question: from which point in time can there properly be said to have been anti-Nazi resistance? There is absolutely no doubt that this applied to the period following the occupation by German troops—though they were indeed greeted by cheers and flowers—on 12 March 1938 and the passage of the law enacting the so-called "reunification" of Austria and the German Reich on 13 March 1938 all the way up to the end of the war in 1945. A beginning in 1938 was put forth as early as 1958 by Otto Molden in what was the first detailed and comprehensive account of the Austrian resistance, a work that has been reissued unrevised several times since then, although it devotes only seven pages to a treatment of Communist resistance. "Resistance and Persecution," DÖW's edition of source materials that has come to comprise thirteen volumes and cover five Austrian provinces, begins, however, with the year 1934, that is, with the Civil War of 12-15 February 1934 and the subsequent outlawing of the Social Democratic Party. Just like the Austrian Communist Party (KPÖ) that had been banned since May 1933, "illegal" opposition to the authoritarian/Fascistic Corporatist State was then the only option left open to the Social Democrats as well. In June 1933, the NSDAP was outlawed in the wake of a hand grenade attack on a Christian-German gymnastics association. But fully a decade before, in early April 1923 in Vienna, National Socialists and Social Democratic *Schutzbündler* had already faced off in the "Battle of Exelberg," in which a skirmish line of 300 Nazis led by a German National Socialist advanced with "shouts of 'hurrah!' from their ranks" against ninety members of the Social Democrats' paramilitary auxiliary. From April 1932 on, hardly a week went by in which the Nazis did not attack and injure political opponents. They began their bombings in June; the first victim was a Viennese Jewish jeweler named Futterweit.

According to a compilation by Gerhard Botz, the death toll due to acts of political violence from 12 November 1918 to 11 February 1934 alone—and not including the victims of the events of 15 July 1927—was 157 Marxists (including thirty-five Communists), ten Catholic conservatives (including seven members of the *Heimwehr*), fifteen policemen and *gendarmes*, seventeen civilians, and sixteen Nazis. Thus, to have been a political opponent of National Socialism or of Jewish descent was perilous long before 1938. Botz regards the acts of violence between 12 February 1934 and 11 March 1938 as having been committed "under circumstances of dictatorship," whereby he includes Nazis among both the perpetrators and the victims. DÖW has not classified the illegal National Socialist Party, "which fought as an underground movement from 1933 to 1939," as a resistance group because its avowed goal was the destruction of Austria and that country's incorporation into the totalitarian dictatorship of Hitler's Germany.

Indeed, without going so far as to equate the Corporatist State with National Socialism, the Dollfuss-Schuschnigg regime's fight against the Nazis was not found to be germane here "since—no matter what comes out of the ongoing discussion of the Fascist character of this system—this was played out on a completely different level— namely, that of the state power structure." Going into this standpoint in greater detail would presuppose an elaboration of theories of Fascism, which cannot be presented within the scope of this chapter. Despite wide-ranging critique of what led up to this situation and the policies pursued by the Corporatist State, it will also begin with 1934 for the simple reason that the machinery of state did indeed put up resistance, albeit not very efficiently and in spite of the resolutely Pan-German convictions of many of its most prominent supporters. This was emphasized by the official *Red-White-Red Book* of 1946: "Austria was the first free country, and for five years the only one, to put up tangible resistance to Hitler's policy of aggression." I cannot go along with many points in Gottfried-Karl Kindermann's hagiography of Dollfuss; nevertheless, I consider the following formulation to be tenable: the Austrian Corporatist State was the first state-level, organized resistance movement to oppose National Socialism. Of course, it is true that this movement—aside from it having put down the attempted Nazi *putsch* in July 1934, during which Dollfuss was murdered in the chancellor's office—was, for a number of reasons, only temporarily successful, just as it is true that numerous functionaries of the Corporatist State were arrested after the Anschluß. These facts cannot be passed over in silence.

## The Resistance in 1938

Otto Habsburg, one of the Austrians already living abroad in March 1938, called for armed resistance in a protest published in

Paris on 15 March. Among those who were already prepared for action on 11 March were Catholic, *bündische* youth movement groups like the *Graue Freikorps*, a student volunteer corps within the Austrian *Jungvolk* organization. This force, armed with machine guns and rifles, planned to engage the advancing German troops on the narrow roads of Leopoldsberg and Riederberg. The *Freikorps'* "Helmuth Wenger" troop—from which the *Österreichischer Kampfbund* would later emerge—mustered on the afternoon of 11 March. With weapons from the arsenal of the former *Heimatschutz*, they and several other young allies waited for the order to deploy. Historian Klemens von Klemperer was among them, and the disappointment that he and his comrades felt when, after hours of waiting, they heard about Schuschnigg's call not to resist and went home, is still palpable to this day. The masterminds of this group were *Freikorps* national commander Helmuth Jörg, who was arrested on 23 April and sent to the Dachau concentration camp, and Otto Molden, who founded the *Freikorps* Leadership Group in the early summer. They soon established contacts with the Innsbruck *Freikorps* that was also carrying on its work underground. Junior-high-school-age boys were recruited, and information was passed on—for example, to the Vatican—during trips abroad that were still possible at this point. When Otto Molden returned from one such trip, he was arrested. The Gestapo accused him of belonging to the Austrian secret organization *"Eisen"* (Iron), whose members had painted over street signs on Vienna's Höhenstraße with "Dollfußstraße," and had painted a huge white *Kruckenkreuz* (the cross symbolizing the Corporatist State) and the slogan "Hail Austria" on the pavement of Schwarzenberg Square in Vienna. Since Molden could prove that he had not even been in Austria during the previous weeks, he was released after ten days in prison. No one ever solved the mystery of who was behind this group. Otto Molden rightly pointed out "that it was only after the collapse of the Nazi regime, if at all, that we heard anything about many of the other elements of the resistance movement, even, in many instances, groups that had been quite active." That is particularly true of many Communist groups, some members of which were later killed while carrying out acts of sabotage or were shot immediately thereafter—for example, in the dynamiting of the Floridsdorf Locomotive Factory.

The nascent resistance movement in the period after 11 March 1938 deserves a detailed and comprehensive treatment here because the opinion is still widely held that Austrians did not put up any resistance against National Socialism until the Third Reich's defeat was already immanent. The previously mentioned thirteen volumes published by DÖW (including several thousand pages) alone contain a few hundred documents just about resistance in the year 1938. Since it is impossible to go into detail about even a significant part of this material, this chapter focuses on Vienna and Tyrol—on east and west Austria—and elaborates on initial and typical manifestations of resistance on the part of various political groups or individuals during the period from 11 March to the end of 1938.

First, however, mention must be made of the Austrians who were regarded by the Nazis as enemies or potential opponents, tens of thousands of whom were arrested immediately after 11 March. The *Red-White-Red Book* puts their number at 70,000; even if the actual figure was somewhat lower, Gestapo reports from the spring of 1938 that have since been published nevertheless contain numerous lengthy arrest lists for almost every Austrian province. They contain the names of leading politicians from the "system era," officials of the *Vaterländische Front*, the *Heimwehr* and the judiciary, such as Linz Police Chief Viktor Bentz, who was murdered immediately, or Dr. Karl Tuppy, states attorney in the Nazi *putsch* trial of July 1934 who was stomped to death in the Buchenwald concentration camp in 1939, journalists, priests, Revolutionary Socialists and Social Democrats, veterans of the Spanish Civil War, Communists, and Jews. Thus, these rolls are evidence that clearly corroborates one aspect of the definition of Fascism put forth long ago by Ernst Nolte: hostility toward all other groups.

On the other hand, this also raises a question that is sometimes hard to answer: whether resistance and persecution did not sometimes occur in reverse order. Here as well, our best recourse is to Stadler's definition, which simply states that everything the Nazi regime persecuted and punished as resistance is rightly to be assessed as such. Therefore, even membership in certain organizations such as the *Vaterländische Front* or being discovered listening to foreign radio stations can properly be considered resistance, and did indeed pre-exist persecution. This is not possible only in the case of the

Jews, who were already being mercilessly persecuted in the Third Reich in 1933 and in the *Ostmark* from 1938 on. Nevertheless, some persecuted Jews put up resistance too.

The fact that Austrian police files had fallen into the hands of the Gestapo facilitated the first wave of mass arrests in the spring of 1938. These documents contained the names of the Social Democrats' and Communists' underground organizers. Thus, even the very first English diplomatic note protested "the treatment of Catholics, Jews and Socialists." Moreover, this first group of Austrian arrestees—some of whom were held for only a short time— included those men who, after their release, reorganized the Austrian resistance after it had been almost totally decimated by the Gestapo in 1939 and 1940.

But the first acts of resistance were carried out in the spring and summer of 1938. As early as the night of 11-12 March the KPÖ— which, as previously mentioned, had been outlawed since May 1933—released a manifesto that read:

People of Austria! Defend yourselves; resist the foreign intruders and their agents. Join together, now more than ever, in a united front of all Austrians. All differences pale in significance in the face of the sacred task now confronting the Austrian people! Stand together against Hitler, stand together to drive Hitler's hordes out of Austria!People of Austria! Defend yourselves! Turn the slogans into deeds: Red-White-Red to the death!

Chancellor Schuschnigg had used this slogan in his speech before the Austrian National Assembly on 24 February 1938; now it was being taken up by the Communists.

The Communist youth organization *Ostmarkjugend* put out several issues of a clandestine paper for young people entitled *Jung Österreich* in 1938. In them, Austrian youth was called upon to "work to enlighten others about capitalism and the rapacious nature of the foreign domination by German Fascism . . . within the ranks of the Hitler Youth, in the League of German Girls and in other legal organizations, in sports clubs, the *Kraft durch Freude* recreational association," and other groups.

In late September 1938, the Vienna Gestapo informed the Chief of the Security Police about Communist and Marxist activities, which consisted of the formation of underground cells. Collections were taken up among members, and the attempt was being made to sell party insignia and distribute illegal material among grass-roots supporters. Industrial accidents and similar incidents in factories were said to have been intentional sabotage. Surveillance operations up to that point had observed eighty upper- and middle-level functionaries and approximately 150 other individuals going about illegal activities, and these were slated for arrest. The Trotskyite "Combat Troop for the Liberation of the Working Class" maintained in the April 1938 issue of its publication *Arbeitermacht* that the second imperialistic world war was now unavoidable: "If the sacrifices of this second imperialistic world war are not to be in vain, then the international working class must strive to transform this imperialistic war into a civil war." One means to achieve this end was said to be active sabotage.

The defendants in the first trial at the Vienna People's Court in April 1939 were Friederike Nödl and six other Revolutionary Socialists who, between March and July 1938 in Vienna and other Austrian localities, had collected money for the Socialist Workers' Aid organization that had been founded in 1934; for this, they were accused of high treason. For the years 1938-39, it would be possible to cite any number of similar acts of resistance in all the districts of the *Ostmark*; due to space limitations, I will discuss just a few examples of early resistance in western Austria (that Tyrol). Then, I will attempt to show, through the use of illustrative examples presented in chronological order, that *all* types of resistance categorized by Botz were being carried out in the *Ostmark*.

Of particular note in Tyrol are the five high treason trials involving Socialists and Communists that had already taken place between September and November 1938. Here, protests against obstructions of or restrictions on Corpus Christi processions were much more frequent than in Vienna. Such restrictions provoked dissent, particularly among peasant farmers, in other provinces as well. Adrian Hoch, the Premonstratensian pastor of Hötting in Tyrol, was arrested by the Gestapo on 5 July 1938 on orders from *Reichskommissar* Bürckel. On the day before Corpus Christi, the priest had a notice of a mass for former Chancellor Schuschnigg, a Tyrolese native, posted on the doors of his church; he also announced it from his pulpit, and went on to celebrate this mass as well.

Beyond the confines of concentration camps and prisons, developments continued after 11 March 1938. Following the wave of arrests by the Gestapo, the Revolutionary Socialists, who had merged with the illegal free unions in May 1938, and the Communists remained operational underground. Although they had certainly become accustomed to illegal status, this had now become far more dangerous, despite the fact that the Nazis had taken some well-publicized steps to win over former Social Democrats in the spring of 1938. A few Catholic and legitimist groups also took a concerted stand and continued operating illegally.

## Catholic Resistance

The first large-scale demonstration against National Socialism that could not be kept out of the public eye and therefore provoked brutal retaliation from the Nazi authorities was the work of the Catholic Youth of Vienna. Following a short prayer service in St. Stephan's Cathedral on 7 October 1938, there was a gathering on the square in front of the church that featured cheers and ovations for Vienna's Archbishop Cardinal Innitzer that consciously played on Nazi slogans of praise to Hitler: "We are thankful to our bishop! We want to see our bishop!" Hermann Mitteräcker, in his account of Austrian resistance that places the greatest emphasis on the activities of the Communists, expressly acknowledged that this rally was the first and only such public display. This demonstration and the act of revenge that answered it the very next day—the Nazi-organized storming of the Archbishop's Palace—were milestones on the Austrian Church's way from pursuing a policy of appeasement toward the National Socialist regime between March and October 1938 to resistance and persecution.

As far as the victims of the resistance put up by the official Church—that is to say, the clergy—there are, in contrast to almost all other resistance groups, precise figures available. From 1938 to 1945, 724 Austrian priests served time in prison, and seven of them died; 110 were sent to concentration camps where ninety of them perished. Fifteen were sentenced to death and executed. Almost 300 priests were expelled from their district or province, and over 1,500 were banned from preaching or giving instruction. Most of the arrested priests were affiliated with the Innsbruck-Feldkirch Apostolic Administration and with the Dioceses of Linz, Seckau, and Salzburg. Sister Restituta (Helene Kafka) was the only nun to be executed in German-controlled Central and Western Europe; she copied and distributed an anti-Nazi "Soldiers' Song," for which she paid with her life in a Vienna military hospital. Based on their total numbers, the Austrian clergy, railway workers, and Jehovah's Witnesses (who refused any form of war-related service) had the highest proportion of victims among all Austrian resistance groups.

In the fall of 1938, Klosterneuburg Canon Karl Roman Scholz and his friend Dr. Viktor Reimann founded the illegal German Freedom Movement, which, following the outbreak of the war, renamed itself the Austrian Freedom Movement at around the turn of the year 1939-40. Secret SS situation reports from this period indicate that, even then, resistance against National Socialism in Austria was relatively stronger than in the rest of the Reich.

Just a few months after the German victory over Poland, walls of factories in the metal industry were painted with slogans like "Down with Hitlerism!" or "Proletarians of the World, Unite!" which the SS attributed to Communists.

Likewise in 1938 in Wiener Neustadt, which was a center of resistance by the Austrian industrial labor force during the entire Nazi period, Communist youth functionaries under the leadership of Karl Flanners reached the decision to organize a Communist Youth League—which had already been founded prior to 1938—in and around Wiener Neustadt, and to publish their own youth newspaper. This paper entitled *The Young Communist* came out until the arrest of Flanners and his co-workers in August 1939.

The aim of Scholz's Austrian Freedom Movement, according to the Nazi's bill of indictment, was to overthrow the National Socialist state, bring about the secession of the Danubian and Alpine districts, and establish a new Austrian state that would include Bavaria and extend all the way to the Main River. The organization comprised several subgroups including a branch at the Cistercian Monastery in Wilhering, Upper Austria. Membership reached 400, each of whom took an oath of allegiance. Despite this oath, in June 1940, Otto Hartmann, a not-very-successful and highly frustrated actor at

Vienna's Burgtheater and a Gestapo spy, betrayed Scholz's Austrian Freedom Movement, the Austrian Freedom Movement led by Dr. Karl Lederer that worked closely with it, and the Greater Austrian Freedom Movement headed by Dr. Jakob Kastelic, a leading member of Catholic Action and a friend of Chancellor Schuschnigg. On the basis of Hartmann's detailed denunciation, all of the three movements' members whose names had been known to Hartmann were also arrested over the following days and weeks; "the People's Court responded with 11 death sentences, nine of which were carried out; there were nine additional deaths as a result of bitter cold and hunger while in custody, 1,974 years imprisonment in the penitentiary and 117 years in jail, with 362 years actually served."

Karl Roman Scholz was not brought to trial at the People's Court in Vienna until 22-23 February 1944; until then, he was held in eleven different prisons. He was convicted of high treason and sentenced to death by the guillotine. The execution of Scholz and eight other resistance members took place on 10 May 1944 in Vienna's First District Court. In a farewell letter addressed to his fellow brothers at the Klosterneuburg Monastery that he had written even prior to his conviction, he expressed the hope that his deeds and his death "will, please God, help bring about the glorious resurrection of our House." This letter was thoroughly justified. Today, although the Klosterneuburg brothers do not believe that the dissolution of the monastery in 1941 was a result of Scholz's activities, they nevertheless cannot identify with the way he went about them. This position is most likely in accordance with views expressed by Austrian priests age sixty and above in the context of a 1979 survey on the subject of "The Church and National Socialism" (2,700 received written queries, 327 responded). Scholz and others were characterized as "isolated cases" who had still not received adequate recognition; sixty-nine disagreed; eighty-eight explained that they had not heard of these men until after 1945, had never been informed, or still did not know the whole story. Some of the responses included far-reaching criticism: "It may well be asked if it made sense to use a human language to speak to wild beasts."

## Socialists, Communists, and Legitimists

Even before the Gestapo broke up the circle surrounding Scholz, it dealt a blow to other resistance groups. As early as May 1938,

Albini, the leader of an opposition group of Catholic students, was executed in Vienna. In the fall of 1938 and the summer of 1939, there were waves of arrests of Communists who had been putting out two mimeographed publications, *The Red Flag* and *Path and Destination*, as well as numerous flyers. These appeared regularly until 1940. It was above all during the summer of 1939 that the Gestapo carried out mass arrests of Communists in order to wipe out resistance in the Austrian hinterland prior to Germany launching World War II. Hundreds of members of Communist resistance groups fell victim to this second great wave of arrests. Styrian organizations, above all those in Graz, Knittelfeld, and Kapfenberg, received the brunt of the impact. Eighty Carinthian and about fifty Viennese Communist activists and leading functionaries were arrested. This wave had already peaked by early winter, but did not completely subside until the summer of 1940.

After the outbreak of the war, the panel of judges of the People's Court handed down a whole series of death sentences. Among the first to be executed from the Styrian group were a book printer named Neuhold and the actor Kurt Drews, who, together with their collaborators, produced the KPÖ manifesto *Austria Will Rise Again* and distributed it in Styria. Neuhold died as a result of being tortured in detention while awaiting trial; Drews was sentenced to death in Graz District Court and executed. These waves of arrests as well as the shock of the Hitler-Stalin Pact of 23 August 1939—one consequence of which in the U.S.S.R. was the closure of the Moscow home for children of *Schutzbund* members—meant a set-back for the Communist resistance movement from which it was not able to recover until after the German attack on the Soviet Union in 1941.

In the fall and winter of 1939, those arrested included the legitimist-Socialist Müller-Thanner group as well as the Meithner group that had contacts to the Communists. The first session of the People's Court in Vienna in the summer of 1939 was devoted to the Revolutionary Socialists. All of these groups had been betrayed by spies; one of them, Hans Pav, had even infiltrated the ranks of the RS leadership. Among the victims of these betrayals was Käthe Leichter, a Revolutionary Socialist and former head of the women's department of the Chamber of Labor in Vienna who was transported from the Ravensbrück concentration camp to Magdeburg and gassed in February 1942. She was the author of one of the most deeply moving Austrian concentration camp poems that describes her dreams of home and family while she and those suffering alongside her in German concentration camps hoped for liberation.

## Concentration Camps and Forced Labor

The very names of the concentration camps mentioned in this poem (Ravensbrück, Sachsenhausen, Dachau, and Buchenwald) make it plain that members of the Austrian resistance were very intentionally assigned to camps far from Austria. On Austrian territory, there was only the Mauthausen concentration camp built in 1938 and its more than forty subsidiary camps. Over 335,000 people from all European nations were imprisoned in them up to 1945, including Germans, Austrians, Luxemburgers, and several hundred Gypsies. Almost half of all Mauthausen inmates were murdered—thousands of Austrians among them—or they succumbed to the inhuman living and working conditions, above all in the camp's notorious quarry. This was so despite the fact that Mauthausen was not one of the extermination camps. Indeed, on 2 January 1941, the head of the Security Police and the Security Service declared it to be a camp for worst-case (Level III) prisoners. "Transfer to these camps was thus tantamount to a death sentence." However, with the expansion that camps including Mauthausen underwent in 1942-43 in order to speed up arms production as part of the "total war" effort, the authorities no longer adhered to the ranking of camps in categories I-III. From the central installation in Mauthausen, the above-mentioned network of subsidiary camps was spread over Linz, Steyr, and Wels, as well as throughout the industrialized region from Vienna to Wiener Neustadt. All inmates who were "fit for work" had to expend their last ounce of strength in the service of armaments manufacturers.

Research into the history of forced labor in the Third Reich began relatively late both in Austria and other countries due to the especially difficult situation with respect to source material, though this is particularly true of Austria. Aside from the accounts of surviving contemporary eyewitnesses, scholarly studies have been carried out and published only since the 1980s. Florian Freund and Bertrand Perz deserve prominent mention in this connection. They collaborated on the publication *Das KZ in der "Serbenhalle"* that investigated metal workers laboring to construct rockets, locomotives, and ships. Florian Freund investigated the history of the Zement labor camp in Ebensee that was involved in rocket production. Bertrand Perz focused on Project Quartz, an effort to manufacture military vehicles, rifles and aircraft motors in Melk. One of the numerous publications by Hans Marsálek, a Mauthausen survivor who had been the official camp historian, deals with the history of the subsidiary camp at Gusen whose inmates were forced to work in quarries and weapons plants.

In these forced labor camps, Austrians functioned primarily as overseers, though not to the same extent as was the case in extermination camps. Indeed, there were also Austrian inmates like the political prisoner Albert Kainz, who was held in Gusen from 1941 to 1945. The major arms manufacturers made extensive use of cheap forced labor for which they paid thirty Pfennigs per prisoner per day until the end of 1942; from May 1943, the rate was fifty Pfennigs and up to five Reichsmarks for skilled laborers. After 1945, only a few of these firms had to answer for this in court, and the punishments they received were mild. *IG-Farben, Henschelwerke, Steyr-Daimler-Puch* and others were thus able to maintain their leading position in their respective sectors. Here as well, there would be no new beginning that totally expunged all continuities with the past.

There were also many POWs—particularly Frenchmen and Poles—who had to perform forced labor in the agricultural sector. Their situation was considerably better than that of inmates who were transported from a concentration camp to work in factories. Nevertheless, "private" contacts with forced laborers on farms was forbidden and severely punished. For example, the administrator of a Nazi women's group in Baden, Lower Austria, was caught entertaining a French prisoner in her apartment, for which she was sentenced to serve two and then four months in prison. For such "transgressions," and above all for those of a sexual nature, the foreign laborer was usually sent to a concentration camp.

In spite of the increased intensity of the persecution measures following the outbreak of war and also despite the almost total obliteration of the first Austrian resistance groups by the previously mentioned waves of arrests in 1939 and 1940, the re-establishment of a resistance movement was begun in 1941, for the most part by men and women who already had done time in concentration camps. As a result of their experiences, they were harder, more resolute, and more conspiratorial than their predecessors in 1938. In their certainty of being in constant danger of betrayal, they adopted the methods of the Communists and began to work together only in tiny cells of three or four members, most of whom had no knowledge of the overall organizational structure and therefore could not provide additional names if they were arrested. Nevertheless, it was necessary to maintain or re-establish connections extending throughout Austria and beyond. Dr. Becker, previously the chief of propaganda for the *Vaterländische Front*, returned to Vienna in May 1941 after his release from Dachau; he proceeded to re-establish the operations bureau that had been an outgrowth of his former political information office and began to assemble a staff:

> Liaison offices were soon set up in Linz, Wels, Innsbruck, Graz and Klagenfurt. A good connection was later established with Salzburg. In Vorarlberg, independent work was going so well that all that was necessary was a communications link via Innsbruck. The task of these liaison offices was to coordinate the assignments of the various individual groups as much as possible though by no means to centralize everything. In most cases, the local cells had to proceed independently in their own operational sphere.

Moreover, the leaders of the bourgeois resistance groups in Austria who were netted in the first wave of arrests and held in Dachau had already reached agreement during their internment on a three-point program that they now began to implement in step-by-step fashion: "1.) to subvert German military and civilian facilities, and undermine the Germans' will to achieve victory and ability to resist; 2.) to establish connections abroad; 3.) to enhance our own strength, though without pointlessly sacrificing our people to the Third Reich's tightly woven network of surveillance."

## 20 July 1944

As for the men of 20 July, it can be said with certainty that they

were striving to achieve a revolutionary—or rather, restorative—
change of political leadership and of the National Socialist system,
though not of society as a whole, and that long and meticulous
planning also went into their undertaking. It is hard to say what
would have happened if Claus Stauffenberg's bomb had killed Hitler
as planned. In any case, a successful assassination and immediately
suing for peace would have spared Germany the sacrifice of more
human lives and more destruction of its cities than it had already
suffered from the beginning of the war until 1944. Ludwig Jedlicka
has investigated these events and provided a detailed account of what
transpired in Austria.

In summarizing Jedlicka's work, it can be said first off that
relatively few Austrian officers had been let in on the plan of the
men of 20 July. Thus, in Military Headquarters XVIII, Salzburg on
20 July, there was absolutely no sign of anything amiss in relations
between the regional armed forces command and the district
government. On the other hand, the fact that the "Valkyrie" plan
could be partially carried out to a greater extent than in Berlin was
due to the convergence of a series of favorable factors—first and
foremost to Captain Carl Szokoll decisively carrying out orders
issued by Kodré and Esebeck, two officers who had not even been
party to the conspiracy. Szokoll, actually the chief protagonist in the
events in Vienna on 20 July 1944, was never discovered as a result of
Bernardis' and Marogna-Redwitz's refusal to talk prior to their
execution on 8 August and 12 October 1944 in Berlin, and also
because his name did not happen to appear on any of the lists
maintained by the men of 20 July. Therefore, even after the
undertaking's failure, Szokoll was still in a position to continue
working to achieve their aim, which he did in preparing for an
Austrian uprising. In doing so, he adopted a few elements of
Stauffenberg's plan.

It was of particular significance for Austria that the German Social
Democratic union leader Leuschner, in going about his wide-ranging
political and personnel preparations in connection with the events of
20 July 1944, had already gotten in touch with Austrian Social
Democrat Dr. Adolf Schärf in the spring of 1943. He held out the
prospect to Schärf of a revolution to overthrow Hitler in the fall of
1943, and expressed hope that the Anschluß of Austria would be

preserved afterwards. According to his own account, Schärf, who had never held the contrary opinion up to that point, nevertheless suddenly came to a realization "as if struck by a flash of inspiration" during this very conversation: "The Anschluß is dead. The Austrians have had their love for the German people driven out of them!" By then, this conviction was already so strongly held by all of the Austrians with whom the men of 20 July held talks that they were no longer able to obtain assurances about maintaining the Anschluß even though they were said to have weighed the possibility of appointing former Austrian Chancellor Schuschnigg to the post of minister for education and cultural affairs in the planned Goerdeler-Beck cabinet. In any case, Schuschnigg himself, who was interned from 1938 to 1945, knew nothing of these plans.

For the codeword to trigger the Austrian uprising in 1945, planners decided to go with "Radetzky," which had already been chosen prior to 20 July 1944. Since November 1944, Szokoll had also been in contact with civilian resistance groups, including one formed by the above-mentioned Dr. Hans Becker. This group, named O5 (code name for Austria), had been striving to organize nationwide resistance efforts since the beginning of the year. In the coordination work necessary to accomplish this, one individual who made a name for himself as a mediator was the young Fritz Molden. It did not take all that long for his efforts to bear fruit: the Provisional Austrian National Committee was constituted on 18 December 1944 in Vienna. It initially consisted of Catholic conservatives, but from the very outset also had contacts to Socialists, above all to Adolf Schärf and to then-Communist Viktor Matejka. Furthermore, the group also succeeded in establishing contact with high-level Allied military and political leaders.

## Politics in Exile

Of these, the Americans—or rather, their President Roosevelt—had a particularly good relationship with Dr. Otto Habsburg, who convinced them in the fall of 1942 to create a separate Austrian unit within the U.S. Army, the so-called Independent Infantry Battalion Nr. 101. Since the opposition to this unit within American government circles, on the part of representatives of the successor states of the former Habsburg Empire, and, above all, among the various mutually hostile groups of Austrian émigrés was considerable, and on 2 April 1943 the battalion consisted of only 199 men who were by no means all Austrians, the unit was disbanded on 3 May 1943. Thus, the symbolic effect for which its initiators had been striving—a manifestation of the rebirth of an independent Austria—could not be achieved. Quite the contrary: it made the disunity of Austrian émigrés strikingly obvious. Nevertheless, one cannot deny that getting the go-ahead to set up this battalion represented "the only successful attempt by a political organization of Austrian émigrés to achieve any sort of recognition of Austria's independence."

Apart from this effort as well as the quite considerable propaganda effect of the newspapers that were being published by Austrian émigrés in several European countries and America, "Austrian resistance" against the Nazi dictatorship—at least in this area—consisted, first and foremost, of the acts of resistance attempted and carried out within the territories controlled by the Third Reich. After all, a collateral effect of these activities was to bring about agreement and unity among Austrian politicians, which was a precondition for the rebirth and reconstruction of Austria. It thus became possible for the outlawed *Arbeiterzeitung* in its first 1945 issue published in Switzerland to voice an appeal for the support of O5 as a nonpartisan Austrian resistance movement. The so-called Committee of Seven, whose members represented the entire political spectrum, had already formed in November 1944 within the framework of O5. This committee's first chairman was Dr. Becker. Following his arrest in March 1945, Dr. Raoul Bumballa took over as head of the committee that would later assume political control of resistance activities during the Battle of Vienna in April 1945.

But things had not yet reached that point. Even in the war's final phase when National Socialism's defeat was only a matter of time, the Nazi authorities gave no quarter. In Vienna, a military revolt planned for 6 April by a branch of O5 and officers from Military Headquarters XVII—Captain Huth and Lieutenant Raschke, close associates of Szokoll—fell victim to betrayal by a Nazi commanding officer. Biedermann, the commandant of the company that was to occupy the train stations and main roads leading into the city, as well as Huth and Raschke, were arrested during the night of 5-6 April and on 8 April—five days before Soviet troops captured the entire city—were barbarously tortured and then hung from sign posts at a street car stop in the Floridsdorf district.

On 5 April in the courtyard of Stein Penitentiary, whose Austrian warden, Franz Kodré, in light of the collapsing front lines, had begun to release his 1,900 mostly political prisoners, a detachment of SS men, *Volkssturm* militia members and *Wehrmacht* soldiers under the command of SA-*Standartenleiter* Leo Pilz shot 391 persons, including 386 prisoners and five guards. Kodré and three other prison administrators were court-martialed, sentenced to death, and executed that very evening.

On 2 April, the City of Vienna was declared an area to be defended at all costs in spite of efforts by Austrian officers to prevent this. Five days later, as the Russians were already occupying the Favoriten district, General von Bünau, commander of the city's defense, reported to the Führer's headquarters: "The civilian population is raising red-white-red flags and concentrating more intense fire on German troops than on the enemy." That same day, *Waffen-SS* Lieutenant General Kramer reported to the headquarters of Army Group South: "There is already shooting in Vienna, but it is not the Russians who are doing so—it is the Austrians." Hitler's answer to Bünau—presumably his final order having to do with Vienna—read: "Proceed against the insurgents with the most brutal means possible!" The SS and a handful of fanatical Nazis did indeed comply with this order for as long as they could.

Despite all of the setbacks, Viennese Sergeant Ferdinand Käs, the official envoy of the military resistance under the leadership of Szokoll, nevertheless finally succeeded during the night of 2-3 April in making it through the front lines and reaching the headquarters of Russian Marshall Tolbuchin in Hochwolkersdorf south of Wiener Neustadt. As soon as Tolbuchin had crossed the former Austrian border near Güns on 28 March, he issued an appeal to the Austrian population in which he emphatically referred to the Moscow Declaration of 1 November 1943, the text of which had not been worded so as to call for the formation of an Austrian resistance, but, presumably, to strengthen the movement that was already in place. In it, Austria was clearly acknowledged as Hitler's first victim; nevertheless, it also admonished the Austrians that they bore inescapable responsibility for having taken part in the war on Nazi Germany's side. Consequently, Austria's contribution to its own liberation would unavoidably be taken into consideration in finally settling the score. Tolbuchin's appeal to the Austrian people's spirit of resistance must, therefore, have made for a more cordial reception being accorded to Käs at Soviet headquarters. On 3 and 4 April, Käs negotiated on behalf of the resistance movement with the Soviets, proposing that the Red Army bypass Vienna—that is, an attack from the west—and suggesting that the city would be surrendered without a fight by the resistance movement. Käs was thus able to come to some important agreements, which he turned over to Szokoll on the morning of 5 April in Vienna. Then during the following night, as previously mentioned, Biedermann, Huth, and Raschke, as well as Szokoll's entire staff, were arrested.

Even though Szokoll's activities had now been betrayed as well, both he and Käs were able to avoid arrest, but carrying out the planned occupation of Vienna by the resistance movement and handing over the city without a fight to the Russians as agreed upon was now out of the question.

The Soviets nevertheless lived up to their side of the bargain they had struck with Käs. Although they had already reached the Schwechat-Mannswörth region on 4 April, they now broke off their attack from the southeast and instead proceeded with the effort to cordon off Vienna from the west. On the morning of 7 April, the actual Battle of Vienna broke out. By the evening of that day, the Red Army had already reached the *Gürtel* beltway. The first link-up of a resistance unit with Russian front-line troops came on 9 April; later that day, the red-white-red flag was flying from St. Stephan's steeple and the Palais Auersperg. The Battle of Vienna was concluded by the evening of 13 April.

In western Austria—the "Alpine fortress" that the National Socialists planned to make their last refuge—liberation took somewhat longer. There, even in the last days of April, the Gestapo carried out a wave of arrests including the round-up of several key members of the Tyrolean resistance movement.

Nevertheless, Tyrolean resistance groups under Dr. Karl Gruber, who had assumed leadership in March, began the step-by-step occupation of Innsbruck on 2 May 1945, and they succeeded in completely restoring public order in their sector even prior to the arrival of the U.S. Army. When the first U.S. troops marched into Innsbruck on the evening of 3 May 1945, they entered a city that had already been totally liberated from National Socialism and was festively adorned with red-white-red flags. During the period 3-5 May, fighting was still going on in Wörgl and Schloß Itter between SS units and resistance groups, and in this final hour, Austrian Major Sepp Gangl lost his life.

On 8 May 1945, the Third Reich ended with unconditional surrender, leaving behind millions of dead, and a Europe that had been largely destroyed and was now occupied by the Red Army.

## Summary and Conclusions

In addition to the 247,000 Austrian soldiers in the German *Wehrmacht* who fell in battle or were listed as MIAs, and the 65,459 deported Austrian Jews who were gassed or killed, Austrian resistance against National Socialism claimed a high toll: 2,700 Austrians were convicted as active resistance fighters, sentenced to death and executed; 16,493 were murdered in concentration camps, thousands of whom died in Mauthausen and its notorious quarry; 9,687 were murdered in Gestapo prisons; and 6,420 perished in penitentiaries and jails in countries occupied by the German *Wehrmacht*. These figures, which are supported by official documentation, do not include the victims of military justice, which have yet to be compiled.

Based on the findings of research done to date, 35,300 Austrians gave their lives in the fight against National Socialism. In light of the total obedience demanded by the National Socialist authorities and the sanctions that threatened those who disobeyed, all of them died for Austria.

Historical scholarship has not yet reached the point of being able to give precise information about the social background and the various motivations of the individual victims. To date, there has been a separate compilation of the resistance activities of only two occupational groups: the above-mentioned priests and the especially politically active railway workers, of whom 1,635 were persecuted by the Nazi judicial system and 154 were sentenced to death and executed. It has also been brought out that of the 213 national assembly representatives of the Christian Corporatist State, 121 were debarred from practicing their occupation and thirty-three were sent to concentration camps, of whom eight died. Of the two women among these representatives, Margarethe Rada was likewise forced into retirement for political reasons. Of all those who headed a ministry department in March 1938, 75 percent were dismissed.

The question of which "crimes" were committed by the tens of thousands of Austrians who were crushed by the wheels of Nazi justice or who were held without even standing trial can be answered only by citing examples, although Radomir Luza undertook an initial attempt a few years ago to do a quantitative analysis, the results of which will be discussed below.

In any case, the spectrum of resistance was broad. It included founding active resistance organizations, carrying on partisan warfare, setting up information services (such as the Socialist Otto Haas), acts of sabotage in the workplace like those carried out by many Communists, the refusal to be inducted into the army or to swear an oath of loyalty out of opposition to the National Socialist system as did Pallotine priest Franz Reinisch from Tyrol and Upper Austrian farmer Franz Jägerstätter, providing aid to those who were persecuted for political or racial reasons, listening to foreign radio stations and disseminating news gleaned from them, or even "unauthorized wage demands" by laborers.

In his work, Luza—as Botz had done—established eight categories of resistance that approximately correspond to these examples. He investigated a random sample of 3,058 cases on the basis of Nazi court transcripts, Gestapo files, and the related secondary literature. His selection criterion was that the subject had committed a significant act of resistance. Although it would certainly be possible to take exception to his political categories—with respect to the "traditionalists" (non-Socialists, meaning major segments of the Austrian People's Party founded in 1945 and encompassing former Christian Socials, Catholics, and liberals) and "legitimists," the activities tend to weigh in favor of the latter; the category "all Austrians" (unaffiliated Austrian patriots) is difficult to get a handle on, just as the boundary between Communists and Revolutionary Socialists is unclear, as the author himself freely admits. A few generalizations can nevertheless be made with a high degree of assurance, of which the following are the most important. The KPÖ played a dominant role in the Austrian resistance (44.5 percent). The non-Communists were led by "all Austrians" (17.7 percent) and "traditionalists" (16.1 percent). Although Tilly Spiegel held the opinion that men and women "balanced one another out" in the active resistance, Luza's findings indicate that this was a male movement (11.6 percent women). The resistance movement consisted mostly of younger men (64 percent under age forty). A relatively larger proportion was non-Catholic or had no religious affiliation than in the population as a whole; on the other hand, the proportion of married/unmarried did correspond to that of the general public. Skilled workers and middle-class intellectuals gave the movement a predominantly urban character. Members of the resistance had a relatively high level of education, with a considerable proportion having attended college. The center of the Austrian resistance was Vienna and the surrounding areas of Lower Austria, followed by Styria and Tyrol. (For those who are knowledgeable about modern Austrian history, the rank of Styria is astounding.) In any case, the methodological approach begun by Luza ought to be carried on, whereby his women-centered "Profile of an Elite" would surely stand to benefit.

As far as the percentage of women in the Austrian resistance is concerned, Luza's figures have already been mentioned. Otto Molden's earliest list of names contained twenty-two women, even though there were thirty-three women from the Scholz group alone who did time in prison. Fifty female prisoners were executed in the Vienna District Court, including forty female blue- and white-collar workers and housewives. Thus, Tilly Spiegel's opinion that men and women "balanced one another out" in the Austrian resistance movement may well be much closer to the truth than the figures Molden cites. It will probably never be possible to come up with exact numbers, although much attention has been focused on women in the resistance since the 1970s, especially in research done by female masters and doctoral candidates. Since the Communists had the strongest organization and suffered the highest losses, resistance by Communist women has always been the object of the lion's share of this interest. The dissertation by Inge Brauneis deserves particular mention here. Remarkable results have also been produced in this area by the use of oral history techniques. Increasingly, contemporary eyewitnesses—that is, women who were active in the resistance—have decided to publish their memoirs. On the other hand, there is still relatively little secondary literature about Austrian women held in concentration camps. Thus, a great deal of research work still needs to be done on Austrian resistance as a whole and resistance activities by women in particular. This is vital not only for contemporary historical scholarship, but also to strengthen Austrian identity.

As previously mentioned, there has been in recent years an increase in interest in the "perpetrators"—that is, in the long-repressed active participation by Austrians in the Nazi regime and its crimes. This, of course, is an integral part of the rehabilitation of our political culture. Nevertheless, it would be a mistake to lose sight of Austrian resistance efforts while this process is going on, although it is equally impossible to surround Austria with a collective aura of resistance. After all, as a result of Austria's difficult situation during the interwar period, too many people believed all too long that the Anschluß would be a way to achieve, if not a better future, than at least a politically and, above all, economically more stable one. A small fanatical minority held firm to this belief until the end of the war and therefore viewed any kind of resistance as treason. A far greater number allowed themselves to be intimidated by the terror of the Nazi regime and resigned themselves to political abstinence or apathetic indifference. Seen in this light, even greater tribute is due to those 35,300 Austrian men and women—one half percent of the total population—who did resist and paid for it with their lives, and those additional tens of thousands who spent months and years in prisons and concentration camps. They made that contribution that the Allies demanded in the Moscow Declaration of 1943 from the Austrians themselves for the re-establishment of a free and independent Austria.

# III. THE SECOND REPUBLIC

Reconstruction – A "New Deal" for Austria: The Kaprun hydroelectric power plant built largely with Marshall Plan funds for the electrification and industrialization of the country.

Source: Austrian Institute for Contemporary History, Vienna

# Allied Plans and Policies for the Occupation of Austria, 1938-1955

*Günter Bischof*

"There is no political entity in European history more dominated by forces from the outside than Austria" (Friedrich Heer)

## A Case of Rape or Seduction? The 1938 Anschluß and Its Aftermath

Allied wartime planning for postwar Austria had to confront a key problem early on: how to interpret the "Anschluß" of March 1938 (the Nazi invasion and annexation of Austria). Undoubtedly, Hitler's *military invasion* of Austria on 12 March was an act of force; international law was broken as it was in the invasion of Czechoslovakia and Poland in 1939. As such, it was an important event in Europe's descent into World War II since democratic nations failed to confront Hitlerite aggression (a policy that would quickly be denounced as "appeasement"). During the war, Allied leaders felt that letting Austria down in 1938 was a fateful mistake which sent the wrong signal to Hitler; this needed to be corrected.

Careful historical study of the Anschluß has demonstrated that it was a highly complex and confusing historical event. It needs to be understood at least on three levels. First, there was the seizure of power of local government by *Austrian* Nazis in the provincial capitals *prior* to the German invasion. Second, Austrian Nazi leaders, who had been appointed to the last cabinet of Chancellor Kurt Schuschnigg upon direct pressure from Hitler in the infamous meeting at Berchtesgaden, seized power in Vienna on the evening of

Provisional Chancellor Karl Renner, "founding father" of the two Austrian Republics, in an early meeting with the deputy high commissioners of the four occupation powers in Vienna (1945).

Source: National Archives, College Park, MD (#111-SC-220741)

11 March, hours before the German *Wehrmacht* crossed the border. Third, the imperialist invasion of the German Army on 12 March completed the *fait accompli* of the previous night. But the cheerful giddiness of untold numbers of Austrians welcoming the German Army columns and, later, Adolf Hitler himself left a bad impression. It suggested to the world that many Austrians supported the Anschluß of Austria to the Third Reich, which Hitler announced to the world in Vienna on 13 March. Some scholars think that, given how ill-prepared the German Army was for an Austrian invasion and the chaotic advance of their divisions into Austria, determined resistance by the much smaller Austrian Army could have thrown the German invaders into even bigger disarray (Lassner). The German advance could have been retarded for a few days, if not stopped.

Such *resistance*, of course, did not happen. Yet it would have made Austria's case for victimization during the war and independence after the war more credible.

At the time, international observers spoke of the "rape" of Austria. Yet British voices of caution in particular proffered a more complex view: "It should be remembered that Austria yielded with so little opposition and afterwards accepted her violator with such enthusiasm that it was legitimate to wonder whether it was a case of rape or seduction." Another high Foreign Office official remarked: "We may argue about the percentages in Austria that wanted or did not want the 'Anschluß' with a Germany Nazi or pre-Nazi, but we are always left with a more or less considerable residue that did want it" (both citations in Bischof/1999). The fact of the matter is that the British quickly recognized the Anschluß *de facto* and *de jure*. The Americans recognized it *de facto* by not resisting Hitler's incorporation of Austria into the Third Reich, but never explicitly *de jure* (Keyserlingk). This allowed the State Department to later proclaim pragmatically that the United States never recognized the Anschluß. The French approached the Anschluß with similar ambiguity. Even though the French had the strongest armed forces on the European continent, they failed to confront Hitler militarily over the invasion of Austria as they did in the case of Hitler's pressure on Czechoslovakia in 1938 and invasion of Poland. Such failure of nerves in 1938, with its fateful consequences for the abysmal "fall of France" in June 1940 (French historians call 1940 "*l'abime*"), left the French with a deep-seated "Anschluß trauma" for years to come (Angerer).

Austrians during the war were both *victims* of Hitlerite aggression and *contributors* and *accessories* to Hitlerite war crimes; they languished and died in the Gestapo's jails and the T-4 euthanasia killing machine and were murdered in the SS's concentration camps; Austrians were "sacrificed" in large numbers in the *Wehrmacht*'s war of aggression and perished under the hail of Allied bombs. A younger generation of scholars has vigorously pointed out in the past twenty years that Austrians were also often eager *perpetrators* of war crimes. Vienna after the Anschluß became a "model" for dehumanizing its Jewish population for the *Altreich*. The Viennese expropriated ("ayranized") Jewish property on a massive scale and invented enormous skullduggery to force Jewish emigration—and thus *radicalized* German anti-Jewish policies. Austrians played a prominent role in the implementation of the "final solution." Mauthausen concentration camp outside Linz, along with its dozens of subcamps, became one of the most murderous camp systems inside the Third Reich. In Castle Hartheim outside Linz, some 18,000 Austrian handicapped people were killed in the Nazi "euthanasia" program by Austrians. In the final weeks of the war, Jews were murdered in cold blood by ordinary Austrians. The Jews were employed as slave labor to build defenses against the Red Army, or embarked on "death marches" to Nazi concentration camps. These crimes committed in the final days and weeks of the war stand for one of the ghastliest chapters of Austria's World War II history. Numerous Austrians were "bystanders" to these events as they had been in the course of numerous Nazi atrocities committed in the *Ostmark* throughout the war. A majority of Austrian public opinion supported the Hitler regime until its bitter end (Bukey). Half a million of Austrian fellow travelers in the Nazi party allowed Hitlerite Germany to build its firm grip on Austrian society during the war.

The Austrian government after the war quite understandably put the best spin on these ambiguous events of 1938 and Austrians' subsequent roles during World War II. It eagerly jumped on the *"rape-of-Austria"* thesis (Austrians as victims and resisters) rather than acknowledge the *"seduction-of-the-Austrian-coquette"* view (Austrians welcoming the Nazi invasion and becoming accomplices of Nazi war crimes). Austrian history during World War II is marked by a complex mix of Austrians being both victims and perpetrators. It was never either/or. Austria was never the exclusive victim of Hitlerite Germany that the Allies maintained in their wartime Moscow Declaration and the Austrian government eagerly echoed after the war, taking the high ground. Austria's best legal minds constructed the *"occupation thesis"* right after the war, shrewdly putting the best spin on Austria's role during the war (Stourzh). It maintained that Austria was invaded in 1938 and occupied during the war and thus seized to exist as a state—it was wiped out on the map of Europe during the war. Austria was re-established as a state within its borders on 10 March 1938, with the "declaration of

independence" by the Provisional Government of Karl Renner. This
new Austrian republic (Second Republic) rose like a phoenix from
the ashes of history and could not be burdened with any Nazi war
crimes (although Austrians who may have been involved committing
such crimes would be punished individually like Ernst Kaltenbrunner
and Arthur Seyss-Inquart at the Nuremberg Trials). Austria,
therefore, would not have to pay reparations to states overrun by
Hitlerite aggression or restitution to Jews and other victims of the
Nazi killing machine. Legally, this "occupation doctrine" came to
prevail over the "*annexation thesis*," which held that Austria was
"only" annexed in 1938—it maintained its existence as a state and
international legal entity, but this statehood lay dormant during the
war. As such it would have to shoulder responsibility for Nazi war
crimes and pay reparations and restitution to victims.

The success of the occupation doctrine gave credence to an
Austrian historical memory that arose after the war and dominated
thought on the issue until the 1980s:

> In March 1938 Austria was occupied and annexed by Germany
> against its will; it was liberated in April/May 1945 by Austrian
> resistance fighters and the Allies. The years 1938 and 1945
> were described as a period of foreign rule and, as far as
> Austria's role and participation in the war was concerned, these
> were portrayed as a period of resistance and persecution, of the
> nation's fight for its liberation. (Uhl in *CAS* vol. 5)

## Between Responsibility and Rehabilitation: Allied Planning
## for Postwar Austria, 1942-45

As the Allied armies marched into Central Europe towards victory,
the Allied planners in Washington and London were cognizant of
Austria's ambiguous international status. They were aware of the
Austrians' modest resistance record and culpability in Nazi war
crimes. But they also knew that they needed to ignore some of
Austria's contributions to Hitler's war of aggression and
extermination, if they wanted to re-establish an independent and
viable Austrian nation. They were particularly interested in
supporting "all appropriate means of fostering the growth of
pronounced Austrian national feeling along democratic

lines" (Mitten in *CAS* vol. X). Both reawakening Austrian identity and making the economy viable would effectively promote the revival of Austria. In negotiating Austria's future international status, the Allied powers soon encountered serious disagreements among themselves.

Anglo-American wartime planning for postwar Austria was part and parcel of their rethinking the future of Germany and East Central Europe. It revolved around three basic options: 1.) in early plans, Austria was a sideshow in a Carthaginian peace with radical German dismemberment, 2.) Austria as part and parcel of Eastern European integration (con/federation and/or customs union schemes), or 3.) the re-establishment of an independent Austria. All options had in common both the goals of drastically weakening Germany after the defeat of National Socialism and containing communism in Eastern Europe. Anglo-American expert planning was started early in the war by the "sister institutions" the Royal Institute of International Affairs in London and the Council on Foreign Relations in New York. By 1942/43, these expert staffs were formally incorporated and broadened in the Foreign Office and the State Department—the "Foreign Office Research Department" and State's "Advisory Committee on Postwar Foreign Policy." There was a big institutional difference in the wartime governing processes in London and Washington. Whereas in Whitehall's very structured wartime planning process, expert plans eventually filtered up into the highest policy-making bodies and most suggestions were eventually adopted by the Cabinet and Prime Minister Winston Churchill, in Washington's chaotic wartime administrative environment and President Franklin D. Roosevelt's polycratic governing style, much of the planning expertise gathered dust in drawers and never was officially utilized by higher decision- making bodies.

The "Big Three" were on top of the policy-making pyramid, yet had very different approaches to reordering Europe after the war. Roosevelt had a tendency to procrastinate on difficult political decisions during the war. He wanted to win the war first and then embark on the political reordering of Europe. He was confident he could do business with "Uncle Joe" (Stalin) after the war. Churchill, on the other had, knew that the military advance of the armies would determine the political landscape of postwar Europe; he made old-

fashioned spheres-of-influence deals with Stalin, which was
repugnant to the Americans. Stalin certainly was convinced that
armies in place would dictate political outcomes and fashioned his
strategy accordingly.

By 1943 Austria was left "hanging between East and West" in
Anglo-American planning. Should it remain part of a South German
state, or a member of a future Danube confederation ("Danubia")?
While American wartime planners initially treated the Austrian
question as an appendix to German dismemberment schemes, they
soon came to accept that Germany should not be rewarded for its
aggression by leaving Austria in the German sphere after the war.
The various federation and customs unions' schemes from the
interwar period that American officials and experts dug up in their
brain-storming sessions as *models* for a future Eastern European
confederation did not hold much promise either, as the Soviets were
expected to determine the future of East Central Europe once the Red
Army liberated these areas. So Austrian independence emerged by
1943 as the most realistic option. Prescient State Department
officials suspected that Austrian nationality might be crystallizing,
and Austrians were learning their lessons about "Prussians" from
their incorporation into the "Third Reich." One American diplomat
noted that "he looked forward to a future of Austria with a status
possibly analogous to Switzerland" (Cannon cited in Bischof,
*Austria in the First Cold War* 23).

It was the junior British Foreign Office diplomat Geoffrey
Harrison who contributed the lion's share to the notion of re-
establishing a politically independent and economically viable
postwar Austria. His basic 1943 memorandum "The Future of
Austria" presented the most focused discussion of the Austrian
question in World War II. The first sentence gave the cue other
nations would follow in interpreting Austria's role: *"Austria was the
first free country to fall victim to Nazi aggression."* The
memorandum envisioned a two-staged process (Stourzh): first, the
re-establishment of an independent Austria after the war; second, the
possibility of Austria joining an East Central European (con)
federation sometime in the future, which was Churchill's favorite
option. In 1943 many British officials in the propaganda departments
thought that Germany was ripe for collapse. With a major statement

in favor of an independent Austria, they hoped to rouse the spirit of resistance in Hitler's "Danube and Alpine *Gaus*" and thus hasten the collapse of Germany. But by dangling the carrot of postwar independence, they also used the stick of reminding the Austrians that their fate would largely depend on their own actions.

These ambiguities about Austria's postwar position were carried into the major Allied wartime statement on postwar Austria, the key "Moscow Declaration." The initial British drafts reflected the equivocations of planners and the progress from a major propaganda statement to a basic political document (Stourzh). Austria was termed the "first free country to fall victim to Nazi aggression." Even though the British had recognized the Anschluß, for postwar purposes they now considered it "null and void." They wished to re-establish a "free and independent" Austria, but wanted it later to associate with neighboring states. But after the carrot came the stick: "The Austrian people must, however, remember that they have a responsibility which they cannot evade, and that in the final settlement account will taken of the part they play in assisting to expel the German invader." While historians later christened this final paragraph the "guilt clause," British diplomat Geoffrey Harrison who drafted this declaration on Austria, rejected that interpretation. It was simply "a warning to the Austrians that they must earn the restoration of their independence." The American State Department accepted the British draft, but cautioned the British that future Austrian independence should not be conditioned on future "association with neighboring states." The Soviets rejected any reference to future Eastern European federations outright just as the Americans had anticipated.

The amended British draft declaration was discussed in the crucial Moscow Conference of Foreign Ministers in later October 1943. A drafting subcommittee deliberated the British draft without any references to Eastern federations or Danubian schemes like the Soviets had demanded. But the Soviet representative also put further teeth in the draft by insisting that "Austria" and not "Austrians" had to shoulder responsibility. The Anglo-American representatives recognized that the Soviets indeed tried to saddle the international legal subject Austria with "full political and material responsibility for the war." Moscow was laying the groundwork for demanding reparations from an independent Austria after the war. The Foreign Ministers accepted the revisions and published their Declaration on Austria as Annex 6 of the Moscow Conference Protocol on 1 November 1943.

When the Soviet archives began to open after the end of the Cold War, it became clear that the wartime Soviet Foreign Ministry set up a small planning staff of its own, headed by former Foreign Minister Maxim Litvinov. These planners rejected all British Eastern European confederation plans because they correctly suspected that the Western powers were trying to build a conservative-Catholic *glacis* as a new *cordon sanitaire* against Communist expansionism. All such Western political and economic Danubian blocs "would be instruments of anti-Soviet policy." Stalin expected the continent fragmented and weakened at the end of the war. This would make him the arbiter of the Europe (Zubok et al.). Even before the Red Army created *faits accomplis*, he expected Eastern Europe to be the Soviet sphere of influence. In the infamous "percentage agreement" of October 1944, Churchill accepted this Soviet sphere and sealed the fate of Eastern Europe by conceding it to Soviet influence (Roosevelt, who did not come to this Moscow meeting, tacitly accepted this division of Europe as well). Austria was not part of the "percentage agreement," for Moscow did not expect it to be in its sphere of influence. Austria would be independent; Moscow's planners expected it to be part of a mid-European *neutral* zone.

The French were not represented during the Moscow meetings but Charles de Gaulle, the leader of the "Free French" committee in Algiers, acted as if France, which in 1943 was still occupied by Hitler's armies, were a great power. De Gaulle was determined to re-establish France's great power status. De Gaulle also accepted that Stalin would control Eastern Europe. Independent of De Gaulle, a study group of diplomats in Paris were thinking about the postwar order. In the case of Austria, they hoped to re-establish an independent and neutral Austria. Two weeks after the Moscow Conference of Foreign Ministers (where the French were not represented), De Gaulle's Algiers Committee issued its own statement on Austria on 16 November 1943. The French declaration was positive and unambiguous. Without any "responsibility clauses," the French were looking forward to the re-establishment of an independent Austria. The French intended to treat Austria much better than Germany after the war and insisted on an occupation zone along with the other three great powers. De Gaulle's thinking predicated treating Austria as a *"pays ami"* after its liberation. It is astounding that all powers envisioned the possibility of a *neutral Austria* after the war, the Americans even contemplating the *Swiss model*!

After Moscow, British planners also concentrated on *economic* planning for postwar Austria. The question was to what extent Britain should "eschew penalizing Austria for her past misdeeds." Some planners wanted Austria to pay short-term reparations "but on a lower scale than Germany." The British anticipated the complexity of the postwar "German assets problem" and the untangling of German from Austrian property. In the end, the postwar viability of the Austrian economy was given highest priority, and the British decided not to burden the Austrian economy with reparations. Austria would be favored, and the costs of the war would be loaded on the Germans. But some British planners, like John Troutbeck, remained highly skeptical about giving Austria preferential treatment: "Were it not for the strategic importance of keeping Austria separate from Germany, we would let this flabby country stew" (Bischof/1999).

The Moscow Conference of Foreign Ministers set up an "European Advisory Commission" (EAC) in 1944 to determine future occupation policies and zonal divisions in Germany and Austria. While the zonal division of Germany was worked out by the EAC in the course of 1944, with regard to Austria, Roosevelt initially refused to accept responsibility for an occupation zone in Austria. The ailing Roosevelt did not want to be pulled too deeply into postwar European politics by accepting too many responsibilities. But John G. Winant, his ambassador in London, warned him that failure to work out advance agreements with the Soviets would lead to "a grab as grab can policy." If the United States failed to shoulder any responsibility in the occupation of Austria, British interests would be pitted against Soviet interests. The case of Bulgaria, where the Red Army had set up a Communist puppet regime, was already showing that "physical participation" in occupations would guarantee respect for American interests. In

December 1944, Roosevelt reluctantly accepted an American occupation zone in postwar Austria. At the same time, British pressure on Roosevelt also succeeded in granting the French participation in the Austrian occupation. It would take another half year of tough negotiations among the four powers to finally arrive at a precise sectoral division of Vienna and a detailed control agreement for Austria in the EAC. It was finally signed on 4 July 1945, two months after the war in Europe had ended and Austria had been liberated by the Allied armies. In Vienna an Allied Council would be the supreme political Allied body governing the occupation regime, just as the Control Council in Berlin was governing Germany. Vienna was divided up into sectors, but the inner core of the city (the 1. District) would be governed by a quadripartite regime (the famous "four in the jeep").

This delay had the advantage that Soviet intentions in postwar Austria became more clearly visible. Among other things, it led to an insistence on the part of the Western powers to write down exact transit rights into Vienna through the Soviet zone (details that the Allies had felt to explicitly agree on in the case of Berlin).

## From Tutelage to Emancipation: Allied Policies toward Occupied Austria, 1945-1955

Historians have characterized the ten-year quadripartite Allied occupation *vis-à-vis* Austria as "a nation under *tutelage*" (Bischof and Leidenfrost). While the initial occupation period under the first control agreement was one of "total control" (Stourzh), the second Control Agreement of 28 June 1946, loosened the direct supervision of the Austrian government through the Allied Council. Only *unanimous agreement* ("negative veto") of all four powers could stop regular Austrian legislation. As Cold War tensions heated up between the Soviets and the Western powers, such agreement in the Allied Council became less and less likely as the Soviets began to veto most Austrian legislation (while the Western powers did not). In the fall of 1950, the Western powers "civilianized" their occupation regimes (the military presence was reduced as ambassadors replaced generals as representatives on the Allied Council); the Soviets followed suit in 1953 after Stalin's death. Since Austrian treaty negotiations were coming to a standstill during the Korean War, the

Western powers wanted at least to send a signal that they were mindful of the burdens of the ongoing occupation of "liberated" Austria. The Soviets followed suit only after Stalin's death in 1953.

As the Austrian government took back more and more powers from the occupiers under the second Control Agreement, a gradual process of *emancipation* from Allied tutelage/*tutelle* (supervision) began (Albrich et at.) This emancipation gave Austria growing *leverage* in their dealings with the occupation powers and in their negotiations for the Austrian treaty ("state treaty"). Austria's ten-year occupation was a result of Austria being one of the leftovers of the Third Reich and, therefore, also having to face some undefined responsibility for the Nazi war of aggression and extermination. The Soviet Union insisted on such culpability and inserted legal grounds for it in the Moscow Declaration as has been pointed out.

Austria under foreign tutelage was not a new phenomenon. Ever since its creation in 1918, Austria's fate has been under severe foreign influence and supervision by the international community ("*tutelle*") (Angerer in Ableitinger et al., 165ff). The St. Germain conference in 1919 prohibited Austria's fusion with Germany ("*Anschlußverbot*"). In 1922 the League of Nations' loans for Austria came with severe restrictions on Austrian economic policy and the maneuverability of Austrian foreign policy. During the rise of European fascist regimes, the Austria's authoritarian Dollfuss and Schuschnigg regimes after 1933 leaned on Benito Mussolini's fascist Italy for protection against National Socialist Germany. Caught between the fascist neighbors of Hitler and Mussolini (and Hungary)—and abandoned to potential aggressors by Western appeasement—Austria was caught between a rock and a hard place. Hitler's economic and political pressure forced Schuschnigg to become more amenable to Nazi Germany; this opened the floodgates for Austrian Nazis (who had assassinated Dolffuss in 1934!) to undermine the Schuschnigg regime. We have heard how such corruption within would lead to the collapse of a free and independent Austria and annexation to Germany in 1938.

For the next seven years, the German occupation not only erased Austria from the map of Europe, but also tried to eradicate all signs of Austrian independence and identity. When the Provisional Renner Government re-established an independent Austria even before the

country's complete liberation, Renner only governed the rump—
Eastern Austria—liberated and occupied by the Red Army in April
1945. Renner's government was under Soviet tutelage and not
recognized by the Western powers. Meanwhile, the Western powers
set up their own occupation regimes in their respective zones.
Austria's strict control through foreign powers would continue for
ten more years.

The British were particularly incensed about Stalin's generals
establishing a government in Vienna unilaterally. The conservative-
socialist-communist "national unity" coalition set up by Renner and
recognized by the Kremlin looked very suspect in London and
Washington where governments had *not* been consulted. Stalin
seemed to be following the pattern he set in Poland, Rumania, and
Bulgaria to control the governments with communist minorities
under his strict control. In Austrian postwar history, the communists
were a negligible political force. They never received much more
than 5 percent of the vote in national elections. In Renner's Cabinet,
they had one-third representation and two powerful portfolios—
Interior (with control over police forces) and Education
(propaganda). High-level British diplomats immediately warned that
the Soviets were "following their usual technique of confronting us
with *faits accomplis*." Suspecting that Renner's was a communist-
controlled government under the Kremlin's influence, the Western
powers, following the British lead, refused to recognize it. Given
Austria's vital strategic geopolitical position "at the crossroads of
Europe where Russian and Western influences meet in equal force,"
as the U.S. State Department noted, much was at stake (Bischof).

Western suspicions of Soviet intentions were not only based on the
traditional anti-communist outlook of leaders like Churchill. The Red
Army's behavior was appalling during their crusade of liberating
Central Europe from "fascist influence." The Red Army's wholesale
raping and looting on a massive scale reawakened among many
people in the West and Austria images of Mongol hordes descending
upon Central Europe. This is what Nazi propaganda had preached for
years, so it was natural for Austrians to believe it when they saw it
happen (Stiefel and Fraberger in *CAS* vol. VIII). What was often
forgotten in this deeply rooted "enemy image" of the Russians/
Soviets was the fact that many of these Red Army soldiers had

experienced the reign of terror of the German *Wehrmacht* (about 8 percent of its soldiers were Austrians) in their homes with their own eyes. This was revenge on a scale of biblical proportions. Raping and pillaging was driving home total defeat to the Germans (the regular Red Army soldier perceived crossing the Hungarian border into the "Third Reich" as entry into Nazi Germany, not Austria). Such severe "liberation" practiced in Germany and Austria made many natives root for the Nazis. Apart from the soldiers' pillaging, the Soviet Union sent teams into Germany and Austria to remove "war booty" on a massive scale. The machinery of entire factories, locomotives and railroad stock, as well as engineers and scientists, was removed. During 1945, as much as an estimated $500 million worth of heavy industrial equipment from their Eastern Austrian zone went on railroad cars to the Soviet Union. News of such Red Army behavior reached Western capitals and only added to their suspicions about the unilateral policies of their Soviet allies.

Starting before the war even ended, such depredations led to a veritable cold war between the British and the Soviets during the summer of 1945, with the Americans increasingly acting as *mediators* to reduce these tensions. Washington took a somewhat "rosier view" (Churchill) of Soviet behavior. An internationally inexperienced President Harry Truman, who replaced Roosevelt after his death on 12 April 1945, tried to keep the late president's policy of cooperation with the Soviets going. For one, the Americans had a more positive image of Renner's integrity; they felt he could not be used as a "'front' by political forces of dubious character" (Bischof). After the four occupation powers had finally retreated into their respective occupation zones agreed to in the EAC, by the end of July American advance parties were the first Western forces to move into Vienna and start preparing the set-up of the Allied Council and the beginning of quadripartite control. In August the American High Commissioner General Mark W. Clark urged his Western counterparts to come to the Vienna area and meet the Soviet commander to work out further details, such as getting the difficult food situation in Austria under control. It was largely due to such American mediation that the British agreed to begin meetings of the Allied Council on 12 September 1945.

The advent of quadripartite Allied government in Vienna quickly upgraded the Renner regime and permitted it to finally break out of its "inner exile" in Eastern Austria and govern the entire country. In the course of September, the crafty Renner managed to gather a conference of provincial representatives in Vienna to broaden his government and thus make it acceptable to the Western powers. The *Länderkonferenz* met from 24 to 26 September in Vienna. Given the heavy Soviet presence in Austria, Renner refused to fire any Communists but added representative from Western Austria, such as Karl Gruber, to his Cabinet. The dashing, young maverick Gruber became foreign minister and would put his fierce anti-communist imprint on Austria's foreign policy during his eight-year tenure on the Ballhausplatz. Given this new constellation in Vienna, the Western powers at last recognized the Renner government on 20 October. At this time, preparations were already underway for an Austrian election on 25 November. The conservative People's Party won this first free national election since 1932 with the Socialist Party a close second. To everyone's surprise, the Communists were badly beaten with their 5 percent of the vote. With more than 90 percent of the votes between them, the conservatives and Socialists formed a coalition government under Leopold Figl, a man who had suffered for five years in Nazi concentration camps during the war. Most of the members of his Cabinet had been persecuted by the Nazis; the Figl government thus sported an impressive "anti-fascist" record.

The Kremlin's response to the anti-communist Figl government was to up the ante in the struggle over Austria and increase the pressure through economic exploitation of its Austrian zone. In a hasty move, Truman and the new British Prime Minister Clement Attlee had conceded to Stalin late in the "Big Three" Potsdam Conference of July 1945 that the Soviets could take reparations from the "German external assets" in their Austrian zone. "German assets" was a very broad and ill-defined term, as the Western powers quickly discovered. It included everything Germans owned in Austria—from legitimate prewar German individual and corporate properties, via both the expropriated Jewish possessions ("aryanizations") and oil properties of Western corporations sold to the Nazis "under duress" in 1938, to the massive investments of the Third Reich during the war, which produced huge new heavy industrial steel and aluminum, chemical, and synthetic fiber conglomerates in the *Ostmark*. Even before Potsdam, the Soviets liberally helped themselves to "war booty" from these "German assets" (ignoring the fact that they might be Austrian) in their initial round of removals right after the end of the war. In August, the Kremlin tried to force a trade treaty and a detrimental deal on the vast oil properties in Eastern Austria down the Renner government's throat. The Western Allies arrived in Vienna in the nick of time in early September to stop Renner from signing a deal on a bilateral Austro-Soviet oil company (the Western oil companies wanted to get their Austrian assets back and not see them slip into the Soviets' control).

After the formation of the Figl government, the Soviets went for broke. In February 1946, they began seizing unilaterally all "German assets" in their zone and completed the process in July (some 280 industrial enterprises, including the entire Austrian oil industry, the Danube Shipping Company, huge tracts of highly productive agricultural lands). These assets were organized in the vast "USIA" holding company. Until the end of the occupation, the USIA empire formed a "state within the state" and essentially produced profits and "reparations out of current production" for the Soviet Union. Estimates are that Austria paid one billion dollar in reparations (most likely much more) through USIA to the Soviets. USIA reparations and 1945 removals easily amounted to 1.5 billion dollars in postwar reparations to the Soviet Union. A consensus is emerging among historians that the Soviet refusal to leave Austria quickly after the war was largely motivated by their determination to seize a maximum amount of reparations from their richly endowed zone.

The American-Soviet Cold War broke out in Austria a year before the larger eruption of East-West tensions. In the spring of 1946, in response to this Soviet economic pressure on and Communist propaganda war against the Figl government, General Clark put his foot down in Vienna and also warned Washington about Soviet intransigence and expansionist intentions in Central Europe. Within a year, the media-prone Clark had made a dramatic turn-around from being a Soviet-friendly mediator in Austria to a leading cold warrior. Clark's warnings came right at the time when George Kennan's famous "long telegram" from Moscow also arrived with a similar message. This in turn fed the growing toughness of the Truman administration *vis-à-vis* Soviet depredations in Germany, Eastern

Europe, and the Near East. These growing tensions in 1946 would finally result in the Truman Doctrine and the Marshall Plan in 1947 and the outbreak of the global East–West Cold War.

The American response to Soviet economic pressure on Austria was to increase their economic and financial aid to the Figl government. In the fall of 1946, Figl was confronted with a worsening food crisis. Austrian agricultural production at this time barely managed to contribute half the food needed to feed the population and was heavily dependent on American food aid. A despondent Figl was even thinking of resigning, which would have had fateful consequences during this stage of the exploding Cold War. In the State Department, leading American economic experts of Charles Kindleberger's caliber had to forcefully respond to this food crisis and the growing balance of payments and trade deficits resulting from it. In 1946/47, the U.S. government poured food and economic aid (imports!) into Austria, stuffing an annual $200 million deficit hole in the Austrian balance of payments (Austria export trade would only recover by the 1950s as a result of such American aid infusions!). They would continue to do so during the Marshall Plan years (1948-52).

Austrian sovereignty was to be restored by negotiating an Austrian Treaty among the four powers (Austria officially became a negotiating partner only in 1954). Austrian treaty negotiations got under way in earnest in 1947 during meetings of special treaty deputies in January/February 1947 in London and the Council of Foreign Ministers meeting in Moscow in March/April. Although major progress was made on the negotiating table on many vital issues, differences on the German assets issue remained the major stumbling block in agreeing on an Austrian treaty. The prospect of protracted treaty negotiations greatly upset the Austrian government. On top of this, the Communist party used the ongoing food crisis to organize "hunger riots" in early May to increase the pressure on the Austrian government. Moreover, persistent rumors about Communist "*putsch* plans" scared both the Austrian government and the Western powers. Also, hundreds of Austrian nationals and officials were abducted by the Soviet occupation authorities in their zone — some reappearing from the gulag only years later and others never to be seen again. Anxieties over further Communist depredations in

Austria culminated during the Czech and Berlin crises in the spring of 1948. "Prague is West of Vienna" became the clarion call for those who feared that Austria might be next on the list of Communist takeovers as a result of domestic political and economic instability.

During these crisis years, when Cold War tensions heightened in Central Europe, the Marshall Plan threw a lifeline to Austrian and Western Europeans. Designed as an economic aid program for European recovery by the European nations getting together to "help themselves," it also had the larger strategic purpose of containing communism in Eastern Europe and thereby finalizing the division of Europe. While Marshall Plan aid concentrated on economic recovery in the first two years (1949/50) of the "European Recovery Program (ERP)" (the official name), it became increasingly a military aid program in the final two years (1951/52), once the Korean War had broken out.

Arguably, no European nation benefited more from the Marshall Plan than Austria. While much of the initial aid was food aid and raw materials to get the engines of production going again, it then turned to machine tools and strategies to increase Austrian productivity (including agriculture). The principal goal was to modernize the economy and put the country back on its track towards economic prosperity. The so-called "counterpart funds" (Austrian Schillings earned by selling American ERP-financed products in Austria at market price deposited by the government into bank accounts for future investment) became the most important investment tool in reviving the Austrian economy during a capital-starved time. Long-term, low-interest "counterpart" credits financed huge hydroelectric power stations in Kaprun/Salzburg, modernized steel factories in Styria, and helped restart the Austrian tourist industry. Increasing exports and tourist foreign currency earned from these investments would allow Austria to correct both its balance of trade and balance of payments problems by the mid-1950s. Every Austrian received $132 in Marshall aid (only Iceland and Norway received more). The incalculable psychological effects resulting from growing national and personal prosperity cannot be calculated. This generous American aid program more than any other political measure helped to keep the Austrian nation-building experiment alive during the grimmest days of the Cold War and gave Austrians hope that they might persist in the face of the Communist onslaught (*CAS* vol. VIII).

While economic recovery occurred in steps as a result of the Marshall Plan, there was less progress on Austrian treaty negotiations. Diplomats saw slow progress in 1948 due to the Czech and Berlin crises, almost experienced a break-through in 1949, and had to resign to near failure in 1950. While the Soviets insisted on a major Austrian payment of 150 million dollars for the restoration of the German assets and abandoned their support of Yugoslav territorial and reparations claims against Austria, the Americans became more intransigent due to the mounting Cold War tensions. In particular, the American military leadership became less and less inclined to agree to the signing of an Austrian treaty as a result of perceived military threats from the Soviet side growing in Central Europe after Prague and Berlin. The Pentagon feared that withdrawing from Austria would invite the communists to seize power. Austria would be militarily too weak to resist Soviet depredations or coup attempts by the Communist party. The Pentagon insisted that a future core of an Austrian army needed to be built secretly before the U.S. Army could retreat from the country. In the fall of 1949 when Austrian treaty negotiations seemed close to a final breakthrough, the American military establishment was the major force resisting the signing of a treaty. In the end, the Soviets saved the Pentagon by turning intransigent again on minor issues. In the course of 1950, treaty negotiations totally deadlocked once again due to the Kremlin's pig-headedness. This opened up a window of opportunity for the Western powers to secretly build and train the core of a future Austrian army (the "*B-Gendarmerie*").

In 1948/49 the United States agreed to join the North Atlantic Treaty Organization (the NATO treaty was signed in April 1949) and started its "reversed course" towards a Japanese alliance, once it became clear that Mao Tse-Tung's Communists would win the civil war in China. In August 1949, the Soviets also successfully detonated their first atomic device. American policy was increasingly "militarized" in Austria as elsewhere. Planning for an Austrian police force got under way, which would become the core of a future Austrian army. In 1948/49, the United States also began a program of secret military aid to Austria. The American military set aside hand weapons for the Austrian police force. A major program was started for countering an anticipated blockade of Vienna (located in the Soviet zone) while Berlin experienced a tightening blockade. Similar Soviet pressure on the West was anticipated for Vienna. The U.S. occupation authorities shipped massive food stocks into the Austrian capital—storing it in warehouses all over the Western sectors of Vienna—to counter a potential blockade. These stores aptly code-named "Squirrel Cage" could have fed a blockaded Vienna for ninety days. In addition, material was stored in Vienna to quickly lay out temporary airfields in the Western sectors of Vienna for air-supplying the blockaded city. Preparations were made to evacuate the Austrian political elite to Salzburg so that the Austrian government could continue to operate in case of a communist squeeze play (Schmidl).

When the Korean War began to rage back and forth in the second half of 1950, Washington planners feared Austria might become "Europe's Korea." Consequently, Austria's secret rearmament was sped up in 1951, especially after the Communists attempted a general strike in Vienna and Eastern Austria in the fall of 1950. Many perceived this as the long anticipated "Communist *putsch* attempt." The Western commanders did not think it was a coup and kept a cool head. They aided a jittery Austrian government in defusing the crisis. But military preparations were intensified. The American Central Intelligence Agency stocked some ninety secret arms caches throughout Western Austria for Austrian guerilla resistance in case of a communist attack. The French began to prepare bridges and roads for demolition on the borders of their zone in the Tyrol and Vorarlberg to counter a Communist attack with the reawakened idea of an "alpine fortress"—an "alpine redoubt/*reduit alpine*" (Koppensteiner in Schmidl) The Americans sped up and intensified their efforts to arm and train the core of a future Austrian army and coordinate plans for Austria with larger NATO defense plans.

The "hot war" in Korea sped up the militarization of the West and relegated East-West diplomacy to the backburner. NATO defense planning was sped up, and West German rearmament was seriously debated. The major national security memorandum NSC-68 had stated that, during this phase of strengthening Western defenses, diplomacy with the Soviets would not be a high priority. It would be resumed from "positions of strength." When Stalin offered to unify and neutralize Germany in a major diplomatic initiative in March 1952, Chancellor Konrad Adenauer and the West dismissed it as propaganda and failed to pursue it (Steininger). Western intransigence had major repercussions on Austrian treaty diplomacy. After all, here was one of the few diplomatic venues that seemed promising since the treaty draft had seemingly been ready to sign in late 1949. Austrian griping and a precipitous decline in the morale of the population due to the seemingly unending occupation led the Americans to embark on the "abbreviated treaty" initiative. Right at the time when the Kremlin presented the "Stalin notes" on Germany to the West, Washington (followed by the reluctant French, British, and Austrians) launched its "short treaty" initiative. A radically shortened treaty draft did away with many vital parts of the treaty such as the burdensome German assets provisions. There was never a chance that Stalin and Vyacheslav Molotov would resume negotiations on this treaty draft. The Kremlin rightly dismissed it as a propaganda initiative. During this ice age of the Cold War, diplomacy deteriorated to psychological propaganda. The Austrian treaty deputies tried to revive negotiations based on the old long draft in the course of 1953, but the Kremlin was not interested in making progress on Austria.

In the course of 1953, Austrian treaty negotiations had to come to terms with a dramatically altered geopolitical landscape. The Kremlin was in disarray after Stalin's death in early March and went into an extended succession struggle which was only resolved when Nikita Khrushchev emerged as the primary leader in 1955. In the months after the brutal leader's departure, it appeared like Malenkov and Beria would take over the reigns in the Kremlin. They launched a major new "peaceful co-existence" campaign with the West. Presumably they wanted to defuse the high state of East-West tensions while things were sorted out in the Kremlin. They did make major concessions in their Austrian occupation regime by giving back some German assets to the Austrian government and civilianizing their high commission. They also eased many strict controls in the daily lives of people in their zone. Beria's failure to chart a similar easing of the occupation of East Germany ended in the uprising of 17 June. The protests all over the German Democratic Republic were brutally squashed, and the monstrous Beria was executed on order of his peers in the Kremlin. Nonetheless, in July an armistice was signed to end the Korean War. The Kremlin leaders sent mixed signals about their interest in forging better relations with the West.

The Western powers reacted quite differently to this Soviet "peace offensive." The new President Dwight D. Eisenhower, along with his hardline Secretary of State John Foster Dulles from the conservative, deeply anti-communist, stalwart wing of the Republican Party, dismissed the Kremlin initiative as typical Cold War propaganda maneuvering. Eisenhower challenged the Kremlin leaders in a major speech in April 1953 to follow their words up with "deeds." The hardliners in Eisenhower's party did not want "peaceful existence" with the godless Kremlin but wanted the new president to start a policy of "rolling back" communism. While Eisenhower stepped up the psychological warfare battles with communism through radio broadcasts, leaflets, and CIA covert warfare, he never abandoned basic containment policy. Plans for a "Volunteer Freedom Corps" of Eastern European refugees to be covertly trained and equipped in Germany never materialized (Carafano). The Hungarians had to learn the hard way in 1956 that, in spite of the booming propaganda rhetoric, the Eisenhower administration was not prepared to risk nuclear war over rolling back communism in Eastern Europe (Borhi).

The old British Prime Minister Winston Churchill reacted dramatically differently to the Kremlin's "peaceful coexistence" campaign. He urged his old wartime ally and friend Eisenhower to test the seriousness of intentions by the new leaders in the Kremlin in a summit meeting. He bombarded Eisenhower with letters asking to get together with Malenkov and announced his desire for a summit publicly. In 1954 he even traveled all the way to Washington and personally pleaded with Eisenhower to meet the Kremlin leaders. After the apocalyptic H-bomb test in the South Pacific, Churchill felt an even greater sense of urgency to defuse Cold War tensions. On his trip back from Washington to London, he announced that he would meet the Kremlin leaders. But his own Foreign Office did not think such a high-level meeting was the right signal to the Kremlin, and Eisenhower was appalled about Churchill's threatened *Alleingang*.

The meeting did not materialize. In 1954 American intransigence prevailed over Churchill's desire for exploring a Cold War settlement (Bischof and Dockrill).

Next to Moscow, Washington, and London (Churchill had resumed power in 1951), there was also a new government in Vienna. In April 1953, Julius Raab from the conservative People's Party renewed the coalition with the Socialists as chancellor of the new government. Raab had been a short-lived Secretary of Commerce in the Schuschnigg government at the time of the Anschluß. Due to his "Austrofascist" past and his open resistance to Soviet economic depredations in their zone, the Soviets did not accept him as a Cabinet member in the 1945 Figl government. For the next eight years, he operated behind the scenes and pulled the strings as the *eminence grise* of the People's Party. In 1953 the new leaders of the Kremlin tolerated him as chancellor, and they would not have to regret it. Raab welcomed the "peaceful coexistence" policies of the Kremlin and their easing of the occupation regime in Eastern Austria (where Raab was from) and even explicitly thanked the Soviets for their concessions. At the same time, he realized that Austrian treaty negotiations probably could not be revived with the old formulas. In the course of 1953, Raab began to explore directly with the new leaders in the Kremlin the potential of a *neutral* Austria, one *not aligned* with any of the military blocs in Europe. Such exploratory Austro-Soviet low-level diplomatic contacts in Berne and Washington started as early as 1952. Foreign Minister Gruber had the Indian ambassador Menon directly test Austrian neutrality with Molotov in June 1953. The hardline Stalinist Molotov, who was slowly frozen out of the Kremlin's inner circle, rebuffed the initiative. He refused to pullback from territory the Red Army had liberated with its blood at the end of the war. Raab was not discouraged and kept the neutral, non-aligned option discreetly in his arsenal of diplomatic options (Stourzh).

The Western powers, above all the United States, were unhappy about the Vienna Ballhausplatz's growing emancipation from both the cover and restrictions of Western diplomatic priorities. They felt Raab was too inexperienced and weak to be negotiating directly with the Kremlin. They did not like a small power, such as an Austrian, using his limited leverage to maneuver between the power blocs.

They also feared that the Soviets were aiming at using Austrian neutrality as a model for Germany. The West's highest priority was to incorporate West Germany into their defense network without discussing neutral options. In Eisenhower's National Security Council, views on Austrian neutrality clashed. Just as in 1949, the Pentagon still represented the hardline position and did not want to abandon Austria. The generals particularly feared the repercussions of a neutralized Austria on the German question. A more pragmatic Dulles argued that the United States could not stop the Austrians if they wanted to be neutral. Essentially, the key observation of 1952 by U.S. ambassador to Moscow, George Kennan, was still correct: "[...] Soviets would like to reserve their position on Austria until the they know roughly what shape the German settlement is to take" (Bischof). Austria was overshadowed by the unresolved German question.

For Raab and the Austrians, 1954 started with East-West impasse, but ended with a breakthrough in the German question. In spite of much hope, no breakthrough had occurred during the February Berlin Council of Foreign Minster's Meeting. Preparing for Berlin, President Eisenhower gave Dulles the green light for accepting Austrian neutrality if it were a Swiss-type, armed neutrality. But, in Berlin, Molotov stopped all talk about a neutral Austria with his insistence that an Austrian treaty would not be signed without agreement on the German question. This Soviet linkage persisted throughout 1954. The dramatic turning point on the German question came in the fall of 1954. When the French National Assembly rejected the scheme of a "European Defense Community," a quick solution to the problem of West German rearmament took on highest priority status. British Foreign Secretary Anthony Eden took the initiative. In October 1954, the Western powers decided in the "Paris Agreements" to directly incorporate West Germany and German troops into NATO (Steininger). West German rearmament within the North Atlantic framework represented a major defeat for Molotov's diplomacy whose aim throughout the early 1950s had been to block such West German rearmament with various diplomatic rear-guard actions (such as linking the Austrian and the German questions). Because the Paris Agreements were quickly ratified by the German and the Western parliaments in the spring of 1955, the Kremlin had to reassess its entire European diplomacy. NATO, strengthened by West German manpower on the frontlines of the Cold War in Central Europe, constituted a major new threat to the Soviet strategy of keeping the West divided and militarily weak in the conventional field. In the nuclear arena, the arms race was heating up with powerful hydrogen bombs becoming available and theater nuclear weapons being added to the defense of Western Europe. Raab had patiently waited for such a breakthrough on the German question and anticipated its potential for paving the way for an Austrian solution.

It was Khrushchev's emergence as the chief Kremlin leader that brought the crucial breakthrough on the Austrian question in the spring of 1955. In February Molotov announced on Khrushchev's insistence that the Austrian question was no longer linked to a German settlement. Raab's ambassador in Moscow, Norbert Bischoff, immediately began to explore the meaning of this reversal with Molotov and the chances for a neutral solution. Legal experts around Stefan Verosta in the Vienna Foreign Ministry had been carefully working out the legal context of an Austrian status of neutrality following the Swiss model. In mid-March, Bruno Kreisky, the Socialist State Secretary in the foreign Ministry, explored Swiss-style armed neutrality with Soviet diplomats in Vienna. Both Kreisky in Vienna and Bischoff in Moscow were encouraged to pursue the neutral option further. When in late March Chancellor Raab and an Austrian delegation were invited to Moscow in mid-April to negotiate with the Kremlin leadership directly, the breaking of the logjam on treaty agreement and four-power withdrawal so long awaited in Austria seemed to get close.

In the Western capitals, this direct bilateral Austro-Soviet diplomacy outside the framework of multilateral Western supervision was viewed with disdain and even horror. The old fear that the Kremlin leaders were playing their old game once again still had not subsided. The Western powers feared the Kremlin aimed at snagging the West in negotiations on Austrian neutrality to reopen the German question and block West German rearmament, almost at the point of completion, in the last minute. Eden, who had done nothing to stop the Anschluß in 1938, complained: "I am sorry that [the] Austrians were not more firmly warned against Moscow's wiles." The West felt Raab and Austrian diplomacy were meeting a challenge that they could not master, as one British observer noticed: "The Austrians seem intent, like the Gadarene swine, on rushing over the precipice to their own doom" (Bischof). Such hyberbole was exaggerated, and Western fears were unfounded. April 1955 would not be another March 1938 for Austria. This time, the Ballhausplatz's active diplomacy took matters into their own hands.

The bilateral Austro-Soviet Moscow negotiations brought the decisive breakthrough in the Austrian question. The top Kremlin leadership wined and dined the Austrians, while the Western ambassadors eyed the bilateral Austro-Soviet honeymoon suspiciously from the sidelines. Not only did Khrushchev and Molotov agree to a Swiss-type Austrian armed neutrality that did not have to be written into the Austrian treaty, but they also offered major economic concessions. The 150 million dollar pay-off for the exhausted German assets in Eastern Austria could be paid through industrial deliveries over a period of years. Due to Marshall Plan aid, Austria had recovered sufficiently to agree to these final "reparation" payments without needing any Western aid (in 1949 their economy would not have been strong enough to do this!). Ironically, some 1.5 billion dollars in American financial and economic aid through the entire occupation decade had put Austria in the position to take matters into their own hands, which was exactly what the Marshall Plan had intended, to "help people to help themselves..." Raab's delegation returned to Vienna and was widely cheered by the population for their triumph in bilateral Cold War diplomacy at this stage of the Cold War (Stourzh). They demonstrated to the world that one could do business with the new Kremlin leaders if it suited their changing geopolitical vision. Had Raab failed, a continuation of the interminable occupation, or worse, a division of Austria would have been one of the likely outcomes.

The Austrian State Treaty was signed on 15 May 1955 in Vienna's magnificent Belvedere Palace. The Austrian population was ecstatic to see the end of the ten-year four-power occupation (following on the heels of seven years of Nazi occupation) nearing. The Western ambassadors and Foreign Minister Figl had put the finishing touches to the fifty-nine article treaty with major annexes. Negotiations were tough to the very end. In this final round, Figl's major success was to get the powers to strike "Austrian responsibility for her participation in World War II" from the preamble of the treaty. This further reinforced Austria's gelling historical World War II memory as a "nation of victims." In this spirit of "letting bygones by bygones," the four Foreign Ministers—Molotov, Dulles, Macmillan, and Pinay—met in Vienna in mid-May to sign the treaty with Figl (Stourzh). Dulles had come to Vienna from Paris where he had presided over a NATO meeting in which the Federal Republic of Germany was officially admitted into NATO after the ratification of the Paris Agreements. Molotov would go on to Warsaw after Vienna to put his signature on the Warsaw Pact treaty. In 1955 the Cold War division of Europe into two powerful military blocs was completed with West Germany's inclusion into NATO and the formation of the Warsaw Pact in response to West German rearmament within NATO.

After the occupation soldiers had retreated from Austria three months after the signing of the State Treaty, the Austrian Parliament passed a law of permanent neutrality on 26 October 1955. Austria was free again and would be a neutral throughout the Cold War. Speculations still abound over Soviet motivations for abandoning Austria in 1955. Most likely it was a combination of economic and political factors. Soviet economic exploitation of its Austrian zone had been bleeding it white. The returns from German assets were diminishing. On top of this, the Soviets would get 150 million worth of industrial equipment and raw materials from Austria over the next six years for handing back these exhausted German assets. After West Germany's integration into NATO, a neutral belt in Central Europe that included Austria and Switzerland and seemingly split the northern and southern NATO flanks appeared advantageous to Soviet strategy. Also, the Austrian solution also led to easing of tensions with Tito's regime in Yugoslavia. After Stalin's "cold war" with Tito, Khrushchev rang in a détente in Yugoslav-Soviet relations. The neutralization of Austria not only led to a withdrawal of Soviet troops but also of Western forces. Some historians think the Kremlin intended the Austrian "neutral solution" to be a model for Germany (Gehler in Albrich et al.); others think that the Eisenhower administration hoped it might be a model for Austria's Eastern neighbors and help "roll back" communism in the Soviet satellites (Gehler in *CAS* vol. IX). The Pentagon felt that secret Austrian rearmament had progressed sufficiently so that a projected 53,000-man Austrian Army could be quickly built with further U.S. military aid from the "core" of the 8,000 strong "*B-Gendarmerie.*" Pentagon strategists expected this Austrian Army to be strong enough to resist potential Communist subversion at home.

The Western powers pushed Eisenhower and Dulles to use the opportunities opened up by the Austrian solution and probe the Soviet "peaceful co-existence" rhetoric for a possible détente in the Cold War in Europe. After Vienna, the Americans could no longer resist British and American entreaties for a summit. The Western leaders met with the new Kremlin leadership in Geneva in mid-July. The "Geneva Summit" did not bring the breakthrough for which many had hoped. The intensifying nuclear arms race and the division of Germany were already too deeply entrenched to pull back from Cold War tensions (Bischof and Dockrill). As the Soviets showed in their 1956 Hungarian intervention, they were not prepared to pull back any further from their Eastern European security sphere (their "*cordon sanitaire*" against Western anti-communism and roll-back!). American "militarization" had progressed too far to seek a general settlement in the Cold War. The "Austrian solution" of 1955, however, offered a signal of hope that genuine diplomacy offered hopes for détente. Austrian neutrality and independence helped overcome Austria's deep Anschluß trauma. The Second Austrian Republic would chart a course of emancipated foreign policy that would be less dependent on great power tutelage.

# Austria Under Allied Occupation

*Klaus Eisterer*

## The End of the War

*The Invasion*

Allied armies liberated Austria from National Socialism. On 29 March—Maundy Thursday in 1945—units of the Red Army's 3rd Ukrainian Front under Marshall Tolbuchin crossed the Third Reich's borders into Burgenland. Mounting an offensive in which they suffered staggering losses, the Soviets succeeded in taking Vienna and St. Pölten by mid-April. They then halted their advance in this sector in order to transfer units to the 2nd Ukrainian Front that was engaged in operations north of the Danube and would go on to pierce deeply into the Mühlviertel district. By the time hostilities ceased, Soviet troops had occupied Burgenland, Vienna, and Lower Austria; in the south, they continued to advance (even after 8 May) beyond Graz, and occupied most of Styria.

In the west, French 1st Army troops crossed Vorarlberg's borders on 29 April and advanced all the way to the Arlberg mountain range. Units of the U.S. 7th Army penetrating south from Bavaria entered Tyrol and Salzburg in early May, while elements of the U.S. 3rd Army occupied Upper Austria, liberating the Mauthausen concentration camp on 5 May. The V Corps of the British 8th Army—fighting alongside units of Tito's partisans—did not cross into Carinthia until 8 May, the very day on which the Third Reich surrendered, and went on to occupy East Tyrol, portions of Salzburg's Lungau region, and western Styria.

In the east, the *Wehrmacht* and the SS—often with support provided by the *Volkssturm*, local militias raised in autumn 1944 whose ranks included men between sixteen and sixty who had not

Postwar de-Nazification: An American questionnaire about Nazi affiliations during World War II.

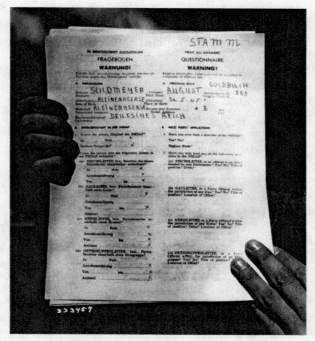

Source: National Archives, College Park, MD (#111-SC-333957)

yet been called up—struggled bitterly against Red Army units, whereas resistance in the west was essentially a matter of holding out via rearguard actions. Soviet losses have been estimated at approximately 18,000; those of all the Western Allies put together certainly did not exceed a few hundred.

The Austrian resistance was also active on both fronts. These outlawed groups formed in clandestine fashion during the days leading up to May 1945 and generally worked in isolation from one another. Individuals and tiny units—demonstrating tremendous personal courage and literally putting their lives on the line—succeeded during the final days of the war in conducting small-scale operations designed to support the Allied advance or to thwart the final acts of insanity of the disintegrating regime. By doing so, their objective was to make a contribution to the liberation of Austria.

In Vienna, for example, the group led by Major Carl Szokoll was able to feed information to the Red Army on *Wehrmacht* strength and troop concentrations in that theater of battle. However, a planned uprising within the city itself did not come off, and Major Biedermann, Captain Huth, and Lieutenant Raschke, members of the Austrian resistance movement whose plans had been uncovered, were summarily executed. As U.S. forces approached Innsbruck, the resistance movement succeeded in assuming power in the Tyrolean capital, where U.S. troops entered a liberated city in which red-white-red Austrian colors—and not white flags of surrender—were flying, and they were greeted by the resistance movement's chairman, Dr. Karl Gruber, and anti-Nazi segments of the population. The Americans found that they were generally "cheered as liberators in Austria, and when there are tensions, then it is mainly with the Germans."

## Liberation

The end of the war had many faces. How people experienced it essentially depended upon their own personal circumstances as well as the behavior of the liberators who had marched into their country. The prevailing mood of the populace during those days was no doubt one of relief that the carnage—in battle at the front and as a result of the bombardment of Austria itself—was over; hope that the men in uniform had survived and would soon be returning home; and, to be sure, a more or less vague sense of anxiety about what the future would bring to a land that would now be occupied by the armies that had liberated it. Among those liberated were the victims: survivors of the concentration camps (Mauthausen and its dreadful subsidiaries) and inmates of "re-education camps," POWs and foreign forced laborers, prisoners of the Gestapo, the handful of Jews who had survived in hiding, and the Gypsies who had not yet been rounded up. Also justified in feeling that they had been liberated were those who now saw bright prospects for the future: advocates of a unique Austrian identity and an independent Austria, Catholics and Communists, Jehovah's Witnesses, and proponents of the new democratic parties. On the other hand, National Socialists—who, after all, made up about a fifth of the adult population—must have perceived these days as a time of collapse and the end of the war as a defeat. Many knew that they now had every reason to fear punishment and retribution. For some, the consequences were drastic, and there was a dramatic increase in the suicide rate.

Even the first statements issued by the Renner government that had been installed by the Soviets show clear signs of ambivalence. For example, the government's declaration of 27 April 1945 (presumed to have been composed by Karl Renner himself) referred to a war "that had long since been lost" and stated it was now time "to put an end to it." In response to this, Alfred Ableitinger wrote, "Thus, it was not characterized as the war that also liberated Austria and which now ought to be brought to a successful conclusion. The government thereby adopted a view that was probably held by most of the population—enough of this war, in which it had been the Allies rather than the Third Reich that had been the enemy."

Thus, the end of the war in 1945 was not a collective experience, since the circumstances, perspectives, and perceptions of the people who lived through those days were, even in spite of long years of ideological indoctrination, absolutely dissimilar. Particularly for soldiers in the *Wehrmacht*, it was probably not easy to realize that they had been defeated and liberated, defeated and, therefore, liberated.

## The Behavior of the Victors

It was not only people's personal attitudes towards the Nazi regime but also the behavior of the troops who marched into their country that determined the relationship between the Allies and the Austrian people, and it was above all the soldiers of the Red Army who often made it difficult to speak of liberation. In the initial phase, murders and rapes, plundering and theft were daily occurrences, and the local Soviet commanders seemed powerless to stop it. Various sources report that between 70,000 and 100,000 women of all age groups were raped in Vienna alone through June; in the Soviet-occupied parts of Styria, 5,000 women and girls were raped; in Lower Austria during the month of July alone, over 1,000 rapes and 112 murders were committed by Soviet soldiers, along with several cases of kidnapping. It is impossible for these raw numbers to capture the existential, mental, and physical suffering of these women, the victims of the "liberators."

It was not until Tolbuchin and Malinowski's units were relieved by the occupation troops under Marshall Konev at the beginning of July that there was a distinct improvement in the public safety situation in the area under Soviet control. In the west and south, on the other hand, there were only isolated instances of physical attacks or rapes; the troops were more disciplined, and, at the same time, the soldiers could fraternize more liberally and with other means. The French considered Austria a friendly country, and most of their soldiers conducted themselves accordingly. The Americans, however, initially did not differentiate between Austrians and Germans, and the Austrians' painful realization that the American authorities regarded them as a vanquished and not as a liberated nation was long a source of disappointment. The British were also forbidden to fraternize at the start; nevertheless, the relations between the Anglo-Americans and large segments of the population seem to have developed well for the most part. The troops became less and less observant of the ban that was designed to prevent non-official contacts with the locals. In the words of one GI, there was a lot of "fraternizing material" around.

For one thing, contact with occupation soldiers promised material advantages. Scenes depicting an American GI showering his blonde girlfriend (played by Marlene Dietrich perhaps) with coffee and nylon stockings became virtually a cinematic cliché. The soldiers had access to foodstuffs and other luxury articles of which civilians could only dream. Soldiers could give them as gifts to someone for whom they cared, or they could use them as payment for "services rendered" (prostitution).

Moreover, fraternization was also an attractive option for Nazis, many of whom attempted to use their wives or daughters to gain the sympathy of key representatives of the occupation powers. Tyrolean Governor Karl Gruber alluded to this phenomenon in his inimitable fashion when he assured the occupation authorities that "there aren't any werewolves around here; at the very most, there are 'were-cats.' But the means that the Counter Intelligence Corps is using won't catch them."

A few other aspects that may be assumed to have played a role in this were, briefly noted, fascination with the victors, and—in cases where women had relationships with black GIs or soldiers from French or British colonies—the exotic attraction of that which is new and strange, rebellion against Nazi racial teachings that had been hammered into them over the years.

Some Austrians were very strongly opposed to fraternization. Women who got involved with occupation soldiers were called whores, were threatened, and had public campaigns organized against them, whereby moralizing zeal, more or less blatant racism, and perhaps even jealousy played a role. In such instances, macho, reactionary, and even Nazi stereotypes came out into the open. Finally, those women whose amorous relationships had predictable consequences were not infrequently abandoned—"the 'burden left over' from the occupation era was theirs and theirs alone to bear."

## Liberated—Occupied

Austria in 1945 actually did display a "double character"—it was liberated and occupied. The longer the occupation lasted, the more the aspect of liberation became overshadowed in people's minds as well as in the political rhetoric of the day, and that of occupation, which was increasingly perceived to be unjustified and, indeed, brought with it massive restrictions on state sovereignty and the imposition of the occupation powers' will upon Austria, became ever-present. A number of more or less clearly defined stages can be identified during the ten-year occupation era.

### The Military Administration (from the end of the war to the First Control Agreement)

The immediate postwar period was marked by chaos and by modest, localized attempts to organize everyday life. Everything depended on the military administration that had been installed, and which, on the divisional level, had put officers in charge of the civil administration. Conditions differed not only among the four occupation zones and from province to province, but also with respect to individual divisions, and a great deal depended on the skill and goodwill of the particular local commander. This initial phase was marked by what Kurt Tweraser called "military Josefinism" in the sense of "everything for the people, nothing by or through the people."

Nevertheless, some commonalities can be identified. The military commanders had to ensure the security of their troops as well as to maintain law and order, and to do so as military circumstances dictated. Their mission was to dissolve and ban the Nazi Party, its organizations and subsidiaries, and intern leading Nazis; to arrest war criminals; to consider National Socialist laws null and void; to halt all forms of discrimination based on racist ideas or other National Socialist thinking; to ban political activities until further notice; to purge the civilian administration of *"Reichsdeutsche"* (those originally from Germany) and National Socialist elements; to keep control of and provide for refugees and displaced persons (DPs), whereby Allied citizens and victims of Nazi barbarism were to be given preferential care and treatment, and all DPs were to be repatriated as quickly as possible; and finally, to supply the civilian population with foodstuffs, to make it absolutely clear to them that Austria had been separated from Germany, that Nazi rule was over, and that the Allies, as they had already set out in the Moscow Declaration, wished to see a free and independent Austria re-established.

The Red Army carried out orders to immediately turn over the civilian administration to Austrians. Even while fighting was still raging in eastern Austria, Soviet officers were installing mayors and re-establishing district administrations, whereby they frequently followed the suggestions of the local populace. In the west and south as well, Austrian civilian administrations were set up relatively quickly—sometimes too quickly, so that embarrassing snafus were the result. In the U.S. zone, for instance, old National Socialist mayors often remained in office "for the sake of expediency—subject to removal and/or arrest later by other units of the Military Government."

By the end of May, provisional provincial governments had been installed in all Austrian provinces, though the processes of setting them up covered a wide spectrum—ranging from the transfer of administrative duties from old Nazi officials to representatives of the re-established democratic parties (in Styria and Carinthia), the assumption of power by the executive committee of the resistance movement (Tyrol), and installation by the military authorities (Vienna, Lower Austria, Salzburg, Upper Austria, Vorarlberg).

As the *Wehrmacht* was collapsing, all the Allies were attempting to occupy as much territory as possible by the end of the war, so that the borders of their respective zones were not congruent with the definitive occupation zones that the European Advisory Commission had designated in early April. The first Allied Control Agreement on Austria was not signed until 4 July, followed by the agreement on occupation zones of 9 July 1945. In July, the "zone swap" took place—the French replaced the Americans in Tyrol, the British took over most of Styria from the Soviets, Tito's partisans (in the south) and the Americans (in the northwest), and the Soviets got the remainder of the Mühlviertel, which had been in American hands until then.

At this point, military governments were installed in the zones as well as the individual provinces, and these were installed to control the provincial governments. Military commissioners for Austria were named at the beginning of July: Marshall Ivan S. Konev for the Soviet occupation zone, Lieutenant General Richard L. McCreery for the British zone, General Mark W. Clark for the American zone, and General Marie-Emile Béthouart for the French zone. At the same time, as members of the Allied Council, they were the supreme authority on all questions having to do with Austria as a whole—though certainly acting in accordance with the instructions from their respective governments. The Allied Council met for the first time on 11 September 1945. In contrast to Berlin, all four major powers in Vienna expressed from the very outset their will to cooperate, and the Allied Council remained functional even during the hottest phase of the Cold War.

Before the Western Allies had even entered Austria, the Soviet Union had agreed to the establishment of a provisional federal government under Karl Renner in Vienna on 27 April 1945. This government was the Soviets' contact for issues having to do with Austria as a whole, although its authority initially did not extend beyond the Soviet-occupied portion of Austria. Nevertheless, from the outset, the "provisional government" acted "as if it spoke for all of Austria, and, in doing so, received broad support from the Soviets." But this was a fiction—even three months after it had been constituted, the central government knew practically nothing about conditions in the provinces outside the Soviet zone, and its ability to exert its influence there was virtually nonexistent.

The members of the Austrian government regarded the First Control Agreement of 4 July as the turning point in occupation policy. During the cabinet meeting of 10 July 1945, Chancellor Karl Renner stated: "Up to now, actually, has been war. [!] Now we want to start working on the peace." Leopold Figl also had the impression that a dramatically positive change had taken place, particularly in the relationship to the Soviet occupation authorities. What also had a tremendous impact on the government's work was the fact that, at the beginning of September, the Western powers finally moved into Vienna, opening up new latitude for action and constituting a counterweight to the Soviet presence.

Now the Renner government also had to be established upon a broader footing before the Western powers would recognize it. At the first all-Austrian "provincial conference" held 24-26 September, two key changes were made to the government: in light of the elections that were to be held as soon as possible, authority over the Federal Election Commission was taken away from the Communist secretary of the interior and transferred to a People's Party (ÖVP) undersecretary, and Tyrolean Karl Gruber was named foreign secretary. At last, the four Allies resolved their differences with respect to recognition of the Renner government. On 20 October, they voted to expand the authority of the federal government to include all of Austria, which amounted to *de facto* recognition.

*The Phase of "Direct Administration" by the Allies (from the First to the Second Control Agreements)*

After the Austrian people impressively demonstrated its capacity for democracy in the elections held for parliament and the provincial legislatures on 25 November 1945—the conservative ÖVP had won 49.8 percent of the votes and eighty-five seats in parliament, the Socialist Party 44.6 percent (seventy-six seats), and the Communists 5.4 percent (four seats)—Austrians considered continued Allied occupation to be senseless.

Of course, the Allies did not see things quite that way. The recognition of the Austrian government and the democratic elections was a political watershed for them as well, but first they wanted to ascertain whether and how the central administration in Vienna would be able to help them. Indeed, the First Control Agreement stipulated that "once a freely elected Austrian government recognized by the four powers has taken office," a new agreement concerning the control mechanism was to be worked out and implemented. Now, the "direct administration" that had been necessitated by the absence of a central government could actually be transformed into an indirect one consisting of supervising the administration that had once again been placed in Austrian hands.

The Allies already began discussing this issue in late 1945, but the negotiations dragged on and on, and it was not until 28 June 1946 that the so-called Second Control Agreement went into effect. In it, however, the four occupation powers still retained the right of direct intervention in a few areas that they considered absolutely essential to guarantee the security of the occupation troops, to maintain order in the land, and to look after their political and economic interests in Austria. The most important new element of this control agreement was contained in the provisions of Article 6, which allowed Austrians to pass legislation (with the exception of constitutional changes) and to implement simple legislative measures, and these would go into effect automatically if the Allied Council did not unanimously veto them within one month. Doing so would require consensus among the occupation powers. On the one hand, this provided Austria with a buffer to absorb any potential shocks that might result from global tensions developing among the "Big Four" as the World War II alliance made the transition into the Cold War; on the other hand, differences among the Allies had the effect of increasing the latitude in which Austria could maneuver. This control agreement considerably expanded Austria's sovereignty.

The removal of restrictions on passage from one zone to another— though the Allied checkpoints remained in place—enabled progress to be made in standardizing the federal territory in an economic respect as well. Up to this point, the inter-zone checkpoints had all too often proven to be an insurmountable barrier in many respects, and sealing off the respective zones had led to each of them pursuing their own trade policies.

The significance of the Second Control Agreement as a milestone in the Allies' Austrian occupation policymaking, as a decisive step forward "in the process of turning over Austria to the Austrians" in the words of a report by the American high commissioner for

Austria, has been recognized not only by contemporary observers but also by historical scholars.

In the wake of the Second Control Agreement and its implementation regulations, the occupation authorities were relieved of certain tasks and prescribed new working methods. The military governments were then reduced in size. Some of their areas of authority were transferred to the Austrians, and these organizations increasingly became oversight bodies whose direct intervention was more and more limited to the prerogatives specified in the Second Control Agreement.

## The Occupiers Stay—Until 1955

Although the Second Control Agreement had meant considerably increased autonomy for Austria, this did not bring independence and sovereignty, which could only result from the withdrawal of the occupation troops and the conclusion of a State Treaty. This took a long time to occur. The longer it took, the clearer it became that Austria had become enmeshed in the "machinery of power politics," as Manfried Rauchensteiner has said, and the fate of this country—and thus the end of the occupation as well—would be decided chiefly in the four Allied capitals.

A proclamation issued by the Council of Ministers on the occasion of the fifth anniversary of the founding of the Second Republic thus stated:

Five years after its rebirth, Austria is still not free. Austria is still occupied, although it has been called the first victim of Hitler's aggression, and the Allied powers have expressly declared that the re-establishment of a free Austria is one of their objectives. The Allied powers bear sole responsibility for the continuation of this unfair occupation.

These feelings of frustration then also gave rise to that mental image that would become fixed by 1955—that of Austria as the victim of prolonged occupation, whereby, in many instances, outrageous oversimplifications that played fast and loose with the facts equated the period from 1938 to 1945 with the postwar era.

In the phase beginning in 1947, it became increasingly clear that the intensification of the Cold War would also have consequences for the relationship between the occupiers and the occupied. The fault lines of the global conflict ran right through Austria, and in the view held by the overwhelming majority of Austrians, who had already sent a clear anti-communist signal in the 1945 elections, the occupiers in the western zones—the Americans, British and French—now became guardians, and the Soviets were what they had always been for most Austrians: the foe.

This image was reinforced by some of their actions. Immediately after they marched into Austria, not only did the Soviets lay claim to and dismantle machinery and even entire factories, they also requisitioned all assets stemming from so-called "German property" located in their zone in 1946. The reaction of the Western powers was to demonstratively renounce their share of German property, a move that they were then able to capitalize on for political and propagandistic purposes. While the USSR was siphoning off assets worth a total of $2-2.5 billion from its zone up to 1955, $500 million in financial assistance—coming primarily from U.S. sources, and even before the Marshall Plan—flowed into the Austrian economy. Marshall Plan aid came to almost $1 billion, whereby Austria, with $132 per capita, received the second-highest proportionate amount of European Recovery Program (ERP) funds, as compared to $19 *per capita* for West Germany. Whereas the Soviet zone thus had to pay reparations, the western zones received the lion's share of U.S. aid (over 80 percent). The Marshall Plan launched the economic take-off and also made an essential contribution to the psychological stabilization of the country.

The Austrian budget was deprived of tax remittances from the businesses amalgamated within the Administrative Authority of Soviet Assets in Austria (USIA), and the fledgling republic also had to pay the costs of the occupation as set by the Allied Council. But once the Allies realized in 1946 that the burden they had imposed upon Austrian economic output was greater than that which Hitler's occupation forces had squeezed out of the western European countries, a 35 percent limit was placed on occupation costs as a proportion of all Austrian state expenditures. (Of this amount, 1/2 went to the Soviets, and 1/6 to each of the Western Allies.) Up to this point, the Red Army maintained about 150,000 men in Austria, as compared to slightly more than 40,000 GIs and approximately 55,000 British troops. French troop strength had been 15,000 in January 1946 before being reduced to 7,000 by the following May.

In the summer of 1947, the United States waived further reimbursement for its occupation costs, and even refunded to Austria all such sums paid since 1945! Over $300 million was returned to the republic, prompting Chancellor Figl to emphatically note that from then on the Americans were "paying guests" in Austria. It was not until 1953-54 that the other powers followed suit. The Soviets showed the way, and the British and French did not want to get shown up. Indeed, during the intervening years, expenditures to cover the occupation costs had declined to about 3 percent of the state budget—an amount that Austria would have had to spend anyway for a modest armed force of its own. Once they started to pay their own way, London wished to reduce its occupation contingent to a single battalion, and Paris withdrew all troops with the exception of 400 men in Vienna and a few officers and *gendarmes* in Tyrol and Vorarlberg. American units thus became the sole remaining countervailing force to the approximately 40,000 Soviet soldiers in Austria.

The thaw of 1953—what Rauchensteiner called the "Russian weeks"—brought even more relief to the occupation regime: the zone borders became lines of demarcation, and the often painstaking and always feared inspections conducted there became a thing of the past; Allied censorship was discontinued; the Soviet Union (as the last of the four powers) now replaced its military commissar with a civilian diplomat, Ambassador Iljitschov; and the Raab government let Moscow know how interested Austria was in resuming the State Treaty negotiations.

Julius Raab became chancellor in April 1953. His policies were able to take advantage of a global political window of opportunity—in Washington, a new administration under Dwight D. Eisenhower had taken office in January, and following Stalin's death on 5 March, new men were in charge at the Kremlin—and were crowned with success. More than anyone else, Raab recognized how important it was to pay attention to the Soviets' frame of mind and to take their security interests seriously. One of the best expressions of this was his now-classic line that there was no point in "delivering resounding soap-box oratory that only succeeded in pinching the tail stump of the Russian bear now encamped in the middle of Austria's garden."

During the decisive negotiations in Moscow in April 1955, it was Raab who got the Austrian government delegation to insert a declaration of intention in the Moscow Memorandum to the effect that, after the consummation of the State Treaty and following the withdrawal of Allied troops, they would throw their weight in parliament behind legislation mandating future Austrian neutrality based on the Swiss model. This decision was not only the result of Soviet pressure; as Raab later explained to Swiss diplomats, there was a second motive behind it—solidly establishing Austria's own independence:

In certain circles, particularly among the followers of the party of the 'Independents,' the idea of an Anschluß with Germany had never really been laid to rest. In his opinion, there would be no better way to cut the legs out from under it than precisely this declaration of Austrian neutrality. He indicated that the case of Switzerland, which had already existed for centuries as a separate country independent from Germany, is one that he personally bore in mind as a vivid example worthy of imitation. He was thoroughly convinced of the necessity of neutrality as Austria's guiding tenet.

## "Intervention" by the Allies? Two Case Studies

The re-establishment of a free and independent Austria was the declared aim of all four powers—whereby, naturally, over the course of the ideological-political confrontations of the Cold War, each superpower proceeded under the assumption that this could be realized in exemplary fashion only in its camp. What follows here is an elaboration on two aspects of the Allied occupation policy that were designed to help reach this goal, two aspects of that "process of 'making Austrians' in which almost nobody wanted to admit having been a Nazi anymore, and rather everyone maintained having been a 'good Austrian'": first, the primarily mental and psychological process of separation from Germany, and secondly de-Nazification, which the Allies saw as an effort on behalf of European security.

### The Severance from the "German Reich"

The Third Reich was defeated and destroyed. Nevertheless, the Allies considered all possible varieties of pan-German thought and advocacy of a "greater Germany" to be still virulent in Austria, and they wanted to actively oppose it by means of propaganda and concrete actions. The governmental and economic severance specified by Allied policies was designed to bring about the ensuing mental separation. First, the removal of all *Reichsdeutsche* from civil service jobs was a component of the de-Nazification and re-Austrification efforts undertaken during the first weeks and months after the war. By early summer of 1945, there began the forced repatriation of *Reichsdeutsche*, who had again become foreigners in Austria as a result of legislation passed in the early days of the Second Republic. The expulsion of Germans from Austria was meant to be interpreted as a de-Nazification measure and an effort to make a clean break with the past. Of course, it was inevitable that this program would run up against limitations sooner or later, and many exceptions were made. After all, many Germans had settled in Austria and assimilated even before the Anschluß, and many of those who had come after March 1938 were valued technicians, businessmen, and professionals.

A second measure was designed to support this process of growing apart from a shared past—the expedited release and return of Austrian *Wehrmacht* soldiers who had been taken prisoner. Here, the Western powers led the way. The Americans had already repatriated their last Austrian POW in early September 1946, trusting that those soldiers who had been treated well in the United States and had received "instruction in democracy" in the POW camps would constitute a strongly democratic, anti-Nazi element of the population. The British also began to release POWs shortly after the end of the war, and completed repatriation by mid-June 1947.

Paris had decided to go ahead with the release of "non-incriminated" Austrian POWs as early as the beginning of September 1945. Whereas hundreds of thousands of captured German *Wehrmacht* soldiers remained in France until 1948 to work on postwar reconstruction, the vast majority of Austrian POWs were home by May 1946. The decisive factors leading to their quick return were not only Austria's lead in re-establishing the institutions of a sovereign state, but also economic, humanitarian, and propagandistic considerations. Most significantly, this effort supported the "de-annexation" propaganda campaign. For instance, Radio Paris reported: "The recognition of Austria as a free, independent state also liberates its prisoners who, as soldiers of the German *Wehrmacht*, were drawn into the German catastrophe. It was the

German uniforms that held them in bondage for the entire duration of the Third Reich."

Even the Soviet Union repatriated the Austrians faster than the Germans; half of all Austrians were home by the end of 1947, whereas half of all Germans did not return until the end of 1948. In 1948-49 those who remained were "sieved"—some were released, some were sentenced. An amnesty program began in 1953; the majority of the prisoners returned to Austria in 1955, with the rest following the next year. The Soviet Union held its POWs the longest, the conditions in Soviet camps were by far the worst, and the sentences handed out by the repressive Stalinist apparatus made a mockery of Western conceptions of justice; nevertheless, coming as it did during the Cold War, all of this overshadowed the fact that Soviet Foreign Minister Molotov's 1947 declaration that Austrians would be released preferentially actually was the truth. Finally, it must be pointed out that, aside from Poland, the Soviet Union was the country that had suffered the most under the *Wehrmacht*, and the POWs' labor was considered by Moscow as justified reparations.

The generally better treatment given to the Austrians, as well as the emphasis on the differences between them and the Germans and between Austria and the Third Reich, however, also had undesirable side effects. Thus, the American *chargé d'affaires* in Vienna, after reviewing the results of a poll on the subject of war guilt according to which only 15 percent of Austrians questioned acknowledged a "partial guilt," was forced to admit: "It stands to reason that the emphasis on Austria's separateness from Germany results in a corresponding feeling of guiltlessness. Since as a matter of national policy we encourage a separate Austrian nationalism, we cannot be surprised, and should in fact find comfort in the fact, that most Austrians deny ever having had anything to do with Germany."

Indeed, there were also bizarre manifestations of this "differentiation movement." For example, Austrian report cards of the 1940s and 1950s used English, French, and Russian as the names of subjects taught in school, but not German, which was then referred to as the "language of instruction"!

## De-Nazification

The Report of the United States Commissioner released in April 1946 stated: "While it may seem easy to one who has never faced the problem to tell who is a Nazi, that problem is relatively simple compared with the related problem of what to do with those who have been identified as Nazis." The three parties represented in parliament then agreed on a new, multifaceted program of de-Nazification that provided for not only punishment of the guilty ones but also the political and social rehabilitation of former Nazis. Beginning in 1946, de-Nazification in Austria was pursued jointly by the three parties and the four occupation powers. "In Germany, one could have criticized de-Nazification as a policy of the occupation powers, a policy of the victors that had been imposed upon the country from outside, but this was impossible in Austria. Parliament unanimously passed all de-Nazification legislation, and the four occupation powers approved all important de-Nazification measures."

In the immediate postwar period, de-Nazification was conducted in accordance with the Allies' military security needs; at the same time, the National Socialist system in Austria was to be radically rooted out. Mass internments (based on the "automatic arrest lists" and, ultimately, the discretion of military commanders) were the consequence. In contrast to the Western Allies, the Soviets relied from the very outset almost totally—except for a few isolated arrests—on the Austrian authorities. Indeed, there were also forced repatriations of Cossacks and Vlassov soldiers who had fought on the side of the *Wehrmacht*, Soviet POWs and Eastern European laborers. A massive number of persons in whom the Soviets had an interest for some reason or other were transported off to the U.S.S.R.

Following the establishment of the zones and their military governments, the Western Allies' security organizations took over the conduct of the purges in their sectors. At this point, there was only very rudimentary coordination. For instance, the British and, to some extent, the French made use of the Americans' famous seven-page questionnaire, an instrument designed to make it possible to politically comb through the population of a country with which they were unfamiliar—an undertaking destined to fail, especially in light of the limited data processing capabilities of the day. Moreover, the system was based on the assumption that the questionnaire would be filled out correctly and honestly, which certainly could not be presumed. Up to 1946, however, tens of thousands of suspicious persons continued to be arrested and interned by Allied as well as Austrian agencies, who were increasingly integrated into the de-Nazification efforts in the western zones.

Shortly after it was constituted, the Austrian government passed the two fundamental laws that would serve as the state's basis for de-Nazification: the *Verbotsgesetz* (Constitutional Law Banning the NSDAP) dated 8 May 1945 and the *Kriegsverbrechergesetz* (Constitutional Law on War Crimes and Other National Socialist Misdeeds) of June 26, 1945. The *Verbotsgesetz*, which was repeatedly amended and assumed its final form in February 1947 as the National Socialists Law (*Nationalsozialisten Gesetz*), banned the Nazi Party, its branches, and subsidiary organizations. Recidivism was made punishable by death. Whoever had been a member of the NSDAP or one of its paramilitary units between 1 July 1933 and 13 March 1938—when the party was outlawed in Austria—was one of the "illegals" guilty of the crime of high treason. They were considered "the hard core of National Socialism in Austria. Whoever joined the party after the Anschluß was deemed to have exhibited a conformist mentality or to have been put under duress. In 1946, 536,000 former Nazis were registered in Austria including approximately 100,000 'illegals.'" The *Kriegsverbrechergesetz*, the "actual criminal law of de-Nazification," mandated punishment of war crimes in the narrow sense, warmongering, torture, and mistreatment, crimes against humanity and human dignity, expulsion of human beings from their homeland, unjust enrichment, denunciation and high treason against the Austrian people. This law was made retroactive, and was thus unique in modern Austrian lawmaking. Special courts were to be set up to enforce it—People's Courts consisting of two professional judges and three lay judges whose verdict could not be appealed.

At first, the existence of this legislation did not mean very much since the government was not recognized by the Western occupation powers, and the Allied Council had not approved the laws. Recognition finally came at the end of October 1945, and in early November, the Allied Council began to authorize Austrian legislation, with the *Verbotsgesetz* and the *Kriegsverbrechergesetz* approved in the very first session. Until then, the western provinces had the option of adopting the de-Nazification legislation that had been passed in Vienna in an autonomous acknowledgment process, or they could have declined to do so and carried out the purges according to guidelines authorized by the occupation powers. After 10 November 1945, though, the Allied Council decreed that de-Nazification was to be conducted by the Austrian government and the Austrian authorities under supervision of the Allied Council.

There were occupation officials who, for a variety of reasons, approved of this approach. For example, General Béthouart sent the following communiqué to French President Félix Gouin:

The Allies have made complete de-Nazification the chief prerequisite for reducing the pressure they have been exerting. Now, if a purge is necessary, then it must be done quickly, be limited to the active heads of the old Nazi Party, and avoid black-and-white thinking in order to permit the immediate resumption of social and economic life in this country. In fact, recollection of the Nazis' crimes is fading, while the occupation continues to constitute a heavy burden. The Nazis who have been excluded from their occupations or incarcerated are increasingly regarded as victims of the occupation powers and not as criminals. National solidarity is at work in enabling them to increasingly profit from donning the halo of resistance fighters against the occupiers, a halo that can only benefit Germanic thinking of which National Socialism was just one aspect.

At present, the purges are being conducted poorly. Spurred on by the Allies and by the Figl government as well, they run up against the veiled resistance of sympathizers and "defiant ones" occupying positions in the civil service, and the undeniable difficulties in finding capable replacements for a considerable number of experienced officials and trained personnel. If the slow pace [of de-Nazification] prolongs the occupation, the Allies will fail to achieve their objective, and one will wonder whether it would not have been less risky to let the Austrians do it themselves.

That is precisely what happened next.

The Allied Council, for whom the initiation of special legal proceedings in Austria was moving forward too slowly, sent a note to the federal government in March 1946 exhorting it to speed up the trials of Nazi criminals as much as possible. The People's Courts had gotten to work as early as August 1945, though only in Vienna; in the western zones, they were not set up until the spring of 1946—that is, practically a year after passage of the enabling legislation. Until they were disbanded in 1955, the People's Courts in Vienna, Graz, Linz, and Innsbruck initiated legal proceedings against more than 136,000 persons (comprising about 2 percent of the entire population) suspected of violating the *Kriegsverbrechergesetz* or the *Verbotsgesetz*. Charges were filed against 28,148 persons, of whom 13,607 (48.3 percent) were found guilty, and forty-three were sentenced to death.

In addition to the convictions by the People's Courts, there were also a number of—still not adequately researched—guilty verdicts returned by Allied courts in cases involving violent crimes committed by Nazis. Death sentences were handed down fifty-three times in the British occupation zone alone, of which twenty were for war crimes. In the French zone, military courts convicted over 5,000 defendants, many of whom were Nazis accused of violent crimes.

In February 1947, following protracted negotiations and numerous revisions, the Allies finally passed a new law, the National Socialists Law (*Nationalsozialisten Gesetz*). The objective of the *Verbotsgesetz* had been to individually screen over 500,000 registered Nazis; furthermore, it provided for a major exception—the sentences specified by law could be suspended if "the individual in question never misused his membership in the NSDAP . . . and if his behavior prior to the liberation of Austria gave certain indication of a positive attitude toward the independent Republic of Austria."

The *Verbotsgesetz* had thus proven to be impossible to implement. Fully 85-90 percent of all registered Nazis took advantage of this exception provision, and the administration was flooded with petitions for clemency accompanied by attestations of the individual's clean prior record, harmlessness, and positive disposition toward Austria. The new law mandated going over to a collective process. In addition to persons subject to the criminal code, war criminals and, in some cases, illegals as well, the law now provided for persons required to atone for their deeds, subdivided into "incriminated" and "lesser incriminated" categories based on an individual's position within the Nazi system. The "lesser incriminated" Nazis included simple party members and candidates for membership. Of the 537,000 registered Nazis, 42,000 were considered "incriminated." The forms of punishment ranged from forfeiture of political rights to the loss of employment and debarment from practicing a particular profession, all the way to pay cuts and fines.

Even while the provisions of the law were being worked out, the Austrian side came out in favor of placing a time limit on the penalties, which the Allies nevertheless rejected. Finally, in 1948, the Soviets raised a suggestion that led to an amnesty for "lesser incriminated" Nazis that affected about 90 percent of all those registered. Thus, de-Nazification as a mass phenomenon ended in 1948.

At the same time, the legal prosecution of Nazi perpetrators also began to decrease in intensity. Approximately 80 percent of all cases before the People's Courts had been initiated before the beginning of 1948. The cutback in investigational activities was attributable to numerous factors, not the least important of which was that, with the Cold War and greater orientation toward the West, the overall social climate in Austria was slowly changing.

In 1955, after the State Treaty was signed and the occupation troops withdrawn, the People's Courts were dissolved and violent Nazi criminals were tried before a jury. Some of these proceedings ended in scandalously egregious miscarriages of justice; some verdicts had to be reversed due to legal errors on the part of the jurors. In 1957, the Austrian parliament passed the National Socialist Amnesty law which not only resulted in the dismissal of a whole series of charges, but also increased the tendency to trivialize Nazi crimes.

From 1945 to 1955—the time of occupation—the People's Courts handed down 13,607 guilty verdicts; during the next twenty years (1955-1975), there were eighteen findings of guilt out of a total of thirty-nine verdicts. After 1975, not a single defendant accused of Nazi crimes or war crimes was tried in Austria. This recapitulation makes it clear that, in Austria, the criminal prosecution of violent crimes committed during the Nazi period took place almost exclusively during the People's Court era from 1945 to 1955. "De-

Nazification in the sense of eliminating National Socialist organizations doubtlessly did take place in postwar Austria," is how Dieter Stiefel summarized his findings. "De-Nazification in the sense of reducing totalitarian and radical currents, however, is a task that cannot be done once and for all; rather, it is one that a democracy faces continually."

# The Austrian Economy:
# Basic Features and Trends

*Franz Mathis*

As in other European countries, the process of industrialization determined socioeconomic development in Austria during the twentieth century. Beginning in the nineteenth century, it took about 100 years to completely revamp relations of production and the Austrian population's way of life. In place of a predominantly agrarian economic structure with only slight market orientation, little division of labor, and low productivity, there emerged an incomparably more productive economy characterized by non-agrarian activities—initially industrial and commercial and then including a steadily growing service sector—and that also featured a high degree of market integration and division of labor. A mostly rural way of life in which the majority of people went about daily production and reproduction near the subsistence level and which featured high birth and mortality rates was replaced by a visibly more urban lifestyle with smaller households, relatively lower mortality rates and intra-family relations that placed greater emphasis on emotions, as well as a society in which the majority, and not just the select few, could enjoy a rising standard of living and an ever-growing selection of goods and services.

All these transformations, though, did not occur uniformly either with respect to time or geographic location. An initial spurt of industrialization prior to World War I in which only a portion of the Austrian population participated was followed during the crisis-torn interwar years by stagnation or deceleration of the process. After 1945, the transition from an agrarian to an industrial and, finally, to a service economy was completed, so that modernization ultimately encompassed virtually all of Austrian society. At the same time,

Economic reconstruction: The VOEST steel plant in Linz, Austria's largest state owned industrial plant, built by the Nazis during the war and expanded with Marshall Plan funds after the war.

Source: Austrian Institute for Contemporary History, Vienna

these macroeconomic changes were continually accompanied by a plethora of discrete microeconomic events that all too often provided a stark contrast to the generally positive basic trend. The many individual hardships that resulted from the continually arising need to adapt and that were, in many cases, connected with severe adversity and great economic distress constituted—together with the ecological damages that have become increasingly visible of late— the price to be paid for the previously mentioned advances. Indeed, in assuming a critical perspective on the past and with a view toward future developments, it might well be asked whether the price was not too high, and if the goodwill and best efforts of all involved could not have lowered that price somewhat.

As an initial approach to reconstructing a chronology of the secular transformation of the Austrian economy and society, two relatively easily quantifiable criteria come into consideration: the respective degree of urbanization and the structure of the workforce. The lower the proportion of the population that lived in rural regions and/or was engaged in agriculture, the greater the extent to which the economy and society had moved away from the traditional, pre-industrial past and in the direction of a modern industrial and service economy. At the beginning of the twentieth century, approximately 58 percent of the six million inhabitants of present-day Austria lived in communities with a population of over 2,000, a widely accepted statistical boundary between rural and urban living. Thus, even then, the majority of Austrians could no longer be characterized as country folk—as had been the case thirty years before—but were already city dwellers. Yet it must be kept in mind that the largest proportion of this relatively high degree of urbanization was attributable to the disproportionately large imperial capital Vienna, the inhabitants of which comprised 29 percent of Austria's population. About half of the population who registered statistically as residing in "urban" communities lived in Vienna. On the other hand, the rural element clearly predominated in the remaining Austrian provinces. Only Vorarlberg, Upper Austria, and Salzburg had already achieved a degree of urbanization that even approached the national average that was so inflated by the inclusion of Vienna, whereas the situation in the other provinces showed little change from pre-industrial conditions.

On the topic of occupational structure, it is again clear that the statistics for Vienna do not clearly represent conditions for the majority of Austrians. On the basis of statistics for Austria as a whole according to which only 44 percent of the population of the territory within the borders of present-day Austria was engaged in agriculture, the country could no longer be properly described as agrarian; rather, it could already almost be characterized as an industrial state. A look at available data, however, shows unmistakably that industrialization was initially confined to only a few regions, of which the Vienna metropolitan area, due to the size of the imperial capital, exerted a disproportionate influence on the Austrian average. Among the other provinces, it was above all Vorarlberg where, even as early as the turn-of-the-century, industrialization was comparable to that in the Vienna area. In all other provinces, however, a clear majority of the workforce was still employed in agriculture. Except for a few sub-regions like the Vienna Basin and Upper Styria, the industrialization process was still only in its infancy.

Taken alone, the striking deviation of Vorarlberg with respect to both urbanization and industrialization suggests that a close connection existed between the two, and this confirms what has long been known from the experience of other countries: that industrialization triggered urbanization in Austria as well. On the other hand, the example of Vienna shows that urbanization and modernization by no means resulted from industrialization alone; rather, the traditional "centerpoint" functions of a governmental and administrative center like Vienna that tend to foster the formation of urban centers are also still capable of providing a decisive impetus to growth. Thus, increasing urbanization and modernization could also take place by means other than industrialization alone. Aside from the industrial regions already mentioned, the first signs of the transformation of the economy and the society were thus to be observed particularly in larger cities such as Graz, Salzburg, Innsbruck, Linz and Klagenfurt, many of which were provincial capitals. It remains to be shown, therefore, whether the proliferation of the modernization process over the course of the twentieth century was also based on more than industrialization alone.

Before investigating that, though, it is helpful to elaborate on the economic and social changes that began, at least to some extent, in the nineteenth century and proceeded up to the beginning of World War I. These changes were initially accompanied by rapid population growth. The number of inhabitants of the territory that today comprises Austria increased by about 50 percent from the mid-eighteenth to the mid-nineteenth century from 2.7 to 4.1 million, but after 1857, it took only about half as long to achieve the same percentage growth—though the absolute increase was almost double—and reach 6.6 million by 1910. Once again, the impact of this accelerating population growth differed among the individual regions, and the city of Vienna again led the way. Due to its previously mentioned central function within the vast realm of the Habsburg Monarchy and the industrialization going on in the Vienna metropolitan area, the city was particularly attractive to potential immigrants. This was the primary reason—aside from the incorporation of some suburbs in 1890—why the population of Vienna grew so much more rapidly that that of the rest of Austria. In fact, the population grew from 600,000 in 1869 to 2.1 million in 1910. Outside of Vienna, on the other hand, the much slower population increase was attributable to a greater extent to natural growth, that is, to an excess of births over deaths. Indeed, demographic changes could also be considerably more complex, such as in the case of Vorarlberg, where emigration almost entirely cancelled out the natural population increase and the growth that did occur, at least up to the turn of the century, was mostly attributable to immigration.

Nevertheless, the so-called demographic shift took place in Austria as well toward the end of the nineteenth century as a side effect of nascent industrialization and modernization. This was at first characterized by a decline in mortality rates; birth rates initially remained at pre-industrial levels and did not fall significantly until after the turn of the century. These two fundamental values of demographic development got back into alignment at a significantly lower level over the course of the twentieth century. However, there were clear differences here as well between Lower Austria, including Vienna, and the rest of Austria. These differences become even clearer by including data for Vienna alone. First, mortality rates in Vienna had already begun to sink in the mid-nineteenth century; whereas outside of Vienna, this long-term trend did not set in for another forty years, or until shortly before the turn of the century, and birth rates in the rest of Austria remained at pre-industrial levels until the very eve of World War I. Thus, in this respect as well, the inclusion of data from Vienna skews the national average, which yields a distorted picture that does not apply to large parts of Austria. However, both birth and death rates, including infant mortality, initially were significantly higher in Vienna than in the rest of Austria, and that these then declined earlier and faster than elsewhere as industrialization progressed. On the other hand, the processes of industrialization and modernization initially had almost no impact on marriage statistics. The available data do indicate a slight difference between urban and rural practices, but hardly a long-term shift. Rather, the fluctuations evident on a nationwide basis from one census to the next can be traced back to business cycle-related, and thus short-term, changes in economic framework conditions: a good economic climate was reflected in a higher—and bad times in a lower—rate of marriage.

Age at marriage, though, was subject to a long-term shift. If the relatively high average age at marriage in a primarily agrarian society can, in many instances, be regarded as a means to regulate the precarious relationship between a growing population and a limited supply of arable land, then an industrializing society—in which agricultural yields are also drastically increasing—will be increasingly able to dispense with such control mechanisms. The consequence was a long-term drop in the average age at marriage that can be observed throughout Austria from about the 1860s onward. Until then, up to two-thirds of men and far more than a third of women were over age thirty when they got married, whereas the median age then shifted into the 24-30-year-old age group among men and into an even younger bracket among women. Once again, this long-term process that continued up to the outbreak of World War I had already progressed much further in the statistics of the Crownland of Lower Austria—dominated by its capital Vienna, which in 1910 included almost 60 percent of its population—than in the other provinces that were still strongly oriented on agriculture.

Increasing urbanization and industrialization, however, presupposed corresponding changes in agriculture that would enable the urban and non-agricultural population to be supplied with sufficient foodstuffs. Basically, this could be achieved in two ways: either by increasing the productivity of the workforce that was still engaged in agriculture or by importing foodstuffs from abroad—in Austria's case, mostly from Hungary. As far as domestic production was concerned, annual harvests of the most important foodstuffs (wheat, rye, barley, oats, and potatoes) rose between the early 1870s and the last pre-war years in the crownlands that make up present-day Austria from an average of 1.86 million to 3 million tons. This increase of 62 percent thus surpassed the 44 percent population growth rate during the same period. Two components were at work here: increased productivity of land and of labor. Planted acreage remained almost constant with the exception of land used to grow potatoes, which was for the most part associated with previously fallow fields increasingly being converted from a three-field system to a crop rotation system of cultivation. The higher yields per acre resulted from both improved crop rotation and intensified fertilization of fields, which, in turn, was made possible by keeping farm animals in stalls and by the increased use of mineral fertilizer.

Both resulted in a greater volume of work, which initially led to the increased use of the labor of the agricultural workforce and subsequently to greater mechanization of farm work. This brought about a rise in labor productivity, that is, per capita output of the agricultural workforce as measured by the yields of potatoes and grains cited above which can be calculated purely arithmetically at about 75 percent. The domestic stock of farm animals did not increase as sharply as harvests over the same period; in 1910, cattle showed a 9.5 percent increase and hogs a 102 percent increase over 1869, whereas sheep numbers declined by 66 percent. At the same time, though, milk output per cow could also be increased to such an extent that total milk production rose from 1850 to 1910—allowing for the rather imprecise data—by about a third.

Of course, there were also distinct regional differences in the area of agricultural production, whereby Lower Austria and, to a lesser extent, Upper Austria and Styria, which were blessed by natural advantages like the proximity of the metropolitan market, almost always showed better results than the inner-Alpine regions, where the only increases were in potato production and swine husbandry. This was also a manifestation of the increasing regional division of labor, which took into account differing conditions in the various provinces regardless of the fact that this was connected with certain hardships for many farmers who could not remain competitive in the modern market economy. Aside from the unfortunate fate of individual producers, though, agriculture throughout Austria was making progress during the years leading up to the turn of the century, as evidenced by the spectacular increase in mineral fertilizer use and the introduction of farm machinery that was taking place in all crownlands. Although it was of course the larger farming operations that could more easily afford machines, mechanization was by no means limited to them; rather, as can be seen from a comparison of mechanized farms with the distribution of farms according to size, even then medium-sized operation had also gotten started.

Besides increasing domestic production, the non-agricultural population of Austria also had greater quantities of imported foodstuffs available. According to average figures for the period 1905-13, for example, over two-thirds of all cattle brought to Vienna slaughterhouses and almost half of all hogs came from Hungary, as compared to a mere 14.5 percent and 8 percent respectively from the territories making up present-day Austria. More than half of all grain consumed in Austria was also imported from Hungary. In this way, the provisioning of a quickly growing urban population could be assured and, in some areas, even improved. Despite rapid population increase, per capita meat consumption in Vienna remained around 70 kg since the 1860s, while milk consumption more than doubled in the period from 1870 to 1910.

This agricultural development set in place an indispensable precondition for successful industrialization as well as expansion of non-agricultural activities in general. In the area of commercial production, the increased use of machinery and the replacement of human and animal power with energy produced first by running water and coal and then by petroleum and in the form of electric power brought about, above all, two fundamental changes: first, the production of incomparably larger output than in the pre-industrial age and second, new places of production in the form of factories in which far more people were employed than in the workshops of the traditional crafts and trades. Although regional distribution was still unequal, the development of Austrian industry up to the beginning of the twentieth century very much conformed to the pattern of other Western and Central European countries. The first phase of mechanization began in Austria, as in other countries, during the *Vormärz* period prior to the Revolution of 1848 and was concentrated in the cotton textile industry. After mid-century, on the basis of extensive iron ore deposits found in Erzberg in Styria, this was followed by the re-organization of iron and steel production including metalworking in the form of a small-scale iron and machinery industry. In subsequent phases, other industrial sectors, including vehicle manufacturing, the electrical industry as well as paper and chemical production, were modernized or came into their own as independent industrial sectors. As a result of this initial stage of industrialization, Austria on the eve of World War I already exhibited a relatively balanced industrial structure. Austrian industry not only produced for the regions that would later become the Republic, but also exported significant quantities to the rest of the Monarchy. Nevertheless, as far as the scope of its business enterprises was concerned, Austria lagged behind other industrialized nations of comparable size, which may well have been attributable to no small extent to the low purchasing power of the Habsburg Monarchy's domestic market.

Up to World War I, only eighty industrial and mining companies had over 1,000 employees and only eleven topped 3,000. Most of these firms, like the vast majority of the much more numerous small and medium-sized enterprises, had been founded by independent businessmen, whereas other segments of the population like the aristocracy, farmers, employees, and women as well as the state and the banks very rarely figured among those founding new companies. Some of those who started up businesses were native Austrians, but a substantial number of them came from abroad. However, foreign firms owned only a relatively small number of businesses in Austria, so that, despite the relatively large number of enterprises that were founded by persons of foreign origin who later became naturalized citizens, one may quite properly speak of a very much Austrian process of industrialization. Nevertheless, as previously mentioned, this process did not at all proceed in a uniform fashion throughout the territory of present-day Austria, and this was reflected in the distribution of the workforce as well as the location of business operations of large-scale enterprises in the industrial and mining sectors. In 1913, no fewer than thirty-two of the total of eighty large Austrian companies were located in Vienna and an additional twenty-four in Lower Austria. There were eleven in Styria, a province richly endowed with natural resources including iron ore, timber, brown coal, and magnesite, and whose capital, Graz, was Austria's second largest city, whereas only six large firms were headquartered in Upper Austria. Vorarlberg with five was represented far out of proportion to its tiny size, while Tyrol,

Salzburg, Carinthia, and Burgenland had only two large firms among them. Thus, with the exception of Vorarlberg in the extreme west, Austrian industry on the eve of World War I was concentrated in a belt—with branches radiating out to Upper Austria—that extended from the Vienna metropolitan area across the Semmering into Upper Styria and down to the Graz Basin.

Parallel to the industrialization and modernization of agriculture—and, indeed, both as a precondition to and a consequence of it—a complete redesign of the system of transportation and shipping was occurring. Along with the new communication technologies like the telegraph and telephone, it was, above all, the railroad and, after the turn of the century, the automobile that replaced the carriage and the riverboat in Austria too and revolutionized the efficiency of transportation. Railroad construction was begun around the middle of the nineteenth century and brought to a certain degree of completion by the outbreak of World War I; after the armistice, the automobile began its rise to pre-eminence. Railroads were faster and not as dependent upon the weather as traditional horse-drawn wagons, and could haul much greater quantities of freight, the effect of which was to make raw materials and finished goods cheaper, and to expand the dimensions of the market.

Besides the railway system, other areas of the tertiary sector also expanded as a consequence of rising agricultural and industrial production, such as wholesale and retail trade including the system of credit, public administration, and the educational system, which could only be expanded on local, regional, and national levels on the basis of a more productive economy. Also flourishing in the tertiary sector were the hotel and food and beverage industries that could profit from rising per capita incomes and tourism, an activity whose roots in Austria go back to the late nineteenth and early twentieth centuries. Although reliable data from this period on overnight stays—which has become the classic indicator for development in tourism—are either unavailable or have not been adequately compiled, the very substantial level of employment in the hospitality industry nevertheless permits certain conclusions. Though the minor differences between the individual provinces should not be overrated, it is certainly striking that just prior to World War I no province had a higher proportion of employment in the hospitality industry than Salzburg, which would later be among the "classic" tourist regions.

In the long-term process of socioeconomic development, the two world wars and the interwar period constituted one long hiatus, so that many aspects of the processes of industrialization and modernization did not resume until after 1945. First of all, the years of World War I brought, besides unimaginable bloodshed, the numerous impairments to economic life which are typical of war. The mobilization for military duty of many male workers and their rather inadequate replacement by women, as well as the increasing orientation of means of production and transportation on the requirements of war led to a sharp drop in production of civilian goods and foodstuffs, and this was tangibly exacerbated by the disruption of foreign trade.

The wartime slump was ultimately of a short-term nature; the new borders drawn after 1918 would prove to have a much more serious impact on subsequent developments. Overall, there were five chief factors that prevented the more positive development of the Austrian economy between the two world wars:

1. The economic shocks of the war years and the immediate postwar period led to considerable bottlenecks in supplying customers with foodstuffs, energy, and raw materials, which led to cutbacks in production and runaway inflation.

2. New international borders, the effects of which were worsened by the nationalistic economic and tariff policies of the Habsburg Monarchy's successor states, cut established trade relationships, blocked access to traditional markets, and thus impeded the return to prewar production levels.

3. The contraction of the domestic market from 51 to 6.5 million consumers confronted some economic sectors with adjustment problems that were difficult or impossible to solve in the face of stagnating real income, relatively high unemployment, slow population growth, and not very receptive foreign markets.

4. Any trends toward a business cycle upswing in the wake of the currency stabilization of 1922 were rudely interrupted by the global economic crisis after 1929, since it meant a brutal setback for the tiny Republic's economy that was now highly dependent on exports, and the rapidly increasing

unemployment and low incentive to invest resulted in decreased domestic demand for consumer and capital goods.

5. The period between the end of the crisis in 1933-34 and the Anschluß in 1938 was too short to allow the Austrian economy to return before 1938 to the production level of 1913, which had been only marginally surpassed in 1928-29.

In light of such unfavorable conditions, the chief indicators of modernization cited above—namely, the degree of urbanization and industrialization of Austrian society—did not change significantly between the wars.

The "urban" proportion of the population, once again measured by communities with more than 2,000 inhabitants, showed an insignificant increase from 62 percent to 63 percent from the census of 1910 to that of 1934. The deceleration of the urbanization process was chiefly attributable to the drop in population of Vienna, which had been deprived of its central geographic location and many of its functions. Vienna's population declined to 1.9 million due to emigration as well as, to a much greater extent, a drastic decrease in births. Nevertheless, the increase in the "urban" population of the provinces was also below its prewar rate. At the same time, the dissimilar developments in Vienna and the rest of Austria resulted in an expansion rather than an acceleration of urbanization during the interwar period. The structural transformation of the Austrian workforce also clearly slowed down in comparison to the prewar years, and this was also accompanied by an initial trend toward evening out regional disparities. On one hand, the proportion of the workforce engaged in agriculture, which had declined by 4 percent nationwide between 1900 and 1910, went down by a mere 3 percent in the twenty-four years up to 1934; on the other hand, the decline in the provinces in which this trend had had less of an impact in the past (with the exception of Burgenland) was now more evident than was the case in, for example, Vienna, Vorarlberg, and parts of Lower Austria and Styria, where industrialization had already been highly pronounced. Thus, if the relative significance of agriculture is regarded as a criterion for greater or lesser modernization, then the distribution of the workforce suggests that, on the whole, the modernization process had indeed slowed down in comparison to the beginning of the twentieth century, but had simultaneously spread out on a regional basis so that a process of convergence of the individual areas began to emerge.

In addition to urbanization and the relative diminishment of the significance of agriculture, the same phenomenon could also be observed in other areas of socioeconomic development. Instead of the relatively rapid population growth that brought Austria's population up to 6.8 million by 1913, there came at first a war-related decline to less than 6.5 million in 1920 followed by an increase by 1937 to 6.75 million, a number slightly below the prewar figure. Behind this stagnant overall demographic development, however, was a regional shift in the direction of more balanced distribution. Primarily due to Vienna's population decline, the number of inhabitants of the three eastern provinces—Vienna, Lower Austria and Burgenland—fell by about 3 percent between 1910 and 1934, whereas population rose by approximately 8 percent in the south and west. Indeed, this shift was only the beginning of a development that would strongly accelerate, particularly in the 1940s.

The divergent development of the Vienna metropolitan area and the rest of Austria was also reflected in basic demographic data. On one hand, the long-term decline of mortality (especially infant mortality) rates—after a short-term rise during the war—continued in both areas at the same speed, with the general rate reaching thirteen per thousand in 1937, and the rate for infants declining to ninety-two per thousand (and even sixty-four in Vienna alone in 1935). Birth rates, on the other hand, fell in Vienna much more sharply than in the other provinces, dropping continuously to a mere five per thousand in 1937, whereas the decrease was only to thirteen per thousand for Austria as a whole. The relatively low mortality and birth rates might give the impression that the demographic shift had already reached its final phase in which the two values had converged at a much lower level. This was indeed the case with mortality rates, but not yet for birth rates, which would take off once again after 1945. Thus, the low values during the 1930s were less the result of a highly developed economy and more the effect of a pronounced crisis that resembled similar situations in the past. Consistent with this picture were also the particularly low values—and even below those typical of modern industrialized nations—recorded in Vienna, which suffered much worse than the rest of Austria from the crises of the interwar years and, above all, from the loss of many of its functions as the capital of an empire with a population of 50 million. The adverse economic conditions, in turn, influenced marriage rates, which, after a certain catch-up phase during the immediate postwar years, fell to an average of only 7.6 per thousand inhabitants in the early 1930s in Vienna, and the national average fell to a mere 6.9 per thousand inhabitants by 1937.

Besides declining birth rates, the reversal of the migration trend also contributed to the stagnation of the demographic development of interwar Austria. In contrast to the late nineteenth and early twentieth centuries when a considerable portion of the population increase was attributable to immigration particularly to Vienna, after 1918 there were more emigrants from Austria than immigrants to it. This also reflected the country's dire economic straits and stagnant development during the 1920s and 1930s, which is discussed in more detail below.

In provisioning its population with foodstuffs, Austria after the collapse of the Monarchy was much more reliant upon its own farmers than before. Despite the fact that domestic producers initially failed to satisfy the population's food requirements primarily as a result of war-related production cutbacks, the situation improved continually thereafter. This was not attributable to an expansion of acreage under cultivation or growth of the agricultural workforce, but—as a continuation of trends established earlier—resulted from the increasing productivity of land and labor. Although productivity growth was considerable in comparison to the war years and immediate postwar period, it remained relatively modest compared to the last years before the war. The average total harvest of wheat, rye, barley, and oats during the period 1930-37 exceeded the 1910-14 figure by a mere 4 percent. Only potato and sugar beet harvests exceeded those of the prewar years by 87 percent and 109 percent respectively. There was a negligible increase in the total stock of cattle, while the number of hogs grew somewhat faster, though sheep continued to decline. The number of dairy cows and their milk production, though, was clearly higher. Nevertheless, since the agricultural workforce had declined by only 11 percent between

1910 and 1934 and the total volume of agricultural production rose by a mere 4 percent, the increase in labor productivity remained a modest 16 percent. Additionally, the mechanization of agriculture in Austria continued though at a slower pace than before. In 1930, the approximately 433,000 Austrian farms were already using a wide variety of machinery to chop feed, reap, mow, and sow, but only about 70,000 were powered by electrical or gasoline engines, and there were only 720 tractors.

Stagnation instead of ongoing development also characterized industrial production between the wars. Many firms struggled to adapt to the new conditions since they were oriented on a much larger market than existed in the new post-1918 Austria. Certainly, over the course of the 1920s, there was a successful effort to better utilize existing overcapacity, but the production volume of 1913 was never equaled by 1929, much less following the decline in production in the wake of the global economic crisis. Things were not any better in the crafts and trades, and the situation was especially bad in the construction industry, in which the 1937 output was, respectively, three-quarters and a mere one-half of the prewar level. The sole success story was electricity production, which, after earlier starts and thanks to plentiful and inexhaustible hydroelectric power that made for far more favorable natural preconditions in comparison to coal, went through an initial expansion phase during the interwar period and grew continually to over twice its prewar level.

Structural and business cycle problems during the interwar years had a particularly strong impact on large Austrian firms—that is, companies with over 1,000 employees. During the period between 1913 and 1937, their number declined from seventy-four to only forty-nine, and they employed almost 50 percent fewer people than the large firms of the last prewar years. The Austrian character of their ownership remained intact, despite the fact that the proportion of foreign companies—though not their absolute number—rose from about a fifth to somewhat more than a quarter. However, this was not, as is often presumed, the result of increased penetration of Austrian industry by German capital. In both 1913 and 1937, Germans owned only five of thirteen large foreign companies in Austria. This would not change until after the Anschluß, when, along with many small and medium-size enterprises, nineteen large Austrian companies were taken over by Germans. As far as the regional distribution of large Austrian firms is concerned, it reflects the shift away from the Vienna metropolitan area already cited with respect to population, and in fact the decline there was somewhat stronger than in the rest of Austria.

This same regional shift can also be observed in the tertiary sector. Employment in the service industry in Vienna, Lower Austria, and Burgenland fell by 5 percent between 1910 and 1934, while rising by 9 percent in the other provinces. Factors combining to generate this trend included the population decline in Vienna and the increase in the rest of Austria, and at least the beginnings of the further development of tourism, which, among other effects, created new jobs in the hospitality industry and did so to a greater extent in the western provinces than in the east. Overnight stays (still mostly during the summer season) totaled about 14 million in 1925 and almost hit 20 million in 1929-30. In the wake of the world economic crisis and the 1,000 Mark "barrier" instituted by Nazi Germany, the figure fell to 16 million, before climbing back to the 20 million mark and even slightly surpassing it in 1936-37. Tourism had not yet become a central factor in the Austrian economy, but this development did establish a broader basis for modernization that would go on to assume much greater significance, especially in the less industrialized provinces of Tyrol, Salzburg, and Carinthia.

In summary, it can be said that the process of industrialization mostly stagnated during the interwar period but, at the same time, sectors with great potential for future growth like the electric utility industry and tourism expanded the basis for the modernization of the Austrian economy and society. The stagnation of older areas of the economy and the still rather slow development of new branches that would prove to be driving forces behind modernization went hand in hand with the beginnings of a process of evening out regional disparities, whereby the more highly developed regions were rather stagnant while those in which development had previously lagged were now somewhat more solidly integrated into the modernization process. The interwar period was thus characterized, on the one hand, by a deceleration and, on the other hand, by the first signs of proliferation of socioeconomic development. The groundwork for successful modernization had been done; the ingredients still missing were favorable economic and political framework conditions, which would not be added to the equation until 1945.

Although the Austrian economy experienced a brief upswing after the Anschluß and the population could once again look with optimism to the future—as indicated by skyrocketing marriage figures and birth rates—a precipitous plunge into the deprivation and misery of World War II quickly followed. Despite the initial expansion of industrial production capacity in the form of several large companies located particularly in the Upper Austrian region, war-related destruction, production cutbacks, and the post-1945 dismantling of industrial assets necessitated yet another new beginning. In contrast to 1918, however, a much more positive basic attitude prevailed both with regard to the will of Austrians to carry out reconstruction as well as the international cooperation proffered and the not completely selfless aid provided by other countries to Austria. The most visible and best-known example was the Marshall Plan, which helped the Austrian economy to more quickly overcome bottlenecks in satisfying demand for foodstuffs, raw materials, and capital goods. The pent-up demands of a population that responded in kind to this positive motivation, was relatively well-educated and highly trained, and, thus, increasingly productive and possessing ever more purchasing power, combined with favorable business conditions in the export markets, led to full capacity utilization of both older production facilities—many of which had recently been overhauled—as well as newly constructed plants. By the end of the 1940s, important industrial sectors, public utilities, and the construction industry were surpassing 1937 output levels; instead of a relatively high level of unemployment that rose to a quarter of all non-self-employed persons during the Depression, there was full employment in Austria during the 1960s and 1970s.

In concert with the overall economic upswing that lasted, subject to certain ups and downs, into the 1970s was a marked acceleration of the structural transformation of the economy and society that had commenced in the nineteenth century and slowed during the interwar years. Both urbanization and industrialization quickly got back on track and reached a certain level of consummation in the 1960s and 1970s. Since the divergence of the economic developmental paths that Vienna and the rest of Austria had been on since the interwar period became even more pronounced due to Vienna's peripheral location in post-1945 Europe, more and more regions of the country underwent urbanization. As a result, by 1951 individual provinces displayed a higher degree of urbanization than the Austrian average. Finally, about three-quarters of all Austrians were living in communities of more than 2,000 inhabitants.

But industrialization was not the sole factor responsible for this, since, beginning in the 1960s and by the 1970s at the very latest, employment in the tertiary (service) sector overtook that in the secondary (production) sector. Service industries developed—as they continue to do today—into an additional force promoting modernization, not only as an accompaniment to rising production volume and increasing division of labor, but also as a result of expanding tourism. Urban and, therefore, modern lifestyles were restricted less and less to the cities themselves; rather, thanks to modern communication technology and the mass media, they increasingly spread to rural areas as well. Although there were, of course, regions that hardly or only partially felt the effects of the modernization process, one characteristic that particularly distinguishes Austria is this modernization that initially manifested itself in only a few regions and has since become an almost totally pervasive phenomenon.

Initially, however, the tendency toward regional distribution that was already evident in the case of urbanization could also be observed in the industrialization process. The differences among the nine provinces with respect to the proportion of their respective populations employed in the secondary sector decreased between 1934 and 1951, and once again up to 1961. This was primarily a matter of less industrialized provinces catching up to Vienna, Lower Austria, and Vorarlberg. Nevertheless, the results of later censuses indicated that this industrial catch-up process in several provinces was itself quickly overtaken by another trend.

Even before Salzburg, Carinthia, and Tyrol had reached the degree of industrialization of Vienna and Vorarlberg, for example, the tertiary sector there began to grow faster than the secondary sector. This suggests that the relative decline of agriculture in those three provinces was less the result of increased industrialization than of an expansion of service industries—in this case, tourism above all. Over the course of the gradual transition to a service economy, which, as a rule, occurs only after a corresponding expansion of the industrial sector, they skipped over this phase of increased industrialization to a certain extent. Vienna was the first to achieve a service economy, but Salzburg, Carinthia, and Tyrol approached this state before both the early industrializers (Lower Austria and Vorarlberg) and the later ones (Upper Austria, Styria, and Burgenland). The population of these five provinces and Vienna encompassed the vast majority of the Austrian workforce, so that their path of development constituted the norm, and the experience of the three smaller provinces of Salzburg, Carinthia and Tyrol was the exception.

Besides the degree of urbanization and industrialization and the relative size of the service sector that occurred later, other changes in the economy and society also expressed the continuation, spread and, to some extent, consummation of the process of modernization. As in the years before World War I and in contrast to the period of stagnation between the world wars, population again grew quickly and simultaneously spread out more evenly across the country. In 1971, Austria had 11 percent more inhabitants than in 1937, though this rate of increase slowed considerably into the 1980s and was not reversed until the upheavals that rocked eastern Central Europe after 1989 triggered a renewed acceleration of growth to 7.8 million in 1991. The east-to-west shift that had begun after 1918 assumed larger proportions; between 1939 and 1991, the population of Salzburg, Tyrol, and Vorarlberg had grown by 85 percent, and this area was now the home of a fifth instead of a ninth of all Austrians. On the other hand, Vienna, Lower Austria, and Burgenland showed an almost continual decline in population, and growth did not resume until the second half of the 1980s. Styria, Carinthia and Upper Austria occupied the middle of the field with growth rates between 16 percent and 44 percent. Regional population shifts resulted from a highly complex combination of natural changes and those caused by migration. One very striking feature was that the disproportionately high increase in the western provinces since at least 1951 was chiefly attributable to a temporary increase in birth rates resulting from a need to catch up after a period of extremely low rates, a phenomenon with numerous precedents from prior centuries. It was not until the

1970s that rates again declined sharply in conformity with the final phase of the demographic shift associated with an advanced stage of modernization. This phase had already been reached in eastern Austria and especially in Vienna, so that deaths outnumbered births in Vienna from 1951 to 1991. Nevertheless, despite its decline in size and its now-peripheral location, Vienna obviously remained so attractive that more people immigrated than emigrated, and this prevented an even more dramatic population decline. As had previously been the case with birth rates and, even earlier, death rates, marriage rates throughout Austria began to reflect the general state of modernization as well. Thanks to improvements in the general standard of living, which was, in turn, the result of higher per capita income, more people could then afford to start a family at an earlier stage in life. Soon, though—as was also the case with birth rates—marriage figures also declined, a phenomenon often referred to as the "prosperity effect" and which provides a stark contrast to human behavior during pre-industrial and pre-modern times.

At least as profound as this demographic shift was the transition from an agrarian to a non-agrarian society, a development that likewise was concluded during the postwar decades. The enhanced productivity of agricultural land and labor that had begun prior to 1945 now accelerated, and the result of this was that fewer and fewer farmers were necessary to feed the population of Austria. Whereas in 1951 one agricultural worker's output covered the nutritional requirements of four persons, this figure had already climbed to twenty-three by 1980.

This progress in productivity was triggered by ongoing migration from rural to urban areas as well as by competitive pressures, and was made possible by rapidly accelerating mechanization and improvements in soil cultivation methods and animal husbandry. As in previous decades, this flight from the countryside primarily had to do with non-self-employed agricultural laborers like farm hands and members of farm families, whereas the number of farms decreased much more slowly throughout this process. However, the farms' character changed in that fewer and fewer of them were operated on a full-time basis: only a third in 1980 as compared to almost two thirds in 1950. Simultaneously, Austrian agriculture became even more dominated by medium-size operations as, most notably, the proportion of very small farms declined in favor of those with between ten and fifty hectares of usable land. Probably the most spectacular development was the increase in tractors as perhaps the most visible sign of modernization, although other machines like all-purpose electrical motors quickly became very widespread. There were slightly over 7,000 tractors in 1939; the number was ten times as high by 1957, and there were no fewer than 326,000 in 1982, when the number of horses was one-seventh of the 1950 total. As a result, wheat yields, for example, were two and a half times as high; milk output per cow doubled.

The logical consequence of this progress in productivity was that more and more people were available for employment in the industrial-commercial and service sectors, and since their productivity rose as a result of escalating mechanization and automation, the scope and selection of non-agricultural goods and services increased disproportionately. Between 1955 and 1975 alone, the value of non-agricultural goods produced almost tripled. Rising productivity also resulted in higher incomes—thanks to the distribution of this "growth dividend" in the annual negotiations conducted by the so-called "Social Partners"—and in greater purchasing power. One consequence of this was the enhanced ability of the Austrian populace to acquire consumer durables. To mention just a single example of this development, the number of automobiles rose continually from a mere 51,000 in 1950 to top 3 million in 1991.

All of this—ongoing automation, rapid expansion of the volume of material goods produced, and the somewhat slower and irregular increase in purchasing power—brought about the previously mentioned structural shift that has been underway since about the 1960s and can be regarded as the transition from an industrial society to a service economy. The increasing volume of production tended to lead to at least the partial satisfaction of the demand for material goods and thus to a waning of demand. This, together with the ongoing automation pursued in order to hold down production costs and remain competitive, meant that jobs could now be cut in the industrial sector as well. Since, at the same time, the purchasing power that was still available or even growing was generating greater demand for services instead of material goods, employment in the tertiary sector could continue to increase, though obviously not fast enough to absorb all those whose jobs had been cut in agriculture and industry, which is why unemployment began to rise again beginning in the 1980s, although the yearly average in, for instance, 1992 was still a relatively low 5.9 percent.

Industrialization in the narrow sense reached its highpoint around 1960, and one reflection of this was the number of large industrial and mining companies, which increased after the war to ninety-four in 1960 and then dropped to eighty-six in 1979. One striking feature was the relatively high proportion of state-owned enterprises, which could be traced back to the Nationalization Law of 1946 that transferred former German property to Austrian state ownership. However, these state-owned enterprises—in contrast to those of the Eastern European centrally-planned economies—were integrated into the market economy from the very outset, operating without state-mandated production quotas and, as a rule, behaving like private companies. Any difficulties that any of these companies encountered were attributable to their specific sector of the economy rather than to their ownership structure. Among private sector firms, foreign companies once again took on increasing significance, but they ultimately remained a valuable complement to a core of Austrian-owned firms.

Over the course of the transition to a service economy, tourism became an even more independent sector and one of critical importance to Austria. Focusing specifically on tourism here is justified by the fact that it has contributed more than any other area of the tertiary sector to furthering the modernization process in those Austrian regions in which industrialization alone might not have been sufficient. Although Tyrol, Salzburg, and Carinthia consistently accounted for less than 20 percent of the Austrian population, these three provinces have generated over 60 percent of all overnight stays since the 1960s, resulting in up to ten times as many overnight stays per capita as in the other provinces. The result of this as reflected in the structure of the workforce was that more than twice as many individuals were employed in the hospitality industry in Tyrol, Salzburg, and Carinthia than in the rest of Austria, not to mention the stimulating effects guests' purchasing power had on other sectors of the economy.

Since then, rates of growth in the tourism industry have clearly declined; since the 1980s, the number of overnight stays has fluctuated between 90 and 100 million per year. Furthermore, continued growth will increasingly be inhibited by the ecological stresses associated with it. As with industrial production, further increases in quantity will hardly be the future of tourism; rather, a commitment to environmental friendliness, social responsibility, and excellence of the services provided is a much more promising path. The concept of "quality not quantity" is also completely consistent with the previously mentioned transition to a service economy, a transition that has been underway for several years since the Austrian economy completed the industrialization process, and one that will doubtlessly determine the further course of the modernization of Austrian society.

# "The Big Two": The Grand Coalition, 1945-1966 and 1987-2000

*Manfried Rauchensteiner*

### Introduction

It was the end of March 1945. Soviet armies had penetrated into Austria as part of their offensive operation to take Vienna and had begun to liberate the country from National Socialism. Within a month, American and French troops, and finally the British, Yugoslavs, Romanians, and Bulgarians as well, stood on Austrian soil. In May, they celebrated their victory over the German *Wehrmacht* and its allies—above all Hungary and Croatia. The time had arrived to rebuild Austria. There were, to be sure, preparations being made underground, but it was not until the moment when the Soviets made it clear that they would permit an Austrian administration in the territory the U.S.S.R. occupied that political life actually began. Thus, the Grand Coalition was born.

To go about describing it today seems tantamount to speaking of something as typically Austrian as Lipizzaner horses, the Vienna Boys Choir, yodeling, and skiing. Nevertheless, what appears at first glance to be a political constant of the Second Republic is revealed upon closer inspection to be something rather more closely connected with expediency or even necessity. Actually, it is not very difficult to explain the reasons for this or to elaborate on its consequences, though, in doing so, it can be noted at the very outset that we are addressing an issue that is an essential aspect of the Austrian soul in that it corresponds to the need for peace and orderliness. After all, periods like the Biedermeier Era do not just happen by accident in Austria, and these can certainly not be explained by citing a single cause or even a few factors. Another

The end of the postwar "grand coalition" in 1966: New Chancellor Bruno Kriesky, SPÖ (right), and former Chancellor Josef Raab, ÖVP (left) after the Socialist election victory of 1970.

Source: Institute of Contemporary History, Innsbruck

element that undoubtedly plays a role here is the one that places a peaceful and orderly process of political decision-making right at the side of orderliness as the citizen's utmost duty. Or, to quote Bruno Kreisky's retrospective comment on the end of the first decades of the Grand Coalition:

> When the coalition had finally broke down . . . I deeply regretted it, but for one reason only: not because I believed that we still could have accomplished a great deal more together that could not have been accomplished between the government and

the opposition, but rather because I feared the reemergence of old diametrical opposites and stirring up memories of past conflicts in domestic politics, knowing that the consequences of this would be difficult to foretell.

The key concepts here are fear, diametrical opposites, stirring up memories, and consequences. And, to a certain degree, the Grand Coalition in Austria ebbed and flowed within this range.

For the Grand Coalition of the Second Republic, though, there were at first hardly any opportunities to have recourse to past experience since the short period of cooperation after World War I that lasted from 1918 to 1920 was insufficient either to allow shared approaches to become clear or to enable the partners to point to accomplishments achieved together. Despite their clear success in getting a republic up and running in 1918, the Treaty of Saint Germain soon assumed much greater importance, and it was precisely this peace agreement that was seen as the debacle of the Grand Coalition. Thus in 1945, as the Third Reich and its National Socialist rule were still in the process of collapsing and a community of expediency summoned by the Soviets began to constitute itself in eastern Austria, about the last thing these men had on their minds was to invoke their former ties, which were all of twenty-five years in the past.

This union born of necessity was a rather unusual one in that the people who entered into it were the products of highly dissimilar experiences in political life. At the head of the provisional federal government formed on 27 April 1945 was Karl Renner, a man who had been one of the co-founders of the Republic of German Austria after World War I. Alongside him stood a number of people with at least some political experience, but, otherwise, most were members of the underground or, in the case of the Communists, who had also been invited to participate at first, those who had been in exile—that is to say, inexperienced individuals with good intentions.

The successful formation of that provisional central government brought to a close the initial phase of the Second Republic that had not even been formally established yet. At this point, it was above all Renner, a Social Democrat, who tirelessly brought up incidents from the past—namely, those having to do with the authoritarian regime in

Austria between 1933 and 1938—in order to then segue into the
conclusion that the successors of the Christian Socials would indeed
be invited to participate in the reconstruction of Austria, but their
role would nevertheless be that of a type of junior partner. But
particularly in times such as these, when there is little that can be
said about the balance of political power and the situation was
changing almost from day to day, there were certain intentions that
did not even remain operative beyond the very day on which they
were formulated.

In April 1945, Renner had to come to the realization that his own
position within that community of likeminded individuals that
became the Socialist Party of Austria (SPÖ) was indeed
acknowledged, but not totally uncontested, and that there were
factions both in his own party as well as in the successor party to the
Christian Socials, the Austrian People's Party (ÖVP), who not only
advocated cooperation without preconditions, but also were
democratic in a new way. The fact that the Soviets designated the
Communists as a sort of third force to join in with the Socialists and
the People's Party was not the source of significant difficulties in this
initial phase, though it did provide Austrians with their first taste of
something they would get to know much better later on—the
*Proporz* system. In the provisional central government, the rule was
that a state secretary would be paired with an undersecretary from
one of the other parties in order to assure a nearly foolproof system
of reciprocal oversight. Examining this construction gives rise to the
impression that major coalitions or even unity governments
presuppose a lack of trust and embody the institutionalization of the
motto "trust is good, oversight is better," but in this case, such
assertions were tempered by actual practice which enabled the
provisional federal government to become a viable instrument of a
new beginning for Austria.

Misery and destruction, on one hand, and the Allied occupation of
Austria on the other constituted the framework conditions of this new
start. The beginnings of the Grand Coalition in Austria on the federal
level, however, can only be understood by taking into account the
situation in the provinces and, above all, by considering that the
collaboration of the various political forces there was quickly
institutionalized in that, in the overwhelming majority of the
provinces, the allotment of political responsibility was made in

accordance with the balance of power given by the voters at the polls, and this was officially established in most provincial constitutions. From this perspective, the Grand Coalition on the federal level loses even more of its distinctiveness, since it ultimately appears to be only a sort of concentrated unity government.

Nevertheless, what prevailed at first was not—or least of all—consensus, but rather, first and foremost, constraint—the necessity to assure the survival of the Austrian population, the obligation to re-establish a civil administration, and to re-endow politics with credibility in what had become a political wasteland. In addition, there was the pressing requirement of dealing with the Allies both in direct confrontation within the individual occupation zones and as a collective authority.

The Grand Coalition that already began to take shape in the autumn of 1945 and assumed more distinct contours in the wake of the first free elections of the postwar period on 26 November still maintained its character of a union born of necessity since, after all, its primary task was to get a grip on the pervasive suffering, hunger, and postwar chaos. These circumstances then led the ÖVP, which achieved an absolute majority at the polls, to pass up the opportunity to use this victory as grounds to form a government on its own, but rather—sensibly—to once again form a coalition with the two other parties represented in parliament. Ultimately, it became obvious that the presence of the occupation powers turned out to be an externally imposed military dictatorship. It was quadripartite, though the fact that there was not always unanimity among them was not very significant at first. They did agree that Austria ought to have at least limited sovereignty for a time, and it was only gradually that they gave up the idea that Austria should either be divided up or merged with other states. On this issue, Hungary played a very crucial role. The Moscow Declaration of 1 November 1943 had stated that Austria as well as other countries confronted by similar postwar problems ought to be given the opportunity to enter into economic and political unions "that are the sole basis for a lasting peace." This referred primarily to Hungary. In the meantime, however, a development of a totally different sort had emerged. Austria found itself faced with territorial demands by Yugoslavia and Czechoslovakia, and, in turn, lodged territorial demands of its own. The country's continued existence was more than questionable. But

Hungary never considered even the slightest involvement with Austria, and the Soviets, in particular, made it clear that their postwar plans were of a very different sort. These factors were part of that chaotic initial situation that placed particular demands on the occupied as well as the occupiers.

It is, therefore, easy to see what it entailed to do a responsible job in politically administering a country that was controlled by an Allied Commission, which in turn formed a committee consisting of the Allied Council and its executive board, in which the individual Allies were of relatively limited importance in comparison to the executive committee that held supreme legislative and executive authority. Following the passage of the First Control Agreement of 4 July 1945, all legislation passed by the provisional federal government and, later, by the Austrian parliament had to be approved by the Allied Council before it actually took effect. The only way to deal with this was for Karl Renner's provisional government and then, after the first free elections, for Leopold Figl's first government to present a totally unified front to the Allies. This took the form of a unity government. However, after the elections, the ÖVP and the SPÖ secretly got together on an exclusive coalition agreement that omitted the Communists and laid down the structure of cooperation. There were only a few points formulated at that time, but they clearly demonstrated the intention to divide power between them—that is, to indeed formally involve the Communists, the third party represented in parliament and the government, in the affairs of state, but to not actually permit them to participate in the exercise of power on the federal level. The Christian-Conservative and the Social Democratic camps thus succeeded in reconciling their respective interests and coming up with an agreement that, although not consciously patterned on the historical example of the *Ausgleich* between the Austrian and Hungarian halves of the Habsburg Empire in 1867, did yield a result that was not totally dissimilar.

The very first sentence of the coalition agreement is remarkable: "*Proporz* will apply not only to the formation of the federal government but also to the formation of the provincial and municipal governments." In addition, the ministerial posts were divided up, a coalition committee was formed and given responsibility for "settling differences of opinion and writing bills to be submitted to parliament," and the essential objectives for the next legislative term were outlined. Indeed, the areas to be regulated were merely hinted at, and there was absolutely no consideration given to, for example, the facts that starvation was looming in the winter of 1945-46, that gearing up with reconstruction was proving to be a tough job, that the exact duration of the occupation was unforeseeable, and that the Allies were beginning to make themselves at home in Austria. Nevertheless, the very points addressed in the last paragraph of the coalition agreement of December 1945—namely, remuneration of civil servants, the treatment of Nazis, nationalization, as well as the Chamber of Labor, a health insurance plan, labor unions, and works committees—make it clear that not only was there a tremendous amount of work to be done, but also that the country's unity could be assured only when conjoint regulations were established.

The unity of the land was the issue that the Grand Coalition regarded as its greatest challenge. In facing it, the alarming example of Germany was already acting as a deterrent by 1945-46. The disintegration of the country into a western and an eastern occupation zone and the impossibility of forming a central government and centralized democratic institutions were outcomes that Austrians used all of their power to avoid. In this spirit, all sides were prepared to defer—or "to repress" in the terminology that would later come into use—certain items on their agendas. But it was precisely this process of repression that seemed to be the only way to assure the physical survival of the population and the political survival of the country. The partners knew from the very start that this Grand Coalition was not exactly a match made in heaven, but perhaps they did not realize at the outset how stormy the marriage would be.

By 1946, there were already a series of critical incidents, whereby past history played a role in the sense that things were repeatedly brought up to discredit a particular individual or group. However, the Grand Coalition did hold a day of reckoning with the past by enacting a National Socialist Law in 1946 that provided for punishment of all 540,000 Austrians who had been Nazis. Of these, 470,000 were considered less incriminated, the remainder as incriminated or severely incriminated. All were initially deprived of some of their civil rights. Death sentences were handed down in forty-four cases, as well as prison sentences totaling 30,000 years.

The less incriminated had to at least pay a punitive tax over a period of years. Then, of course, something occurred that is seemingly immanent in every political system: de-Nazification was abruptly terminated, since a half million people were, after all, a half million voters, and each party figured it had better chances of getting them when they came out on behalf of the integration of former Nazis. This led to an explosive growth of the major parties, but could not prevent the formation in 1949 of a new liberal party that succeeded in attracting the lion's share of former National Socialists to its camp.

Perhaps it seems rather strange that in 1946 Austria sent a note to the still-extant League of Nations stating that its membership was still in force. This was meant to suggest continuity as well as to make a clear statement in response to the question of whether Austria had been occupied or annexed: Austria was being occupied.

## Austria, a Land that is Mostly Ruled in Tandem

Certain areas were matters attended to jointly, including, above all, interactions with the occupation powers, the consideration accorded to the prerogatives of the head of state, and the working out of a compromise with the provinces. However, within the Grand Coalition, each of the two major parties began to establish its own "turf." Traditionally, the Socialists sought to set up and expand their organization in areas having to do with the workforce, industry, transportation, and the social welfare system. The supporters of the People's Party, on the other hand, were farmers, industrialists, and small businessmen. Since 1945, there were provinces that were dominated by the SPÖ and those that were dominated by the ÖVP, and the consolidation of this dominance had to be undertaken on a number of different levels: *vis-à-vis* the occupation powers who did not cede their authority—at least in the provinces—until 1953, their coalition partner, as well as the Communists, and the "League of Independents" (VdU) that was founded in 1949 and sought to present itself as the heir to the mantle of both the German Nationalists as well as the traditional Liberals.

The process that then got underway came to be termed "horizontal integration" by political scientists, since, after all, the tendency toward the expansion of power that is inherent in every organization and especially in every political party very quickly encounters its limitations in the realm of "normal" politics. Thus, not only did each party seek to increase its influence by setting up its own organizations for laborers, civil servants and white-collar workers, the self-employed, and the farmers; they also had their subsidiary charitable organizations, rescue squads, and automobile associations, and there were—and still are—even sports organizations, soccer teams, and recreational facilities affiliated with a particular party.

In going about this, the parties achieved an astoundingly high degree of organizational density. Within ten years, both major parties had over 500,000 members. Thus, by the end of the occupation period in 1955, party membership exceeded a million, and the trend was still growing. In absolute numbers, there were as many people organized in the major democratic parties in Austria as there were in West Germany, which had a population eight times as large, meaning that Austria exhibited an organizational density that was eight times as high.

There is no simple answer to the question of why that was so, but a few contributing factors can certainly be cited. In Austria, there seems to have traditionally been a greater readiness to join organizations. Even today, every Austrian—from newborn to senior citizen—is, statistically speaking, a member of at least three associations. In the postwar period, there was the additional problem of de-Nazification. Former Nazis were debarred from practicing their profession as well as having to bear the burden of punitive taxes and all sorts of reparations measures. For those whose only contact had only been with the periphery of National Socialism and above all for the so-called lesser incriminated, it was, therefore, an expression of one's commitment to democracy to join one of the major parties. Thus, it had the effect of softening some of the harsh consequences of having been associated with the Nazi Party. ÖVP or SPÖ membership facilitated (re)entry into one's chosen field and advanced one's career. Then came reconstruction, another area that was dominated by the major parties and their housing construction organizations. Whoever needed an apartment did not simply apply to the government's housing office, but also frequently resorted to party membership to speed up the process. Thus, the parties of the Grand Coalition grew inexorably and expanded their influence.

Nevertheless, merely showing how relatively quickly power corrupts and how, in the present day and age as well, the division of the political spoils takes place and dualism continues as the most quintessentially Austrian form of coexistence and collaboration do not by any means do justice to the Grand Coalition. Without a doubt, this arrangement made a considerable contribution to the positive course of postwar Austrian history and thereby facilitated a form of identification.

In seeking the reasons behind this "success story" of the Grand Coalition, one must almost unavoidably return again and again to the occupation period, since nothing cited as yet has made it possible to understand why this community of necessity developed into something that ultimately allowed a truly historical compromise to take place. The formation of blocs in Europe played an essential role in bringing about this transformation in the internal content of the Grand Coalition. The changes in Hungary in 1947 and, to an even greater extent, the coup in Czechoslovakia in 1948 were shocking to Austria, and this shock was so profound that suddenly those demands that were operative in the formation of this union born of necessity— namely, the conclusion of the State Treaty and the withdrawal of the occupation forces—were dropped. Indeed, we know very well that beginning in 1948 there were repeated protestations that a withdrawal of the Western occupation forces was quite undesirable as long as the country had not been provided with a security guarantee and, above all, prior to the elimination of the danger that many saw in the potential encroachment of Communism from Hungary or Czechoslovakia. The fact that the ongoing stay by Allied troops was desired did indeed change the quality of the occupation, but did nothing to lessen Allied control, arbitrary use of authority, and illegal encroachments that also took place in the western occupation zones. The more or less unspoken but latent readiness to accept the occupation forces ultimately included the acceptance of the material aspect as well, since, with the exception of the Americans, all the occupation powers demanded reimbursement for the considerable costs of stationing troops in Austria and special taxes had to be levied to cover them. Not least of all, Austrians also had to continue to bear the disadvantages of restricted sovereignty, since, for example, until 1955 it was the right of the Allies, according to the Second Control Agreement, not only to supervise the legislative process, but also to veto particular laws. All of these were burdens born to avoid the disintegration of the state, since in 1948 and in the years thereafter as well, there were continual fears that the country would be divided into an East Austria and a West Austria.

The importance of this security concern for the Grand Coalition was such that the continuation of this form of cooperation was from 1948 on actually no longer called into question, and that there was a secret agreement to carry on the coalition until the end of the occupation. The objective of the collaborative effort was thus made unmistakably clear—conclusion of the State Treaty and withdrawal of the Allies.

During the time of occupation, the parties of the Grand Coalition were repeatedly subjected to pressure and concerted efforts to exert influence on them, but they too repeatedly sought the support of one or more of the occupation powers in order to implement their own agendas. The United Kingdom's Labor government, for example, clearly backed the Austrian Socialists; the Americans at first tended to side with the Socialists, and then seemed to favor the People's Party, but ultimately treated the "Big Two" pretty much equally. The Soviets could not work up much enthusiasm for either of the coalition parties, but generally comported themselves with correctness. They were initially able to avoid taking a more direct approach since to do this they had the Austrian Communists who, even as late as 1947, were attempting to break up the Grand Coalition. Indeed, there were other episodes as well that made it clear that the Soviets—in contrast to the Western powers—were not interested in the continued existence of the coalition. For this reason, the Soviets supported the formation of new parties and basically had no objections when the former Nazis who had come together in the VdU began taking on the trappings of a political party and attracting dissatisfied protest voters. However, that could be described at best as an attempt using inadequate means to break up the Grand Coalition and perhaps to allow the Communists to take on more significance in political life.

Among those who brought their influence to bear and occasionally even constituted a truly countervailing force were the Austrian presidents who, all the way up to the 1970s, undertook vigorous efforts to help overcome crises within the Grand Coalition. In so doing, the most active of these heads of state, Karl Renner, and the party that had put him in this office became embroiled in a bitter conflict, since the Socialists viewed such a politically activist presidency with great mistrust. Finally, Party Chairman Adolf Schärf sent a message to Renner reading: "Nip this in the bud!"

In 1955, three processes got underway: the Federal Republic of Germany was invited to join the North Atlantic Treaty Organization (NATO), the Soviet Union sought to restructure its alliance, and it ended its postwar economic regime in that the firms that the U.S.S.R. had confiscated as German property in a whole series of eastern and northern European states and most of which were being operated as bilateral corporations were reorganized, sold, or liquidated. All three processes had, among other effects, direct consequences for Austria and led to the conclusion of the State Treaty, which had indeed been readied ever since 1947 but was now being finalized under totally different preconditions. The two most important of these were neutrality being imposed upon Austria and the settlement of Soviet demands for material compensation.

The effect of both of these was that the alliance of the two major parties in Austria became even closer. After all, the decision in favor of permanent neutrality was a commitment that was supremely in the interest of the state, but one which nevertheless was associated with problems since Austrians had to then fear being cut off from Western Europe. Furthermore, substantial material obligations were assumed in connection with the State Treaty and were provisionally arranged for an additional ten years. All of this together gave rise to the necessity of continuing to work together to wind up the period of occupation.

In a most telling scene following the signing of the Austrian State Treaty, American Secretary of State John Foster Dulles invited the leaders of the major parties, Chancellor Julius Raab and Vice-Chancellor Adolf Schärf, to a meeting at which he rather insistently questioned them about Austria's future political course, and was visibly pleased when both assured him that they would support continuation of the Grand Coalition.

But this was, after all, much more than a domestic political problem, and one ought not lose sight of the fact that even though it proceeded on the basis of a known quantity—namely, the perpetual neutrality of Switzerland upon which Austria sought to orient its course—imposing neutrality upon Austria was a risk. There were two political blocs in Europe at the time, and the danger of a war was very real. We must only recall what Henry Kissinger wrote while the Korean War was raging. He stated that this was the wrong war in the wrong place, and that the real one would be waged in Europe. On 14 May 1955, a day before the signing of the Austrian State Treaty, the Warsaw Pact Treaty was signed in Warsaw, and shortly after these two events, the Federal Republic of Germany's entry into NATO was consummated. Indeed, bloc formation initially has a stabilizing effect since it diminishes individual states' latitude for independent action, but if a conflict does develop, then it is that much larger and more devastating. The worries about subsequent developments being voiced in 1955-56 were surely not exaggerated. Immediately prior to the signing of the State Treaty, the Federal Republic of Germany recalled its *chargé d'affaires* from Vienna, and was the only neighboring state that did not congratulate Austria on having regained its sovereignty. Italy, Belgium, and certain circles in France and elsewhere were skeptical. Thus, it was also a problem of foreign policy calculability, which had initially hardly changed with respect to Austria. Additionally, there were hardly any personnel changes either, since the men at the top were almost all the same. Of course, that also turned into a problem because the change of the generational guard within the parties proceeded only by fits and starts and, for example, it was extraordinarily difficult to get a man like Julius Raab to step aside.

The comparative stability then was useful when it came to managing crises like the Hungarian Revolution that had spillover effects upon Austria; during this time, it was not only a matter of processing approximately 200,000 refugees, but also of responding to the possibility of the fighting spreading onto Austrian territory. During a fire fight in Burgenland, one Soviet soldier was killed and others were captured and held prisoner. Such occasions not only proved the worth of the collaboration between the Big Two; they also showed how advantageous it was to have people with extensive crisis management experience in top leadership positions.

Not the least of the problems facing Austria during the immediate post-occupation period was the considerably retarded development of the former Soviet occupation zone. The enterprises that had been confiscated by the Soviets—that is, most heavy industry in eastern Austria—were run according to the management principles of a planned economy. As a consequence, the entire petroleum industry, shipping on the Danube, and many other sectors had been left with serious developmental deficits. They had been cut off from Western credits, investment, and innovation. Now, they had to catch up, and the only way to accomplish this was for their counterparts in western Austria to scale back some of their plans. Nevertheless, it was without a doubt easier to overcome ten such years as opposed to many decades, as parts of Central Europe and the former German Democratic Republic are now being forced to do.

## The Fear of the Past

As early as the late 1950s, however, it became apparent that despite its tendency to solidify, the Grand Coalition could become unstable as well. Even after the end of the occupation period, the confrontation with some issues, like the question of the validity of the Concordat with the Vatican, was simply postponed. The People's Party, which of course continued to cultivate its Christian heritage, would have liked to quickly normalize relations with the Holy See, but the Socialists threatened to launch a *Kulturkampf*. Consideration of Austria's rapprochement to and closer ties with the West was likewise delayed. Indeed, it had been the Socialists who had voiced concerns about Austria's mandatory neutrality because the country would thereby forfeit the opportunity to participate in subsequent European initiatives. Foreign policy problems were also part of the mix, including the South Tyrol question that led to severe tensions with Italy in the late 1950s and early 1960s.

It ultimately turned out that resolving matters left unsettled from the occupation period, and, above all, compliance with the demands of American, British, and French firms as well as the demands of those who had been expelled from the country or had been racially persecuted by the Nazis, could not easily be managed by the coalition parties, and this led to increasingly unpleasant delays. Of course, problems with the division of political power had an even more powerful impact, which was to more tightly circumscribe the discretionary latitude not only of political policymaking, but of public administration as well. This ultimately gave rise to a bland mush of compromise views which did not stand up to criticism particularly well.

For quite some time, *Proporz* had no longer been limited to the federal level; rather, as provided for in the initial and subsequent Control Agreements, it also applied to the provinces and municipalities with more than 10,000 inhabitants. In all state-owned industries, among higher-level civil servants, teachers, and in all areas to which the parties had extended their influence as part of their "horizontal integration" efforts, *Proporz* ruled. Parliamentarism became atrophied as the national legislature came to be used not to actually conduct debates, but merely to express opinions on bills that had already been adopted in the committees and in the Council of Ministers before a vote was then held. Indeed, since 1956 there existed a coalition-free realm that afforded the possibility of free votes in parliament, but this was hardly used in practice. The second chamber of parliament—besides the *Nationalrat*, the *Bundesrat*—led a shadowy existence. But since the parties, at a time when so-called postmaterialism was emerging, unavoidably failed to find common ground sometimes, and since differences in their basic approaches became increasingly apparent in numerous areas, the Grand Coalition became ever more inelastic. Bills were continually being shelved since they could not be submitted to parliament due to differences of opinion. When it finally came to concluding another coalition agreement following the 1964 elections, not only did the negotiations take four months, but the most ridiculously trivial matters in it also had to be regulated.

This was an expression of how collaboration in the existing form had survived. Interestingly, though, there was hardly any consideration given to a "small coalition," and when this idea was even brought into play, it was the Socialist side that did so. However, since it was above all one man pursuing this course—namely Minister of the Interior Franz Olah, who had launched a struggle to assume power in the SPÖ—a short-term split developed within the Socialist ranks. It was precisely in this moment of Socialist weakness in the spring of 1966 that parliamentary elections were scheduled, and these resulted in an absolute majority for the ÖVP. Indeed, negotiations on a continuation of the coalition were begun immediately, but since the fundamental preconditions for this had long been absent, the readiness to relinquish power that was the actual basis for any such form of cooperation was not present anymore. The People's Party was no longer prepared to dispense with the exercise of power since it was, after all, in a position to govern alone. What had been valid in 1945 no longer applied under these totally changed circumstances. Therefore, the ÖVP negotiators demanded not only more ministerial posts, but also a complete revision of the form of cooperation. Ultimately, though, this would have led to a coalition "on call" for the time being. Even as the negotiations were proceeding, the Socialists were adjusting to the new situation. Finally, it was a single man who argued vehemently and right up to the end for the continuation of the Grand Coalition— namely, Bruno Kreisky. In doing so, he was hardly motivated by the belief that this would be an ideal form of government; rather, his sole consideration was that the historical compromise had not been in practice long enough, and that this step would lead to the formation of a new oppositional mentality between the political camps and might again produce severe conflicts. But the ensuing four years would make him aware that a new day had dawned, and perhaps he had given too little consideration to the fact that, in the meantime, the Grand Coalition had created possibilities of perpetuation that might insure its continued existence under any form of government.

One of the constitutional realities of the Republic of Austria is that constitutional laws can be passed only with a qualified two-thirds majority of all representatives in parliament, and it takes both major parties to put together such a majority. However, since a constitutional clause had come to be inserted in the very first paragraph of a number of bills, there could be no unilateral political initiatives in social policy areas of a highly sensitive nature. This applied to school legislation as well as to economic agreements, matters having to do with domestic and foreign security, and a number of other areas, too.

As if that were not enough, the effort to institutionalize the reconciliation of the interests of the major segments of society had already begun in 1948. Initially, this took the form of yearly wage and price agreements that would continue until the wage-price structure had been brought into order. Then in 1958, there came the creation of the Parity Commission, in which each of the major organized interest groups would have a seat and a vote, and, just like in the Council of Ministers, decisions had to be made unanimously. In its expanded form following the Raab-Olah Agreement, the Parity Commission for Wage and Price Issues took on the character of an extra-parliamentary decision-making body in which the parties of the Grand Coalition concurred on social policy measures, and in doing so excluded all third parties. In this form, the collaboration of the Big Two also survived the decades during which close cooperation between them had seemingly been interrupted.

## The Return to Dualism

The question that now must be asked is whether we may properly regard the Grand Coalition that took shape in 1986 to have reassumed stewardship over the affairs of the Republic of Austria after a twenty year intermezzo of solo governments and a small coalition as a typically Austrian form of cooperation in the political and social welfare sphere. This is not a question that can be responded to with a simple "yes" or "no" answer—after all, what is typical? Usually, the enumeration of typical characteristics merely serves to reinforce clichés.

What is certain is that postwar Austrian history can be rather cleanly divided into the following segments: about three years of a unity government with a simultaneous Grand Coalition, followed by approximately eighteen years of a pure Grand Coalition, then seventeen years of solo governments, three years of a small coalition, and, once again, a Grand Coalition for thirteen years. With the Grand Coalition thus having prevailed for a total of almost thirty-five years, the dominant characteristics of this form of government are quite easy to identify. However, the institutionalization of the key functional areas in which the collaboration of the two major parties was necessary actually resulted in what amounted to a fifty-five year duration that extended practically throughout the entire Second Republic.

In many areas, the mechanics also disguised the differences that existed. That it is eminently reasonable to seek out consensus when it comes to attaining major state objectives goes beyond the typical. Moreover, since rationality in politics can sometimes be a rather short-lived phenomenon, one may well proceed under the assumption that even large coalitions cannot become so solidly established that they function forever. Furthermore, the chief precondition for this is that there exist sufficiently large parties that are capable of forming a major coalition from which they can successfully exclude other parties. It is precisely at this point that the Grand Coalition of 1987-2000 began to diverge from its predecessors. Those who had been major players had to increasingly struggle to maintain their place in the political landscape. Nevertheless, they also brought a certain degree of nostalgia into play when a new political objective announced itself in the late 1980s, and voters obviously wanted to rely on a tried-and-true course to achieve it. In the mid-1980s, a new "real utopia" began to emerge—namely, the long-delayed and frequently postponed turn to the West that had been steadily coming together and developing from an economic community into a political one. But since a change of direction such as this had to necessarily go hand in hand with an overall correction in the course of postwar Austrian politics, the rapprochement of the two no longer large and dominant parties to form a new Grand Coalition was practically unavoidable.

The history of the Grand Coalition up to the end of the century, however, did not begin with parliamentary elections, but actually began a half year before in June 1986 with the election of Kurt Waldheim as president. The first presidential candidate successfully nominated by the ÖVP had set in motion a whole series of mechanisms that most certainly called into question the basic pattern of political culture and the *"cohabitation Autrichienne."* Waldheim's election produced polarization and a highly emotionally charged atmosphere. What ultimately was triggered, in a wanton manner and by no means with the intention of enabling historians to do a solid job of interpreting this period, grew into a clash that simply refused to die. Austria's past had caught up with it, but this was not, as one might have suspected, the history of its involvement in World War II, but its postwar past.

For decades, the past had been dismissed merely as events that had taken place. In doing so, Austria had most certainly not proceeded in lockstep with Germany, but had endeavored to navigate its own independent course. This had not been some sort of precarious balancing act, nor—as Andreas Hillgruber and others have noted—

was Austria "living a lie." Rather, this was the result of the joint force of two political cornerstones—on one hand, the Moscow Declaration and the shared responsibility clause that had been deleted from the State Treaty at Austria's wish and with Soviet support, and, on the other hand, neutrality. Both were used during the 1960s and 1970s to learn to avoid this issue; both were also instrumentalized and contributed to Austria's drifting off into isolation. As it did so, of course, it was obvious that, whereas Austria was not among the victorious powers of World War II, it nevertheless did all it could to distance itself from the losers in decisive issues. This went well for a time, but Austria gradually overdid it. It once again began to constitute a special case, though no longer in the sense of the occupation period or, subsequently, as a result of its role in the "Cold War of the pacts," but rather during the Kreisky years and thereafter in the form of the frequently conjured-up image of the "island of the blessed spirits." In doing so, Austria could no longer proceed under the assumption that it would be entering into one of the most important political phases simply on the basis of its international legal status, its reputation as an honest middleman, and its full sovereignty. Rather, Austria was increasingly called upon to elaborate on the political course it had been pursuing since 1945, to explain and justify itself. It did this by repeatedly evoking 1938 and the occupation period, the State Treaty and neutrality. But no one wanted to hear this anymore, and Austria had what Chancellor Vranitzky described as a heightened obligation to provide an explanation.

But there were also other factors at work in the mid-1980s. For years, it had been apparent that things were stagnating, that bottlenecks were preventing innovation, and that important past decisions that certainly had been right and proper for the early years of the Second Republic were no longer viable. A whole plethora of buzzwords were associated with this: budget crisis, crisis of the social welfare state, crisis of state-owned industries, crisis of the political system, crisis of the "social partnership" system, crisis of the parties, and many more. Of these, the easiest to quantify seemed perhaps to be the crisis of state-owned industries, a colossus that could no longer be run with the means allocated for this purpose, and the mismanagement of which had suddenly become extremely expensive. One had no way of grasping the sums involved—ös 20, 40, or 80 billion—but everyone realized that they were enormous. In solving these problems, social partnership, one of the great achievements of the Second Republic, was more detrimental than useful. On balance, it could be said that Bruno Kreisky's SPÖ was no longer capable of being reformed, and both he and many of the individuals with whom he surrounded himself came across more like members of a Soviet-style gerontocracy than of a Western democracy. The small coalition, into which Kreisky did not wish to enter in 1983 because coalitions as such seemed to him to be a much too difficult and trying form of domestic political collaboration, had been offered as a historical compromise. But this coalition was unsatisfactory, and the ÖVP continued on its way to becoming the strongest party, one which could perhaps even manage to put together a new solo government.

Among the factors that contributed to the failure of the small coalition were not only the problems, frustrations, and minor scandals that had begun to pile up or even the emergence of diverging basic political principles; rather, for the first time, this was particularly attributable to Europe. Alois Mock's ÖVP had begun to focus increasing attention on European questions, and the Socialist Party (as it was still called in those days) lagged behind. Perhaps a key date can be said to have been 16 December 1985, the day on which the ÖVP filed its "Europe Motion" in parliament. According to the assumptions it set forth, a sort of political "triple jump," as Andreas Khol has said, from full participation in the internal European market to full European Community (EC) membership would have been conceivable. The motion was not adopted. With that, however, the ÖVP acquired a reputation as the party of Europe, oriented on the future and more modern, once again "the" quintessential party of business, and very definitely capable of governing without a coalition partner. In 1986, there were upcoming elections not only for president, but for parliament as well. At this point, though, the SPÖ became the beneficiary of events taking place within the ranks of its small coalition partner, the FPÖ. A new chairman took over that party, and this move was taken as an opportunity to dramatically stir things up in the SPÖ as well. However, since Chancellor Vranitzky made it unmistakably clear that a continuation of the small coalition with the FPÖ under its new chairman Jörg Haider was out of the question, this paved the SPÖ's way to a new Grand Coalition. It must be pointed out that a whole series of preliminary moves had been made to prepare for this course, that Kreisky had nothing against Haider, and that Haider himself was prepared to continue the small coalition. Nevertheless, Vranitzky's clear refusal ultimately prevailed upon Kreisky and others. Parliamentary elections were held in November 1986. For a while, it appeared that the clear victor would be the ÖVP, but they eventually emerged from the race as the second strongest party. Two factors contributed to this: first, personal appeal, whereby Vranitzky came across much better than Mock, and then the unexpected comeback of the FPÖ. Then, in light of the looming Grand Coalition, the alternative that offered itself to the opponents of Socialist policymaking in tandem with the FPÖ was without a doubt a more radical solution than the "other" policy being propagated by Mock.

## The Unique and the Recurrent

When the Socialists and the People's Party agreed to form a new Grand Coalition in 1987, the country breathed a sigh of relief. The "Big Two" had gotten back together. Interestingly, the approval rating among the Austrian population for the Grand Coalition was approximately 70 percent, although from the very start there was no lack of recollection of those scenes from the previous coalition that had led many to view with a certain degree of skepticism that which had seemingly been the basic pattern of the Second Republic.

What was still a fresh memory in 1987—or at least could still be recalled then—were those structures and processes that had been referred to as "horizontal integration" and that had brought about the complete saturation of all spheres of life by the parties of the Grand Coalition—from sports clubs to renters' alliances and automobile associations to organizations of workers and employees, and, of course, the institutions of the Social Partnership. Even the old style reconciliation of conflicting interests, which was formally referred to as "bargaining," but was usually just called "backroom dealing," seemed to be threatened by a new coalition. But at first, it was only the good intentions that mattered. In 1987 following brief negotiations, a new Grand Coalition was formed. The coalition agreement differed from previous pacts; it was relatively short, although eighteen working papers were appended to it. The new "Big Two" renounced the old way of doing things. They promised that everything would become more "transparent" (the fashionable new word making the rounds). Nor was it even a question of whether the coalition agreement would be made public or not—it was! With that, the partners could get on with the job at hand, and do a bit of cleaning up as well.

The differences between this coalition and the "Big Two's" first long period of cooperation were striking. First of all, the chancellor's office changed hands, and the SPÖ assumed leadership of the coalition. Moreover, there was a meticulous listing of agendas and the forms of cooperation, though without committing the mistake of going into absurd details that had been the foundation of the previous coalition agreement between the two. Finally, the ministerial posts were reassigned, although this was ultimately an agreement of the chancellorship and the leadership of the government, which had to do primarily with the finance ministry. After all, parliament should not just be a rubber stamp. The fact that this was the case was attributable to an opposition that had become larger and more self-confident. Otherwise, the parties making up the governing coalition reverted to their old habits in that they once again secured precisely those ministries that they had always dominated or sought to dominate. The impression that one could be relatively satisfied with the performance of a minister who could simultaneously manage his large-scale farming operation is very prominent, but the actual problem of the new Grand Coalition was in a totally different area.

For some time, the coalition succeeded, at best, in giving the impression of being an effort to keep things from falling apart. There were no real ideas behind it. The country struggled forward and, at best, reacted indignantly when, during the course of the Central Europe Movement that was heading toward its climax at the time, it was suggested that Austria ought to play a role, but at the same time the suspicion was articulated that the country harbored thoughts of restoration and dreams of achieving major power status. Therefore, the Central Europe debate was only just tolerated as a discussion of architectural styles, cafés and Franz Josef Land, though not concerning that desolate island of ice near the North Pole, but the question of whether the Austria of yore had really been such an orderly, multicultural country inhabited by more or less harmoniously coexisting ethnic groups as it was occasionally being portrayed at that time. Nevertheless, there was nothing new about any of this.

In 1988 the isolation of Austria in the person of its head of state was complete. The conclusion of work by the Historians' Commission was seen as a guilty verdict, and, whether intentionally or not, this conviction was immediately extended to include Austria as a whole. To be an Austrian did not automatically mean that one could expect a friendly reception. That eventually passed, but it also triggered a process of rethinking in Austria, although the charge of having done a shoddy job of coming to terms with the country's Nazi past does not tell the whole story. More concrete was the German accusation that the *Ostmärker* were up to their old tricks again, or the charges made by the Western allies that the lazy Austrians were exploiting their neutrality, not making adequate provisions for their own security and relying on others to take care of them. But at last, the EC crystallized as the key issue within the Grand Coalition, and the intention emerged to establish stronger ties with the by now twelve signatory nations of the Rome Protocol.

The decision to take this step was only partially the result of economic data, budget balancing efforts, and market considerations. In a time of particular isolation, Austria's intention to strengthen its bond with the West was also a signal and a conscious show of allegiance, and it was a sort of Western European trump card that had to be played. It produced new and unaccustomed comparisons. Austria—still to some extent fixated on Sarajevo—was reminded that the Habsburgs ruled longer in Brussels than they did in Bosnia-Herzegovina. To a certain extent, the Central Europeans replied with the slogan "Prague is located further west than Vienna." But things were still proceeding on parallel tracks: Central European Movement and orientation on the West. Then, however, things began to happen in rapid succession. On 17 June 1989, Austria formally applied to join the Western communities. The famous "letter" could not have been formulated more simply—a one-sentence request for membership, as well as a somewhat more detailed elaboration of Austria's intention to maintain its neutrality.

The discussion of pros and cons was wide-ranging. One occasionally got the impression that Austrians were engaged in a dialogue in which their very future was at stake; at other times, it seemed to be merely a matter of statism. Of course, it was no mere coincidence that it was precisely at this time that Austrian patriotism was reaching a new high. One felt as if one were living in the best of all possible worlds, and things were bound to get worse in the future. However, it was precisely this line of argumentation that made it easy for the proponents of EC membership to depict closer ties with the West as a means of enhancing Austria's chances of survival and of assuring its future.

Another explanation that might also sound plausible is that events of 1989 had positively forced Austria to act out of concern that looming changes in Eastern Central Europe would have consequences for Austria to the extent that a whole crowd of applicants might soon be forming on Brussel's doorstep. If that was indeed the case, then Austria's step actually was something like flight from its historic responsibility toward Central Europe, even when the line was added with increasing frequency that as a member of the EC in Brussels, Austria could much more effectively further the interests of the Czechs, Poles, Hungarians, and others than it could if it were not a member of the European communities.

After four years of the Grand Coalition, economic development received high marks. The partnership to get Austria's affairs back in order had worked; it had accomplished what could have been expected and, indeed, what was expected of it. There had been victims of the turnaround. Not everyone could go along with the changes, nor did everyone want to do so. They began to flee into retirement, and the powers that be allowed them to do so whenever possible. Other victims of the turnaround sought to apportion the blame solely to the governing parties, and they then sought a new political home within another camp. Nevertheless, the governing parties had more or less no alternative. The upcoming negotiations concerning joining the EC were by no means the least of the reasons why the Grand Coalition was never called into question; it was basically the only possible form of cooperation. However, the goal was clear: EC membership. Everything else was of secondary importance. Now, there were even opportunities to do some Central European policymaking.

In another area, a certain degree of closure was being achieved. In 1992, Kurt Waldheim's term in office ended, and he chose not to run for a second term. Once again, a certain amount of relief could be felt. Not only were the "Big Two" a couple again, but, with the election of Thomas Klestil, there was once again normality surrounding the man at the top. In addition, 1992 was also the year that shuttle diplomacy got back into full swing. The posters bore the slogan "We are Europe," and it became clearer by the day that no other issue would even come close to EC—or, by now, European Union (EU)—membership in the demands it would place on the attention of Austria and the coalition. Meanwhile, there had come to be absolutely no doubt that Austria also wanted to take part in the more narrowly-defined community, one to which—in a strict sense—the 1989 letter had not even been addressed.

As the negotiations leading up to joining the EU accelerated, efforts to bring about reform and innovation gained momentum too. In political jargon, it seemed as if every second word were paired with "reform": parliamentary electoral reform, tax reform, party reform, the reform of agricultural market regulations and the national railway, army and university reform, reform of the Social Partnership system, and so forth. Then in 1994, it was time to decide, and of the major political groupings, only the FPÖ finally came out against joining the EU. That party's declared goal was to deliver a decisive defeat to the government in the EU plebiscite, but its effort failed miserably. Once again, there had been a sort of return to political fundamentals—in 1955, the VdU had been the only party represented in parliament to vote against neutrality, and now the FPÖ was opposed to joining the EU. Following the plebiscite, the FPÖ immediately shifted its focus to domestic policies and successfully established itself as a middle-sized party with 22.5 percent of the vote in the 1994 parliamentary elections. It seemed that the EU and Austria were two altogether different spheres.

The rest can be rapidly recapitulated. In 1995, one year after the EU plebiscite and parliamentary elections that had produced relatively substantial losses for the parties of the Grand Coalition, parliamentary elections were held again. The nineteenth legislative period had been the shortest since 1918. The process of putting together a budget led to the break. In going about it, some things were done too hastily and others overlooked. For example, there had been a lot of business—not least of all having to do with the EU— that had to be attended to prior to year's end. Therefore, a special session of parliament was called. This turned into a difficult balancing act, since the government had, after all, resigned and had only been entrusted with carrying on official business, and the coalition agreement was no longer in force. The two partners had no desire to create bad blood between them, since an additional period of the Grand Coalition was in the offing. Nevertheless, bills were proposed for which majorities had to be sought outside the Grand Coalition. Of course, the elections did not produce the expected results, and one might well have gotten the impression that the collaboration between the SPÖ and the ÖVP certainly was desired at least for another legislative term. Both coalition parties picked up seats, and could thus make up some of the losses they had suffered in 1994. But these times were a typical aftermath. The facts that one could also have regarded what took place as an indication that the work was completed, that politics would no longer be so interesting, that personal merit could no longer become so clearly manifested in the hands-on work of day-to-day politics, and that commitments which had been made could no longer be fulfilled without giving up ever-larger shares of privileges that had, so to speak, been rightfully acquired over the years triggered a movement to do some political housecleaning. Obviously, Chancellor Vranitzky's domestic political efforts were also totally wrapped up with joining the EU; once that had been accomplished, he lost interest relatively quickly and did something very unusual: he withdrew from politics. The minister of finance did the same. These were more or less voluntary resignations. Thereafter, it was no longer possible to make out a well-defined phase, except to say that domestic policymaking focused on the budget and relatively insignificant matters. Obviously, only the EU had established the necessary basic consensus, whereas everything else could lead to problems within the coalition.

The discussions of how things could go on in the future began long before the end of the legislative period. It was above all journalists who were racking their brains over what sort of government Austria would have after the 1999 elections. A continuation of the Grand Coalition was deemed to be most probable. Anything else—a government of the best and brightest, some sort of small coalition, a so-called "rainbow" coalition of Social Democrats, Liberals, Greens, and others—was already being ridiculed in 1998. Thus, no one of any great significance was initially irritated when the October 1999 elections produced results that were certainly not unexpected, but still hard to come to grips with. Up until January 2000, one could still proceed under the assumption that the government would eventually come to a new version of the Grand Coalition, even if the Social Democrats had lost strength and the FPÖ had become the second strongest party followed by the ÖVP in third place. It was not until union leaders refused to subscribe to a new coalition pact that the situation went to "condition yellow." By this time, the state of affairs was written all over the faces of the political leaders who had once been partners, but now had a hard time finding something to smile about with one another. Perhaps the only question left at this point was who would get their political "walking papers" from whom. Then on that fateful day in February came the realization that another thirteen years of the Grand Coalition had come to an end. It had lasted almost as many years as the previous one decades before.

Perhaps it would be a good idea not to bet against this being the last we will see of this form of political collaboration. Nevertheless, the Grand Coalition of 1987-2000 may also be properly characterized as unique an expression of one's decisive refusal to simply regard it as a sort of continuation of the Grand Coalition of former days, even if there are a number of obvious instances that support the case of precedence. This was the latest edition of an "ad hoc alliance"—and by no means a group sharing a common fate—whose development over the course of its political history or within its social and economic context is simply to be regarded as a "succession of unique framework conditions."

But these unique features were only half the story, since, of course, there were recurrent processes. Moreover, it is precisely because both the unique and the recurrent have their place in this period that it must be regarded as more than just a collection of new elements and those that are seemingly familiar, and invites the question of how and why things developed as they did. Thus the historical investigation of this latest chapter of Austrian history is already underway.

# The Kreisky Era, 1970-1983

*Oliver Rathkolb*

## Can One Properly Speak of a Kreisky Era?

In recent decades, it has been primarily scholars doing historical research oriented on the social sciences who have begun to criticize the "history of cabinets and personalities" and to replace it with history focusing on political, economic, and social influences. Even leading figures that dominated the political decision-making process for long periods of time came to be regarded as a part of developments that were themselves hardly able to influence long-term trends.

Political scientists like Peter A. Ulram thus characterize the period during which the socialists were the sole ruling party under Chancellor Bruno Kreisky as "Social Democratic hegemony" based on a "voter alliance, a voter coalition . . . bringing together Social Democrats and progressive, liberal forces" (according to Kreisky's own definition in an ORF interview on 8 April 1975).

For the editors of the anthology *Austria 1945-1995*, the 1970s were characterized by "social welfare-liberal reforms under Kreisky" and the "Social Democratic Keynesians'" efforts to help the economy through the two global economic crises. Indeed, a few contributors repeatedly mention the political decision-making process and thus also the chancellor's possibilities to influence or determine the outcome of events as a matter of fact, though without going into an exact analysis of them. Nevertheless, the current trend in the social sciences is indeed proceeding in the direction of "era formation" for the years 1970-83 (with certain aftereffects, interrupted continuities, and diverse caesuras).

Only a few years ago, however, Elisabeth Horvath left the "era or episode" question unanswered in her monograph. Even Social

Chancellor Bruno Kreisky (right) meeting President Richard Nixon (middle) and
Secretary of State Henry Kissinger (left).

Source: Bruno Kreisky Foundation Archives

Democratic President of Parliament Heinz Fischer entitled his
monograph *The Kreisky Years*, and it was only within his text that he
addressed the "era discussions" of Johannes Kunz (1975) and, in the
field of foreign policy, Erich Bielka and others (1983).

Social scientific studies that have appeared up to now demonstrate
that Bruno Kreisky grasped, like no other politician, the social
upheavals and trends that had been underway since the mid-1960s
and, within the framework of generally prevailing conditions, made
them the goal of his political work. In this sense, it does seem
justified to speak of an era, even if there were indeed instances when
Kreisky's policies ran up against limits (for example, minority rights
for Slovenes in Carinthia) or took positions contrary to emerging
socio-economic trends (environmental movement against the
Zwentendorf atomic power plant up to 1978).

In a number of essential areas, Kreisky, as "inventor and
preserver" of the social welfare-liberal consensus that reached its
highpoint in 1979 when the SPÖ took 51 percent of the vote in
parliamentary elections, made possible the implementation of
measures contributing to the transformation of Austrian society that

had already begun to manifest itself in the mid-1960s. In certain questions—such as the political discussions of the Nazi past of Austrian men and women—Kreisky, however, intentionally remained in the background due to general social pressure and his own Jewish descent, only to subsequently become even more intensely involved both as participant in and subject of domestic political discussions (ranging from the Peter Wiesenthal affair to the Waldheim debate). Such instances clearly show that even defining personalities can themselves become part of the trend in sensitive, socially tabooed subjects, even if they attempted—as Kreisky did— at least subjectively to keep from suppressing the discussion of basic principles ("Fill in rifts without forgetting them").

As far as the discussion about the continuities among the elites in the SPÖ as well as the FPÖ were concerned, Bruno Kreisky, who had been arrested by the Gestapo in 1938 and forced into exile in Sweden, was confronted by a *fait accompli* upon his return. All key political parties with the exception of the KPÖ very quickly went from a de-Nazification policy to a policy of reintegration of former members of the NSDAP. The social policy effort to come to terms with the Nazi past was abandoned. When he clearly voiced his critical position toward automatic de-Nazification, Kreisky himself was firmly put in his place by "party friends" whose line of argumentation pointed out that he had, after all, not been in Austria at the time. As vice-director of the cabinet in 1953, he backed President Theodor Körner's refusal to accept the clearly "Nazified" VdU in a coalition government with the ÖVP and the SPÖ.

On the other hand, in the 1960s and 1970s above all, he expressed a great deal of understanding for the "little former NSDAP members," basing his attitude on the dire socio-economic straits during the time of the Dollfuss-Schuschnigg dictatorship, when Kreisky, like thousands of others, was arrested and imprisoned for almost a year and a half. The contacts between the FPÖ and the SPÖ also remained intact during the 1960s and ultimately resulted in the parliamentary support of the SPÖ minority government in 1970 by the FPÖ under the leadership of Friedrich Peter. Kreisky, for his part, subsequently saw to the reform of election laws that had considerably disadvantaged the smaller parties, but the SPÖ nevertheless achieved an absolute majority in the 1971 parliamentary elections.

The often extremely heated debates between the head of the Jewish Documentation Center in Vienna, Simon Wiesenthal, and Kreisky—with aggressive lines of argumentation and vicious insinuations used on both sides—had already escalated in 1970 when Kreisky attacked Wiesenthal, who had provided information to the German newsmagazine *Der Spiegel* and the Catholic weekly *Die Furche* about the NSDAP membership of three members of Kreisky's first government. It was also Wiesenthal who had revealed the SS membership of Minister of Agriculture Hans Öllinger. Kreisky defended his cabinet appointments, but arranged for Öllinger, whom he hardly knew, to resign from his post for health reasons. Without going into greater detail here, it can simply be said that Kreisky demanded evidence of culpability during the period of Nazi rule in order to justify excluding former NSDAP members from holding political positions. Wiesenthal, on the other hand, was the object of his acrimonious attacks because Kreisky regarded Wiesenthal's political affiliation with the ÖVP as the real motivation behind his revelations about members of the SPÖ government. There is no question that Kreisky was way out of line in the public criticism he voiced both in this discussion as well as in the subsequent conflict having to do with the SS membership of Peter, who had belonged to a unit that had committed war crimes, with Kreisky referring to Wiesenthal as a "Jewish fascist" and later even accusing him of "collaboration with National Socialists" in concentration camps. Wiesenthal, for his part, had begun the second conflict in 1975 when, a few days after parliamentary elections, he released a dossier containing documents that proved Friedrich Peter's membership in an SS death squad. Nevertheless, Wiesenthal has to this day been unable to come up with concrete proof that Peter was personally involved in war crimes. A press tribunal twice condemned Kreisky for the unproven charges of "Nazi collaboration" he had made against Wiesenthal.

The extremely heated and emotionally exaggerated discussion must be regarded in light of the Austrian chancellor's own life experiences. Into the 1970s, his Jewish background had given rise to both veiled and open anti-Semitic attacks, whereby, in the 1960s, it had been above all ÖVP functionaries who had made unbridled use of such tactics.

Kreisky was consciously—and sometimes also unconsciously—aware that his Jewish descent would be repeatedly thrown up to him as a "negative trait" in political debates, and he most certainly was cognizant of the fact—although he publicly disputed it above all in the 1970s and early 1980s—that widespread and deep-seated anti-Semitism still had the power to influence public discourse in Austria. Thus his reactions were even more ferocious when he suspected political motives behind Wiesenthal's revelations, the ultimate effect of which was to force him into the role of the "Jew." Therefore, Kreisky long steered clear of all "Jewish questions," and it was only very late in the process that he got involved in arranging the "Jewish indemnification negotiations."

## Socioeconomic Framework Conditions of the Transformation of Society Beginning in the Mid-1960s

The latest studies—most recently by Ernst Hanisch—have shown that signs pointing in the direction of deep-seated social reform efforts could even be noticed in the early 1960s when information technology was already signaling the coming computer revolution, job opportunities were shifting from the agrarian sector to service industries, and self-employment was undergoing a rollback. The basic configuration of party politics of the interwar years that had remained in effect in a modified form during the reconstruction period had started to become more permeable, while the dominance of the Catholic Church and the influence it exerted upon its faithful gradually began to diminish. The economic, social, and political reconstruction of the postwar years had reached the point at which efforts were no longer a matter of survival and repairing the damages of war; rather, what was called for was the elimination of authoritarian structures and adaptation to current European and global trends. In Austria, this increasingly meant rejection of the Grand Coalition and the *Proporz* system, and the direct influence exerted by the parties in many areas of life, such as in broadcasting (broadcasting petition drive).

It is remarkable that this need to catch up in various social policy areas could already be felt in many respects before the "1968 movement," and that in Austria, it was above all the Austrian People's Party (ÖVP) under Josef Klaus that was able to harness this potential. Among the forces for reform, it was primarily young voters and communities with fewer than 5,000 inhabitants who were the driving forces behind the end of the Grand Coalition between the ÖVP and the SPÖ. Among these segments of the population, there was obviously a palpable desire to dismantle traditional structures and to adapt to current economic and social conditions. The ÖVP did a considerably better job than the SPÖ in attracting scholars to their ranks (Action 20) and in signaling their leading role for reform in the direction of modern technological developments ("Information Society").

At the same time, Kreisky himself was attempting to lead a permanent discussion and, as early as the late 1960s, to carry out a reform of democratic institutions and processes in Austria. The most important reason for this was that, as a result of his international experience and contacts as well as his exile in Sweden from 1938 to 1950, he clearly recognized the authoritarian constraints and continuities from the nineteenth century and the undemocratic regime thereafter that were still intact in the bureaucracy, in the legal and educational systems, and in the parliamentary process. On this issue, Kreisky could also count on the support of voters from conservative backgrounds who were nevertheless politically prepared "to go a part of the way together" with the SPÖ.

Kreisky's claim to be a "liberal" in this sense also manifested itself in an open and supportive understanding of art and culture, which in turn explains why many artists became active political supporters of Kreisky in the early years. Of course, the call for "saturating all aspects of life with democracy" encountered the most diverse forms of resistance in its actual implementation and produced a wide variety of conflicts, but nevertheless always remained a component of his fundamental political values. At the same time, though, the chancellor did not shrink from clearly expressing his own opinions, and he certainly was prepared to make decisions that could not initially be counted on to receive broad approval.

## SPÖ Party Chairman Against the Will of the Party Establishment

The SPÖ had to take action in the wake of a painful defeat at the polls in 1966 that was attributable to, among other factors, internal turbulence having to do with the exclusion from the party of Franz Olah, the former president of the Austrian Federation of Labor (ÖGB) and minister of the interior, who then ran with his own Democratic Progressive Party and got almost 150,000 votes (3.28 percent).

Kreisky personally went public in the media with a call for the dismissal of party chairman Bruno Pittermann, which made him the object of harsh criticism by Viennese party functionaries and led to him being *de facto* ejected from party headquarters on Löwelstraße in Vienna. Kreisky retreated to the headquarters of the Lower Austrian SPÖ, the provincial organization which he would one day lead and which constituted his grassroots support in the "movement." For quite some time, the former foreign minister (1959-66) was unsure of his own political future in the party. He turned down an offer to run for secretary general of the UN since he saw no possibility to implement his own political agenda in that position.

In spite of his public reputation and international recognition, Kreisky feared that "due to Austrians' tendency to judge people according to their religious background, my candidacy would constitute a liability to the party. Of course, I had always identified with the Austrian people, but I was aware of certain anti-Semitic tendencies and I did not want to stand in the way of my party."

Indeed, during the 1970 campaign, the ÖVP put up posters describing Josef Klaus as "the real Austrian" and thereby indirectly playing up Bruno Kreisky's Jewish descent in order to bring out anti-Semitic reservations in the voters. A number of ÖVP officials appealed over and over again to anti-Semitic prejudices in campaigning against him; once, swastikas were even painted on his garage door. It is, therefore, reasonable to assume that the average voter was aware of his Jewish descent. Even in his own party since his days as a youth organization official, Kreisky was repeatedly confronted by veiled as well as open anti-Semitic attacks.

That he succeeded in being nominated at the SPÖ convention on 1 February 1967 was primarily attributable to the fact that Hans Czettel, a functionary from Lower Austria who was the candidate of the inner circle of the party's executive board (Bruno Pittermann, Karl Waldbrunner, and Anton Benya as ÖGB president), refused to submit to a contested vote. Since the defeat at the polls in 1966, the provincial party organizations had gained considerable influence, and they threw their support to Kreisky in the hope that he could bring about fundamental reforms while still maintaining party traditions.

After Bruno Kreisky had been elected SPÖ chairman in 1967 in a secretly held contested vote, he set about the effort to regain the reform initiative for his party that had already been prefigured in his acceptance speech at the convention, in which he focused on the challenges of the emerging Computer Age and the Information Society. Thereafter, he also proceeded to implement the theoretical demands for "analysis of social conditions . . . through the use of science" in concrete platform commissions.

This concept of employing experts was part of one of Kreisky's key strategies in the direction of an open party in the sense of a "catch-all party system:

> The economic platform, for instance, was not put together by a small group of politically reliable economists, but rather was the work of 300 scholars who were not subjected to any restrictions whatsoever. The "people" platform is also characterized by the fact that it was worked out by experts without regard to their political affiliation, and we are particularly pleased about this.

Indeed, long before the 1970 election, Kreisky repeatedly emphasized: "Our party is an open party. It is open to everyone who wants to work with us."

Another aspect of this "open party" concept was the continuation of the effort to work out an agreement with the Catholic Church, a course that the agnostic Kreisky consistently pursued (for example, in a public discussion sponsored by the Lower Austrian SPÖ with leading Catholics on 3 November 1967). Sensitive issues like the decriminalization of abortion in conjunction with the "trimester solution" were not aggressively pursued prior to 1970, and would not play an important role in domestic politics until after that date.

The supposition that with these pragmatic concepts the SPÖ suddenly became a "liberal People's Party" is by no means consistent with the facts. In 1969, it was clear that the SPÖ under Kreisky had augmented its "working class voter" potential. Fully 59 percent of workers questioned said they favored the SPÖ; meanwhile, a trend began to emerge in 1970 whereby an increasing number of better-educated individuals (those who attended college and college prep school grads) voted SPÖ (1969: 18 percent; 1972: 29 percent; 1977: 30 percent). In 1970, a growing preference among women for the SPÖ also began to manifest itself in parliamentary elections (1969: 39 percent; 1972: 45 percent), and, among younger voters, the party even achieved an absolute majority that year.

The SPÖ's concepts for reform—supplemented shortly before the parliamentary elections by the slogan "Six months are enough" in reference to the term of compulsory military service—were received very well in small communities that had previously been dominated by the ÖVP and, above all, among the upper middle class, women, white collar workers, and young voters. A total of 158,000 voters switched directly from the ÖVP to the SPÖ. The core areas of SPÖ growth, furthermore, were those where the impact of primary structural shift was particularly great. Peter A. Ulram summarized the 1970-79 parliamentary election results with the following hypothesis: "The SPÖ thus succeeded in transforming the social welfare-liberal coalition of interests and values into a voter coalition that held together for more than a decade, and thus ascended to the position of hegemonic power in the Austrian party system."

The input of young, independent experts appeared in a new economic platform, as well as in other platforms. The development of the economic platform was coordinated by Ernst Eugen Veselsky, whom the Chamber of Labor had nominated to head the Advisory Council for Economic and Social Welfare Questions, and this was to be only the beginning of an effort to also bring other key areas of life into the political discussion. There were still halfhearted attempts to block these initiatives, but the project's momentum and impact upon the public—as well as in the independent press and newspapers read by the middle and upper classes—had already become too strong. Moreover, the new party chairman had very quickly succeeded in reunifying the SPÖ by means of concrete integration measures and concessions of power; his predecessor Pittermann, with whom there had been heated conflicts in the past, was granted great latitude to coordinate parliamentary strategy, and "reconciliation" was very soon arranged with ÖGB chief Benya and others. A total of "1,400" experts participated in these reform commission meetings, although the core editorial staff was, of course, much smaller. A "people program" containing strategies having to do with "Healthcare Policy and Environmental Hygiene" was also worked out by a staff under the leadership of Hertha Firnberg. Additional areas of emphasis were the "Higher Education Platform" coordinated by Heinz Fischer and the "Judiciary Platform" by Christian Broda.

At the same time, it was becoming obvious that the ÖVP was not in a position to fulfill the expectations placed on it to open up the social policymaking process; this manifested itself, for instance, in the area of judicial reform, where patently regressive measures stemming from pressure exerted by the Catholic Bishops' Conference had been incorporated into the government's proposed amendments to the legal code. Franz Pallin analyzed the government's 1968 bill as follows:

> The idea of retribution was accentuated; abortion, incest, and blasphemy were 'raised' from misdemeanors to felonies; special measures to protect the honor of the Church, and higher penalties for attacks against priests were proposed; homosexuality between adults and illicit relations with a married person would continue to be punishable offenses; there would be heavier penalties for adultery, and much, much more. The legislation proposed by the government in 1968 was not only judicially amateurish, but also a provocation to anyone who felt committed to pluralism in our society.

On the other hand, judicial development stagnated in the area of divorce law in clear opposition to the general—which is to say, actual—trend.

Bruno Kreisky succeeded both as a result of his opposition policies and the above-mentioned reform initiatives as well as the reform deficits and reactionary steps on the part of the ÖVP government under Chancellor Josef Klaus to pick up new supporters primarily in smaller communities that had previously been dominated by the ÖVP (upper middle classes, women, white-collar workers, and young voters), whereby a total of 158,000 voters switched directly from the ÖVP to the SPÖ in 1970. At the same time, the SPÖ's reservoir of loyal voters remained fully committed to the party.

## Setting a New Ideological Course

Bruno Kreisky, who had made it a point to get intensively involved in ideological debates since the interwar period, although he conducted these discussions almost exclusively in conjunction with concrete political work and did not immerse himself in theoretical publications, now made the effort to put his own stamp on the party's line. Proceeding from the 1958 platform, on which he had worked as a member of the editorial committee without having had any really decisive input, he continued the trend to utilize Austromarxist methods and hypotheses for analytical purposes, but ultimately to develop "historical compromises" in concrete policies both in economic and social areas. Since 1967, he had been promoting dialogue between receptive representative of the Catholic Church and the SPÖ, an undertaking that had already been officially initiated by Franz Olah and Felix Slavik in 1959. He also made this dialogue personally credible, especially since he considered himself an agnostic (that is, one for whom supernatural phenomena remain unknowable without, however, denying others the right to make such supernatural phenomena the basis of their religion).

The importance to him of finally putting aside this conflict that seemed to have been raging ever since the beginnings of Social Democracy is revealed by his assessment of the consequences of the "trimester solution" that Minister of Justice Christian Broda had successfully gotten passed against the express will of the Catholic Church and the ÖVP, and, ultimately, the SPÖ as well. Kreisky's first reaction was that this would cause a loss of votes at the next election, but it turned out that he had erred in underestimating society's dynamism in this area.

The centerpiece, however, was the element that had also been at the core of his efforts in the opposition—a new economic platform based on solid scholarly underpinnings, designed to launch the SPÖ's new pragmatic course and to eliminate once and for all Social Democratic policymaking's old image that was a relic of the interwar period and that had remained operational after 1945 as well. In 1970, Kreisky propagated an "economic platform for Austrian Social Democracy, which still seems to have the reputation of being an especially radical, Austromarxist party . . . a new approach that lays down the principle of the equality of all productive assets," which in turn meant the express recognition of the "equality of private property and publicly-owned property of any kind."

It would be a misjudgment, though, to believe that the "Social Democrat" Kreisky—he preferred the term Social Democrat to the official designation "Socialist"—dispensed with social reforms and political visions for that reason. One outstanding feature of the first years of the SPÖ minority government as well as the years during which it was the sole governing party was the implementation of thoroughly controversial political concepts in spite of the high probability—for example, in the case of the "trimester solution"—of a loss of votes in future elections. Kreisky and his ministers understood how to sound the depths of the reform potential in society as a whole and to come up with concrete measures that made a difference in everyday life for the benefit of socially disadvantaged groups (such as free use of public transportation by students and free school books). In many cases, though, this was not a matter of redistribution, since all classes could take advantage of these programs regardless of income. Only in the areas of special salary supplements and pension payments were adjustments made in the mid-1970s that applied only to those on the low end of the economic spectrum.

The theoretical ideas of the SPÖ chairman and chancellor increasingly focused on the implementation of "social democracy," and Kreisky characterized himself as a "centrist" and as an "enlightener" in a positive sense. Nevertheless, the SPÖ stuck with its fundamental effort to achieve a "classless society" in order to at least have a theoretical corrective to new class-like developments in the welfare state.

Kreisky's long-term political goal was by no means to turn the SPÖ into a "leftist People's Party," although in 1972 at the party convention in Villach, he stated that "there are a lot of people who are prepared to go a considerable piece of the way together with us, without wishing thereby to subscribe to all of our goals." Particularly over the course of the internal party debate about the new 1978 platform, the SPÖ once again consciously attempted to establish new and old social policy visions—not only to engage "the leftists" within the party, but also to intentionally take steps against the abuse of power by those in office and to prevent them from becoming self-satisfied and losing their competitive edge. Austrian *Realpolitik* of the late 1970s and early 1980s was increasingly dominated by corruption scandals (Vienna General Hospital scandal) in which socialist politicians were involved. The conflict between Kreisky and Hannes Androsch, his vice-chancellor, finance minister, and the man long presumed to be his successor, triggered by the business expansion of Androsch's tax accounting practice Consultatio by the trustee administering it, and charges of tax evasion that ultimately led to a court conviction are paradigmatic of Kreisky's failed effort to implement in all areas of society—and especially in the SPÖ—a permanent process of reform as a corrective featuring high moral values.

The *realpolitische* core of the Kreisky-Androsch confrontation, however, went all the way back to 1974, when both Androsch and Vienna Mayor Leopold Gratz wanted to use the occasion of President Franz Jonas' death to kick Kreisky upstairs into the candidacy for president. At the same time, early elections in 1974 were designed to lay the groundwork for a Small Coalition with the FPÖ under Friedrich Peter. Androsch would take over as chancellor and Gratz would become party chairman. By 1974, many in the top ranks of the SPÖ no longer believed the party would be able to obtain an absolute majority once again.

To more fully illustrate the scope and impact of Kreisky's leadership, a specific re-examination of a few areas in which reform efforts were launched during the Kreisky era follows.

## Economic and Social Policies on the Way to "Austro-Keynesianism" and the Welfare State

Even before the 1970 parliamentary elections, the SPÖ had made economic policy one of the central elements of its political preparations in order to finance and implement corresponding social policies. Like the ÖVP before 1968, the SPÖ chose a course of structural improvements through state investment, and they profited from the business cycle upswing between 1968 and 1973. Good preparation had been done domestically by Finance Minister Stefan Koren in the form of well thought-out tax increases and budget cuts introduced without forewarning. The social partnership system, which in fact exerted autonomous control over income policy, was already functioning when the ÖVP was the sole governing party, and would retain its significance for Austria's "path to assume its place among the advanced nations of Europe" in the early 1970s by means of growth-enhancing legislation and structural improvements. A high level of state investment boosted growth. The "bridge" built between the EWG and the EFTA (to which Austria belonged), improved foreign trade possibilities, which, among other effects, made a liberalization of trade possible.

It was not until Austria felt the negative consequences of the first oil shock of 1973-74, when a cartel agreement among oil-producing Arab states drove oil prices up to ten times their previous levels, that the Kreisky government intentionally employed other economic policy instruments. An expansive fiscal policy was designed to increase public investment and enable Austria to weather the storms of the global economic crisis. At the same time, Finance Minister Hannes Androsch and National Bank President Koren intentionally pursued a hard currency policy, and thus the *de facto* linkage of the Schilling to the Deutschmark, in an effort to rein in inflation.

Indeed, Austria succeeded in maintaining growth and cushioning the impact of the crises on employment, though at the price of high budget deficits (1973: 1.3 percent of GNP; 1975: 4 percent). It would be naive to presume that Kreisky and his finance ministers Androsch and Salcher had completely ignored the question of budget consolidation; actually, the facts show that this was one of their most important goals from 1976 on, but, in doing so, they always took the international economic situation into account. Thus, 48 percent of the federal debt stems from the Kreisky era of 1970 to 1983, whereas 46 percent of all debt was issued in the years 1984-88. It is also essential to point out that the question of state expenditures must also be seen from the perspective of their positive effects on the Austrian economy as a whole, the infrastructure of the country, and the lives of its people, since by no means did these investments and outlays simply vanish into a black hole.

Decisions made primarily in the late 1970s and early 1980s to invest massive amounts in state-owned enterprises as well as private firms despite the fact that, as we now know, these operations were already beyond structural reform, were errors from a business management point of view, but, from an economic perspective, at least these poor investments went for wages and salaries and thus had ripple effects throughout the entire economy. Nevertheless, these "efforts to try to put out the fire" did nothing to change the prospects for preserving these jobs on a long-term basis.

This policy of deficit spending was made possible by a process of establishing political priorities that Kreisky carried out on the basis of his personal experience as well as that of his entire generation with the exploding unemployment and hyperinflation of the interwar period. His famous line, "I'd rather be a couple of billion Schillings deeper in debt than have a couple of hundred thousand more unemployed," became a political credo that defined the special case of Austria, and the social partnership contributed to a certain extent in carrying this out. But the effort to "stay the course" through the second world economic crisis in 1979 revealed the limits of this national economic policy that was based upon a mixture of political framework conditions, the economic and social partnership, correspondingly flexible fiscal and hard currency policies, and a high level of employment in state-owned industries. In 1982, the jobless rate began to rise, and the situation of the state-owned enterprises turned critical as the federal budget deficit rose. Kreisky's efforts to get the budget back into balance through tax measures ("the Mallorca package") without radically cutting public investment at the same time was something the voters no longer supported, and resulted in the loss of five seats and the absolute majority in 1983.

Essential to a proper understanding of Kreisky's policy of the primacy of employment is the fact that he belonged to a generation of politicians for whom joblessness was not just a numbers game in the larger round of political poker. He was convinced that "unemployment . . . means, first and foremost, the sum of the fates of individual men and women for which a responsible politician cannot and must not be responsible for causing. And it also means that the breeding ground for all sorts of radical political experiments is once again in place."

Kreisky's commitment to stimulating the Austrian economy also went so far that he was very much in a position to throw his excellent reputation among Arab statesmen as well as among the oil-exporting states of the "Third World" into the balance in order to more favorably structure the terms of oil imports and simultaneously open up new markets for the Austrian economy.

## Legal Reforms

The need for Austria to enact reform in this area was especially great. With permanent reference to "legal security" and the fear of social changes associated with it, the judicial system had appealed in numerous respects to very traditional legal principles in order to block the recognition of social developments that had been completed long before. For example, the most important elements of family law were based on the General Civil Law Code of 1811, and the core of criminal law had been laid down in the Criminal Law Code dating from 1804.

Christian Broda had already tried, during his term as minister of justice back in the 1960s and within the framework of the Grand Coalition, to put through a complete overhaul of the criminal code based on proposals developed by a panel of experts between 1954 and 1962. The ministerial draft that subsequently emerged in 1964, however, was filed away once again after the ÖVP's success at the polls in 1966, and, other than the restorative counterproposal by Hans Klecatsky in 1968, it was not until Kreisky's minority government in 1970 and the years thereafter that an attempt was made to put through a comprehensive legal reform. For Christian Broda:

legal reform in a democracy . . . is designed to serve the purpose of conformance whereby the legal order is adapted to a changed society. However, changing the legal order and the process of social conformance is by no means without consequences for the subsequent development of society. Changes to the legal order are the source of stimuli that exert an effect upon society and, in turn, influence its subsequent development.

Nevertheless, the first Kreisky government initially went about these changes very cautiously. Even the government declaration of 27 April 1970 reflected this pragmatic approach, the goal of which was, above all, to institute the formal equality of all citizens before the law fully in the sense of the failed liberal Revolution of 1848. The so-called small criminal law reform of 1971 was also focused to correspond to this approach; among other changes, it decriminalized homosexual activity between adults and illicit relations with a married person, and provided for fines instead of imprisonment for minor traffic offenses.

It was not until 16 November 1971 during the second Kreisky administration that Broda introduced into parliament the government's bill for a major criminal law overhaul. At the same time, opinion seemed to have basically swung in favor of a total reform among the other parties represented in parliament as well, but the abortion issue remained the absolute point of confrontation. The ÖVP, as well as, in particular, the Catholic Church and some FPÖ representatives, rejected the proposed "indication solution" as going too far. Finally, an intra-party discussion that reached its climax at the 1972 convention in Villach led to a revision of the original proposal in the direction of a "trimester solution" which decriminalized abortion during the first three months of pregnancy.

In Villach, the chancellor himself kept out of this sensitive question and also voted for the convention resolution. The reason for this is provided by Heinz Fischer's eyewitness account of the events. Once the criminal law bill, revised in accordance with the convention resolution (including the trimester solution), was presented on 29 November 1973, Kreisky stated that the SPÖ's insistence upon this resolution was "the cardinal error of our efforts. This resolution will cost us the majority. It is Broda's third mistake—after Habsburg and Olah-Kronenzeitung—that will end up deciding an election. Basically, this destroys 20 years of effort on my part to bring about reconciliation with the Church. They will never forgive us—not the Cardinal . . ."

It is remarkable that, in this question, Bruno Kreisky misjudged changes that had been taking place throughout society. Despite a massive opposition movement within the Catholic Church, the "Action for Life" petition drive that collected almost 900,000 signatures, and political resistance on the part of the ÖVP, it turned out that even the ÖVP gradually began to move away from the official Church position on this issue, or rather no longer exerted the same political pressure in its advocacy. Moreover, Franz König, the cardinal to whom Kreisky referred, had indeed strongly criticized the SPÖ, but ultimately prevented a massive *Kulturkampf* from getting started. Kreisky, on the other hand, had expressly given free rein to Broda and Firnberg even before the Villach convention, even though the international debates about the trimester solution—for example, in Germany—made him feel even uneasier. But ultimately he would fully back all provisions of the party resolutions and get actively involved in the debate and vote on the bill in parliament.

Divorce reform, the second highly controversial point—in parliament and elsewhere—within the framework of changes to family law, ultimately proceeded as well in the direction of the SPÖ, which was going along with a social trend toward no longer placing an official "imprimatur" on traditional religious constraints. As early as 1951, the ÖVP had gotten behind efforts, primarily in the area of family law, to do away with the obligatory civil marriage that the National Socialists had introduced into Austria in 1938. The lines of argumentation from this time—including a sort of vulgar biology that sought to justify the different treatment of men and women in family law—would be deployed again in the 1970s. Actually, the SPÖ's approach to family law carried on certain traditions that went all the way back to the Monarchy (1901) and the interwar period (equality of the spouses, the legal status of the offspring of the marriage, the relationship of the spouses with respect to marital assets). In the area of family law, however, no new, unitary legislation was passed; rather, particular sections of it were amended, including granting equal rights to children born out of wedlock, implementing new regulations concerning the legal status of the family's children (parental rights and duties instead of parental authority), and revision of the legal relationship of the spouses to one another.

Viewed as a whole, the area of legal reform in a narrow sense was certainly one of the most essential reform efforts of the 1970s for the development of the Second Republic, the effects of which would be felt for decades. Furthermore, developments in the field of education meant that there was not only a corresponding formal legal framework available, but also an increasing number of young judges, state's attorneys, and lawyers who were in a position to add positive and progressive social content to this framework, although the "prisonless society," another one of Broda's visions, still appears to be a utopian fantasy.

Broda, as well as Kreisky, made the effort to bring together a broad majority behind these reform proposals; they succeeded with two exceptions: the new regulation of abortion through the trimester solution, and divorce over the protest of one of the spouses in cases in which the partners had been separated for many years (although this was an issue to which the FPÖ agreed).

To an increasing extent, Minister of Justice Broda's aim was not only to establish formal equality before the law, but also "to bring about . . . more equality through the law" (Broda 1980). The SPÖ's new 1978 party platform took this approach into account. Whereas the concept of civil rights did not take into consideration real social inequality, those who put together the new party platform sought to argue in the direction of a concept of social rights—that is, a "right that is not derived from abstract concepts, but rather one that regards human beings in their concrete economic and social situation and intentionally treats them differently on that basis."

A concrete example of this endeavor is the trustee law for handicapped persons. Other projects of Broda's, such as the federal law regulating social jurisdiction, the legal aid law for the mentally ill, and the juvenile court law, were not enacted during his term as minister.

## Reform of Elementary and Higher Education

*School Reform*

Even in the 1960s, the educational system was being increasingly overtaken by social trends not only with regard to substantive pedagogical issues, but also in a quantitative respect as well. Between 1960-61 and 1970-71, the number of students attending general high schools (AHS) rose from 38,500 to approximately 97,000. Enrollment at schools offering compulsory basic education was also exploding, though without anything having been done to provide more classrooms and teaching personnel. In 2,713 elementary and high schools, class size exceeded the permissible limit of forty; almost a third of all AHS students were in classes with thirty-six students or more.

The political discussions about maximum class size dominated the debates in parliament in the late 1960s along with the question of eliminating the ninth school year for AHS students, which had been successfully put through by means of a national petition drive initiated by some ÖVP politicians against the will of the ÖVP minister of education.

In spite of dissimilar approaches in areas of pedagogy and access to education, however, educational questions basically lacked the sharply defined ideological contours they had during the First Republic. Here as well, convergence of positions and compromise were the result, although it was always the ÖVP that filled the post of minister of education during this period. Above all, it was the Education Law of 1962 that signaled the highpoint of political cooperation on educational questions on the level of the Grand Coalition.

The discussions within the SPÖ focused primarily on equal opportunity, that is, ensuring that all children have the same chance to pursue an education. Whereas educational legislation required a two-thirds majority, it was possible to enhance the overall educational picture with a number of ancillary regulations. As early as the first Kreisky minority government, AHS entrance exams that had been mandatory until then were discontinued. In 1971 above all, the SPÖ concentrated its arguments on the element of equal opportunity through free schoolbooks, free transportation to and from school, and the expansion of subsidies for students running parallel to a school construction program that had already been started by the ÖVP when it was the sole governing party.

A few school reform measures having to do with the democratic participation of students and parents' representatives to enable them to have input into pedagogical framework conditions (School Instruction Law of 1974) were successfully implemented, as were intensified efforts to redesign course content in the new area of "political education" to replace traditional "civics instruction." A series of educational experiments and changes in school organization would also be launched, but a central element of the SPÖ reform program, the unified middle school for ten- to fourteen-year-olds, remained positively taboo for the ÖVP.

In no other area was such a pronounced "reform on little cat's feet" carried out during the governmental era of Chancellor Kreisky. This was due to both the traditionally controversial nature of school-related issues and the fact that such legislation required a two-thirds majority. Socialist school experts like Josef Hieden therefore came to the conclusion that the "fundamental principles of socialist school policy could be implemented only on a limited basis." The core element of the party's reform efforts—the unified school on the lower secondary level—was abandoned in 1983 in favor of high school reform.

## Institutions of Higher Education

Bernd Schilcher explained the "malignancy afflicting Austrian universities" since 1945 with "their isolation": isolation of specialized disciplines from each other, isolation from new scholarly currents, isolation from society, isolation from the pluralism of diverse worldviews. During the Monarchy, the *Weltanschauung* at the universities had been dominated by conservative forces (Christian Socialists and, increasingly, German Nationalists). When Liberals and Social Democrats were even present among the faculty, they were totally marginalized, and during the First Republic, the pressure on this minority and the influence of the radical pan-German movement and its anti-Semitic attitudes increased. Austrofascism and above all National Socialism had "liquidated" the most progressive and open-minded university professors.

Therefore, 1945 would by no means signal new beginnings, but rather the restoration of conservative structures with dominant authoritarian elements. It was thus no accident that all international trends, particularly in the arts and humanities, seemed to have passed by the Austrian universities in Vienna, Graz, and Innsbruck without having left a trace. Socialists continued to be intentionally excluded from those faculties, solely because of their political views and regardless of their scholarly qualifications.

At the very latest, by the advent of the 1968 student movement—which was hardly felt in Austria—dissatisfaction and pressure in the direction of reform became increasingly apparent among both young Catholic student activists closely associated with the ÖVP as well as the minority of Socialist students. Even during the Klaus years when the ÖVP governed alone, at least a first step was taken toward reform by the educational administration ("Council for University Issues" consisting of politicians, bureaucrats, professors, teaching assistants, and students that was set up to work out the basics of university reform). The antipathy to planning of the Heinrich Drimmel era was brought to an end, and the first systematic analysis of the need for academicians was carried out. Up to this point, only one legislative initiative had been put forth by the Ministry of Education—the Student Aid Law of 1963. The so-called University Organizations Law of 1955 (UOG) had merely compiled and reissued various different decrees and regulations from the time of the Monarchy.

But it was precisely in this area in which the SPÖ had almost no opportunity to have input into policy measures that one of the most comprehensive reform undertakings would be initiated. Even during the opposition period, SPÖ Club Secretary Heinz Fischer—who had, among other activities, made a name for himself in the student movement opposed to Taras Borodajkewicz, an anti-Semitic and racist professor at the Vienna Economics University—was at work on a university concept in cooperation with several university professors and some socialist students. Kreisky himself as SPÖ party chairman also made sure to keep up contacts during the opposition period with Catholic student organizations and the *Cartellverband* (CV) in order to build broader grassroots support for his projects.

Even during the first phase of solo administration, the Socialist minority government founded a new federal Ministry for Science and Research and thus severed the umbilical cord that had always connected the universities to the educational bureaucracy. Hertha Firnberg, who had originally chaired the working group for the party's "people platform," was the first head of this new ministry. Within a short time, a six-member working group had developed a proposal for a UOG, which was submitted for discussion in 1971. However, this measure, designed to guarantee greater openness and democratization at the universities, was not passed by parliament until 11 April 1975. One subject of especially heated discussions was the tripartite parity of university professors, the "middle strata" of academicians, and students which was meant to bring more democracy into university decision-making processes—including the appointment of professors and the acceptance of postdoctoral theses—and to provide for more objectivity. The social explosiveness of the UOG was manifested by the fact that it was one of the longest-debated laws of the Second Republic.

Meanwhile, ancillary measures like the repeal of university fees and the establishment of new universities in Linz and Klagenfurt were part of an effort to expand access to higher education to all social classes. Just as in the legal field, a catch-up process was launched here as well, accompanied by certain long-term reform efforts that are still evident to this day. Basically, however, assurance of the solid position of the newly founded ministry itself was the chief carryover. On the other hand, in the current reform of the reform phase, the dominant elements are at least a partial decentralization of the universities in the sense of enhancing the autonomy of university agencies, deregulating numerous commissions, and strengthening evaluations of various kinds.

## Military Reform: "Six Months are Enough" and the Search for a New Defense Doctrine

Shortly before the 1970 parliamentary elections, Bruno Kreisky took up a suggestion from Leopold Gratz and Peter Schieder, the chairman of the Socialist Youth Group, to decrease the mandatory term of service in the Austrian Army from nine months to six. Although this idea was by no means new—as early as 1964, Otto Rösch, who was then the SPÖ secretary of state in the ÖVP-dominated ministry of defense, had proposed a substantial reduction of the mandatory term of service—Kreisky made it into an important campaign issue for the first time, and it was well received, particularly by young male voters. Doing alternative public service instead of going into the army, another idea that was advanced by Socialist Youth functionaries, was not addressed in concrete terms during the election campaign, but was very much a part of the discussions conducted in 1970 and over the following years.

Although this proposal was met with widespread and massive opposition within the officers' corps, Kreisky attempted to fulfill this campaign promise as quickly as possible. But in order to ensure a wide-ranging discussion of the necessary basic framework conditions, he set up an army reform commission as an advisory panel.

The chancellor himself made the effort to steer the discussion away from a pragmatic argument about the time required to train troops and toward a fundamental debate about "military doctrines." His personal concepts ran in the direction of broad-based national resistance that would also be supported by the workers through civil resistance to an aggressor. Furthermore, in his view, the process of socially anchoring the "political defense of the nation" should also be supported by the other bodies representing the interests of the people. In keeping with the Swedish model, Kreisky attempted to create a new committee as a forum for national defense questions—besides the National Defense Council—consisting of experts and elected officials as well as representatives of businessmen, workers, and farmers.

It would take until 1972, however, for an effort led by Minister for Foreign Affairs Rudolf Kirchschläger to produce the "Draft of a Declaration of Fundamental Principles Concerning Austrian National Defense," and this was also unanimously adopted in 1975 by parliament as a constitutional law entitled "Comprehensive National Defense."

With regard to an internal defense doctrine, however, Kreisky did not receive ideas from his own ranks, but from a group of officers centered on General Spanocchi, who sympathized with the ÖVP. Their conceptions of the transformation of the Austrian Army in accordance with the concepts of an organized militia, "special forces"-type warfare, and zone defense would play a key role in the subsequent concrete reform discourse. Such conceptions most closely approached Kreisky's ideas about a "political defense of the nation" and established the trend for at least the following decades toward a quasi-professional army.

### Foreign Policy and the Internationalization of Austria through an Active Policy of Neutrality without "Ideological Celibacy"

There was certainly no area in which Chancellor Kreisky himself attended to the details more meticulously than in the field of foreign policy. Here, it is important to note—also as a line of continuity carrying over from the chapter on Austria's defense doctrine—that, in his view, the best defense policy was to anchor the tiny state of Austria as broadly as possible within the international community of states (UN, policies to reduce international tensions, disarmament). Here as well, we notice continuities stemming from Austria's experience with Anschluß in 1938, which had been accepted in silence by the states of Europe. The prevailing opinion was that Austria should never again withdraw into an isolated position during the Cold War, but ought to attempt to create positive framework conditions on its own.

Kreisky himself never made a secret of the fact that in this Cold War, the ideological-military-economic confrontation between the Communist Bloc under Soviet leadership and the "West" under the aegis of the United States, his allegiance was clearly and uncompromisingly on the side of the West. Containment of the Soviet zone of influence was just as much a part of his basic convictions as straightforward confrontation with the ideology and political practice of communism. Here as well, he remained true to his basic principles from the interwar period.

Nevertheless, due to Austria's geographical situation between the blocs, the conditions imposed by the State Treaty, and the country's policy of neutrality, even in the late 1950s he was pursuing an active "good neighbor" policy toward the adjacent communist states (Yugoslavia, Hungary, and Czechoslovakia), and in the 1960s he also attempted to pursue a policy of peaceful coexistence in Austria's bilateral relations with countries like Poland and Rumania that were amenable to reform in order to thus increase the security of Austria and the region as a whole. In the country's relationship with the major powers as well, he had been striving since the late 1950s to assume an active communications function—that is, in certain concrete issues like the Berlin question or the Cuba crisis, Austrian politicians and diplomats would engage in intensive contacts and dialogue in order to keep the particular negotiations running smoothly, or to submit their own suggestions in order to steer processes in a positive direction.

The highpoint of this new role for the tiny neutral state of Austria was certainly the negotiations before and after the Conference for Security and Cooperation in Europe (CSCE) in 1975 in Helsinki, where Austria succeeded both in coauthoring measures for the reduction of tensions and in implementing resolutions having to do with concrete mechanisms for the observance of human rights. Today, following the collapse of the Stalinist form of communism in Eastern Europe and the Soviet Union, these political steps toward a reduction of tensions and cautious intervention by Austria on behalf of the observance of human rights are being dismissed as "naïve" and even misinterpreted as having contributed to maintaining the system of communist regimes. Actually, these interventions, which Kreisky was also the only politician to raise in his address at the

CSCE in Helsinki, were an important part of the effort to keep opposition movements politically active, and, in case their members were arrested, to at least do something to make their lives somewhat easier. In light of the nuclear confrontation that was also taking place in Europe, this was the only possible way to provide at least long-term support for reforms and to prevent a "Hot" War. It was only in the early 1980s that this form of Eastern European policy was sharply criticized by the United States under President Ronald Reagan, though without denying the great contribution that Kreisky had made to the implementation of human rights on that side of the Iron Curtain. Thus, it was also no coincidence that Chairman of the Presidium of the Supreme Soviet Leonid Brezhnev and U.S. President Jimmy Carter signed the SALT II agreement on 18 June 1979 in Vienna.

In contrast to the interwar period, Vienna would become a permanent meeting place between East and West, and this is why the SPÖ solo government also took over an ÖVP project from the Josef Klaus administration to erect a third headquarters for the United Nations and establish an international conference center there, implementing these plans in the face of domestic political opposition and a national petition drive. Incidentally, it was the tremendous size of the conference center and the positive effect this project would have on employment in the construction industry that ultimately played a decisive role in getting the go-ahead.

But it was above all Kreisky's Middle East policy that provoked an international sensation and contemporary criticism. As early as the 1960s in his capacity as foreign minister, he sought to give consideration to Arab positions in the Middle East peace process to a greater extent than Western Europeans and Americans ordinarily did (for example, he visited the Egyptian president and revolutionary leader Gamal Nasser in 1964). Both in the 1960s and in the 1980s, though, Kreisky was far ahead of his time, and he was sharply criticized from many quarters. While his Middle East fact-finding missions within the framework of the Socialist International were praised and his policy of integration of Egyptian President Anwar Sadat garnered recognition as well as acceptance in the Camp David Accords on the part of Israeli and American politicians, Kreisky succeeded only in Europe in making Yassir Arafat's Palestine

Liberation Organization (PLO) a "socially acceptable" negotiating partner and in gaining acceptance for the position that a solution to the Middle East problems would have to be combined with a solution to the Palestinian problem with that people's active participation. The peaceful solution currently being pursued, that is, the inclusion of the PLO and Arafat, was the source of considerable political controversy and negative reactions in the media in the United States and Austria even far into the 1980s. Behind the scenes of the public debate, however, Kreisky was a much sought-after partner in conversations, particularly in the United States and even for Republican politicians. The official contacts with Arafat and the recognition of the PLO by the Republic of Austria were well received in the Arab world, but in Israel these moves came across positively only with the peace movement. Among extremist Palestinian organizations and some Arab states, however, Kreisky's Mid-east policy also sometimes evoked skepticism or a negative reaction. Obviously Kreisky's visions were decades ahead of their time.

Kreisky's foreign policy conceptions were not limited to the Middle East; rather, as far back as the late 1950s, he began to get involved in the so-called North-South conflict, in which he was a strong voice in favor of the interests of developing nations. Even as a student, he had displayed his commitment to the fight against colonialism, and he remained true to this cause as foreign minister and chancellor. The highpoint of this consistent foreign policy line, which had led to the founding of the Vienna Institute for Development Issues in the mid-1960s, was the first North-South Summit Conference in Cancún, Mexico, in 1981, which Kreisky organized as co-chairman. Despite the failure of what was then a unique confrontation of presidents and heads of government of eight industrialized nations and fourteen developing lands, it nevertheless managed to ultimately positively influence the subsequent dialog in the direction of a more deliberate development policy. A fundamental revision of existing disparities, that is, a policy of reconciliation and solidarity between the economic capacities of the North and the South, did not come about. Nevertheless, young people, particularly in recent years, have been made more attuned to the problems of development policy.

## Summary and Review

A final evaluation of the consequences of the reforms outlined above is certainly not yet possible. Nevertheless, it is already apparent that the period beginning in 1970 accelerated the long-term trend toward *westernization* of the political culture in Austria, meaning that the political camps as well as the influence exerted by the parties on social developments were subject to a process of erosion. Due to the explosive growth of education and advanced training, citizens have also become increasingly conscious of their democratic rights, and have by no means been shy in coming out against views that have prevailed in governing or opposition parties on particular issues. The 1978 plebiscite vote against the Zwentendorf atomic power plant was the first example of the emerging breakdown of citizens' unquestioned subservience to policies handed down by the leadership of a particular political camp, although this process did not become really blatant until the early 1980s. Parallel to this, "Austria consciousness" reached a highpoint during these years and became strongly anchored among broad segments of the population in the form of an unemotional, occasionally relatively simple, Austrian patriotism. The traditional image of a provincial and Catholic Austria gradually began to disappear and was replaced by the myth of the "island of the blessed spirits" and the *de facto* acceptance of the country's tiny stature, neutrality, and strong social welfare safety net.

During a speech in Innsbruck in 1975, Heinz Fischer attempted to discuss the question "The Kreisky Era: An Era of Social Policy?" and made it clear that

the time of socialist governmental activity in Austria since 1970 has been without a doubt a particularly fruitful period of reform in the Second Republic. It has brought change and innovation to many areas, but it did not demolish the structure of our social order, so that, according to its view of itself, this has been a period of reform activities that have conformed to the basic rules of the system and not a period of radical change to that system.

This statement is important because it also explains the relatively broad consensus—despite bitter opposition in some instances—in favor of the reforms outlined above, which political scientist Peter A. Ulram defines as the "social welfare-liberal consensus." However, this consensus also concealed the signs of internal decay of its socialist-Social Democratic core, which manifested itself even more dramatically during the 1980s.

A key communications instrument in shaping this "social welfare-liberal consensus" was Chancellor Kreisky's highly effective media persona, and a significant element contributing to his success at the polls was surely the rapid increase during the mid-1960s in the number of private homes with television sets. For the first time, it was possible for thousands of voters to compare the candidates in the privacy of their own homes, so to speak, by watching a televised confrontation between Chancellor Klaus and the challenger Kreisky, who was absolutely masterful in employing this medium.

The television was surely an important factor in reaching new groups of voters. Between 1965 and 1970, private ownership of television sets rose from 30 percent to 67 percent, and thus also made possible a considerably more private process of opinion formation as compared to viewing in a group setting at a tavern or in a neighbor's home where all viewers were usually members of the same political camp. At the same time, the broadcasting reform measures that had been passed with the votes of the ÖVP and the FPÖ on the basis of the broadcasting petition drive resulted in a professionalization of television under the leadership of the conservative journalist Gerd Bacher, and this intensified *Americanization* also brought politicians face to face with new challenges and opportunities. In his direct confrontation with Chancellor Josef Klaus, Bruno Kreisky used this medium much more effectively. Kreisky also had much better relationships with both Julius Raab and Alfons Gorbach than he did with Josef Klaus. Furthermore, over the course of decades, Kreisky's relations with the media were considerably more open than was typically the case in Austria during the 1950s and 1960s. The fact that Kreisky himself had worked as a professional journalist during his stay in Sweden and secretly desired to continue to pursue these activities exerted a positive effect here. Moreover, his experience abroad as secretary of state and foreign minister had inculcated him with an open style of communication.

Also in the question of distancing himself from the Communist Party of Austria, Kreisky, who was a consistent ideological anti-communist despite his deeply felt commitment to a comprehensive policy of reducing international tensions, had delivered in his Eisenstadt Declaration an unmistakable rejection of support by the communists. In spite of his basic ideological positions, Kreisky reacted towards criticism from the left wing of his own party—for example, from Günther Nenning—just as uncompromisingly, though in such cases he was satisfied to fire off put-downs that came across well in the media (thus, at the SPÖ's nineteenth party convention, Kreisky called Nenning a "nerd").

A transformation of values and the mobility of the employees of the new middle class would accompany the "spurt of modernization" which came into its own in the 1970s but had already begun to emerge in the late 1960s. In contrast to many other industrialized nations, this development proceeded relatively quickly in Austria and was also intensified by means of concrete political programs and projects, which thus made it identifiable as an "era."

Some lines of development—for example, equal rights for women and the reordering of the relations between the genders—did not get underway until the end of the Kreisky era, without causing for the time being radical social or party political changes up to 1983. By appointing four women as secretaries of state in 1979, Kreisky made an intentional effort to conform to an emerging social trend, even though the majority of the male party functionaries were not yet ready to follow the "Sun King" (*Sonnenkönig*) on this issue. At least in some areas, individual provisions of the gender equality platform could be successfully implemented during these years. Female voters accorded recognition to this effort to take more of an interest in the cause of women, so that the SPÖ could clearly establish itself as the women's party at the polls in 1983—despite all social deficiencies within its own ranks and its ideological work.

Significant for the long-term consequences of educational reform as well as, for example, for granting equal rights to women was the fact that they did not become socially and politically effective until the end of this era or even into the 1980s. Some of these developments would end up turning against the Social Democrats and reach their culmination in the conflict with the environmental movement (first Zwentendorf, but then especially the movement in opposition to the Hainburg power plant). "Social Democracy" as a movement had failed to link up with the new environmental movements and also increasingly fell out of touch with young voters. Only as an elder statesman a few years before his death did Bruno Kreisky himself change his basic attitude towards the Green and anti-nuclear movements, since he instinctively sensed that new demands on modern society also called for new answers.

# Austria and Europe, 1923-2000:
# A Study in Ambivalence

*Michael Gehler and Wolfram Kaiser*

## From Pan-Europe to the European Parliamentary Union

The priority awarded by the Austrian governments between 1945 and 1955 to the maintenance of Austria's territorial integrity over full participation in West European integration tends to divert from the significant contributions made by Austrians to the public discourse about closer European cooperation in the interwar and in the immediate postwar period. In promoting the idea of a united Europe, Richard Nikolaus Coudenhove-Kalergi in particular played a leading role in this debate, which initially remained largely restricted to individual politicians and intellectuals. Based on his multinational descent and his cosmopolitan intellectual background, Coudenhove-Kalergi was an early advocate of closer international cooperation. As early as 1920, under the impression of the breakup of the Austro-Hungarian Empire, he advocated separating Vienna from the rest of Austria and converting it into the seat of the League of Nations. Coudenhove-Kalergi believed that, after the breakdown of the old monarchic order in Central Europe, European civilization faced two threats: the first orginated from modern mass culture epitomized by the United States and the second from the Soviet Union and its strategic aim of worldwide communist revolution. For Coudenhove-Kalergi the central question was how best to safeguard the position of the old continent between the United States and the Soviet Union, foreshadowing the postwar debate about Europe as a cultural, political, and military "third force" between these two powers.

Coudenhove-Kalergi specifically called for a European federation of all nations from Poland to Portugal. This federation, he hoped,

Austria joins the European Union in 1995: After the June 1994 plebiscite, Austria's *Neue Kronen Zeitung* proclaims, "A Two-third Majority for the EU: A Resounding YES for Europe!"

Source: *Neue Kronen Zeitung* cover, Institute of Contemporary History, Innsbruck

would include the progressive introduction of a customs union, mutual border guarantees, and a common defensive posture against the Soviet Union, finally leading to the creation of a "United States of Europe" similar to the United States of America. Due to its worldwide obligations and orientation, Britain was not expected to be part of this united Europe, but Coudenhove-Kalergi consistently emphasized the need for a cooperative relationship with it. To promote his ideas of closer European unity, Coudenhove-Kalergi founded the Pan-European Union in 1923, whose headquarters were situated in the Vienna Hofburg, the old imperial palace of the

Habsburgs. Among its members were well-known Austrian politicians like the leading member of the *Christlich-soziale Partei*, Ignaz Seipel, Austrian chancellor during 1922-24 and 1926-29 and foreign minister in 1930, and the Social Democrat Karl Renner, head of the Austrian delegation at St. Germain and Austrian chancellor during 1919-20, who later became chancellor in the first provisional postwar government in 1945 and Austrian president during 1945-50. In October 1926, Coudenhove-Kalergi organized the first Pan-European Congress. More than two thousand politicians, including prominent European leaders, gathered in Vienna. In his keynote address, Coudenhove-Kalergi particularly emphasized the need for reconciliation between Germany and France, a major motivation behind the closer integration of the core Europe of the Six—that is France, the Federal Republic, Italy, the Netherlands, Belgium and Luxemburg—after the Second World War. During the 1930s, however, growing political radicalization, economic protectionism, and international tensions sidelined the ideas of Coudenhove-Kalergi and other early supporters of European integration. On entering Austria in 1938, the Nazi regime banned Coudenhove's Pan-European Union; Coudenhove himself went into exile in Paris where he unsuccessfully tried to put together an Austrian government in exile.

During the war, having moved to the United States, Coudenhove-Kalergi temporarily converted to the idea of a monarchic restoration in Austria as a safeguard against pan-Germanism. When the allies recognized Edvard Benes' Czech government in exile, he demanded similar treatment for Austria. His efforts were not, however, supported by either the allied powers or, indeed, by the Austrian republicans in emigration in the United States who continued to blacklist Coudenhove-Kalergi for his support for the interwar authoritarian regimes of Engelbert Dollfuss (1933-34) and Kurt Schuschnigg (1934-38). Coudenhove's political activities during the war were thus restricted to his role as adviser to Archduke Otto von Habsburg. Together they developed the concept of a European confederation under Western tutelage which would include Germany and exclude the Soviet Union. The institutional structure of such a confederation would follow closely the Swiss constitution. The American government did not support this plan, nor, as was to be expected, did the Soviet Union. It was, however, at least noticed by the British Prime Minister Winston Churchill, whose rather vague idea of a Danubian confederation to ward off Soviet influence in Central and South-Eastern Europe, which he temporarily favored, closely paralleled Coudenhove and Habsburg's concept.

In June 1946, Coudenhove returned to Europe—to Gstaad in Switzerland where he founded the European Parliamentary Union (EPU). The EPU encompassed leading Austrian politicians like Eduard Ludwig, Hans Pernter, and Bruno Pittermann, although none of them played a very prominent role in the new organization. With the creation of the EPU, Coudenhove-Kalergi expected to exert public pressure on the European governments and parliaments to move towards the realization of his pan-European ideals, hoping to utilize the economic dynamism of the Marshall Plan for the political integration of Europe. Once more, however, Coudenhove-Kalergi's ambitious concept of a European federation, which would originate from a constituent assembly, proved unrealistic. Due to British pressure for a strictly intergovernmental structure, the Council of Europe, which was finally created in 1949, was and remained purely an advisory body. European integration became largely restricted to the economic sector, first with the creation of the European Coal and Steel Community (ECSC) in 1951-52 and subsequently with the creation of the European Economic Community (EEC) in 1957-58.

Recent research on European integration history has established that the influence of European pressure groups such as Coudenhove-Kalergi's EPU on the integration process in the first decade after the war was, in fact, limited. Instead, economic interests and wider foreign policy goals, as defined by the governments involved, were decisive in determining the shape of institutions and the policies followed. Moreover, even among the pressure groups that were engaged in promoting the idea of European unity, Coudenhove-Kalergi played only a marginal role after the war by comparison to the interwar period. The European Movement, created in 1947 by Winston Churchill and Duncan Sandys, was much more visible in the public debate about European integration and organized the Hague Congress, which took place in May 1948. Nonetheless, Coudenhove-Kalergi's initiative at least contributed to the formation of a political climate among the political elites in Western Europe which was increasingly favorable toward the idea of closer integration.

## Austria, the OEEC, EPU, GATT, and ECSC

After the Second World War, Austrian attitudes to participation in closer European cooperation were overshadowed by the overriding strategic aim, which was almost universally accepted in Austria, of negotiating the withdrawal of allied occupation troops and regaining national sovereignty. At a time of growing tension between the two superpowers, to participate fully in West European integration that went beyond intergovernmental economic cooperation threatened to impede Austrian efforts to preserve the unity and territorial integrity of the country in its pre-1938 boundaries. In the Moscow Declaration of 1 November 1943, the allied powers—for legal as well as for opportunist foreign policy reasons—had agreed on the interpretation that Austria had been the first free country to fall victim to German aggression. They regarded the so-called Anschluß of 1938 null and void and declared their intention to recreate Austria as an independent and sovereign state. The recognition of the Renner government in October 1945 and the signing of the Second Allied Control Agreement in June 1946 were milestones towards the re-establishment of an independent Austria. Thereafter, however, the Austrian question became entangled in the deepening East-West conflict and was eventually only resolved with the signing of the Austrian State Treaty in 1955.

The key dilemma for Austrian European policy-makers before 1955 was the need to manage Austria's dependence on American financial aid and its fast growing economic interdependence with Western Europe without, however, antagonizing the Soviet Union. In the summer of 1947, the Austrian government decided to accept the invitation to the Paris conference which was to decide the institutional and policy framework for the administration of the Marshall Plan, an initiative which the United States hoped would not only support the short-term economic recovery of Western Europe, but also lead to its long-term political reconstruction and integration. In 1948, Austria joined the Organization for European Economic Cooperation (OEEC) despite the refusal by the Soviet Union and its East European satellites to participate. During 1948-52, Austria received $962 million from the Marshall Plan, or 13.5 percent of all funds. According to one estimate of mid-1951 by Ludwig Kleinwächter, Austria's ambassador to Washington at that time, Austria had until then received no less than $789 million from the United Nations Relief and Rehabilitation Administration (UNRRA) and interim and congressional aid and from the Marshall Plan. It could also make use of $152 million of drawing rights and of $80 million initial positions within the European Payments Union (EPU), founded in 1950, of which Austria was initially an associate member and then a full member from 1953 onward. Overall, Western aid amounted to over $1 billion until 1951. This does not include the substantial sums donated by private charities or those released by the so-called counterpart funds. In addition, the United States disclaimed a large part of the payments to which they were entitled under the terms of the occupation accord. Some Marshall Plan money also made its way into the Soviet zone of occupation and thus helped overcome the food crisis and related social problems. It could not, however, compensate for *de facto* reparations to the Soviets through the dismantling of industrial plants, the control of production and the appropriation of German assets, payments that have been estimated at between $1 and $2 billion.

The greater long-term significance of the Marshall Plan was of course its impact on the liberalization and the accelerated redirection of trade. In the interwar period, the traditional Austrian trade links within the former territory of the Austro-Hungarian Empire already had been eroded. After Austria's annexation by the German Reich in 1938, the economic and trade ties with Germany were greatly strengthened, a trend that was subsequently reversed only temporarily due to the economic and trade distortions after 1945. In 1948 Austrian exports went mainly to Italy (17 percent), Switzerland (13.3 percent) and Czechoslovakia (7.5 percent). At that time, more than 15 percent of Austrian exports still went to the Soviet Union and its satellites, the highest proportion of trade conducted with Eastern Europe of all OEEC countries. However, OEEC and EPU membership in conjunction with American restrictions on the export of modern technology to the Soviet bloc, which Austria had to accept, led to a decline of the share of Austrian trade with Eastern Europe. By 1955 imports from Eastern Europe were down to 8 percent compared with 32 percent in 1937, and Austrian exports to the region also had declined to eight per cent compared with 28 percent in 1937. By contrast, imports from other OEEC countries rose sharply from 40 percent to 75 percent, and exports to these countries from 53 percent to 71 percent. As part of this development, Austrian economic dependence on Germany increased again in the wake of economic recovery in the newly created Federal Republic, a potentially sensitive domestic political issue in Austria. By 1960, 27 percent of Austrian exports went to the Federal Republic and 40 percent of Austrian imports came from there. Austria also largely depended on the Federal Republic for its income from tourism which helped finance a chronic trade deficit.

In addition to the OEEC and the EPU, Austria also became a member of other Western economic organizations: the International Monetary Fund (IMF) and the International Bank for Reconstruction and Development (IBRD) in August 1948 and the General Agreement on Tariffs and Trade (GATT) in October 1951. The Austrian government, however, took great care to emphasize that, due to its economic dependence on Western Europe and its political dependence on Soviet goodwill, it ought to be treated as a special case. Within the OEEC, for example, Austria occupied a special status during 1948-52, before an improved balance of payments position allowed it to follow OEEC rules and participate fully in trade liberalization. While safeguarding its core economic interests through participation in the OEEC and EPU, the Austrian government acted very cautiously in its policy towards European institutions of a more overtly political character. In 1947, for example, Foreign Minister Karl Gruber advised the Austrian ambassador to Paris, Alois Vollgruber, to "tread softly" and not to "put yourself into the forefront" in order to avoid antagonizing the Soviet Union. The Vienna government made clear that Austria, before it had regained its sovereignty, could not participate in full economic integration in the form of a customs union with supranational institutional features, a concept that the United States strongly favored. Austria also did not join the Council of Europe when it was created in 1949 and only accepted an invitation to send a delegation of observers, which did not comprise members of the government, to the sessions of the Parliamentary Assembly in Strasbourg in November 1951. The Austrian government was particularly careful to avoid any association with Western defence organizations. It stated clearly that it could not join the Brussels Pact of 1948 or the North Atlantic Treaty Organization (NATO), founded in 1949, a policy that was not seriously disputed within Austria.

To follow a policy of non-alignment was seen as essential for the negotiations on the Austrian State Treaty ultimately to succeed. These had made rapid progress in 1949, but stalled during 1950-53 at the time of the Korean War. In 1953 the Austrian government, now led by Chancellor Julius Raab (1953-61), initiated a new approach that allowed for the possibility of Austrian commitment to a policy of permanent neutrality in exchange for securing Austria's territorial integrity and regaining full national sovereignty. On this line there was broad bipartisan agreement between the governing Christian Democrat *Österreichische Volkspartei* (ÖVP) and the Social Democrat *Sozialistische Partei Österreichs* (SPÖ). Even Gruber, who is often depicted as unequivocally pro-American and a "cold warrior," did not support full Western integration over national unity, as the West German Chancellor Konrad Adenauer did under different external conditions after 1949.

As a result, the Austrian government had very little freedom with which to manoeuvre regarding matters of European integration. In his book *Die Politik der Mitte*, published in 1946, Gruber argued that a confederation of states was only conceivable on a worldwide basis and that it should comprise the continental European countries as well as the Anglo-American nations. With respect to Austria's future role in Europe, Gruber specifically concluded in 1947 that it was no viable alternative for Austria to be thinking in terms of a separate state for the Western zones only, fully integrated into all Western organizations. Such an entity would hardly be viable, for the Soviet Union in its zone controlled most of Austria's industry, whereas the Western powers enjoyed its Alpine scenery. Moreover, Gruber argued, it would result in the economic and political disintegration of the country and would mark "the end of Austria." Gruber welcomed, in principle, progress made by the Six towards closer West European integration, such as the creation of the ECSC in 1951-52. He hoped that, in the long run, Austria could fully participate in this process. In that case, Austria would also be able to play a much more active role in initiating common policies in Europe.

Ultimately, neutrality was the price Austria paid in 1955 in exchange for the Soviet Union's approval of the State Treaty and the withdrawal of their troops from eastern Austria. During the bilateral negotiations in Moscow in April 1955, the Austrian delegation agreed to follow a policy of permanent neutrality. The fact that the neutrality status was formally enacted not in the State Treaty of May 1955, but in a separate parliamentary constitutional law of October 1955 underlined that the Austrian government considered that the solution agreed upon in April allowed it to define the extent of Austria's neutrality and the related obligations itself and that it left room for a continued policy of Western orientation. The Soviet Union had to accept Austria's accession to the United Nations in December 1955 and to the Council of Europe in April 1956. It was unclear, however, what degree of economic integration, if any, involving the transfer of national sovereignty to common institutions, the Austrian government would consider compatible with its new neutrality policy. The Soviet safeguard here was Article Four of the State Treaty that prohibited economic or political union with Germany, but this was, of course, a provision that from the very beginning was open to conflicting interpretations.

In 1955 the exact shape of Austria's future neutrality policy and how it would limit Austria's policy choice in matters of European integration still had to be defined. Within the ÖVP, many leading politicians of the older generation regarded the armed neutrality of Switzerland, adapted to Austria's special needs, as exemplary and well suited for safeguarding Austria's security under the *de facto* political shield of NATO. According to the dominant Swiss view, such an interpretation of the neutrality status would, for example, exclude the possibility of participation in a customs union. In their post-imperial search for a new international role for Austria, some Conservatives hoped that the neutrality status might assist future Austrian governments in playing a mediating role in Central Europe and between the two blocs and thus enhancing Austria's diplomatic influence and international standing. Austria's independence in foreign policy, however, would be backed up with a strong ideological Western orientation that only the Christian Democrats could guarantee.

Accordingly, in the first decade after the war, the ÖVP continuously emphasized its role in transnational party cooperation within Western Europe. As early as June 1946, Gruber had established contacts with French Christian Democrats of the *Mouvement Républicain Populaire* (MRP). ÖVP politicians subsequently played an important role in establishing contacts between French and German Christian Democrats which eventually led to the integration of representatives of the German *Christlich-Demokratische Union* (CDU) and of its Bavarian sister-party, the *Christlich-Soziale Union* (CSU), in transnational party cooperation within the *Nouvelles Equipes Internationales* (NEI) founded in spring 1947. ÖVP politicians also took part in the informal Geneva circle. These meetings in Switzerland were organized by the French journalist Victor Koutzine, a special adviser to Georges Bidault, and the German emigrant writer Jakob Joseph Kindt-Kiefer, co-founder of the all-party group *Demokratisches Deutschland* and of the *Vereinigung Christlicher Demokraten* in Switzerland. They brought together leading West European Christian Democrat politicians like Bidault, French foreign minister in 1947-48 and minister president in 1949-50, the Belgian Jules Soyeur and the Germans Konrad Adenauer, Jakob Kaiser, and Josef Müller. The Austrian participants hoped to avoid too narrow a concentration on the Six in the emerging core Europe. Unable to participate fully in the integration process, they argued for an active Christian Democratic movement in Europe. They also continuously stressed their strong ideological Western orientation. At the NEI youth congress in the Austrian resort of Hofgastein in July 1949, for example, the ÖVP General Secretary Felix Hurdes declared emphatically "that we here in Austria will hold out in this advance post of Christian occidental culture."

The SPÖ, too, accorded priority to the territorial integrity of Austria and thus to its neutrality over Western integration, although initially with less enthusiasm than many Christian Democrats. Having left behind the anachronistic politics of class struggle, the SPÖ, which had been working together with the ÖVP in a grand coalition since 1945, found it easy to accommodate itself with the economic concept of the Marshall Plan. The Social Democrats actually advocated early Austrian membership in the Council of Europe, although they, too, were skeptical about the possibility of Austrian participation in the ECSC and, more generally, in core Europe institutions, particularly when they were of a more overtly political or even military nature. Unlike its German sister party, the SPÖ did, however, welcome in principle the creation of NATO, the plan for a European Defense Community (EDC) and the eventual creation of the Western European Union (WEU) in 1954-55, although it ruled out Austrian membership.

Between 1945 and 1955, the priority awarded by the Austrian governments to securing Austria's territorial integrity and regaining national sovereignty severely limited its European options, with potential adverse economic consequences. Non-participation in the ECSC temporarily appeared likely to undermine Austria's economic recovery due to its dependence on German coal supplies and its need for markets for Austrian steel. As long as integration among the Six remained restricted to certain sectors, however, the economic effects of reluctance to go beyond economic cooperation along intergovernmental lines were rightly regarded as limited and bearable. When in October 1954 unilateral negotiations with the ECSC about privileged bilateral association failed, the Austrian government thus decided to give up its efforts, a tactical move that in retrospect can be seen as a crucial diplomatic down payment to the Soviets before the signing of the State Treaty.

Unlike Austria, the Netherlands and Belgium, two low-tariff countries with a similar degree of economic interdependence with Western Europe, were under no external constraints and chose a very different strategy to enhance their role in the emerging new Europe by participating in setting up the ECSC and negotiating the EDC Treaty. To them, membership in integrated organizations like the ECSC essentially offered three main advantages: it helped sustain economic and social policies which no longer seemed viable in the context of a small nation state; it provided for disproportionate influence of smaller states, either through independent supranational institutions like the ECSC High Authority or through weighted voting like in the EEC Council of Ministers; and it created a stable framework for interest mediation and thus promised to maximize security against the larger states, particularly against Germany. Belgium had, of course, been neutral before the First World War, and the Netherlands had remained neutral in the interwar period, but their neutrality status had not protected them against German invasion and occupation in 1914 and 1939 respectively.

Their choice was not, however, so obvious as it may seem in retrospect. Denmark and Norway, both NATO members, saw no economic need and showed no political desire to join integrated institutions. Moreover, Switzerland and Sweden, despite a similar degree of economic interdependence with Western Europe, were determined to retain their historically rooted neutrality status, which seemed to have safeguarded their security during the Second World War and had actually enabled them to profit from it economically. Their case reminded Austrian politicians, who were contemplating the most useful definition of Austria's new neutrality status, that attractive alternative strategies to integration in fully or partly supranational institutions existed for safeguarding the economic interests and enhancing the political role of smaller states in postwar Western Europe.

## Free Trade (EFTA) instead of Common Market (EEC)

Soon after the signing of the State Treaty, tacking between neutrality and participation in West European economic cooperation was, however, rendered much more difficult as a result of the decision in principle by the Six at the Messina conference in early June 1955 to proceed with horizontal integration in the form of a customs union, a project that had in fact been discussed on and off since 1947-48. After expert talks under the direction of the Belgian foreign minister Paul-Henri Spaak between July and November 1955, the Six decided at their meeting in Venice in May 1956 to proceed with negotiations. These eventually led to the signing of the Rome Treaties in March 1957 and the establishment of the EEC on 1 January 1958. The EEC Treaty provided for the progressive abolition of all internal tariffs and the introduction of a common external tariff of the Six over a period of twelve years. The potential adverse economic effects on Austrian trade with the Six seemed serious, particularly because Austria's trade was now mainly with the Federal Republic whose tariffs were on average considerably below the future common external tariff and would thus have to be raised against third countries like Austria. Moreover, not least due to its disadvantageous geographical location, Austria could not hope to compensate fully for any possible export losses in the EEC market with greater exports to other OEEC countries.

Despite the potential adverse economic effects of non-membership, the Austrian government never seriously considered during 1955-57 joining the EEC as a full member, particularly after it was reminded of Austria's precarious security position on the iron curtain when the Soviet Union brutally suppressed the Hungarian Revolution in autumn 1956. Although, in contrast to the ECSC High Authority, the EEC Commission had no independent decision-making powers, the EEC Treaty provided for the introduction of majority voting in the Council of Ministers at the beginning of the third stage of the integration program, a permanent transfer of sovereignty to common institutions which the Austrian government now regarded as incompatible with Austria's new and constitutionally enshrined neutrality status. The Austrian government, therefore, welcomed with great relief the British initiative within the OEEC in 1956-57 to create a wider industrial free trade area (FTA) as a trade roof above the EEC, a proposal that promised to avoid competitive disadvantages for Austrian export industry in a common market of the Six. According to the initial British plan, the free trade area would not involve the harmonization of tariffs and would be organized entirely along intergovernmental lines. It would thus ideally safeguard Austria's trade interests without provoking Soviet opposition and diplomatic pressure.

In late 1958, however, France under the new leadership of Charles de Gaulle broke off the FTA negotiations, which had been going on in Paris since October 1958. From then onwards, Austria was caught in the Anglo-French rivalry over the political leadership of Western Europe, which culminated in de Gaulle's veto against British EEC membership on 14 January 1963. The Austrian government initially perhaps underestimated the medium-term diplomatic difficulties to find a suitable multilateral solution to the ensuing West European trade conflict between the Six and the other OEEC member states. Otherwise, it might have directly pursued economic association with the EEC on a bilateral basis, as Greece did in the early 1960s. De Gaulle might have responded positively to such an Austrian approach at that time. Austria's EEC association would have given France some political control over the ever closer economic links between Austria and the Federal Republic and would have weakened Britain's political position in Western Europe. Instead, the Austrian government decided unanimously in the summer of 1959, albeit without great enthusiasm, to participate in setting up the EFTA of the so-called outer Seven, that is—apart from Austria—Britain, Sweden, Norway, Denmark, Switzerland and Portugal, an option that Raab had mentioned for the first time in summer 1958.

The EFTA Treaty, which closely resembled the original British plan and provided only for a weak secretariat in Geneva for administrative purposes, was initialled in Stockholm in November 1959 and came into force in May 1960. The Austrian government initially hoped, as did the British, that the creation of EFTA would provide enough counter-pressure on the Six to induce them to agree to renewed negotiations about multilateral association within a wider FTA, but this time between the two European groups, EEC and EFTA, rather than between the EEC and individual countries, as had been the case in Paris. Leading ÖVP politicians in particular, who had close links with Austrian export-oriented business that became increasingly concerned about possible Austrian exclusion from the EEC market after the breakdown of the FTA negotiations, initially hoped that EFTA would provide a bridge to the EEC and a wider economic solution acceptable to all sides. The Austrian ÖVP Trade Minister, Fritz Bock, with support from Austrian industry, was successful in getting this common aim enshrined in the preamble of the EFTA Treaty.

The main reason for initial Austrian support for EFTA membership was the hope that Austria could thus continue to enjoy the advantages of economic interdependence and of political independence at the same time, minimizing any legal obligations and avoiding a commitment to long-term political integration. In the early 1960s, however, neutrality and EFTA membership also began to acquire several secondary domestic and external functions, in any case for leading SPÖ politicians. This is particularly true for Austria's new foreign minister since 1959, Bruno Kreisky, who later so successfully shaped the changing definition of Austrian neutrality and formed the self-perception of Austrians when he was chancellor between 1970 and 1983. Because it would have enraged the ÖVP and industry circles, Kreisky was careful not to discuss these evolving secondary functions explicitly in the domestic political context, but he spoke about them much more freely to foreign politicians.

One secondary function—and to Kreisky perhaps the most important one—was that neutrality and EFTA membership would facilitate the ongoing Austrian nation-building process in conscious demarcation from Germany. Kreisky's thinking on Austria's role in Europe was strongly influenced by the Anschluß syndrome. Even by the early 1960s, Kreisky continued to see the Federal Republic, and particularly German economic penetration, as a serious threat to Austrian independence. Talking to the British Foreign Secretary Selwyn Lloyd in London in February 1960 shortly after the creation of EFTA, Kreisky emphasized that, in his view, "Austria was confronted with two dangers, the Soviet Union and Germany. The best way to preserve her security against both was internal stability combined with neutrality." Before the visit the British ambassador to Vienna, Reginald James Bowker, had advised the Foreign Office that to Kreisky, EFTA was a potent political symbol in that it marked "a significant break from Austria's traditional policy of close association with Germany." Kreisky would continue "to look to the United Kingdom, as the strongest partner in the new association, for continuing support in carrying through a policy which is unpopular in many influential quarters in Austria."

For Kreisky, to play up the dangers of economic dependence on the Federal Republic and—with the help of EFTA membership—to contain artificially the bilateral economic and trade ties regardless of the potential adverse effects on the Austrian economy, were major strategic aims. Kreisky made it clear to the German Foreign Minister Heinrich von Brentano during a meeting in Bonn in March 1960 that, in his view, the crucial point was that "to join the EEC would indirectly mean to join Germany." In the early 1960s, Kreisky strongly encouraged Austrian constitutional lawyers to develop a progressively narrower interpretation of neutrality that included non-participation in economic organizations that might prevent Austria from taking independent action in economic and trade policy at times of war. This was a theoretical construction that was also fashionable in Switzerland, but that legal advisers in the British government, Austria's key ally in the West European trade conflict, regarded as far-fetched in terms of international law and entirely politically motivated. For Kreisky, the progressive reinterpretation of the obligations of neutrality was a useful pseudo-academic cover for his main concern that Austrian EEC membership was undesirable on political grounds and would be in contradiction to the State Treaty's Anschluß prohibition.

In the early 1960s Kreisky also played on the fear domestically that, as the Soviet Union treated the EEC as the economic wing of NATO, Austrian EEC entry might provoke unpredictable Soviet reactions, possibly even including military threats or measures. In reality, however, Kreisky did not believe in the 1960s that it would. He freely confessed to von Brentano that, "if Austria joined the EEC, the Soviet Union would *not* regard this as a *casus belli*." Instead, Kreisky feared that EEC membership would not allow Austria to play the role of arbiter between East and West or, as the new British Ambassador in Vienna, Malcolm Henderson, noted sarcastically in 1963, that it would put an end to the special treatment of Austria by the Soviets as their diplomatic "pet canary," which was designed to demonstrate what pleasant life neutral countries could lead and, more generally, to help create an inoffensive image of the Soviet Union in the world at large. As foreign minister and later as chancellor, Kreisky was indeed keen to develop Austrian foreign and European policy with full regard to Soviet interests and sensitivities. Early benefits of this strategy of accommodation included, at the political level, the prestigious hosting of the summit between John F. Kennedy and Nikita Khrushchev in Vienna in spring 1961 and, at the economic level, the stabilization of Austria's protected trade with the Eastern bloc. Kreisky admitted to von Brentano that his real concern about the Russian reaction to possible Austrian EEC membership was that the Soviets would no longer conclude favorable treaties with Austria and would not, for example, allow the international test control organization to be located in Vienna, "to which Austria attaches the greatest importance."

The British government was fully convinced that in order to shore up domestic support for his foreign and European policy, Kreisky was grateful for mild Soviet threats that helped rationalize his stance against Austrian EEC membership. Henderson noted about an informal conversation between Kreisky and the Soviet Ambassador to Austria, Victor Avilov, during a Viennese *Faschingsball* in February 1963 that "Dr. Kreisky has been under fire here from the People's Party for allegedly failing to press the Austrian application

for association with the EEC with sufficient vigour; and the Socialist
Party in general has been accused of being too anxious not to upset
the Russians by commiting Austria to un-neutral courses. It is
therefore probable that he was not really displeased at the nature of
Mr. Avilov's remarks." Three months later, Henderson noted about a
Soviet protest against the possibility of independent bilateral
association of Austria with the EEC after the breakdown of the
British entry negotiations: "I have no doubt that Dr. Kreisky is
pleased with the Russian *démarche*. It will support him and the
Socialist Party in their relations with Dr. Gorbach [the ÖVP
chancellor] and may help to keep Dr. Bock under some sort of
control."

In 1961-63, however, Kreisky was still too weak politically to
carry his particular vision of Austria's future role in Europe and the
world with the larger coalition partner, the ÖVP. When the British
government decided in the summer of 1961 to apply for EEC
membership, which finally put an end to the search for a multilateral
solution to the trade conflict between the EEC and EFTA, the
Austrian government decided to apply for economic association
according to Article 238 of the EEC Treaty alongside the two other
neutrals within EFTA, Sweden and Switzerland, in December 1961.
Apart from a few Europhiles, EFTA membership and, after 1961,
EEC association necessitated by the changing external
circumstances, was as far as most Social Democrats, not just
Kreisky, wished to go. Kreisky thus strongly supported the modified
European strategy, according to which the EFTA neutrals would
coordinate their European policies closely during the negotiations in
Brussels to achieve the common aim of multilateral EEC association.

Leading ÖVP politicians, on the other hand, had always regarded
EFTA membership as a temporary arrangement before a multilateral
solution could be reached. They were rightly concerned that, even if
Britain was allowed to join the EEC, strong United States and French
opposition to allowing the neutrals all economic benefits of
association without the financial burden and the political
responsibility of full membership, could well make association
impossible to achieve. As a result, Austria might need once more to
play on its economic dependence on the EEC market in conjunction
with its precarious security situation in order to be awarded special

treatment by the EEC. Within the ÖVP, Bock was particularly concerned about the economic dangers of long-term exclusion from the EEC market and pressed for a more active association policy, if necessary on a bilateral basis and without close rapport with the other EFTA members. Bock was strongly supported by the ÖVP "modernizers" around Josef Klaus, finance minister during 1961-63 and chancellor during 1964-70, who regarded a closer relationship with the EEC as one element in their strategy for the domestic economic and political modernization of Austria.

These differences between the ÖVP and the SPÖ erupted into the open when de Gaulle's veto against British EEC membership clarified that there would be no wider solution, comprising the EEC and all EFTA countries, for the foreseeable future. Up to this point, the corporatist decision-making structures and the established grand coalition policy-making patterns, based on the lowest common denominator between the two parties, had excluded the possibility of a substantial innovation in Austrian European policy. However, the breakdown of the Brussels negotiations, which led to sharply increased pressure from Austrian export industry for a unilateral approach to the EEC, in conjunction with slight ÖVP gains in early national elections in autumn 1962, facilitated a change of course. In an internal coalition trade-off, Kreisky, not least in order to secure his position as foreign minister, ceded ministerial responsibility for European integration matters to Bock. The renewed grand coalition now decided against the advice of Kreisky, but with his reluctant cooperation, to pursue the association option independently in bilateral talks with the EEC and on 26 February 1963 renewed its association request.

Eventually, two rounds of negotiations with the EEC Commission took place. However, the negotiations between the Community and Austria finally failed in 1967, ostensibly over Italy's veto in the wake of a crisis in the bilateral relationship with Austria over the bomb attacks in South Tyrol. Within the EEC, only the Federal Republic, not least because of its own export interests in the Austrian market, had vigorously supported the Austrian application for association, which would have been in the form of a *de facto* customs union, probably with special arrangements for agriculture. Early on after de Gaulle's veto, the Adenauer government—at this stage with the support in principle of the French government—began to press for the privileged treatment of Austria as a special case. Otherwise, however, the Austrian desire to conclude an association treaty according to Article 238 of the EEC Treaty from the very beginning met serious objections that were initially underestimated in Vienna. The Italian government, for example, insisted that a simple trade agreement was entirely sufficient to safeguard Austria's economic interests. They managed to delay first, the consideration of the merits of the Austrian case by the EEC Commission, which finally submitted its generally favorable report in June 1964, and subsequently, the start of exploratory talks. Neither were the Benelux governments happy about the Austrian policy of going it alone—the so-called *Alleingang nach Brüssel*—though for different reasons. Enraged by de Gaulle's unilateral veto of British EEC entry, a cornerstone of their own European policies, the Dutch and Belgian governments were primarily concerned in 1963-64 with avoiding any action which could upset the internal cohesion of EFTA, of which for the time being Austria remained a member, in order at least to sustain some degree of counter-pressure on the Six, particularly de Gaulle.

In addition to these objections in principle among the Six, it was obvious that the Community would not treat the Austrian case as a political priority. The veto had plunged the EEC into a serious internal crisis, and in 1963-64, the Six were preoccupied with at least establishing a suitable basis for consultative talks with the British government and with finding an economic *modus vivendi* in the form of a liberal policy towards the Kennedy round of the GATT and continued progress towards the protectionist Common Agricultural Policy. The constitutional "empty chair" crisis of 1965-66, when France boycotted the ministerial council meetings to prevent the transition to majority voting at the beginning of stage three, further burdened the Austrian application.

Although, ultimately, Austria's talks with the Community failed, they were pioneering in that they represented the first serious negotiations about economic association according to Article 238 of the EEC Treaty between the EEC and an advanced industrial country. The key issues, which were controversial then, were later to come up once more in the negotiations between the Community and the remaining EFTA countries about the creation of the European Economic Area (EEA) in the early 1990s. For example, the Six—the Italian government in particular—were not prepared to award Austria all economic advantages of integration in a *de facto* customs union without compensatory financial contributions to the EEC's development and social funds. This controversy foreshadowed the dispute in the negotiations in the early 1990s about payments by EFTA countries into the so-called cohesion fund, which would benefit the poorer Community states. The Austrian government, on the other hand, insisted that its neutrality status absolutely required it to retain the principal right of autonomous rather than automatic adaptation of EEC legislation, the so-called *acquis communautaire*. Then, as over the EEA Treaty twenty-five years later, however, this demand was rejected outright by the Community which regarded such an arrangement as a serious threat to its legal integrity and, moreover, as an undeserved reward for a country that was not prepared to join as a full member.

Two years after the breakdown of Austria's efforts to reach a separate agreement with the EEC, de Gaulle's retirement from French politics in April 1969 finally permitted the wider solution which the EFTA states had set out to achieve ten years previously. On 1 January 1973, Britain, Denmark, and Ireland joined the Community. The other EFTA members, including Austria, signed free trade agreements with the EEC and the ECSC, which had been amalgamated to become the EC in 1967. In Austria's case, the successful conclusion of bilateral negotiations with Italy about South Tyrol had previously removed the most difficult diplomatic obstacle. According to the free trade agreement, all tariffs on industrial goods between Austria and the EEC were to be abolished by 1977. Unlike in the case of a *de facto* customs union, which the Austrian government had aimed at during 1963-67, Austria preserved its treaty-making power in trade relations with third countries in accordance with the initial British FTA concept of 1956-57, favored throughout by Kreisky.

The 1972 free trade agreement safeguarded Austria's core economic interests in the EC market. At the same time, it left Kreisky, who was elected Austrian chancellor in 1970, free throughout the 1970s and early 1980s to pursue his political vision of a neutral, pacifist Austria as a mediator between East and West and increasingly also in the North-South conflict. This policy temporarily secured for Austria a prominent international diplomatic role out of all proportion to the country's size, economic strength, or strategic importance. The benefits of the new strategy of political and, increasingly, mental equidistance to the two blocs in Europe were now substantial. They included, at the political level, the elevation of Vienna to third seat of the United Nations with the construction of a UN conference center in the 1970s and, at the economic level, extremely low defence expenditure for a token army under the continued *de facto* political shield of NATO.

## Application for Full EC Membership (1989) and Joining the EU (1995)

Before the 1972 free trade agreements, Austrian economic gains in terms of greater exports to other EFTA countries had not compensated for losses in trade with the EC, one reason among others for the comparatively weak performance of Austria's economy in the 1960s. After 1973 the share of trade conducted with the six founding members of the EC rose once more. But despite a certain amount of reallocation of Austria's European trade in the 1960s and the resulting disadvantages for the Austrian economy, it is correct to point out that "all 'precise' economic prophecies of the 1950s and 1960s that Austria could not survive without joining the EEC [were proved] wrong." The main reason why the adverse economic effects of non-participation in the EEC were limited, as in the case of Britain, was that tariff barriers were not only continuously being negotiated downwards within the GATT, but that they proved the lesser obstacle to increased trade by comparison with non-tariff barriers, such as industrial norms. After a period of political stagnation within the Community in the 1970s, the EC Commission suggested in 1985 to abolish these non-tariff barriers and to create an internal market in goods, capital, services, and people by 1992. This initiative started a dynamic phase in European integration, which lasted until the signing of the Maastricht Treaty in 1992. Like the decision by the Six to create a customs union in 1955-57, the new internal market program completely changed the external economic context for Austrian European policy by increasing once more the economic price of non-participation in the Community. Moreover, the decline of the Soviet Union as a superpower in conjunction with the easing of East-West tensions after Gorbachev's assumption of office in 1985 also fundamentally changed the external political context for Austrian European policy. It sharply reduced the political eroticism of the neutrality status, and it completely excluded the possibility of serious political sanctions in case of Austrian EC membership.

It now seemed increasingly that only by joining as a full member could Austria prevent a severe competitive disadvantage in the enlarged EC, which by 1986 comprised twelve countries, and facilitate the modernization of the still highly regulated service sector. Moreover, by the mid-1980s, the corporatist economic system was seen to be in need of structural reform, and EC membership was to provide the necessary external pressure to cushion politically the economic and social effects of deregulation. Against this changing economic background, the Federation of Austrian Industrialists first demanded EC membership in May 1987. In January 1988, the smaller of the two coalition parties, the ÖVP, which had joined a new grand coalition in 1986, followed. Finally, the SPÖ party leadership eventually voted fifty-four to four in favor of applying for EC membership in April 1989, and the application was lodged in July 1989. Six months previously, the EC Commission President Jacques Delors had proposed the participation of EFTA countries in the internal market program without actual EC membership, an initiative that was designed to delay the enlargement of the Community until after its institutional deepening in the Maastricht process. The resulting EEA Treaty was signed on 2 May 1992. It was linked with a transit treaty between the EC and Austria that was supposed to regulate transit traffic between EC countries through Austria for a period of twelve years. By 1992, however, the Austrian government did not regard the EEA solution as a suitable substitute for full membership of the Community. Throughout, the Austrian government emphasized the importance of the inclusion of agriculture as well as full participation in EC decision-making.

Austria's entry negotiations began on 1 February 1993 and were concluded on 1 March 1994. After protracted negotiations during the winter of 1994, solutions were eventually found to the three problem areas of greatest domestic political concern to the government. These were agriculture, transit traffic, and regulations restricting the sale of property in Alpine regions. In Austria, unlike in Scandinavian countries, a referendum on membership in what is the European Union (EU) since 1 November 1993 was obligatory under the constitution and was called by the government for 12 June 1994. The referendum debate was characterized by a marked and stable elite consensus on the desirability of EU membership. This consensus encompassed the two governing parties, SPÖ and ÖVP, the small opposition *Liberales Forum* (LIF), founded in 1993, all major interest groups other than environmental organizations, the four institutions of Austrian organized corporatism, or *Sozialpartnerschaft*, and the overwhelming majority of the media. Only the right-wing populist *Freiheitliche Partei Österreichs* (FPÖ), the Greens, and the small and weak communist party opposed EU entry. On voting day, turnout was 82.4 percent; 66.6 percent voted in favor of EU membership and only 33.4 percent against. After the parliamentary ratification process was concluded, Austria joined the EU on 1 January 1995.

The Austrian political elite secured the two-thirds majority for EU entry chiefly by stressing that membership was entirely in line with Austria's postwar European policy and that it would require no major domestic adjustments. But this was true only insofar as the EC application was the attempt to adapt Austrian European policy to the fast changing external economic and political circumstances at the end of the Cold War era, essentially to achieve the same strategic objectives of guaranteeing sustainable economic growth and securing political manoeuvrability and influence, when the neutrality-EFTA strategy no longer provided sufficient benefits. It conveniently ignored, however, that the two principal strategies, neutrality and integration, were geared towards broadly similar objectives, but that over a period of forty years they had very different repercussions for the economic and political systems and the prevailing mental structures of the smaller states and that, as a result, Austria would be confronted with the need for considerable internal change after EU entry.

Accession to the EU has not only caused severe economic and financial adaptation problems, but it has also affected the institutional balance within the Austrian political system by accelerating the disintegration of the postwar, consociational patterns of governance. EU entry has reinforced the existing trend towards much greater competition and confrontation in the political system. However, EU membership exerts perhaps the greatest pressure on the entrenched paradigms in which Austrians have learned to perceive themselves and the wider world since the Second World War, and particularly since the Kreisky era, and in which Austrian politicians are used to contemplate politics, articulate interests, and pursue policies. Their post-entry irritation extends, for example, to the difficulty of getting used to thinking and acting as part of a wider community of states with an enormous and long-established network of intersocietal and intergovernmental contacts and a certain degree of supranational decision-making.

Two illusions of the postwar era, which over time became to a varying extent part of the belief systems of at least the SPÖ and the ÖVP, cause particular problems. These are first, the superficial internationalist rhetoric, so carefully cultivated by Kreisky in the 1970s, which has ever only superficially concealed a distinct lack of European or international orientation in the economy, in education, and other spheres of Austrian society; and second, the idea of the moral superiority of a neutral and peace-loving country. By the mid-1990s, this idea has been shattered by the growing awareness that the outside perception of Austria's neutrality policy, in any case since 1989, varies from, at best, indifference to the sarcastic view that neutrality is and always has been a cheap policy of hanging on the coattails of NATO. By comparison with Sweden and Switzerland, who throughout the Cold War pursued credible defence policies, respect in other EU states for the neutrality policy of Austria, which spends only a slightly greater portion of its GDP on defence than Luxembourg or Iceland, is very limited, indeed. Unlike Britain, Austria is at least geographically "at the heart of Europe." Experience since EU entry suggests, however, that much more substantial domestic adjustments may still be needed before the Austrians can themselves make a significant contribution to the future development of the Union.

## Austria within the EU, 1995-2000: Economically Integrated, but Politically Isolated?

Austria not only joined the EU, but also the European Monetary System (EMS), the precursor to the Economic and Monetary Union (EMU), as a net payer. Thanks to its unbroken economic policy of integration before 1989, it joined the EU in an economically advanced stage. The attempt was made by the Grand Coalition— consisting of Social Democrats and Christian Democrats, under both of the SPÖ Chancellors Franz Vranitzky (1986-97) and Viktor Klima (1997-2000) and the Christian Democratic Vice Chancellors Erhard Busek (1991-95) and Wolfgang Schüssel (1995-2000)—to adhere to the criteria for convergence in the form of austerity programs and tax increases. These provoked criticism within the country.   The influence of the FPÖ opposition leader and right-wing populist, Jörg Haider, grew steadily—from 8 percent in 1986 to 27 percent in 1999. But in 1997, the initiative for a petition for a referendum against the EURO (for which the present-day Vice Chancellor, Susanne Riess-Passer, was responsible) was rejected by the people in relatively clear terms.

Austria's assumption of the EU presidency in the second half of 1998 demonstrated its capability of taking on this new role and, with it, the responsibility for community policy. Austria needed "Europe" within a short time, two identity-forming core elements of the Second Republic were removed: the victim thesis was made questionable in the wake of the Waldheim debate and "permanent" neutrality became obsolete through the security policy in Europe (the Common Foreign and Security Policy and, in a new manner, NATO). The "return to the European stage" seemed to offer a sensible replacement for them.  But this hope was deceptive.

Overnight, the country was to become a pariah. The "EU's model student" was hit unexpectedly, unpreparedly, and undeservedly by the decision of the fourteen other EU countries of 31 January 2000 threatening (and later carrying out) sanction measures in the event of the formation of an ÖVP-FPÖ government, which took place on 4 February 2000. In the history of the community, there had never been a precedent for such an action.  This made the Austrians very aware of the political dimension of the political union, the loss of relevance of national sovereignty, and the worries of the other EU members with regard to the change in government in the Alpine republic. People there had simply gotten too accustomed to Haider. The sensitivity in other countries affected by right-wing populist tendencies (Belgium, France, and so forth) was underestimated. The Austrian Foreign Ministry had indeed expected negative reactions, but not to this degree. Even the politicians appeared to be surprised. Critical comments had been counted on, but not such massive punitive measures against a member state. They were unique in the history of the community and thus unforeseeable.

Soon thereafter, there were doubts as to their permissibility and legality. The measures appeared to be disproportionate, and in any case without legal basis. Social Democrats and members of the Green Party were at first in favor of the hard stance of the EU fourteen. They attempted to justify the "sanctions," and they also saw in them a reason for the resignation of Wolfgang Schüssel, who was still Foreign Minister at the time and the presumptive new chancellor.

On 12 September, the EU fourteen announced "the immediate abolition of the sanctions." In a contradictory and ambivalent communiqué by the French presidency of the Council of the European Union, a classic compromise formulation on the safeguarding of the unity of the union, it was stated that the EU fourteen had taken note of the report. The "measures" had proven "useful," but could now be abolished. It would be "counterproductive" if they were to be applied further. Austria had not violated "European values." The development of the FPÖ, however, was "uncertain." This, along with its "nature," was reason for "serious concern." A "special vigilance toward this party and its influence on the government" must thus be maintained. This "vigilance" would be practiced in common. At the end of the communiqué, it stated that the procedures followed by the EU should never again be repeated. The recommendation by a committee of three "wise men" for the creation of a control mechanism in similar situations was judged to be a "useful contribution to these deliberations," but it was not acted upon concretely.

Austria itself was only superficially the issue and the reasons for the measures of the fourteen Union states are not to be found primarily in the actions of the Socialist International as was rashly believed in Austria. Rather, the deep crisis of the German Christian Democrats (CDU) at the end of 1999 and beginning of 2000 was decisive for the absence of mediation in the path of transnational party cooperation and the lack of corresponding political support for the ÖVP-FPÖ government.

From the beginning on there was no unified front of the 14 Union states, despite the German Christian Democrats dropping out. It was therefore foreseeable that these "sanctions" would not hold consistently in the long run and in the end had to become only grotesque and anachronistic. Apart from the absent legal basis, the punitive actions by the EU fourteen can hardly be designated as sanctions; on the whole, they were "sanctions" of a rather harmless sort. The lifting of the measures signaled that the EU fourteen could only carry out a policy contrary to public opinion in their countries for a limited time. In addition, Austria, whose international importance is far less self-evident than is generally assumed within the country, was an example that made evident the fact that, in this action, self-interests clearly ranked above community interests. According to Albert Rohan, General Secretary of the Austrian Foreign Ministry, the country owed the relatively quick end to the EU fourteen measures above all else to its EU membership. But it still remains a question whether Austria is and will be politically isolated within the EU.

# Austria between 1983 and 2000

*Anton Pelinka*

The "Kreisky Era" ended with the General Elections of 1983. The SPÖ lost its overall majority in the Austrian National Council and was forced to make an arrangement with one of the other parties in parliament. Kreisky, already very ill, resigned as chancellor and some months later also resigned as chairman of the SPÖ. But he decisively influenced the strategic orientation of his party. As a consequence his preference since 1970 for compromising with the smaller FPÖ rather with the ÖVP, a coalition was formed between the SPÖ and the FPÖ under Fred Sinowatz (SPÖ) as chancellor and Norbert Steger (FPÖ) as vice-chancellor.

This reflected the beginning of the end of a political pattern that was traditional for the Second Republic: the dominance of the political system by just two parties—the SPÖ and the ÖVP. The pattern of two-party dominance was expressed by the "grand coalition" between the ÖVP and SPÖ from 1945 (until 1947, the coalition also included the small Communist Party of Austria, KPÖ) to 1966 and was also expressed by the seventeen years of one-party governments (1966-70: ÖVP; 1970-83: SPÖ). The end of two-party dominance was mainly expressed by the decline of votes the two parties were able to get. In the 1960s and 1970s, more than 90 percent of the voters preferred either the SPÖ or the ÖVP. This extremely high degree of concentration had begun to decline, favoring in the 1980s and 1990s the partly redefined FPÖ and the newly- established party of the Greens. Additionally, in the 1990s the Liberal Forum (LIF) also benefited from the waning allegiance to the ÖVP and SPÖ. The re-establishment of the coalition between the Social Democrats and the conservative ÖVP in 1986 did not prevent the further decline of the two traditional major parties. The SPÖ-

Fifty years after the Anschluß, the past is still haunting Austria: Cover of the
German news magazine *Der Spiegel* reading "Austria 1938-Austria 1988: Trauma
Anschluß, Trauma Waldheim"

Source: *Der Spiegel* cover, Institute of Contemporary History, Innsbruck

ÖVP coalition lasted until 2000, when—after the parliamentary
elections of 1999—the ÖVP formed a coalition government with the
FPÖ.

The years after the Kreisky era can be seen divided into the
following periods:

- 1983-1986: The "Small Coalition" between the SPÖ and FPÖ;
- 1986-1999: The "Grand Coalition" between the SPÖ and ÖVP;
  and
- since 2000: The "Small Coalition" between the ÖVP and FPÖ.

During these coalition years, Austria was also confronted with a new (international as well as domestic) awareness of the Nazi regime and of Austria's (and the Austrians' role) in that regime. The election of Kurt Waldheim to the federal presidency in 1986 was the first important event which polarized Austria and led to international critique on Austria, based on Austria's post-1945 attitude to define itself just as a victim of the Nazi rule. Some of this critique was deflected by a new attitude of the Austrian government at the end of the 1980s and during the 1990s, when representatives of both traditional major parties—for example, Chancellor Franz Vranitzky (SPÖ) and President Thomas Klestil (ÖVP)—officially accepted Austria's co-responsibility for Nazism. The rhetoric of the FPÖ after 1986, when party chairman Jörg Haider used language calculated to appeal to pro-Nazi sentiments, and the FPÖ's access to the government in 2000 created the second wave of international criticism.

Open debates about Austria's past were typical for the 1980s and 1990s. They also fitted into the new social unpredictability within the country. The new generation did not respect the loyalties firmly established in the past. The new openness was the consequence of Austria's ability to live—as a society, as a political system—with more explicit conflicts, both between the generations and within the (especially younger) generations. In these years, Austria became a much more conflict-oriented society.

The political developments of the 1980s and the 1990s did not only end the pattern of two party dominance; they also reflected a break with the pattern of consociational democracy—a specific understanding of democracy, defined not only as majority rule, but also as power sharing. As a consequence of the experience of centrifugal democracy, civil war, and dictatorship, Austria's "Second Republic" after 1945 had developed a special kind of consensus-oriented democracy. Based on the reconciliation efforts of the two traditional political movements, the Social Democrats and the Catholic Conservatives, the Austrian political system became an example of political "over- stabilization." In the 1990s, this type of consociational democracy increasingly lost its ability to mobilize political loyalties within its traditional framework. The rise of the Freedom Party (FPÖ), redefined after 1986 as a rightist populist party, and the new Green Party indicates the alienation of the traditional elitist network and the younger generation from the traditional model of democracy in Austria..

The basic philosophy behind the consociational type of democracy in plural societies is to reduce the rule of competition in favor of a balance between competitive and coalescent elements, between conflict and consensus orientation. The rules of the game should not be "the winner takes all," but rather that the loser gets something, too. The history behind this philosophy is a deep fragmentation caused by violent domestic conflict.

## Success and the End of "Consociational Democracy"

It is not the Austrian constitution, which explains the Second Republic's inclination towards consociational democracy. After 1945, the constitution was still the same as it had been during the years of the First Republic, an era which certainly cannot be called "consociational." Consociational democracy is the specific political culture as it developed after the catalyst years of authoritarian and totalitarian rule.

The First Republic's political culture fits the pattern of centrifugal democracy in that it was already fragmented along the lines of various camps. Three subcultures divided the Austrian society and its political system: the two major ones, the Socialist and the Christian-conservative, and the smaller pan-German one. The leaders of those three camps responded to this situation by competing according to the rules of liberal democracy. Because nothing could be gained by adopting a moderate attitude toward the political center, this competition set in motion a trend away from the center, a phenomenon known centrifugal democracy.

The most striking aspect of this development was that the camps treated each other according to the logic not of domestic, but of foreign policy. This included an arms race that led directly to the civil wars of 1934. Centrifugal democracy brought about the destruction of democracy.

After 1945, the fragmentation had not disappeared. In his study of Hallein, a town near Salzburg, G. Bingham Powell, Jr., described and analyzed the deep hostility, which still characterized the relationship between "black" and "red" Austrians in the 1960s. There was still an identity between party functions and functions in all the secondary groups which dominated social life. There was no independent life beyond the camps. Moreover, the camps were still characterized by strong, hostile stereotypes. Powell summarized the finding of his study:

1. partisan distrust and hostility are indeed associated at the individual level with pure or cumulative (rather than mixed or cross-cutting) cleavage position and with membership in partisan secondary groups; and
2. hostility and distrust between major political groups complicate and reduce the effectiveness of political decision-making.

Even twenty years of consociational democracy, the fragmentation and the *Lager-Mentalität* (camp mentality) were still there. Politics still was considered to be a battle between the forces of good and evil. The two major camps, in a coalition cabinet jointly responsible for Austria's development, still took a dichotomic view of society. To put it more precisely, because the old stereotypes still worked on society, on the "masses," the elites were free to behave according to the model of consociational democracy.

The powerful political leaders in 1945 and the years immediately thereafter were the elites of the SPÖ and ÖVP, of the socialist and of the Christian-conservative camps. The communists did not really count. As soon as it was obvious that the U.S.S.R. did not plan to integrate Austria into its Marxist-Leninist realm by force, the influence the KPÖ had enjoyed in 1945 was a thing of the past. The KPÖ was not strong enough to build a camp for itself. The SPÖ kept its *de facto* monopoly on the political left because the Social Democrats were able to reestablish their camp with all the familiar structures and organizations of the last decades of imperial Austria and the First Republic: socialist organizations for everyone, fulfilling every social function, from child care to provisions for a true socialist burial. In contrast, the pan-German camp was paralyzed. Identified for good reasons with the Nazi regime, the camp, which had been the Christian Socials' coalition partner between 1920 and 1933, simply did not exist in political terms.

Austrian consociational democracy consisted from the very beginning of two elements: the cooperation between the ÖVP and

SPÖ on the government level, including a parliamentary alliance; and cooperation between employers and employees, or between their respective interest organizations. These two elements were characterized by different logic and competences:

- Government and parliament followed the rule of liberal democracy, which the grand coalition, simply by its existence, restricted until 1966. This rule followed the logic of a zero-sum game. If you don't want to lose, make sure that someone will. Majority rule existed, electoral victories had an impact on parliament, and elections were a competitive procedure on a political market, the same as in other liberal democracies. Government and parliament dominated all non-economic matters, and both government and parliament were under the control of political parties, namely of the ÖVP and SPÖ.

- Business and labor established their own rule of corporatism. Majority rule was abolished, and a mutual veto made compromises unavoidable. The zero-sum game did not exist, and elections had little or at least no immediate influence. Corporatism dominated all economic matters, including most aspects of social policy. Economic interest groups organized to represent employers, employees, or agriculture controlled the corporatist level.

Both levels were integrated by virtue of their amalgam of political parties and economic interest groups. Political decision making was synchronized by the identity of political personnel; the two major camps controlled not only the parties, but also the organized economic interests. There was no significant voice on the corporatist level that was not controlled by the parties, and no significant voice was heard on the government level unless it was under the control of the major economic interest groups.

The structural and personal links prevented the two areas from moving apart. The differences concerning majority versus unanimity rule also implied different tendencies in self-promotion and self-perception: parties in parliament competing for votes are always inclined to go public as much as possible. On the other side, interest groups, which have to preserve their ability to compromise, are always interested in avoiding publicity if possible.

Consociational democracy had survived the end of the coalition in 1966. It survived especially on the level of corporatist decision

**FIGURE 1:**
**The Two Logics of Government and Corporatism**

|  | Government | Corporatism |
|---|---|---|
| **Differences:** | | |
| Players | Political Parties | Economic Associations |
| Arenas | Parliament | Social Partnership |
| Philosophies | Competitive | Coalescent |
| Rules | Majoritarian | Unanimity |
| Tendency | Public Disclosure | Little Disclosure |
| Powers | Non-economic | Economic |
| **Similarities:** | | |
| Structures | Both Government and Corporatism are linked by party factions within economic associations | |
| Personnel | Both are controlled in an elitist, cartel-like way | |

N=2,200

Source: Plasser and Ulram 32

making in the field of economic and social policy, and it survived on the level of regional (state) politics, where almost all Austrian provinces (states) were governed by coalitions between the ÖVP and SPÖ. But this specific kind of consensus-oriented democracy did not survive the social changes of the late twentieth century. The most important factors which are able to explain these changes are:

- Social mobility, the result of economic growth and improvement of general education, put an end to the traditional loyalty of the "camps," for the new generation started to rethink the old patterns of political behavior. Traditional electoral "monopolies" (for example, the SPÖ's quasi-monopoly of blue-collar votes and the ÖVP's quasi-monopoly of Catholic votes) started to break down.
- European (and international) development made it necessary to perceive Austria not as a kind of island governing itself in full

sovereignty, but as a dependent, smaller European country with a selfish interest in strengthening ties with Europe, meaning especially the European Union (EU). Austria and the Austrians became more and more aware of the necessity to accept a new openness, especially regarding Europe.

For the new generation, the traditional domestic enemy, the "reds" (Social Democrats) for the "blacks" (Catholic Conservatives) and vice versa was no longer perceived as a threat. That was the moment when consociational democracy in Austria began to crumble. The preconditions for consociational democracy were undermined by the successes of the concept itself. By reducing social fragmentation, it had also reduced political hostility. The auto- and heterostereotypes had lost their dichotomic significance; the "reds" had a less negative impression of the "blacks" (and vice versa); the enemy stopped being so dreadful anymore.

It was the attitude of the younger generation and the significant changes it underwent in the 1980s which made the walls of consociational democracy start to crumble. When the younger generation realized that the old perception of two hostile camps no longer fit into political reality, they started to leave the camps. For them, the old fragmentation along traditional cleavages was history.

Consociational democracy Austrian-style is the history of self-elimination by success. The old elite groups were able to bridge the deep gaps from the past so successfully that the gaps disappeared. But in closing those gaps, the elites destroyed their power base. The cleavages responsible for the old camps disappeared—and so did the old camps.

But it was also the changes in Europe and the world in general that forced Austria to open up economically, socially, and politically. Austrian industry, protected after 1945 by its high degree of public ownership, had to start a privatization process in the 1980s, as did the nationalized banks. The end of the Cold War caused Austria to rethink its traditional policy of neutrality. As a consequence, Austria decided to apply for EU membership in 1989 and joined the EU in 1995, after a two-thirds majority of the electorate supported this move in a decisive referendum.

Austria becoming member of the EU was the most important development during the years of the SPÖ-ÖVP coalition that lasted from 1986 until 2000. The two traditional major parties, which had been responsible for the Neutrality Act of 1955 and its specific interpretation, did not undo the Neutrality Act, but reinterpreted its meaning. Until 1989, joining the European Community (now the European Union), was thought to violate the best interpretation of neutrality, but came to be seen as incompatible with neutrality. Austrian neutrality, which was a specific Austrian response to the Cold War based on Austria's geopolitical conditions, had lost most of its impact on Austria's international position.

In 1994, when a decisive majority accepted Austria's EU membership in a referendum, it was the SPÖ-ÖVP coalition which was behind this step towards *Europeanization*. It was the last significant action of this coalition.

## The Beginning of the Transformation

The transformation of Austrian politics was first and foremost a dramatic change of the electoral behavior. Beginning with 1986, the FPÖ – the traditional small party of the pan-German camp – had redefined itself without breaking with its roots. It was the first party to profit from the decline of SPÖ and ÖVP. The Greens, which succeeded in entering parliament in 1986, were the second party to receive the benefits of the decrease in numbers of the Social Democrats and the Catholic Conservatives.

The elections of the National Council on 3 October 1999 gave clear evidence of the social factors that were decisive for the election outcome. The most visible (and most decisive) factor was the generation gap; other factors, which must be added in order to understand the outcome, were education (and correspondingly, occupation) and gender. The generation, education, and gender gaps had been already visible since the late 1980s, indicating significant changes in the political system's social environment.

Generation divided Austria into two almost completely different societies. Generational replacement played an important role in the dramatic increase in volatility. The parties, representing the two traditional, major camps—the SPÖ and the ÖVP—still had (and have) an overwhelming hold on the older generation. The third traditional party, the FPÖ, and to an even greater degree the two nontraditional parties, the Greens and—until 1999—the LIF (Liberals) attracted a significantly younger electorate.

During this period of political transformation, in the 1990s, political attitudes were sharply divided by the generation gap, by a deep cleavage created by traditional loyalties to the parties of the traditional camps and by loyalties of a new, distinctly more volatile type.

**TABLE 1:**

**The Party System and the Youngest and Oldest Voters in 1999,**
**Percentage of Age Groups**

|                 | SPÖ | FPÖ | ÖVP | Greens | LIF |
|-----------------|-----|-----|-----|--------|-----|
| Younger than 30 | 25  | 35  | 17  | 13     | 4   |
| Older than 70   | 39  | 25  | 31  | 2      | 0   |

This deep cleavage signifies the end of the "camps." For about one hundred years, beginning with the 1880s, the Austrian camps and their respective parties were able to pass on political loyalties within the borders of the camps. An Austrian was born usually into a particular camp and stayed within it, eventually handing down this loyalty to the next generation. Being born into a camp meant undergoing a political socialization; through youth groups, cultural organizations, educational programs, and leisure activities, a person was more or less completely bound to his or her camp. A person was either "black" (politically Catholic, that is Christian-conservative), or "red" (Social Democrat), or "blue" (pan-German; although in the 1930s and later members were often described as "brown" due to the almost complete takeover of this camp by the National Socialists, NSDAP).

In the 1930s, however, there was a break in this chain, in this continuity; the Austrian Nazi party attracted voters (up to 1933, the year of the last free local elections), members, and sympathizers in numbers far beyond the strength of the traditional pan-German camp. Even before 1938, the Austrian Nazi party became a successful catch-all party, winning acceptance among the traditional Christian-social and the traditional social-democratic electorate by invading political Catholicism and labor. In the 1930s, the traditionally closed camps were no longer so closed.

Between November 1945 and April 1946, the Allies had registered 428,249 Austrians, or about 10 percent of the adult population, as (former) members of the NSDAP. If the many Austrians who were still outside the country during the first year after World War II (for example, in prisoner of war camps) are taken into account, this figure must be adjusted even higher. About 600,000 Austrians had joined the Nazi party, a number that corresponds almost exactly to the membership of the best organized party of the First Republic, the Social Democrats. Considering that the pan-German camp in the First Republic attracted only one-third as many votes as the Social Democrats (and the Christian Socials) were able to get between 1919 and 1932, these membership figures emphasize the success that the Austrian NSDAP had even with Austrians who did not come from the traditional pan-German camp. It is also clear that it was especially the younger generation born into either the "black" or the "red" camp who went over to the Nazi party.

But in 1945 and especially in 1949, when most of the former NSDAP members got back their voting rights, the old pattern was fully re-established. The two major parties, strengthened by the rejuvenated socializing powers of their respective camps, were able to win about the same share of votes as in the First Republic: together they got 82.7 percent in 1949. The pan-German VDU (League of Independents, predecessor of the FPÖ) got 11.7 percent, or 489,273 votes, approximately the same number the two smaller parties of the pan-German camp had received in the First Republic. Compared with the 600,000 members, not voters, the NSDAP had in Austria, the re-establishment of the traditional camp system and of the two-and-half party system had an interesting impact: a significant number of former Nazis had joined the two major parties, at least as voters, but in many cases as members, too. The camp system was back.

Once re-established, the traditional party system and its tradition of socialization within the camps worked rather smoothly to control Austrian politics by means of its hereditary system. Everybody had his or her place in the party system, and in most cases, this place was defined by birth and was, therefore, for life. The system worked about four decades, and only then did things start to change. In the 1980s, the combined voting share of the two major parties started to decline. The FPÖ, the Greens, and later also the LIF were attracting more and more voters. But it was not largely the general electorate that started to leave the SPÖ and ÖVP; it was mainly the young voters who, no longer content to remain within the borders of the camps into which they were born, went over to the FPÖ, the Greens, and the LIF.

Because this was and is happening under the conditions of liberal democracy, it must have a different meaning from the generation gap, which was responsible for the rise of the Austrian Nazi party. In both the 1930s and the 1980s and 1990s, the socialist and the Christian-conservative camps were and are losing control over political socialization. But in the 1980s and 1990s, this could not have been the byproduct of political instability as was the case in the 1930s. It must be seen in correspondence with the stability of the Second Republic. The younger generation's inclination to leave the two major parties was (and is) based on a feeling of (political) stability, not instability. They did and do not go over to a totalitarian party with militant structures like the Nazi party. They were and are attracted either to the Greens or the Liberals, parties with no permanent organization or structure reminiscent of the strict organizations for which the camps were famous, or to the FPÖ, which is a traditional party with vestiges of the pan-German camp that are still important for political recruitment within this party. But the FPÖ did and does not attract its new electorate by binding it through membership or organization. During the eight years when the FPÖ's share of the vote exploded from 5 to more than 20 percent, its membership did not increase significantly. In 1985, the official data for FPÖ membership was 37,057, and in 1994, it was 42,200. Since 1986, the FPÖ has been a much less traditional party that it was prior to that time.

The explanation is that the younger generation was and is not leaving the major parties to join parties of the same type, nor are they leaving traditional parties. An increasing number of the younger generation has not been effectively socialized by the traditional structures of political parties and ideological camps. They never "belonged" to such traditional parties and camps and are now demonstrating their preference for a much looser alliance, for example, by not voting at all. Voter turnout is on the decline in Austria, falling from 92.9 percent in 1975 to 81.9 in 1994, but going up again to 86.0 in the 1995 general parliamentary elections—and falling again to 80.4 in 1999. Younger voters are quite flexible, changing party affiliations much more easily than members of the older generation, and do not view casting a vote as a lifetime decision.

The political behavior of the younger generation must be seen as a process of political polarization. The parties that significant numbers of younger voters prefer are (with the exception of the Liberals) seen by the electorate as less centrist than the SPÖ or ÖVP. The Austrian electorate perceives the Greens as the most left-wing party and the FPÖ as the most right-wing.

TABLE 2:
Perception of Political Parties on a Left to Right Scale

| Greens | SPÖ | LIF | ÖVP | FPÖ | Self-Perception of Electorate |
|--------|-----|-----|-----|-----|-------------------------------|
| 2.26 | 2.37 | 2.86 | 3.37 | 4.02 | 2.93 |

1.0= far left, 5.0=far right

N=2,200

Source: Pelinka 33

The young vote is a polarized and polarizing vote. This can be seen in correspondence with the education gap. Education as an electoral factor, according to traditional assumptions about the correlation between class and education, for decades followed a well-established pattern: voters with a higher level of education thanks to their bourgeois background showed a significant preference for the ÖVP, the party of the moderate right, while a number of voters with less education as a consequence of their non-bourgeois background (with the exception of the agricultural vote, that is, the labor vote), voted for the SPÖ, the party of the moderate left. This is still the case with older voters, but no longer true of the younger generation.

Among younger voters, the left-right dimension is completely reversed: Higher levels of education mean a tendency to favor the Liberals and the Greens, both of which, according to the dominant perception, are to the left of the ÖVP, with the Greens even being left of the SPÖ. The lack of higher education among these voters means a tendency to favor the FPÖ, which is seen as the most right wing of all the Austrian parties.

**TABLE 3:**

**Education Gap in 1999**

|                          | SPÖ | FPÖ | ÖVP | Greens | LIF |
|--------------------------|-----|-----|-----|--------|-----|
| **Elementary School Only** | 21  | 16  | 18  | 3      | 3   |
| **Vocational Training**  | 49  | 55  | 41  | 29     | 24  |
| **Higher Education**     | 30  | 30  | 41  | 68     | 73  |

N=2,200

Source: Plasser and Ulram 39

If the education gap is correlated with the generation gap, the differences become even more significant. Among the blue-collar voters, the FPÖ is the party of choice, ahead of the SPÖ; among the youngest voters with a high school education, the Liberals and the Greens are competing with the ÖVP. But that means that a high school or a university degree is no longer correlated with voting right of the center, and lack of higher education, especially in the case of the blue-collar vote, is no longer correlated with voting left of the center.

This reversal of the traditional correspondence between education and the left-right scale calls for an explanation, which can be found by analyzing the blue-collar vote. Between 1986 and 1999, the blue-

**TABLE 4:**

**Blue Collar Vote, from 1979-1999: Division between the SPÖ and FPÖ's Percentage of Blue Collar Workers**

| Year | SPÖ | FPÖ |
|------|-----|-----|
| 1979 | 63 | 4 |
| 1990 | 53 | 21 |
| 1995 | 41 | 34 |
| 1999 | 35 | 47 |

Source: Plasser and Ulram, 35

collar vote shifted dramatically from the SPÖ to the FPÖ. With respect to the generation gap, this means that, as a group, the younger blue-collar voters have changed their preference from a moderate left-wing party to a not-so-moderate right-wing party.

The education gap must be interpreted as an indicator of a general trend towards modernization. As early as 1960, Seymour Martin Lipset analyzed the authoritarian tendencies among blue-collar workers in the United States. In other Western democracies, the impact of significant numbers of working class voters casting their ballots not for traditional left-wing parties but for those from the right, especially for authoritarian rather than moderate right-wing parties, was felt much earlier than in Austria. The traditional perception of the labor vote as being inclined towards leftist parties had already been corrected, first in the United States and then in Western Europe, before the Austrian party system ever felt the effects of this reversal.

It is not at all remarkable that this trend can be observed in Austria, too. What is remarkable is that this trend is so delayed in Austria. The delay can be explained by the preservative effects the traditional ideological camps—in the case of labor, the socialist camp—had for such a long time. The strength of social democracy in Austria provided the blue-collar element with a political and ideological home which workers claimed as theirs. Now that home is no longer providing shelter, at least not for the majority of the young blue-collar workers. They consider themselves homeless. Now that the camp has lost its function as a subsidiary home for young blue-collar workers, they are responding as workers have done already in other comparable societies; they are moving towards the right and evolving authoritarian tendencies.

Because the socializing powers of the camps and their ability to stabilize political beliefs and behavior within their borders are in decline, the effects of modernization are setting in. But this decline is the impact of modernization. The demographic trend towards the cities (urbanization) and the economic trend towards the tertiary sector (service-oriented industries) are feeding the need for education. Education and social, as well as geographical, mobility are destroying the ability of traditional camps to control political loyalties. Social modernization provokes political transformation, even in Austria.

This can also be seen with respect to the political attitudes, which distinguish male and female behavior. The gender gap that for a long time was an insignificant factor in Austrian politics has now affected voting trends in Austria.

TABLE 5:
### Gender Gap among Party Membership in 1999:
### Percentage of Male and Female Votes

|            | SPÖ  | FPÖ   | ÖVP  | Greens | LIF  |
|------------|------|-------|------|--------|------|
| Male       | 31   | 32    | 26   | 5      | 3    |
| Female     | 35   | 21    | 27   | 9      | 4    |
| Gender gap | +4%  | -11%  | +1%  | +4%    | +1%  |

N=2,200

Source: Plasser and Ulram 32

The gender gap expressed by the difference of male and female vote is especially significant for the FPÖ. The FPÖ is a male party:

the probability of an Austrian man voting for this party is significantly higher than it is for an Austrian woman. The upswing the FPÖ enjoyed since 1986 must be attributed mainly to the male vote.

The gender gap can be explained by means of international comparison. In most Western European countries, the "post-materialist" type of political party the Greens are representing is especially attractive to women. On the other hand, "rightist-populist" parties—a category that clearly includes the FPÖ—attract significantly more men than women. The European division between the "harder," more materialistic orientation of male voters and the "softer," post-materialist orientation of female voters has finally come to Austria.

The surfacing of the gender gap is also an indicator of modernization. Austrian politics is more and more explainable by patterns already established in other socially and economically advanced societies. The idea of specific Austrian behavior and Austrian uniqueness is vanishing.

The increasing importance of generation, education and gender means a decrease in the impact of factors such as religion, *Volk* (ethnocentrism), and class, at least in the traditional sense. The SPÖ, the party of the traditional labor movement, has already lost the majority of young (blue-collar) labor voters. The upswing of the FPÖ, the party of the pan-German tradition, cannot be attributed to pan-Germanism and traditional ethnocentrism. The FPÖ's recent popularity must be explained by the amalgamation of the remnants of pan-German ideology with general Austrian patriotism and the populist protest agenda, which the FPÖ is representing since 1986. (Plasser, Ulram 1995). The SPÖ has retained the old blue-collar vote and much of the new middle-class vote, but this cannot be analyzed as the effect of traditional class orientation. In addition, the decline of the ÖVP can be explained by the decline of political Catholicism and the resulting diminished impact religion as such has on political behavior.

There are, of course, visible new fragmentations. The transformation is not changing Austria into a heaven of perfect harmony; in fact, quite the opposite is true. There is a deep-seated conflict between the winners and the losers of modernization, expressed in the xenophobic attitudes of the latter. There is a significant increase in the importance of gender and education in political behavior. Additionally, hidden behind the generation gap is an explosive potential: those negatively impacted by modernization could identify with Austria's Nazi past. As the FPÖ, the party established by former Nazis for former Nazis, became a decisive factor of the Austrian party system and joined, in 2000, the Austrian government, the explosiveness of this potential became obvious.

But this has almost nothing to do with the old cleavages that constituted and defined the traditional camps. It has everything to do with Austria's integration into Europe, not with Austria's membership in the EU, but with Austria's full participation in the dynamism Western societies have developed, transgressing borders. Austria is not an island, neither of the blessed, nor of the damned.

There has been one factor that still sets Austria apart, despite the trends toward Europeanization. Austria was and still is the country that has the special burden of being the country of Adolf Hitler. Right-wing attitudes in Austrian society and politics, perhaps not so different from parallel tendencies in other countries, has created general suspicion. When in 2000 the new Austrian government included a party widely seen as the party of the extreme right, this suspicion came out into the open and isolated Austria against its will.

### Conclusions: De-Austrification and Re-Austrification

The consequences of the general elections in 1999 have been rather dramatic. The elections saw the FPÖ—for the first time ever—ahead of the ÖVP within an extremely small margin. The SPÖ was able to keep its pre-eminent position despite some losses. The trend, visible since the late 1980s, was strengthened: the SPÖ and ÖVP were increasingly losing the ability to mobilize voters. The FPÖ and, to a lesser extent, the Greens have profited from this the most.

In February 2000, after weeks of negotiations, first between the SPÖ and ÖVP and then between the FPÖ and ÖVP, a coalition government was formed by the FPÖ and ÖVP under the chancellorship of the ÖVP's chairman, Wolfgang Schüssel. The SPÖ went into the opposition after three decades of leading the government.

It is not the end of the grand coalition that makes this development so significant. It is the international, especially the EU's, response to

**TABLE 6:**
**National Council Elections**

|  | Percentage of Votes | Seats in the National Council |
|---|---|---|
| SPÖ | 33.15 | 65 |
| FPÖ | 26.91 | 52 |
| ÖVP | 26.91 | 52 |
| Greens | 7.4 | 14 |
| LIF | 3.65 | 0 |

Source: Official Election Results, Federal Ministry of the Interior

this new coalition that deserves the term "dramatic." What could be seen as "normalization" is seen as very special, very deviant, especially from the European viewpoint.

The SPÖ's farewell to their leading role in government could have been explained as a further step towards "Europeanization" or "Westernization," as time for a change. But this was completely overshadowed by the FPÖ's entry into government. The other fourteen EU governments argued, backed by the European Parliament's resolution, that the FPÖ is not acceptable as a party within an EU government. The fourteen EU governments decided to downgrade bilateral relations with the new Austrian government. The FPÖ's xenophobic rhetoric was used as an official justification. The FPÖ's roots in Austria's Nazi past must be seen as an additional explanation for such a unique response.

The new coalition started to challenge some of the structural remnants of Austrian consociationalism. The Social Affairs portfolio was split between a new "Generational Ministry," led by a FPÖ minister, and the Ministry of Economics, led by a ÖVP minister. The latter, coming from the "Business League" of the People's Party and an entrepreneur himself, is in charge of labor relations, including the control over the Chambers of Labor. For the first time since 1945, labor relations were not in the hand of a politician with special links to the ÖGB, the Trade Unions. Even between 1966 and 1970, during the years of the ÖVP's single party government, the social affairs ministry was run by a representative of the Christian Unions – the minority faction within the ÖGB. For the first time since 1945, labor relations were integrated into an overall economic ministry, which is also in charge of controlling the Chambers of Commerce.

Even before 1999, social partnership was in decline. It was the general perception that social partnership had already lost some of its impact on Austrian politics and that this decline would continue. The FPÖ-ÖVP coalition is a catalyst that quickens this process of decline, weakening social partnership and weakening consociationalism.

This new situation presents an interesting paradox. At the very moment when Austria seems to make the possible last decisive step towards (West) European normality by destroying consociational structures, it is reminded of its still (and even more) special status:

- The challenge to written and unwritten rules of Austria's special political culture can be seen as further adaptation to conflict oriented democracy. It can be argued that Austria is becoming more like the other (West) European democracies with a political culture less consociational and more competitive.
- The inclusion of the FPÖ completely destroys this image. For the EU, the inclusion of the FPÖ in the Austrian government is a throwback to Austria's past and a reminder that Austria is still unique because it was not able to deal sufficiently with its responsibility for Nazism.

Austria has almost ceased to be a special case of consociationalism. But Austria has become another special case: the country which is used for a new European policy of *cordon sanitaire*, for a warning signal that right-wing extremism will not be tolerated on government level within the European Union. In a certain way, Austria has to go back to point zero – to start again in shaping its understanding of democracy.

In September 2000, the governments of the other fourteen EU members lifted the bilateral measures against the Austrian government. The reason was that a report on Austria by three "wise men" had argued that the measures had been productive, but they would become counterproductive on the long run. This report also argued that the human rights situation in Austria is not principally different from the other members' record, but that the FPÖ's specific character is still reason enough to observe the behavior of the Austrian government carefully.

Austria has almost escaped its role as a very special case. But instead of a special case of consociational democracy, Austria is now seen as a special case of rightist extremism. Consociational democracy was an instrument to escape the traps of history. After using this instrument, it seemingly had become obsolete. But Austria is back, detained in a trap again. Again, it has to do with history.

But it is a different Austria in a different Europe, which has to face its role. Austrian society has become more flexible and its citizens better educated. For that reason, the future of Austrian politics has become much less predictable. Austrian voting behavior, extremely stable after 1945, has become—beginning in the 1980s—extremely volatile. It is not the return to the past, which is so specific about the Austrian situation. It is more the opening into a unpredictable future, which is haunted by the ghosts of the past, which characterizes the Austrian situation.

Austria's integration into the European Union—the result of the 1980s and 1990s—has decisively changed the situation of Austria. As a member of the EU, Austria is—intentionally or not—part of a federation, which reduces the importance of national politics significantly. Austria's political situation has changed dramatically during the last two decades of the twentieth century. But it has also deeply embedded Austria in a network of European dependencies.

# Select Bibliography

This bibliography is designed to direct students towards the readings cited in the chapters of this book and beyond. It is not intended to being exhaustive. Since most of these essays first appeared in German, meticulous readers might want to go back to the original German texts and look up the exact citations and bibliographic references at the end of each chapter (Rolf Steininger and Michael Gehler, eds. *Österreich im 20. Jahrhundert*. Vol. I: *Von der Monarchie bis zum Zweiten Weltkrieg*; vol. II: *Vom Zweiten Weltkrieg bis zur Gegenwart*. Vienna: Böhlau Verlag 1997). Chapter bibliographies from these two volumes have been updated with the most recent literature available. Whenever possible, English titles are referenced. As this bibliography clearly indicates, much of the crucial literature for an understanding of modern Austria is not available in English. It goes without saying that any serious student of twentieth century Austria eventually will need to learn German. Both of the two principal periodicals published on Austria in the United States—*Contemporary Austrian Studies* and the *Austrian History Yearbook*—should be consulted for updates on recent publications and historiographical debates. They regularly feature book reviews and review essays on important subject matters. The Internet sites also help in getting the most up-to-date information on Austria.

## Internet

<www.ifz-innsbruck.at> (ZIS – contemporary history information system)
<www.kakanien.ac.at>
<www.demokratiezentrum.org>
<www.centeraustria.uno.edu>

## Important Periodicals

*Contemporary Austrian Studies*
*Austrian History Yearbook*

*Austrian Studies*
*Central European History*
*German Studies Review*
*Journal of Modern History*
*Journal of Contemporary History*
*Contemporary European History*
*Journal of European Integration History*
*Zeitgeschichte*
*Österreichische Zeitschrift für Geschichtswissenschaft*
*Wiener Zeitschrift zur Geschichte der Neuzeit*
*Mitteilungen des Österreichischen Staatsarchivs*
*Vierteljahrshefte für Zeitgeschichte*

## Basic General Works

Armingeon, Klaus, and Markus Freitag. 1997. *Deutschland, Österreich und Schweiz: Die politischen Systeme im Vergleich. Ein sozialwissenschaftlichers Datenbuch* Opladen.

Bachinger, Karl, and Dieter Stiefel, eds. 2001. *Auf Heller und Cent: Beiträge zur Finanz- und Währungsgeschichte.* Vienna.

Barker, Elisabeth. 1973. *Austria, 1918-1972.* London.

Bischof, Günter, Anton Pelinka and Erika Thurner, eds. 1998. *Women in Austria.* (Contemporary Austrian Studies 6). New Brunswick, NJ.

Bischof, Günter, and Anton Pelinka, eds. 1997. *Austrian Historical Memory and National Identity.* (Contemporary Austrian Studies 5). New Brunswick, NJ.

Bluhm, William T. 1973. *Building an Austrian Nation: The Political Integration of a Western State.* New Haven, CT.

Brook-Shepherd, Gordon. 1996. *The Austrians: A Thousand-Year Odyssey.* New York.

Bushell, Anthony, ed. 1996. *Austria 1945-1955: Studies in Political and Cultural Emergence.* Cardiff.

Feichtlbauer, Hubert. 2001. *The Austrian Dilemma: An Inquiry into National Socialism and Rascism in Austria.* Vienna 2001.

Forster, David. 2001. *"Wiedergutmachung" in Österreich und BRD im Vergleich.* Innsbruck.

Gehler, Michael, ed. 1996. *Ungleiche Partner? Österreich und Deutschland in ihrer gegenseitigen Wahrnehmung. Historische Analysen und Vergleiche aus dem 19. und 20. Jahrhundert.* Stuttgart.

Gehler, Michael, Wolfram Kaiser, and Helmut Wohnout, eds. 2001. *Christdemokratie in Europa im 20. Jahrhundert/Christian Democracy in 20th Century Europe/La Démocratie Chrétienne en Europe au XXe Siècle.* Vienna.

*Geschichte der Österreichischen Bundesländer seit 1945.* 1997ff. Ed. Herbert Dachs, Ernst Hanisch, and Robert Kriechbaumer, 9 vols. Vienna.

Good, David, and Ruth Wodak, eds. 1999. *From World War to Waldheim: Culture and Politics in Austria and the United States.* New York.

Good, David, Margarete Grandner, and Mary Ho Maynes, eds. 1996. *Austrian Women in the Nineteenth and Twentieth Centuries: Cross-Disciplinary Perspectives.* New York.

Hanisch, Ernst. 1994. *Der lange Schatten des States: Österreichische Gesellschaftsgeschichte im 20. Jahrhudnert.* Vienna.

Heer, Friedrich. 1981. *Der Kampf um die österreichische Identität.* Vienna.

Jelavich, Barbara. 1987. *Modern Austria: Empire and Republic 1800-1980.* Cambridge.

Johnson, Lonnie. 1989. *Introducing Austria: A Short History.* Riverside, CA.

———. 1996. *Central Europe: Enemies, Neighbors, Friends.* New York:

Johnston, William M. 1972. *The Austrian Mind: An Intellectual and Social History, 1848-1938.* Berkeley.

Kriechbaumer, Robert. 2001. *Die grossen Erzählungen der Politik: Politische Kultur und Parteien in Österreich von der Jahrhudnertwende bis 1945.* Vienna.

———, ed. 1998. *Österreichische Nationalgeschichte nach 1945: Die Spiegel der Erinnerung. Die Sicht von innen.* Vienna.

———, ed. 1998. *Liebe auf den zweiten Blick: Landes- und Österreichbewusstsein nach 1945.* Vienna.

Luther, Kurt Richard, and Peter Pulzer, eds. 1998. *Austria 1945-95: Fifty Years of Second Republic.* Aldershot.

Mantl, Wolfgang, ed. 1992. *Politik in Österreich: Die Zweite Republik. Bestand und Wandel.* Vienna.

Plaschka, Richard G., Gerald Stourzh, and Jan Paul Niederkorn, eds. 1995. *Was heisst Österreich: Inhalt und Umfang des Österreichbegriffes vom 10. Jahrhundert bis Heute.* Vienna.

Pauley, Bruce. 1992. *From Persecution to Prejudice: A History of Austrian Anti-Semitism*. Chapel Hill, NC.

Pelinka, Anton. 1997. *Das grosse Tabu: Österreichs Umgang mit seiner Vergangenheit*. Vienna.

Plasser, Fritz, ed. 1999. *Wahlen und politische Eisntellungen in Deutschland und Österreich*. Frankfurt.

Sieder, Reinhard, Heinz Steinert, and Emmerich Tálos, eds. 1996. *Österreich 1945-1995: Gesellschaft, Politik, Kultur*. 2$^{nd}$ ed. Vienna.

*The Sound of Music zwischen Mythos und Marketing* 2000. (Salzburger Beiträge zur Volkskunde). Salzburg.

Spiel, Hilde. 1987. *Vienna's Golden Autumn: From the Watershed Year 1866 to Hitler's Anschluß 1938*. New York: Grove/Atlantic.

Stadler, Karl R. 1971. *Austria*. London.

Steinberg, Michael. 1990. *The Meaning of the Salzburg Festival: Austria as Theater and Ideology, 1890-1938*. Ithaca, NY.

Steiner, Kurt, et al., ed. 1981. *Modern Austria*. Palo Alto, CA.

Steininger, Rolf. 1997. *Südtirol im 20. Jahrhundert: Vom Leben und Überleben einer Minderheit*. Innsbruck.

Sully, Melanie A. 1981. *Political Parties and Elections in Austria*. London.

Thaler, Peter. 2001. *The Ambivalence of Identity: The Austrian Experience of Nation-Building in a Modern Society*. West Lafayette, IN.

## Biography/Autobiography

Brown, Karin. 1987. *Karl Lueger: The Liberal Years*. New York.

Brusatti, Alois, and Gottfried Heindl, eds. 1987. *Julius Raab: Eine Biographie in Einzeldarstellungen*. Linz.

Clark, Mark W. 1950. *Calculated Risk*. New York.

Dachs, Herbert, Peter Gerlich, and Wolfgang C. Müller, eds. 1995. *Die Politiker: Karrieren und Wirken bedeutender Repräsentanten der Zweiten Republik*. Vienna.

Edwin, Robert. 1988. *Waldheim: The Missing Years*. New York.

Fischer, Heinz. 1998. *Reflexionen*. Vienna.

Geehr, Richard S. 1990. *Karl Lueger, Mayor of Fin de Siècle Vienna*. Detroit.

Gehler, Michael, ed. 1994. *Karl Gruber: Reden und Dokumente 1945-1953*. Vienna.

Gruber, Karl. 1955. *Between Liberation and Liberty: Austria in the Post-War World.* Trans. Lionel Kochan. London.

Jahoda, Marie. 1997. *"Ich habe die Welt nicht verändert": Lebenserinnerungen einer Pionierin der Sozialforschung.* Frankfurt.

Kreisky, Bruno. 2000. *The Struggle for a Democratic Austria: Bruno Kreisky on Peace and Social Justice.* Ed. and trans. Matthew Paul Berg. New York.

Pelinka, Anton. 1989. *Karl Renner zur Einführung.* Hamburg.

Pelinka, Peter. 2000. *Österreichs Kanzler: Von Leopold Figl bis Wolfgang Schüssel.* Vienna.

Petritsch, Wolfgang. 2000. *Bruno Kreisky: ein biographischer Essay.* Vienna.

Rauscher, Walter. 1995. *Karl Renner: Ein österreichischern Mythos.*

Secher, H. Pierre. 1994. *Bruno Kreisky Chancellor of Austria: A Political Biography.* Pittsburg, PA.

Stadler, Karl. R. 1982. *Adolf Schärf: Mensch, Politiker, Staatsmann.* Vienna.

von Klemperer, Klemens. 1972. *Ignaz Seipel: Christian Statesman in a Time of Crisis.* Princeton.

Whiteside, Andrew G. 1975. *The Socialism of Fools: Georg Ritter von Schönerer and Austrian Pan-Germanism.* Berkeley.

## Further Literature for Individual Essays

*World War I and the First Republic*

*Kuprian*

Beller, Steven.1989. *Vienna and the Jews, 1867-1938: A Cultural History.* Cambridge.

————, ed. 2001. *Rethinking Vienna 1900.* New York.

Boyer, John. 1981. *Political Radicalism in Late Imperial Vienna: Origins of the Christian Social Movement, 1848-1897.* Chicago.

————. 1995. *Culture and Political Crisis in Vienna: Christian Socialism in Power, 1897-1918.* Chicago.

Bridge, Francis R. 1991. *The Habsburg Monarchy among the Great Powers, 1815-1918.* New York.

Hamann, Brigitte. 2000. *Hitler's Vienna: A Dictator's Apprenticeship.* New York.

Jászi, Oscar. 1961. *The Dissolution of the Habsburg Monarchy.* Chicago.

Schorske, Carl E. 1980. *Fin-de-Siècle Vienna: Politics and Culture.* New York.

Williamson, Samuel R., Jr. 1991. *Austria-Hungary and the Origins of the First World War.* New York.


*Rauchensteiner*

Albertini, Luigi. 1957. *The Origins of the War of 1914.* 3 vols. London.

Herwig, Holger. 1997. *The First World War: Germany and Austria-Hungary, 1914-1918.* London.

Mamatey, Victor S. 1957. *The United States and East Central Europe 1914-1918: A Study of Wilsonian Diplomacy and Propaganda.* Princeton.

May, Arthur J. 1966. *The Passing of the Habsburg Monarchy.* 2 vols. Philadelpia.

Rauchensteiner, Manfried. 1993. *Der Tod des Doppeladler: Österreich-Ungarn und der Erste Weltkrieg.* Graz.

Shanafelt, Gary W. 1974. "Austria-Hungary and the German Alliance 1914-1918." Ph.D. diss., University of California.


*Maderthaner*

Bottomore, Tom, and Patrick Goode. 1978. *Austro-Marxism.* Oxford.

Edmonson, C. Earl. 1978. *The Austrian Heimwehr and Austrian Politics 1918-1936.* Athens, GA.

Freidenreich, Harriet Pass. 1991. *Jewish Politics in Vienna, 1918-1938.* Bloomington, IN.

Gruber, Helmut. 1991. *Red Vienna: Experiment in Working-Class Culture, 1919-1934.* New York.

Gulick, Charles. 1948. *Austria from Habsburg to Hitler.* 2 vols. Berkeley.

Kitchen, Martin. 1980. *The Coming of Austrian Fascism.* London.

Lewis, Jill. 1991. *Fascism and the Working-Class in Austria 1918-1934: The Failure of Labor in the First Republic.* New York.

Pauley, Bruce. 1981. *Hitler and the Forgotten Nazis: A History of Austrian National Socialism.* Chapel Hill, NC.

Rabinbach, Anson. 1994. *The Crisis of Austrian Socialism: From Red Vienna to Civil War.* Chicago.

————, ed. 1985. *The Austrian Socialist Experiment: Social Democracy and Austro-Marxism.* Boulder, CO.

Spender, Stephen. 1935. *Vienna.* London.

Zweig, Stefan. 1964. *The World of Yesterday.* Lincoln, NE.


*Binder*

Binder, Dieter. 1979. *Dollfuss und Hitler: Über die Aussenpolitik des autoritären Ständestaates in den Jahren 1933/34.* Graz.

————. 1992. *Verlorene Positionen des christlichen Lagers.* Vienna.

Kluge, Ulrich. 1984. *Der österreichische Ständestaat 1934-1938.* Vienna.

Pelinka, Anton. 1972. *Stand oder Klasse? Die Christliche Arbeiterbewegung Österreichs 1933 bis 1938.* Vienna.

Stiefel, Dieter. 1988. *Die grosse Krise im kleinen Land: Österreichs Finanz- und Wirtschaftspolitik 1929-1938.* Vienna.

Tálos, Emmerich, and Wolfgang Neugebauer, eds. 1984. *"Austrofaschismus": Beiträge über Politik, Ökonomie und Kultur 1934-1938.* Vienna.

Wohnout, Helmut. 1993. *Regierungsdiktatur oder Ständeparlament? Gesetzgebung im autoritären Österreich.* Vienna.


*Steininger*

Albrich, Thomas, Klaus Eisterer, and Rolf Steininger, eds. 1988. *Tirol und der Anschluß: Voraussetzungen, Entwicklungen, Rahmenbedingungen.* Innsbruck.

Amann, Klaus. 1996. *Der Anschluß östereichischer Schriftsteller and das Dritte Reich.* Bodenheim.

Botz, Gerhard. 1978. *Der 13. März und die Anschlußbewegung.* Vienna.

Gehmacher, Johanna. 1998. *Völkische Frauenbewegung: Deutschnationale und nationalsozialistische Geschlechterpolitik in Österreich.* Vienna.

Jagschitz, Gerhard. 1975. *Der Putsch: Die nationalsozialisten im Juli 1934 in Österreich.* Vienna.

Kann, Robert, and Friedrich Prinz, eds. 1980. *Deutschland und Österreich: Ein bilaterales Geschichtsbuch.* Vienna.

Low, Alfred. 1985. *The Anschluß Movement, 1931-1938, and the Great Powers.* New York.

Lassner, Alexander N. 2001. "Peace at Hitler's Price: Austria, the Great Powers, and the "Anschluß," 1932-1938." Ph.D. diss., Ohio State University.

Luza, Radomir. 1975. *Austro-German Relations in the Anschluß Era.* Princeton.

Schausberger, Norbert. 1978. *Der Griff nach Österreich: Der Anschluß.* Vienna.

Stourzh, Gerald and Birgitta Zaar, eds. 1990. *Österreich, Deutschland und die Mächte: Internationale und österreichische Aspekte des "Anschlußes" vom März 1938.* Vienna.

Suval, Stanley. 1974. *The Anschluß Question in the Weimar Era: A Study of Nationalism in Germany and Austria 1918-1978.* Baltimore, MD.

Voithofer, Ricahrd. 2000. *Drum schliesst Euch frisch an Deutschland an ... Die Grossdeutsche Volkspartei in Salzburg 1920-1936.* Vienna.

Volansky, Gabriele. 2001. *Pakt auf Zeit: Das deutsche-österreichische Juli-Abkommen 1936.* Vienna.

*World War II*

*Stadler*

Amery, Jean. 1971. *Unmeisterliche Wanderjahre.* Stuttgart.

Austriacus. 1936. "Der Fall des Wiener Professors Schlick - Eine Mahnung zur Gewissenserforschung." *Schönere Zukunft* 12. 7.

Coser, Lewis. 1984. *Refugee Scholars in America: Their Impact and Their Experiences.* New Haven, CT.

Dokumentationsarchiv des Österreichischen Widerstandes, ed. *Österreicher im Exil 1938-1945.* Vienna 1984ff [France (1984), Spain (1986), Belgium (1987), Great Britain (1992), United States (1995)].

Fleming, Donald, and Bernard Bailyn, eds. 1969. *The Intellectual Migration: Europe and America, 1930-1960.* Cambridge, MA.

Hagspiel, Hermann. 1996. *Die Ostmark: Österreich im Grossdeutschen Reich 1938 bis 1945.* Vienna.

Heilbut, Anthony. 1983. *Exiled in Paradise: German Refugee Artists and Intellectuals in America from the 1930s to the Present.* Boston.

Hölbling, Walter, and Reinhold Wagnleitner, eds. 1992. *The European Emigrant Experience in the USA*. Tübingen.

*International Biographical Dictionary of Central European Emigres 1933-1945*. 1983. Ed. Herbert A. Strauss and Werner Röder. 2 vols. New York.

Sauter, Johann. 1936. Sigmund Freud—Der Begründer der Psychoanalyse. In: *die pause. Heft 6*.

Spaulding, E. Wilder. 1968. *The Quiet Invadors: The Story of the Austrian Impact Upon America*. Vienna.

Stadler, Friedrich, and Peter Weibel, eds. 1995. *The Cultural Exodus from Austria*. Vienna.

————. 1987. *Vertriebene Vernunft: Emigration und Exil österreichischer Wissenschaft*. 2 vols. Vienna.

Timms, Edward, and Ritchie Robertson, eds. 1995. *Austrian Exodus: The Creative Achievements of Refugees from National Socialism*. Austrian Studies. Edinburgh.


*Weinzierl*

Botz, Gerhard. 1983. *Gewalt in der Politik: Attentate, Zusammenstösse, Putschversuche in Österreich 1918-1938*. Vienna.

Bukey, Evan Burr. 2000. *Hitler's Austria: Popular Sentiment in the Nazi Era 1938-1945*. Chapel Hill, NC.

Dokumentationsarchiv des östereichischen Widerstandes [DÖW], ed., *Widerstand und Verfolgung*. Vienna 1975ff [Vienna, 3 vols, (1975, 1986), Burgenland (1979, 1983), Lower Austria, 3 vols. (1987); Upper Austria, 2 vols. (1982); Salzburg, 2 vols. (1991), Tyrol, 2 vols. (1984)].

Ehalt, Hubert Christian, ed. 1997. *Inszenierung der Gewalt: Kunst und Alltagskultur im Nationalsozialismus*. Frankfurt.

Exenberger, Herbert. 1998 *Gedenken und Mahnen in Wien 1934-1945: Gedenkstätten zu Widerstand und Verfolgung, Exil, Befreiung. Ein Dokumentation*. Vienna.

Freund, Florian, and Bertrand Perz. 1987. *Das KZ in der "Serbenhalle": Zur Kriegsindustrie in Wiener Neustadt*. Vienna.

————. 1989. *Arbeitslager Zement: Das Konzentrationslager Ebensee und die Raketenrüstung*. Vienna.

*Gerechtigkeit für Österreich.: Rot-Weiss-Rot Buch*. 1946. Vienna.

Hoensch, Jörg K. 1999. *Judenemanzipation – Antisemitismus – Verfolgung in Deutschland, Österreich-Ungarn, den böhmischen Ländern und in der Slowakei*. Essen.

Horwitz, Gordon J. 1990. *In the Shadow of Death: Living Outside the Gates of Mauthausen*. New York.

Kindermann, Gottfried-Karl. 1984. *Hitlers Niederlage in Österreich: Bewaffneter NS-Putsch, Kanzlermord und Österreichs Abwehrsieg 1934*. Hamburg.

Kreissler, Felix. 1984. *Der Österreicher und seine Nation: Ein Lernprozess mit Hindernissen*. Vienna.

Liebmann, Maximilian, ed. 1998. *Staat und Kirche in der "Ostmark."* Frankfurt.

Lingens, Ella. *Eine Frau im Konzentrationslager*. Vienna 1966.

Luza, Radomir. 1984. *The Resistance in Austria, 1938-1945*. Minneapolis, MN.

Molden, Otto. 1970. *Der Ruf des Gewissens: Der Österreichische Freiheitskampf 1938-1945*. Vienna.

Perz, Bertrand. 1990. *"Projekt Quarz": Steyr-Daimler-Puch und das Konzentrationslager Melk*. Vienna.

Rathkolb, Oliver. 2001. *NS-Zwangsarbeit: Der Standort Linz der Reichswerke Hermann Göring AG, Berlin, 1938-1945*. 2 vols. Vienna.

Safrian, Hans. 1993. *Die Eichmann-Männer*. Vienna.

Stiefel, Dieter. 2001. *Die Österreichischen Lebensversicherungen und die NS-Zeit*. Vienna.

————, ed. 2001. *Die politische Öknomie des Holocaust: Zur wirtschaftlichen Logik von Verfolgung und "Wiedergutmachung."* Vienna.

Stadler, Karl. 1966. *Österreich 1939-1945: Im Spiegel der NS-Akten*. Vienna.

Szabolcs, Szita. 1999. *Verschleppt, verhungert, vernichtet: Die Deportation von ungarischen Juden auf das Gebiet des annektierten Östereich 1944-1945*. Vienna.

Walterskirchen, Gundula. 2000. *Blaues Blut für Österreich: Adelige im Widerstand gegen den Nationalsozialismus*. Vienna.

Weinzierl, Erika. 1986. *Zu wenig Gerechte: Österreicher und Judenverfolgung 1938-1945*. Graz.

*The Second Republic*

*Bischof*

Ableitinger, Alfred, et al., eds. 1998. *Österreich unter alliierter Besatzung 1945-1955*. Vienna. (See especially Thomas Angerer's essay on French policy, the Anschluß trauma, and the foreign dependency of Austria).

Albrich, Thomas, Klaus Eisterer, Michael Gehler, and Rolf Steininger, eds. 1995. *Österreich in den Fünfzigern*. Innsbrucker Foschungen zur Zeitgeschichte 11. Innsbruck. (See especially the essays by Günter Bischof on Austria's secret rearmament and Michael Gehler on Austrian neutrality as a "model" for Germany and Klaus Eisterer on the Swiss and Austrian neutrality).

Bischof, Günter. 1999. *Austria in the First Cold War, 1945-55: The Leverage of the Weak*. Basingstoke.

———, and Saki Dockrill, eds. 2000. *Cold War Respite: The Geneva Summit of 1955*. Baton Rouge, LA.

———, and Josef Leidenfrost, eds. 1988. *Die bevormundete Nation: Österreich und die Alliierten, 1945-1949*. Innsbrucker Forschungen zur Zeitgeschichte 4. Innsbruck.

———, et al., eds., 2000. *The Marshall Plan in Austria*. Contemporary Austrian Studies 8. New Brunswick, NJ. (See especially the essay by Alexander Lassner on the disarray of the German *Wehrmacht* during their invasion of Austria in 1938).

———, et al., eds. 2001. *Neutrality in Austria*. Contemporary Austrian Studies 9. New Brunswick, NJ. (See especially Michael Gehler's essay on Austria and the Hungarian crisis of 1956 and Austria's "model function" for Germany and Hungary; and the "Historiography Forum" debate of Stourzh's massive state treaty history cited below).

Borhi, László. 1999. Rollback, Liberation, Containment, or Inaction? U.S. Policy and Eastern Europe in the 1950s. *Journal of Cold War Studies* 1: 67-110.

Bukey, Evan Burr. 2000. *Hitler's Austria: Popular Sentiment in the Nazi Era 1938-1945*. Chapel Hill.

Carafano, James Jay. 2000. "Waltzing into the Cold War: U.S. Military Operations in Occupied Austria, 1945-1955." Ph.D. diss., Georgetown University.

————. 1999. "Mobilizing Europe's Stateless: America's Plan for a Cold War Army," *Journal of Cold War Studies* 1 (Spring): 61-85.

Cronin, Audrey Kurth. 1986. *Great Power Politics and the Struggle over Austria 1945-1955*. Ithaca, NY.

Dockrill, Saki. 1996. *Eisenhower's New Look National Security Policy, 1953-61*. Basingstoke.

Gehler, Michael, ed. 1994. *Karl Gruber: Reden und Dokumente 1945-1953*. Vienna.

————. 1996. *Verspielte Selbstbestimmung? Die Südtirolfrage 1945/46 in US-Geheimdienstberichten und Österreichischen Akten: Ein Dokumentation*. Innsbruck.

Keyserlingk, Robert. 1988. *Austria in World War II: An Anglo-American Dilemma*. Kingston.

Kos, Wolfgang, and Georg Rigele, eds. 1996. *Inventur 45/55: Österreich im ersten Jahrzehnt der Zweiten Republik*. Vienna.

Mastny, Vojtech. 1996. *The Cold War and Soviet Insecurity: The Stalin Years*. New York.

Pape, Matthias. 2000. *Ungleiche Brüder: Österreich und Deutschland 1945-1965*. Vienna.

Rathkolb, Oliver. 1997. *Washington ruft Wien: US-Grossmachtpolitik und Österreich 1953-1963*. Vienna.

Steininger, Rolf. 1990. *The German Question: The Stalin Note of 1952 and the Problem of Reunification*. New York.

Stourzh, Gerald. 1998. *Um Einheit und Freiheit: Staatsvertrag, Neutralität und das Ende der Ost-West-Besetzung Österreich*. Vienna.

Schmidl, Erwin, ed. 2000. *Österreich im Frühen Kalten Krieg 1945-1958: Spione, Partisanen, Kriegspläne*. Vienna. (See especially Erwin Schmid's essay on American planning for a Vienna blockade and Bruno Koppensteiner's essay on French plans for the defense of the "Alpine redoubt").

Trachtenberg, Marc. 1999. *A Constructed Peace: The Making of the European Settlement 1945-1963*. Princeton, NJ.

Wagnleitner, Reinhold. 1994. *Coca-Colonization and the Cold War: The Cultural Mission of the United States in Austria after the Second World War*. Trans. Diana Wolf. Chapel Hill, NC.

————, and Elaine Tylr May, eds. 2000. *"Here, There and Everywhere": The Foreign Politics of American Popular Culture*. Hanover.

Witnah, Donald R, and Edgar L. Erickson. 1985. *The American Occupation of Austria: Planning and Early Years*. Westport, CT.

Zubok, Vladislav, and Constantine Pleshakov. 1996. *Inside the Kremlin's Cold War: From Stalin to Krushchev*. Cambridge, MA.

*Eisterer*

Beer, Siegfried, ed. 1995. *Die "britische" Steiermark 1945-1955*. Graz.

Eisterer, Klaus. 1992. *Französische Besatzungspolitik: Tirol und Vorarlberg 1945/55*. Innsbrucker Forschungen zur Zeitgeschichte 9. Insbruck.

————. 1995. *Die Schweiz als Partner: Zum eigenständigen Aussenhandel der Bundesländer Tirol und Vorarlberg mit der Eidgenossenschaft 1945-1947*. Innsbruck.

Karner, Stefan. 1995. *Im Archipel GUPVI: Kriegsgefangenschaft und Internierung in der Sowjetunion 1941-1956*. Munich.

Mähr, Wilfried. 1989. *Der Marshallplan in Österreich*. Graz.

Meissl, Sebastian, Klaus Dieter Mulley, and Oliver Rathkolb, eds. 1986. *Verdrängte Schuld, Verfehlte Sühne: Entnazifizierung in Österreich, 1945-1955*. Vienna.

Pelinka, Anton, and Rolf Steininger, eds. 1986. *Österreich und die Sieger*. Vienna.

Rathkolb, Oliver, ed. 1985. *Gesellschaft und Politik am Beginn der Zweiten Republik*. Vienna.

Rauchensteiner, Manfried. 1979. *Der Sonderfall: Die Besatzungszeit in Österreich 1945 bis 1955*. Graz.

Sandner, Margit. 1985. *Die Französisch-Österreichischen Beziehungen während der Besatzungszeit von 1947 bis 1955*. Vienna.

Stiefel, Dieter. 1981. *Die Entnazifizierung in Österreich*. Vienna.

Tweraser, Kurt. 1995. *U.S.-Militärregierung in Oberösterreich*. Linz.

Wagnleitner, Reinhold, ed. 1984. *Understanding Austria: The Political Reports and Analyses of Martin F. Herz, Political Officer of the U.S. Delegation in Vienna 1945-1948*. Salzburg.

*Mathis*

Bachinger, Karl, Hildegard Hemetsberger-Koller, and Herbert Matis. 1987. *Grundriss der Österreichischen Sozial- und Wirtschaftsgeschichte von 1948 bis zur Gegenwart*. Vienna.

Bischof, Günter, Anton Pelinka, and Dieter Stiefel, eds. 2000. *The Marshall Plan in Austria.* Contemporary Austrian Studies 8. New Brunswick, NJ.

Bruckmüller, Ernst. 1985. *Sozialgeschichte Österreichs.* Vienna.

Butschek, Felix. 1985. *Die Österreichische Wirtschaft im 20. Jahrhundert.* Vienna.

Good, David F., ed. 1994. *Economic Transformation in East and Central Europe: Legacies From the Past and Policies for the Future.* London.

———. 1984. *The Economic Rise of the Habsburg Empire, 1750-1914.* Berkeley.

Katzenstein, Peter J. 1984. *Corporatism and Change.* Ithaca, NY.

Mathis, Franz. 1987. *Big Business in Österreich: Österreichische Grossunternahmen in Kurzdarstellungen.* Vienna.

———. 1991. *Big Business in Österreich II: Wachstum und Eigentumsstruktur der Österreichischen Grossunternhemen im 19. und 20. Jahrhundert. Analyse und Interpretationen.* Vienna.

Otruba, Gustav. 1968. *Österreichische Wirtschaft im 20. Jahrhundert.* Vienna.

Sandgruber, Roman. 1995. *Ökonomie und Politik: Österreichs Wirtschaftsgeschichte vom Mittelalter bis zur Gegenwart.* Vienna.

Weber, Wilhelm, ed. 1961. *Österreichs Wirtschaftsstruktur gestern – heute – morgen.* 2 vols. Berlin.


*Rauchensteiner*

Dachs, Herbert, et al., eds. 1991. *Handbuch des politischen Systems Österreichs.* Vienna.

Kriechbaumer, Robert, et al., eds. 1995. *Die Transformation der Österreichischen Gesellschaft und die Alleinregierung Klaus.* Salzburg.

———, and Franz Schausberger, eds. 1995. *Volkspartei – Anspruch und Realität: Zur Geschichte der ÖVP seit 1945.* Vienna.

Pelinka, Anton. 1993. *Die Kleine Koalition: SPÖ – FPÖ 1983-1986.* Vienna.

Rauchensteiner, Manfried. 1987. *Die Zwei: Die grosse Koalition in Österreich, 1945-1966.* Vienna.

———. 1981. *Spätherbst 1956: Neutralität auf dem Prüfstand.* Vienna.

Riedlsperger, Max. 1978. *The Lingering Shadow of Nazism: The Austrian Independent Party Movement since 1947.* New York.

Steininger, Rolf, ed. 1997. *Südtirol zwischen Diplomatie und Terror 1947-1969.* 3 vols. Bozen.

Steininger, Rudolf. 1975. *Polarisierung und Integration: Ein vergleichende Untersuchung der strukturellen Versäulung der Gesellschaft in den Niederlanden und in Österreich.* Meisenheim.

*Rathkolb*

Bielka, Erich, et al., eds. 1983. *Die Ära Kreisky: Schwerpunkte Österreichischer Aussenpolitik.* Vienna.

Bischof, Günter, and Anton Pelinka, eds. 1994. *The Kreisky Era in Austria.* Contemporary Austrian Studies 2. New Brunswick, NJ.

Fischer, Heinz. 1993. *Die Kreisky Jahre ,1967-1983.* Vienna.

Fröschl, Erich, et al., eds. 1990. *Die Bewegung: Hundert Jahre Sozialdemokratie in Österreich.* Vienna.

Gatty, Werner et al., eds. 1997. *Die Ära Kreisky: Österreich im Wandel 1970-1983.* Innsbruck.

Schmid, Gerhard. 1999. *Österreich im Aufbruch: Die Österreichische Sozialdemokratie in der Ära Kreisky, 1970-1983.* Innsbruck.

Sully, Melanie A. 1982. *Continuity and Change in Austrian Socialism: The Eternal Quest for the Third Way.* Boulder, CO.

Ulram, Peter A. 1990. *Hegemonie und Erosion: Politische Kultur und politischer Wandel in Österreich.* Vienna.

*Gehler / Kaiser*

Bischof, Günter, and Anton Pelinka, eds. 1993. *Austria in the New Europe.* Contemporary Austrian Studies 1. New Brunswick, NJ: Transaction.

————, Anton Pelinka, and Michael Gehler, eds. 2002. *Austria and the European Union.* Contemporary Austrian Studies 10. New Brunswick, NJ.

Gehler, Michael, and Rolf Steininger, eds. 2000. *The Neutrals and the European Integration, 1945-1995.* Vienna.

————. 1993. *Österreich und die europäische Integration 1945-1993: Aspekte einer wechselvollen Entwicklung.* Vienna.

————. 2002. *Der lange Weg nach Europa: Österreich vom Ende der Monarchie bis zur EU, 1918-2000* (vol. 1); *Österreich von Paneuropa bis zum EU-Beitritt, 1922-1995* (vol. 2). 2 vols. Innsbruck.

Gerlich, Peter, and Heinrich Neisser, eds. 1994. *Europa als Herausforderung: Wandlungsimpulse für das politische System Österreichs*. Vienna.

Griller, Stefan, et al., eds. 1991. *Europäische Integration aus Österreichischer Sicht: Wirtschafts-, sozial- und rechtswissenschaftliche Aspekte*. Vienna.

Herbst, Ludolf, et al., eds. 1990. *Vom Marshallplan zur EWG: Die Eingliederung der Bundesrepublik in die westliche Welt*. Munich.

Hummer, Waldemar, ed. 1991. *Österreichs Integration in Europa 1948-1989: Von der OEEC zur EG*. Vienna.

————, and Georg Wagner, eds. 1988. *Österreich im Europarat 1956-1986: Bilanz einer 30jährigen Mitgliedschaft*. Vienna.

Jachtenfuchs, Markus, and Beate Kohler-Koch, eds. 1996. *Europäische Integration*. Opladen.

Kramer, Helmut. 1990. *Europäische Integration: Perspektiven für Österreich*. Vienna.

Kunnert, Gerhard. 1993. *Österreichs Weg in die Europäische Union: Ein Kleinstaat ringt um eine aktive Rolle in der europäischen Integration*. Vienna.

Luif, Paul. 1988. *Neutrale in die EG? Die westeuropäische Integration und die neutralen Staaten*. Vienna.

Milward, Alan S. 1999. *The European Rescue of the Nation State*. London.

Moravcsik, Andrew. 1998. *The Choice for Europe: Social Purpose and State Power from Messina to Maastricht*. Ithaca, NY.

Pelinka, Anton, et al. 1994. *Ausweg EG? Innenpolitische Motive einer aussenpolitischen Umorientierung*. Vienna.

Scharsach, Gilbert. 1996. *EU-Handbuch. Das grosse Nachschlagwerk der Österreichischen EU-Diskussion*. Vienna.

Schneider, Heinrich. 1989. *Alleingang nach Brüssel: Österreichs EG-Politik*. Bonn.

Schwendimann, Thomas. 1993. *Herausforderung Europa: Integrationspolitische Debatten in Österreich und der Schweiz, 1985-1989*. Bern.

*Pelinka*

Bischof, Günter, and Anton Pelinka, eds.1996. *Austro-Corporatism: Past, Present, Future*. Contemporary Austrian Studies 3. New

Brunswick, NJ.

————, et al., eds. 1999. *The Vranitkzy Era in Austria.* Contemporary Austrian Studies 7. New Brunswick, NJ.

Luther, Kurt Richard, and Wolfgang C. Müller, eds. 1992. Politics *in Austria: Still a Case of Consociationalism.* London.

Mitten, Richard. 1992. *The Politics of Anti-Semitic Prejudice.* Boulder, CO.

Pelinka, Anton. 1998. *Austria: Out of the Shadow of the Pa*st. Boulder, CO:.

Plasser, Fritz, and Peter A. Ulram. 1999. *Analyse der Nationalratswahl 1999 Report.* Vienna: Center for Applied Political Research (ZAP).

Powell, G. Bingham. 1970. *Social Fragmentation and Political Hostility: An Austrian Case Study.* Stanford.

# List of Contributors

*Dieter Binder*, born 1953, associate professor of contemporary history, University of Graz; *Die diskrete Gesellschaft* (2000); *Internationales Freimaurerlexikon* (2000); *Geschichte der Republik Österreich 1918-1938* (1992).

*Günter Bischof*, born 1953, professor of history and executive director, Center for Austrian Culture and Commerce, University of New Orleans; visiting professor at the Universities of Munich, Innsbruck, Salzburg, and Vienna; *Austria in the First Cold War 1945-55: The Leverage of the Weak* (1999); co-editor, *Contemporary Austrian Studies* (10 vols.); for a complete curriculum vita see <www.centeraustria.uno.edu>.

*Klaus Eisterer*, born 1956, associate professor at the Institute of Contemporary History, University of Innsbruck; *Französische Besatzungspolitik: Tirol und Voralberg 1945/46* (1991), also in French translation *La présence française en Autriche (1945-1946): Occupation – dénazification – action culturelle* (1998); for a complete curriculum vita see <www.ifz-innsbruck.at>.

*Michael Gehler*, born 1962, associate professor at the Institute of Contemporary History, University of Innsbruck; editorial board member of the journal *Zeitgeschichte*; board member of the Ranke Society; permanent fellow at the Center of European Integration Studies at the University of Bonn; founding member of the Study Group for European Integration (Austria); *Zeitgeschichte im dynamischen Mehrebenensystem* (2002); co-editor, *Austria in the European Union* (2002); for a complete curriculum vita see <www. ifz-innsbruck.at>.

*Wolfram Kaiser*, born 1966, senior research fellow of the Austrian Science Foundation at the University of Innsbruck; visiting professor at the University of Portsmouth and the College of Europe, Bruges

(Belgium); *Using Europe, Abusing the Europeans: Britain and European Integration* (2000); co-editor, *Christdemokratie in Europa im 20. Jahrhundert* (2001); and *British Foreign Policy, 1955-1964: Contracting Options* (2000).

*Hermann J.W. Kuprian*, born 1955, assistant professor of Austrian history, University of Innsbruck; co-editor, *Ostarichi – Österreich: 100 Jahre – 1000 Welten* (1997).

*Wolfgang Maderthaner*, born 1954, executive secretary of the Society for Working Class History in Vienna; *Mehr als ein Spiel: Fußball und populäre Kulturen im Wien der Moderne* (1996).

*Franz Mathis*, born 1946, professor of economic and social history, University of Innsbruck; visiting professor at the Universities of Salzburg, New Orleans, Bolzano, and Trento; University of Innsbruck coordinator of UNO friendship treaty affairs; *Big Business in Österreich*, 2 vols. (1987-1991).

*Anton Pelinka*, born 1941, professor of political science, University of Innsbruck, and director of the Institute of Conflict Research, Vienna; visiting professor at the universities of New Orleans and Michigan, as well as Harvard and Stanford universities; *Austria: Out of the Shadow of the Past* (1998); co-ed., *Contemporary Austrian Studies* (10 vols.)

*Oliver Rathkolb*, born 1955, adjunct lecturer of contemporary history and co-director of the Ludwig Boltzmann Institute for History and Society, University of Vienna; director of the Bruno Kreisky Foundation and coordinator of the Bruno Kreisky Forum for International Dialogue in Vienna; coordinator of <www. Demokratiezentrum.org>; *Washington Ruft Wien: US-Grossmachtpolitik und Österreich 1953-1963* (1997); editor, *Zwangsarbeit in den Linzer Betrieben der Reichswerke Hermann Göring AG Berlin*, 2 vols. (2001).

*Manfried Rauchensteiner*, born 1942, adjunct professor of Austrian history at the University of Vienna; director of the Museum of

Military History in Vienna; *Der Sonderfall: Die Besatzungszeit in Österreich* (1979); *Die Zwei: Die grosse Koalition in Österreich, 1945-1966* (1987); *Der Tod des Doppeladlers. Österreich-Ungarn und der Erste Weltkrieg 1914-1918,* (1992).

*Friedrich Stadler,* born 1951, associate professor of history and philosophy of science; chair of the department of Contemporary History; member of the Center for Interdisciplinary Research, University of Vienna; founder and director of the Vienna Circle Institute; *The Vienna Circle* (2001); co-ed., *The Cultural Exodus from Austria* (1995).

*Rolf Steininger,* born 1942, Jean-Monnet-Professor and chair of the Institute of Contemporary History, University of Innsbruck; senior fellow of the Eisenhower Center for American Studies at the University of New Orleans; board member of the European Community Studies Association; *Der Mauerbau* (2001); *Deutsche Geschichte 1945-2002,* 4 vols. (2002); for a complete curriculum vita see <www.ifz-innsbruck.at>.

*Erika Weinzierl,* born 1925, professor emeritus at the Institute of Contemporary History, University of Vienna; *Zu wenig Gerechte* (1986); co-editor, *Vertreibung und Neubeginn. Israelische Bürger österreichischer Herkunft* (1992).

# Index

Breinigsville, PA USA
02 August 2010
242856BV00002B/4/P